One Hundred Great Jewish Books

One Hundred Great Jewish Books

Three Millennia of Jewish Conversation

෨෨

Rabbi Lawrence A. Hoffman

BlueBridge

Published by
BlueBridge
An imprint of
United Tribes Media Inc.
www.bluebridgebooks.com

LIBRARY OF CONGRESS CATALOGING-IN-PUBLICATION DATA
Hoffman, Lawrence A., 1942-
One hundred great Jewish books : three millennia of Jewish conversation /
Lawrence A. Hoffman.
p. cm.
Includes bibliographical references and index.
ISBN 978-1-933346-31-1
1. Jews—Bibliography. 2. Judaism—Bibliography. 3. Jewish literature—
Bibliography. 4. Best books. I. Title.
Z6366.H64 2011
[DS102.95]
016.296—dc23
2011022351

Cover design by Stefan Killen Design
Cover art top: Prayer book for a Chazzan. From Poland, 16th or 17th c.
Photo credit: Erich Lessing / Art Resource, NY
Cover art bottom: The library in the small house of Baruch Spinoza (1632–1677).
Photo credit: Erich Lessing / Art Resource, NY
Text design by Cynthia Dunne

Printed in the United States of America

10 9 8 7 6 5 4 3 2 1

Contents

6. The American Experience to World War II:
The Conversation Expands   165

7. The Holocaust and Israel:
The Conversation Is Focused   189

Introduction

The Jewish Conversation

෧ᵥ෧

Judaism is more than a religion. But what else is it? Despite the existence of the State of Israel, it is not a nationality, because not all Jews are Israelis, and not all Israelis are Jews; Jews have inhabited many countries over the centuries, and where permitted to do so, have identified as citizens of them. Nor is Judaism a single culture, ethnicity, or way of life, since Jews have lived differently through the ages, and continue to do so even today; most North American Jews have roots in eastern Europe, while most Jews in Israel hail from countries in the Mediterranean.

Recognizing all this, the great twentieth-century American Jewish philosopher Mordecai Kaplan defined Judaism as a civilization, more specifically as a "religious civilization"—and indeed, for Jews in Boston, Berlin, or Buenos Aires, religion does seem central. But most Israeli Jews would disagree. For the majority of Jews in Israel, religion is associated with Jewish fundamentalism and its ultra-Orthodox political parties that would return Judaism to the Middle Ages if they could. So most Jewish Israelis say they are secular.

Whatever Judaism might be, however, it has consistently demonstrated a particular fondness for books. Since books are nothing if not records of things said, Judaism may be best defined as an ongoing conversation. It evolved from barely recognizable origins in a tiny plot of land we now call Israel and spread from there, over some three to four millennia, mostly throughout Europe and the Americas, but in some form or other to every other continent as well.

Only people have conversations, of course, and as it happens, the traditional way Jews have defined themselves is as a *people*, the Jewish People (*am yisra'el*)—not an easy category to imagine today, at least not in the West. Ever since Napoleon, we have been taught to think in terms of nation-states and religions—hence the notion of Judaism as a religion, which is what Napoleon wanted Jews to be. Seen as a religion, they could fit nicely into his empire—as loyal French citizens by nationality, and as a Jewish version of that citizenry by religion.

Two centuries have passed since Napoleon, however, and Jews no longer have to prove their loyalty to the countries in which they live. There is no reason, therefore, not to return to the original Jewish notion of peoplehood. Jews *are* a people, albeit a people where religion has played an extraordinary role, and what makes them a people is the conversation they all share. This book is an introduction to the written record of this distinctive Jewish conversation, a judicious (but naturally subjective) selection from a massive literature reaching back some three thousand years.

One Hundred Great Jewish Books is, therefore, an altogether new kind of introduction to Judaism, intended to enrich the explanations of Jewish history, thought, and practice that other books provide. It opens the door to three millennia of dialogue and debate, sometimes philosophical but more often down-to-earth, in line with the biblical exhortation (Deut. 30:11–14) that ultimate wisdom "is not too baffling [. . .] nor beyond reach. It is neither in the heavens [. . . nor] beyond the sea [. . .] No, the thing is very close to you, in your mouth and in your heart." Welcome to the heartfelt Jewish conversation about life and death and everything in between!

From the earliest of times, Jews have valued literacy. In fact, Hebrew—the Jewish language par excellence and the original language of the Bible—invented the first vowel system that made reading and writing possible beyond the limited ranks of a priestly elite. The conversation, therefore, made it into book form very early: the Hebrew Bible was already being composed about 1000–900 BCE and was sealed as a finished creation sometime in the second century CE. (Jews tend to prefer BCE [Before the Common Era] to BC [Before Christ], and CE

[Common Era] to AD [*Anno Domini*, i.e., in the year of the Lord].) The final state of these Scriptures was canonized by the Rabbis—leaders and thinkers from late antiquity who gave us rabbinic Judaism, the form of Judaism that all Jews follow today, in one form or another. The Rabbis left us their own library of classics, and from there, the conversation took off in a thousand different directions.

Over the centuries, pretty much nothing has been off-limits: Jews have attended to much more than idealized piety. The Talmud, the most important compendium of post-biblical thought and the pinnacle contribution of the Rabbis, discusses virtually everything—not just formally religious matters such as God and prayer, but issues as diverse as business law on one hand, and eating practices on the other. There are very wide parameters for what counts as conversation that is legitimately Jewish.

This book allows readers to traverse time and space and listen in on the conversation as it has expanded. Part One provides several key books from the Hebrew Bible. Part Two introduces the pivotal period of the Rabbis, whose major works reach from late antiquity to the early Middle Ages. Part Three looks at the age of medieval philosophy and mysticism, a set of books that build upon the rabbinic masterpieces, expanding the Jewish attitude on matters of life and death, God and the world, good and evil, and everyday matters of human relationships—familial, sexual, commercial, ideological, interreligious, and otherwise. It includes obvious religious treatises but also personal diaries, theological histories, and messianic travelogues.

All these literary, conversational strains feed into Parts Four to Nine, which address the cauldron of change we call modernity—beginning with the European Enlightenment of the eighteenth century that culminated a century later in the Jewish emancipation: the transformation of medieval, ghetto-based Jews into citizens of modern states and stakeholders in national and world affairs. In the 1800s, for the first time ever, Jews could easily leave the Jewish conversation (if they wished to do so), just as non-Jews could freely join it, without fear of church reprisals, governmental restrictions, and social stigma. The conversation adapted to this dramatic change by expanding into Jewish versions of more general themes such as socialism (Jewish Marxism), nationalism (Zionism), and modern religion (synagogue denominations). Part Seven of this book pays special attention to the two most critical events in modern Jewish history—the Holocaust and the founding of the State of Israel—while Part Nine addresses the seething questions of the late twentieth and early twenty-first centuries.

Included in these pages are artists and poets, historians and theologians, men and women from around the world who advocate every kind of Judaism imaginable, encouraging readers to add their own voice to this ancient yet forever new conversation, and to take their own authentic stand on the subjects that move them to passion.

For newcomers to Judaism, this book is a unique synopsis of the things Jews talk about—and the sources Jews cite when they do the talking. For veterans of the Jewish conversation, it will fill in gaps in their knowledge by identifying critical books and the worthies who wrote them.

This selection of one hundred great books was of necessity somewhat personal—reading is, after all, an intensely personal experience. So to some extent, these are the books that I have found highly compelling, as I have gone through a lifetime of Jewish conversing. But I have also consulted others whose reading makes us soul mates: professors, publishers, rabbis, and pretty much any avid Jewish reader I could talk to. I made sure they were religiously diverse (Reform, Orthodox, Conservative, Reconstructionist, secular, and people who say they are "just Jewish"). I talked to women and men, North Americans and Europeans, Diaspora Jews and Jews in Israel, and people of all ages: my teachers, now in their seventies and older; my own generation (I was born just before the baby boomers); my students and even my students' students, i.e., Jews in their twenties and thirties.

I had to ask myself, what in fact constitutes a great book? Among other things, I looked for:

(1) *influence*: books that have been insightful forays into new territory, breakthroughs that influenced whole generations and thereby earned a place on the list of Jewish books that truly matter;

(2) *enjoyment*: whenever possible, reading should be engaging, so I looked for books that are entrancing. To be sure, some great books are not so much read as they are slogged through, and I did include some of those, too—but I explained them sufficiently for readers to understand their importance without necessarily consulting them page by page;

(3) *availability*: ancient Jewish classics are in Hebrew, the language of the Bible and of modern Israel; or they are in Aramaic, the language spoken in the time of Jesus and the literary preference of the Rabbis who lived in late antiquity. These, and medieval classics, too, are

largely inaccessible to contemporary readers, but the ones included here are available in translation;

(4) *comprehensiveness*: a volume like this should represent more than a single stream of conversation—it should include fiction and non-fiction, poetry and art, humor and satire, the old and the new, religionists and agnostics, nationalists and socialists, and as many points of view as one is likely to encounter in the Jewish conversation today;

(5) *particular and universal appeal*: the great books included here have shaped the Jewish character, but one need not be Jewish to appreciate the Jewish struggle with history. Judaism emphasizes both particularism (the uniquely Jewish story) and universalism (the general human predicament). Both perspectives are captured here;

(6) *"the classics"*: books that many readers likely have heard of and probably consulted (at least in part);

(7) *author diversity*: I allowed any author included here just one book (or set of books). At times, this decision proved difficult to follow, but I stuck to it. I included one series that I have edited, but I chose it because it is a collection of the views of many others. I trust that teachers, colleagues, and friends whose books are not here will sympathize with the enormous difficulty I had in making my selections. Many of the finest books could not be squeezed into an overview of just one hundred, especially given all the other necessary constraints that I have listed here.

Reading this book should be like reading the minutes of a thousand Jewish conversations over time, an encounter with the Jewish experience in all its sensitivity and genius, but also its failures and foibles. May you find it enjoyable, challenging, and informative; may it exercise the mind, touch the heart, and stir the soul—at least a little.

I

The Bible

The Conversation Is Launched

☙

The greatest Jewish book of all must surely be the Bible, without which there would be no Judaism, no Christianity, and no Western civilization as we know it. More than a single book, however, the Hebrew Bible is a compilation of many independent compositions, spanning almost a millennium of time and put together in its final form only in the second century CE by a group of post-biblical authorities called the Rabbis.

The biblical books that we now have were not the only candidates for rabbinic canonization, however. Many other (and very similar) Jewish texts of the time were passed over, for reasons that we can only guess at. Some, called the *Apocrypha* (meaning, books of doubtful authority or authenticity), were adopted as part of the Roman Catholic and Eastern Orthodox Bibles (but not the Jewish or Protestant Bibles). Others, the *Pseudepigrapha*—writings falsely ascribed to eminent personalities to make their authorship sound authoritative—never made it into any of the recognized sets of sacred writ that are still around today (or, in a few cases, were only included by Eastern Orthodoxy).

The books that did become the Hebrew Bible present a remarkable record of Judaism in its infancy. Its world was an uneasy balance between two geographic areas where the presence of abundant river systems supported major civilizations: the Nile in Egypt and the Tigris-Euphrates in present-day Iraq (Babylonia in the late biblical and rabbinic periods). The biblical people first known as Hebrews—and only eventually as Jews—inhabited a narrow slice of land on the eastern shore of the Mediterranean, known variously as Judah, Israel, Judea, Palestine, and now Israel again. The Bible is, by and large, the intergenerational conversation that describes how that people came into being, suffered slavery in Egypt, made a covenant with God, pioneered a promised land, was taken captive by Babylonia, and found its way back home again.

It is hard to say just how to refer to the Jewish Bible, since Christians, too, have a Bible, part of which is the same as it is for Jews, and part of which is altogether different. The specifically Christian part includes the Gospel accounts of Jesus's life, the book of Acts that chronicles the early church, a series of letters (mostly attributed to the apostle Paul), and a final book called the Revelation, purporting to announce the events that will lead up to the day of judgment and deliverance.

It was once common to call the Jewish and Christian parts "the Old" and "the New" Testament, respectively, but that nomenclature is generally avoided today, because it implies that the Jewish Bible (the "old") has been superseded by the Christian Bible (the "new"). Until relatively recently, Christian theology held that Jews must "graduate," as it were, from the Old Testament to the New Testament, in order to be saved. In some circles that view still exists, but most major churches today no longer take that "supersessionist" position.

However, we cannot call the two testaments the Jewish and the Christian Bible, either, since the "Jewish" Bible is sacred writ for Christians, too, and should not be co-opted linguistically to denote Jewish Scripture alone. The specifically Jewish part is written almost entirely in Hebrew, however, so it is appropriate to call it the Hebrew Bible. The non-Hebrew sections—parts of the late books Daniel and Ezra, and a single sentence in Jeremiah—are written in Aramaic, a language similar to Hebrew that the Persians introduced at the end of the sixth century BCE as a lingua franca for their empire.

Jews divide this Hebrew Bible into three sections: the Five Books of Moses (*Torah*), the Prophets (*N'vi'im*), and the Writings (*K'tuvim*).

Putting together the first letter each of *Torah*, *N'vi'im*, and *K'tuvim* (with a vowel in between for pronunciation purposes) gives us "TaNaK." And because in Hebrew "k," when preceded by "a," changes to "kh," the Hebrew name for the Bible—which is the name that Jews prefer—is *Tanakh*.

The entire Hebrew Bible is sacred to Jews, but pride of place goes to its first section, the Torah (Genesis, Exodus, Leviticus, Numbers, and Deuteronomy), which is said to have been revealed directly to Moses on Mount Sinai. Most modern Jews have replaced that traditional view with a scientific understanding of its composition by a series of successive writers and editors from about 1000–900 BCE (when kings David and Solomon held the Israelite throne) to somewhere in the fifth century BCE, when the final wave of Jews who had been taken captive in Babylonia returned to the Land of Israel.

After King Solomon died—about 931 BCE—the kingdom that he and his father, David, had built disintegrated into a northern branch called Israel and a southern one called Judah, whose capital was Jerusalem. In 722 BCE, Israel was overrun by Assyria, the superpower of the time, located in what is now northern Iraq and southern Turkey. In 586 BCE, Judah, too, was conquered—and the Temple in Jerusalem destroyed—by Babylonia (in today's southern Iraq), which had displaced Assyria as the dominant power in the area. The Babylonians carried off the ruling class of Jews into captivity. Some fifty years later, however, Persia conquered Babylonia and allowed the exiles to return. At first, most exiled Jews stayed in Babylonia, but a century or so later, around 450 BCE, émigrés led by Ezra, a priest, and Nehemiah, a governor, fully reestablished Jewish life back home. It is then that the Torah was canonized (i.e., it was made the "constitutional" basis for the new society). The Jerusalem Temple had been rebuilt sometime earlier, from 520 BCE to 516 BCE.

The prophets (*n'vi'im*) lived from the eighth to the sixth centuries BCE, surrounding these two imperial conquests and the return of the exiles. Within the N'vi'im, the second section of the Tanakh, Jews include not just the books that bear the prophets' names (Isaiah, Jeremiah, Ezekiel, and the so-called Twelve Minor Prophets) but also the historical books of Joshua, Judges, Samuel, and Kings that describe the original conquest of the Land, its monarchical history under David and Solomon, its split into north and south, and the demise of both— the very time when the prophets were active.

The entire era can be divided into (1) Monarchy; (2) Exile; and (3) Return from Exile:

1000 BCE
Monarchy:
        Kings David and Solomon
        Divided monarchy: Israel (north), Judah (south)
900
800
        Prophetic era (8th to 6th centuries)
722   Assyria conquers Israel (north)

Exile:
586   Babylonia conquers Judah (south), exile

Return from Exile:
538   First wave of return from exile
520–516 Temple is rebuilt
450   Second wave of return from exile; Ezra and
        Nehemiah
        Torah is canonized
400 BCE

The third section of the Tanakh, the K'tuvim (Psalms; Proverbs; Job; "the five scrolls," i.e., Song of Songs, Ruth, Lamentations, Ecclesiastes, and Esther; Daniel; Ezra; Nehemiah; Chronicles) is a set of books that are unrelated to each other, and generally dated between the return from exile and the middle of the second century BCE. The book of Psalms stands out as uniquely prayerful and liturgical. Some books (Proverbs, Ecclesiastes) exemplify wisdom literature, treatises that range from serious philosophical discussion on the attainment of knowledge to homespun descriptions of appropriate human behavior. Jews link Ecclesiastes to four other books—Esther, Ruth, Lamentations, and Song of Songs (a lengthy love poem)—as "the five scrolls." Each is read at a different holy day within the Jewish calendrical year. The books of Ezra and Nehemiah describe the return from exile. Job and Daniel are patently fictitious; the former explores the problem of theodicy (Why do good people suffer?) while the latter epitomizes the lesson that in times of persecution, Jews should remain true to their religion.

In the fourth century BCE, Alexander the Great displaced the Persians, thereby inaugurating the Greek, or Hellenistic, period. About

167 BCE, a revolt by a priestly Jewish dynasty called the Hasmoneans (sometimes called the Maccabees) managed to establish independence and a second Jewish Monarchy (or Commonwealth). About that time, a new group called the Pharisees initiated the rabbinic period. They gave way to the Rabbis, who canonized the biblical sections of the Prophets and the Writings in the second century CE.

The Rabbis did more than canonize the Hebrew Bible, however. Not only did they tell the Jews what to read, they also taught them *how* to read it, by providing their own interpretations of what the Bible "really" meant. Draconian legislation such as "an eye for an eye," for instance, was declared null and void, and core stories such as Adam and Eve or Abraham and Isaac were imaginatively embellished to the point where the original story line was practically forgotten. (We will turn to these rabbinic readings in Part Two.) But the Bible exists in its own right, independent of its rabbinic overlay. It was the creation of the Bible that launched the Jewish conversation. The Bible is without doubt the very first set of great Jewish books.

Genesis

"In the beginning, God created the heavens and the earth."

Though it is the first book of the Bible, Genesis is not the first biblical book written. Like much of the Bible, it evolved over centuries, from about 1000 to 900 BCE (when kings David and Solomon established the First Jewish Commonwealth), until roughly 450 BCE (when the priest Ezra and the governor Nehemiah left the Babylonian exile to establish the Second Commonwealth). Sometime in that fifth century, the final form of Genesis was put together and declared holy writ. The Second Commonwealth lasted until 70 CE, when the Romans ended it, and no other independent Jewish commonwealth has existed until the modern State of Israel, which came into being in 1948. For almost two millennia now, Jews who gather weekly for Sabbath worship mark the beginning months of the Jewish year by hearing Genesis proclaimed, bit by bit, from beginning to end.

Genesis recounts the origins of the world, the human enterprise in general, and the Jewish People in particular. The appellation "Jew" is anachronistic, however, since "Judah" originally referred only to the southern kingdom during the divided monarchy. When sailors identify the prophet Jonah as the cause for the storm that threatens to capsize their ship, he explains straightforwardly, *"Ivri anokhi,"* "I am a Hebrew" (Jonah 1:9).

Still, we go by "Jew" today, and see the book of Genesis as the beginning of the Jewish narrative, our identity through time. Many of the tales are fictitious, but so are the mythic accounts of all peoples—the Roman account of Romulus and Remus, for example. No matter. Haven't we all heard of Abraham, Isaac, and Jacob; Sarah, Rebecca, Rachel, and Leah? The Jewish mission through history is set when God makes a covenant with Abraham, promising that his progeny will be a blessing to all humanity.

That is the particularistic Jewish aspect to Genesis. Its universal appeal is the theme of human growth and conflict that its real-life characters embody. None of these ancestors had children easily; when they do, their offspring become as challenging as our own children often are. Isaac is born in chapter 21, and almost killed at his father's hand only one chapter later. The first set of twins, Cain and Abel, invent sibling rivalry to the point of the first fratricide; only Cain survives, a wanderer on the face of the earth, as all of us are wanderers, unless history and nature are kind to us. The next set of twins, Jacob and Esau, wrangle in their mother's womb, then fight it out while growing up. Jacob emerges triumphant (if not very likeable) because he successfully steals his older brother's birthright and paternal blessing. It is hard to hold back tears when we read poor Esau's plea, "Father, do you have no blessing left for me?" Incredibly, the two brothers will be reconciled in the touching account of Esau, who has moved past anger, and Jacob, who sees in his brother's countenance the very face of God. Nobody in the book of Genesis grows up easily, and some barely grow up at all: not only does Cain kill Abel, but Joseph is sold into slavery by his very own brothers.

The Joseph stories are nothing short of a TV series, their various chapters virtually begging the reader to keep going and see how the whole thing ends. Jacob has two sons by his favored wife, Rachel: Joseph (who is the older) and Benjamin. When famine forces Joseph's brothers to seek out food in Egypt, Benjamin stays home, lest his father lose him also. Joseph, who has by now become the pharaoh's viceroy, doles out grain to his brothers, who do not recognize him. He finagles to get Benjamin to come the next time, and then, to keep his beloved little brother close by, he tries to hold him ransom while the others—Joseph's half brothers—return home. One of the most pathos-laden lines in the whole Bible comes when Judah, the oldest brother, offers to stand surety for little Benjamin. "Let me stay instead," he pleads, "lest my father die of heartbreak"—meaning, "My father doesn't love me as much."

When Genesis ends, the brothers gather around their ailing father, who confers a personal blessing that each of them will carry throughout life. Isn't that what we all dream of: moving into adult life with a parental blessing to mark our way? But some blessings are better than others, and that, too, is reality for us: sometimes our parents do not love us all the same.

Genesis begins with not just one, but two accounts of creation, the first one punctuated by God's assurance that the universe is "good"— good to live in and good to worry about. The book ought then to have moved to Noah, who builds an ark and rescues the world (and its goodness) when human evil threatens to overcome it.

Instead we get Adam and Eve and the Garden of Eden. What's the point of that, we might wonder. For Christians it has been the story of the fall, our ancestral couple's primal disobedience in eating the only forbidden fruit of the Garden. For Jews, the climax of the tale is its end, their exile from paradise—rather than the cause of that exile, Adam and Eve's sin. The tale of Adam and Eve was composed relatively late, only after the end of the paradigmatic exile to Babylonia in 538 BCE. The anonymous editor who chose the opening stories in Genesis had experienced the Babylonian claim that their own gods, not the Jewish one, ruled supreme. Thus he began the book of Genesis with not just one, but two accounts of creation—to insist at the very outset that since God alone created everything, God alone has power to direct human affairs.

The same editor included Adam and Eve to prefigure the defining Jewish trauma: exile from home. They personify this state of exiled existence not just for Jews, however, but for all of us—for every human being who feels, at times, homeless, alone, and in despair. The rest of the Hebrew Bible emphasizes this core theme of Jewish history. Prophets repeat it, warning constantly of exile's pending disaster, but then promising the certainty of eventual return home.

The Jewish exile from home and the central human search for belonging come together in this remarkable book of Genesis.

Isaiah

"And they shall beat their swords into plowshares, and their spears into pruning hooks; nation shall not lift up sword against nation, neither shall they learn war any more."

In Jewish tradition, Isaiah is one of three major prophets; the other two are Jeremiah and Ezekiel. Also in the N'vi'im are twelve other, so-called minor, prophets, grouped together as "the twelve." The historical books of Joshua, Judges, 1 and 2 Samuel, and 1 and 2 Kings are also considered part of the N'vi'im, because they form the historical background against which the prophets led their lives. These latter books also refer to other prophets—not the literary prophets who left us writings of their own, but court prophets (such as Elijah) who became advisors or antagonists to kings.

For most of Jewish history, Jews did not study the prophets book by book. Instead, the prophets were known primarily through selections that had become part of a weekly synagogue lectionary that had come into being slowly, over the course of centuries from late antiquity to the early Middle Ages. To this day, a weekly Torah reading is followed by a prophetic addendum called the *Haftarah*. Because the prophetic portion was chosen only with an eye to some inherent connection to the Torah text, and because it was rather short in any event, the larger message of each prophet against the backdrop of his time was easily missed. (The same phenomenon occurred among Christians who were taught snippets of prophetic writings only as predictions of the coming of Christ, and thus knew little or nothing about who the prophets actually were and when they lived.)

The prophets were unveiled as historical personalities only in the nineteenth century, when the study of evolution and a scientific approach to history gave people a modern historical consciousness. Nineteenth-century liberal rabbis in Germany were among the first emancipated Jews allowed to attend university. There, they became excited about the concept of historical evolution as a way to claim their religious tradition, but also as a way to modify the tradition by seeking its relevance for their own era. They seized on the prophetic denunciation of injustice as their own raison d'être as Jews, claiming the Jewish People as God's agents, charged through time with bringing the message of ethical monotheism to the world. The prophets were rediscovered as proponents of this ethical monotheism, untiring champions of the poor and downtrodden—a concept that became especially resonant in the 1890s, when the great migration from eastern and southern Europe made America awash with urban poverty. Ever since, whenever issues of inequality and suffering have been addressed in the public arena—the American civil rights marches of the 1950s and 1960s, for example—the prophets have been widely cited as the biblical model for pursuing righteousness.

Through all of this, no prophet matches the influence of Isaiah, son of Amoz, who inhabited Jerusalem during the last half of the eighth century BCE. The book that bears his name is filled with lines that have become commonplace today—such as the quotation with which this entry begins (Isa. 2:4), or "Come let us reason together" (1:18), "The people that walked in darkness have seen a great light" (9:1), and "The wolf shall lie down with the lamb [. . .] and a little child shall lead them" (11:6).

Chapters 34–35 and chapters 40–66 of Isaiah are by another author altogether, someone we call Second Isaiah. We know neither his real name nor why his work was appended, but he probably lived during the sixth century BCE, and his message is altogether different. The original Isaiah inhabited a world where the once united kingdom of David and Solomon had been split into Israel in the north and Judah in the south (Jerusalem was Judah's capital). In 722 BCE, Assyria conquered Israel and threatened Judah. First Isaiah preached against the folly of forming alliances with Assyria's enemies—especially Egypt, the other major power at the time. God alone could be trusted to save his people, but God would not come to Judah's aid as long as the wealthy and powerful oppressed the poor. Given such widespread social inequity, God would use the powerful kingdoms of the time to destroy Jerusalem. Only then would a "sacred remnant" arise, newly purified and committed to justice and righteousness.

In 586, Jerusalem was indeed conquered, by Babylonia. Second Isaiah wrote mostly from the Babylonian exile, his message inherent in the stirring demand with which his prophecy begins: "Comfort, yes, comfort my people" (40:1). Much of Second Isaiah is known for prophecies on which Jews and Christians have differed. The suffering servant in Isaiah 53 might be the best example: Christians identify the servant as Jesus, while Jews do not. But First Isaiah, too, has proved controversial. Chapter 7:14 says, "A young woman is with child and about to give birth." Classical Christian exegesis translated *almah*, the noun for "young woman," as "virgin," thus foreshadowing Jesus's mother, Mary.

Isaiah is not an easy biblical book to read. Its anonymous editor had little regard for chronological order, and much of the original Hebrew is opaque. It should be studied, not read; picked up for a chapter or two, then pondered when compelling verses capture the imagination. All in all, the book of Isaiah is a sweeping portrait of the most revolutionary era in biblical history, a period of conquest, exile, and restoration. It is steeped in all the grand themes that make the prophets so central to the human enterprise.

Psalms

"The Lord is my shepherd; I shall not want."

Rolling around in the deep recesses of memory is a scene from childhood: someone saying in Yiddish, *"m'darf zogen t'illim,"* "You should recite Psalms." In all probability, the occasion prompting the advice was some family illness, against which reciting psalms was considered a reasonable remedy. The speaker may even have been a member of a *chevra t'illim* (a society for reciting psalms), a voluntary organization devoted to the special piety of psalm recitation. In one custom, the psalter would be divided into seven sections, one for each day of the week; another practice associated psalms with weekly Torah portions and the holiday cycle, so that not a Sabbath or a holiday would pass without some psalm being added because it was indicative of the day in question. Similarly, Psalm 19 was read at weddings, Psalm 12 at a boy's circumcision, and still other psalms to bring rain in times of drought or healing for those in pain.

This privatized recitation of psalms emerged from sixteenth- and seventeenth-century Jewish mysticism—the era in which the kabbalistic tradition flourished in the Land of Israel—and was outfitted with an introductory and a concluding prayer requesting every known (and even unknown) benefit. "Let my recitation be as if King David himself were saying it," said the worshipper, believing (with tradition) that it was King David who had authored the psalms in the first place. Not only the sentences, but the individual words, letters, vocalization schemes, cantillation marks, and the names of God formed by combining the letters of the beginnings and ends of sentences would atone for sin, placate divine wrath, and bring about the *yichudim* (the unification) of the male and the female sides of God that represented the uniquely kabbalistic metaphor for redemption. Kabbalist Isaiah Horowitz (ca. 1565–1630) reported what he thought was an old custom of staying up all Yom Kippur eve (the evening prior to the Day of Atonement), to read through the psalter in its entirety. "Nothing is greater than Psalms," he adjured his readers, "for it contains everything: much praise for the Holy One, Blessed be He, as well as many psalms that evoke penitence and seek divine pardon."

Worshippers prayed that on account of the merit of the psalms' words, letters, mystical names, and so on, sick friends and family would be healed, captives redeemed, travelers protected, stillbirths avoided, pregnancies brought to fruition, and scholarly children born. Unfriendly governments would look kindly on their Jewish populations, evil decrees would be eliminated, business would prosper, and redemption would arrive. "*M'darf zogen t'illim*," indeed!

Scholars today believe that the psalms were authored by many people, all of them anonymous. But Jewish tradition ascribes them to King David himself. Apparently, when Jewish ancestors, some two thousand years back, tried to come up with the best way to aggrandize their most warlike king, they decided he should be a composer, musician, and singer! Whatever the case, the psalms were sung as worship in the Second Temple (sixth century BCE to 70 CE), and in some cases, possibly, even in the First Temple (tenth to sixth centuries BCE).

The 150 psalms get their name from the Greek *psalmos*, a translation of the Hebrew *mizmor* (meaning, a song accompanied by a string instrument). We call it the book of Psalms (or Psalter), but it is in fact a collection of five books, combined by an editor once upon a time, probably on the model of the Torah, the Five Books of Moses. Each of the five Psalm books is itself a compilation of several smaller and prior collections. One such collection, for example (Psalms 105–106, 111–113, 115–117, 146–150), begins or ends with *Hallelujah*. The psalms of another collection (Psalms 120–134) announce themselves as "Song of Ascent," possibly because pilgrims sang them on their way up the Temple mount.

The Hebrew title is *t'hillim*—songs of praise—a reference to the psalms' liturgical function from the very beginning: singing praise to God. They still function that way. While very few Jews today belong to psalm societies, psalms are far and away the most frequently cited biblical material in the Jewish prayer book (the Siddur). Whole clusters of psalms form the bulk of the early morning service, the prayers that welcome Shabbat, and a celebratory addition to the worship for festivals called *Hallel*—literally, praise.

Some of the best-known biblical lines are psalms, none more famous than Psalm 23, which is widely recited in times of distress, especially at funerals. So popular is this psalm that it alone among biblical material has resisted the tendency to retranslate prayers into gender-neutral modern English. It is still most widely encountered in its King James Version: "The Lord is my shepherd; I shall not want. He maketh me to lie down in green pastures: He leadeth me beside the still waters. He restoreth my soul: He leadeth me in the paths of righteousness for His name's sake. Yea, though I walk through the valley of the shadow of death, I will fear no evil: for Thou art with me; Thy rod and Thy staff, they comfort me. Thou preparest a table before me in the presence of mine enemies: Thou anointest my head with oil; my cup runneth over. Surely goodness and mercy shall follow me all the days of my life: and I will dwell in the house of the Lord for ever."

Jesus died with a psalm on his lips. According to Matthew and Mark, it was Psalm 22:1, "My God, my God, why have you forsaken me?"— while according to Luke, it was Psalm 31:6, "In your hand I entrust my soul." Jews recognize Psalm 31:6 as the concluding verse in the most familiar Hebrew hymn in the morning service: *Adon olam*—"Master of the World."

But not all psalms are positive. Their appeal is precisely their balanced view of life's sometimes bitter realities. Psalm 38 wonders why God has not appeared, when "my wounds stink and fester [. . .] I am bent and bowed." And Psalm 74 cries out, "Why, O God, do you forever reject me?"

Faith comes easily to those without pain, and glib statements of faith by people who deny even their own pain's reality are suspect. Psalms have persisted as the Bible's best example of faith that is deep, honest, and true, because they express what suffering is, yet affirm God's presence, even in the midst of it.

Job

"You have not spoken the truth about Me as did my servant Job."

The book of Job is arguably the most profound piece of religious literature ever written. It has intrigued not just readers of the Bible, but poets, playwrights, and philosophers of the human condition who have recast its tale of suffering for their own ends. Archibald MacLeish, for example, has given us *J.B.*, a stunning drama of Job updated for our time, while C. G. Jung's final great work is called *Answer to Job*, possibly because the promise of human meaning seems tied up with the quandary that the book of Job sets for us in terms that cannot be forgotten: why do the righteous suffer?

Job is a brilliant work of fiction, probably composed sometime between the sixth and fourth centuries BCE. It begins with an unforgettable scene of God walking to and fro in heaven, with apparently nothing to do but boast of the righteousness of "my servant Job [. . .] There is no one like him on earth, a blameless and upright man who fears God and shuns evil." For the first time in the Hebrew Bible, a figure named Satan appears, not yet the medieval embodiment of evil but one of God's many minions. Satan anticipates his later incarnation, however, when he dares God to give him power to test Job with suffering.

Why God agrees to Satan's proposal is the underlying theme of the book—the all-time classic statement of what is called the problem of theodicy: why would an all-knowing, all-powerful, and all-good God collude with the forces of evil, whether represented in antiquity by the figure of Satan or recognizable to us moderns in earthquakes, hurricanes, and other disasters that we still call "acts of God"?

In short order, Job's livestock are stolen, his house is burned down, and his children are killed in a cyclone. Job's response is classic: "Naked came I out of my mother's womb, and naked shall I return there. The Lord has given, and the Lord has taken away. Blessed be the name of the Lord." Notwithstanding his trials, "Job did not sin, nor did he cast reproach on God." As the story unfolds, things get even worse: Job himself is afflicted with excruciating pain. "Cursed is the day when I was born," he mourns, "and the night it was announced, 'A male has been conceived.' May that night be darkness."

The rest of the book is commentary on this simple but tragic tale. Will Satan win his bet? Will Job curse God?

Job should be read against the backdrop of two earlier biblical books, Exodus and Ezekiel. Exodus, the story of Israel's journey from Egyptian slavery to Mount Sinai, contains the promise that God visits the sins of the fathers upon the children all the way down through three successive generations. Ezekiel, a prophet living later, after the Jews' traumatic experience of being taken captive by victorious Babylonian conquerors, argues to the contrary: suffering does not depend on what one's ancestors have done. The exiles can plan for a positive future, because from now on, God holds each person responsible for his or her own sins alone.

Job questions even this advance. It would be bad enough if his pain derived from what other people once had done. But attributing it to his own sins won't work either, because (as the book plainly tells us), he is perfectly righteous—and he knows it.

Most of the book of Job is a dialogue between Job and some visiting friends, who insist that he must have done something wrong. God never punishes without cause, says Eliphaz: "Do not reject the discipline of the Almighty. God injures, but He binds up; He wounds, but his hands heal." Bildad concurs. "We are of yesterday and know nothing," he believes. If, however, we "ask the generations past, study what our fathers have searched out," we will learn that "God does not despise the blameless." Yet a third friend, Zophar, is sure it would all be crystal clear if God would only "enter into conversation" with Job. Until then, Job should trust that God knows truths that Job himself is ignorant of.

But Job remains adamant in his own defense. "At least let me know what You charge me with!" he demands of his divine tormentor. And in the end, God finally intervenes.

But Job gets no answer to the problem of evil. Nor do we. God just pulls rank: "Who is this," God asks, "who darkens counsel, speaking without knowledge? Where were you when I laid the earth's foundation? Have you ever commanded the day to break? [. . .] Have you penetrated to the sources of the sea, or walked in the recesses of the deep? [. . .] Can you send up an order to the clouds for an abundance of water?" Near the very beginning of the book, Job had predicted, "Man cannot win a suit against God," and we see now just how right he was. Faced with God's omnipotence, Job realizes he is no match for the Almighty. "I recant and relent," he concedes, "being but dust and ashes."

The story ends with Job restored to his former status, but with more wealth than ever, and with twice the number of children he once had. Job eventually dies "old and content."

Readers, however, are likely to be less content. We get some satisfaction when God at least refutes the simple-minded notion of Job's friends that all human suffering is deserved. In almost a side comment, God assures us, "I do not work that way." But how then *does* God work? That, unfortunately, we never learn.

Job's surrender seems intended as a pious conclusion to remind us to trust God no matter what befalls us. But Job is a book that makes that conclusion difficult to swallow. Why do the innocent suffer? The problem of theodicy remains as unanswerable today as it was two and a half millennia ago, when a brilliant thinker and author wrote this biblical account of suffering without cause—a treatment of the subject that has never been surpassed.

Ecclesiastes (Kohelet)

"'Utter futility,' said Kohelet, 'Utter futility. All is futile.'"

Religions, we assume, should at the very least broadcast life's purpose. But what if there is no purpose to broadcast? Alternatively, if life has no *inherent* purpose, perhaps we can manufacture one—anything from artistic creation to building a financial empire?

But what if that, too, proves elusive? What if even the wealthiest, the wisest, and the most creative geniuses inevitably look back from their deathbeds disillusioned by the grim reality of having pursued lives that were useless?

There are other options—and enjoying family and friends must rank high among them, most of us would say. But doesn't that, too, evaporate upon our deaths? What if the final judgment on life really is "Utter futility; utter futility; all is futile"? That is the nightmarish scenario with which Ecclesiastes begins—and once upon a time, perhaps, also ended.

Jews call this book of the Bible Kohelet, after the name of its narrator, introduced halfway into the first chapter as "Kohelet [. . .] a king in Jerusalem." At some point, someone added an additional one-line preamble, calling him "Kohelet, son of David in Jerusalem." This attribution is almost certainly false, but nonetheless, Jewish tradition identifies Kohelet as King Solomon.

The Hebrew root from which KoHeLet is derived is *k.h.l.*, implying "gathering," so the Septuagint, the ancient Greek translation of the Hebrew Bible, called it Ecclesiastes—from the Greek noun meaning, member of the assembly. The great medieval Jewish commentator Rashi (see page 57) thought Kohelet meant "the one who assembles wisdom," an ironic name for a protagonist who assures us there is no point to wisdom in the first place.

Perhaps the best metaphor here is that of a child playing "connect the dots." There is good reason to be satisfied with the picture created when all the dots are joined. By turning a scattered set of dots into a meaningful design, the child is preparing for the lifetime task of finding meaning in the random dots of life that come one's way.

Kohelet is a collector of his life's dots who discovers that even the "good" dots can prove wearisome. As he reviews his life, he finds only meaningless redundancy. "I have grown richer and wiser than any that ruled before me," he says, "but as wisdom grows, vexation grows; to increase learning is to increase heartache." True, he goes on, "wisdom is superior to folly," since "a wise man has his eyes in his head whereas the fool walks in darkness"—but "the same fate awaits them both." Neither one is "remembered forever. The wise man dies just like the fool." And as for possessions, "I loathed all the wealth that I was gaining [. . .] for I shall leave it to the man who will succeed me."

This is just the book's beginning. In short order, Kohelet tries everything—companionship, for instance, but who can count on that? "When two lie together they are warm, but how can he who is alone get warm?" In the end, we all age: "Better a poor but wise youth than an old and foolish king." And even in the interim, who knows what fate will bestow? "God sometimes grants a man riches, property, and wealth [. . .] but God does not permit him to enjoy it."

Behind the specific examples lies the sickness of spirit we call ennui, the mental weariness that saturates the soul. Not only do accidents foil our planning, but there is no successful plan to be had. At least goodness should be rewarded, but "sometimes the upright man is requited according to the conduct of the scoundrel, and sometimes the scoundrel is requited according to the conduct of the upright."

Yet despite the book's pessimistic main theme, Kohelet prescribes proverbial wisdom for staying in the moment. Yes, long-term planning is absurd, but the long term is made of specific moments—the individual dots that we try to string together into a larger picture of purpose. If there is no larger picture, at least the dots are real enough. "The only future is nothingness," but in the present, "what a delight for the eyes it is to behold the sun." The future may frustrate us, but in the present, "whatever is in your power to do, do with all your might [. . .] go eat your bread with gladness and drink your wine in joy." It is sensible to invest your energy in the moment, while you still have it—to "send your bread upon the waters," as Ecclesiastes puts it. All we get are "fleeting days of life," but we *do* get those days. There may be no higher purpose. But there may be no need for one.

That may be sufficient for most people, as it probably was for the author of Kohelet. But the book ends with a surprising turn. After repeating the opening evaluation, "Utter futility. All is futile," Kohelet offers "a further word [. . .] The sum of the matter, when all is said and done: revere God and observe His commandments! For this applies to all mankind—God will call every creature to account." The God of this book until these final lines is a God of "utter futility," unmoved by human fate. The God with whom the book ends takes note of what we do and then rewards and punishes. The long term is not so futile after all!

Most scholars believe this pious conclusion is an addendum, tacked on to make Kohelet less pessimistic. The original text was composed anonymously, sometime between the sixth and the third centuries BCE. It did not become sacred writ until several centuries later, through Rabbis who either inherited the book with the last part already added, or added it themselves, to make it comport with their views of a personal God who provides an afterlife to make up for inequities here on earth.

Not that it matters—a number of canonical books are composed by at least two, and sometimes more, different hands. The end result here, whether by one author or two, is a jaundiced view of human ambition, studded with sage advice on doing the right things nevertheless—with a final corrective comment that God, perhaps, notices us after all.

The Jewish Study Bible
(2004)

Adele Berlin (*born 1943*) and Marc Zvi Brettler (*born 1958*)
(*editors*)

> *"'O how I love your teaching! It is my study all day long' (Psalm 119:97). These two themes—the love for Torah (teaching) and dedication to the study of it—have characterized Jewish reading and interpretation of the Bible ever since. The love is the impetus for the study; the study is the expression of the love."*

Until relatively recently, vernacular versions of the Bible were as much religio-political tracts as they were "true" translations of the original. What fueled them at first was the Protestant rebellion against the medieval church and its papal tradition that claimed the absolute right to decide what the Bible meant. At stake was not the Hebrew Bible that Jews used, but the Christian Bible, available mostly in a Latin version called the Vulgate.

The most direct way to challenge church authority was to put vernacular versions of the Bible into the hands of would-be critics of Rome. In the 1380s, even before the Reformation began, John Wycliffe, a theologian at Oxford University, produced the first English translation—and was declared a heretic after his death. In the sixteenth century, Martin Luther translated the entire Christian Bible into German; and in 1534, King Henry VIII charged Thomas Cranmer, the archbishop of Canterbury, to prepare an official English translation that became known as the Great Bible, because of its hefty size and weight. The most famous translation into English, the King James Version, came into being in 1611.

Jewish translations of the Hebrew Bible never followed this Christian model of being motivated by denominational infighting, largely because in the various movements of Judaism, translations are used only for convenience, not for official purposes. All Jews agree that the Bible can be read only alongside the rabbinic interpretations of it—and those presuppose complete familiarity with the Hebrew original. Jewish denominational disputes have therefore focused more on these rabbinic teachings than on the actual biblical text itself.

There were, of course, Jewish biblical translations in antiquity: the Septuagint—the classic translation from Hebrew into Greek—dates from around the second century BCE, and a variety of Aramaic translations (each one called a *targum*, Hebrew for "translation") emerged in the first several centuries CE. But Jewish tradition treats the Septuagint as outside the stream of Jewish thought, and the targums are considered part of the rabbinic interpretation of the Bible rather than as an accurate translation of it.

In any event, nothing comparable to the Protestant Reformation occurred in Judaism until the nineteenth century, and when it did occur, the overall challenge for Jews was *not* to establish a theological rationale for political power—Jews had no power to establish—but merely to be recognized as citizens in the body politic. So while Christian translations argued subtle doctrinal differences, Jewish translations sought merely to acculturate Jews into the language of the countries where they lived. The first such modern translation was begun in 1783, in Prussia, by the great Enlightenment philosopher Moses Mendelssohn—an attempt to familiarize Jews with German. Since most Jews could not read German script, Mendelssohn transcribed the German into Hebrew characters. In America, more or less official English Bibles were produced by the Jewish Publication Society (JPS) in 1917 and then again, in stages, from 1962 to 1982. (The JPS is a nondenominational organization established in 1888, with the original goal of providing Jewish immigrants to America with cultural resources in English. *The Jewish Study Bible* uses the 1982 JPS translation.)

These modern English versions of the Hebrew Bible are revolutionary not just because they are translations, but because they come without commentaries—and Jews almost never read the Bible without at least one accompanying commentary, usually the one written by the great medieval scholar Rashi. Independent verses of the Bible were also used as proof texts for lessons taught by the Talmud or by rabbinic teachers in the ancient and medieval synagogue. Modern-day rabbis cite the Bible that way, too, during worship services that feature biblical readings as prayers in their own right, or as an official lectionary—weekly portions drawn from the Torah and the Prophets. The point here is that traditionally speaking, few Jews have ever even considered reading the Bible as an independent literary work, i.e., starting at the beginning and moving through it to the conclusion.

That traditional Jewish understanding of the Bible as a sacred text to be refracted through the lens of the Rabbis and the liturgy conflicted with the modern academic approach of seeing it as an independent literary creation. When Jews were admitted to universities in the nineteenth century, however, they learned to study the Bible scientifically and in its own right. First and foremost, biblical critics revealed the Torah as a set of documents composed by human authors over a lengthy period of time, rather than a single set of teachings imparted by God to Moses on Mount Sinai. Scholars now approached the psalms as cultic poetry, took apart Isaiah as not just one book but two, and saw echoes of other ancient Near Eastern cultures in the stories of Genesis. Archeology, too, had its impact as remnants of excavated material culture shed light on the world to which the Bible testifies.

The Jewish Study Bible returns to the age-old Jewish method of reading the Bible with a line-by-line commentary. But the commentary is modern, a judicious selection of textual, literary, and archeological information. Take Joshua's vaunted capture of Jericho, for example (Josh. 6). The story is compelling: seven priests carry seven ram's horns, as they lead the Israelites around the city walls in circuits for seven days, after which the people shout and (as the well-known spiritual has it) "the walls come tumblin' down."

But according to the commentary in *The Jewish Study Bible*, "Archeological research has shown that the last *city wall* of Jericho no longer existed [by the time of Joshua . . .]; therefore the story of its conquest may be more symbolic than historical." We learn to read the tale as a ritualized account using folk motifs like the number seven, which occurs "14 times (2 x 7) in ch 6—to indicate days, priests, ram's horns, and circuits of the city." This new information is not likely to satisfy biblical literalists, but for readers who already doubt the veracity of a tale where a city's walls collapse because of shouting, the story becomes worth reading all over again, in a new light.

This account of Jericho is just one small example of the way *The Jewish Study Bible* reveals the Bible as a work of literature saturated with symbolism, laced with poetry, punctuated with references to the ancient Near East where it arose, and resonant with echoes of Israel's search for God. We also get sophisticated but accessible essays to introduce the various biblical books, maps that illustrate the narrative, and references to traditional Jewish (and Christian) interpretation, alongside the modern scientific one. The editors, Adele Berlin and Marc Zvi Brettler, are leading contemporary scholars and teachers in the field of Bible studies. With *The Jewish Study Bible* they offer the wealth of modern biblical study not just to experts but to everyday Bible readers—and make the Bible even more well worth reading every day.

2

The Rabbis

The Conversation Is Transformed

☙☙

A familiar story, based loosely on the Talmud, pictures the Palestinian sage Rabbi Akiba (d. ca. 132 CE) explaining Torah to his students. Moses, who has heard of Akiba's greatness, sneaks down from heaven to enjoy listening to Akiba's exposition. As the conversation in the class develops, Moses is shocked to discover that he cannot follow it. Indeed, he cannot even recognize the Torah that they are discussing as the document that he himself brought down from Sinai.

Whether the Torah actually goes back as far as Moses has been a matter of debate among Jews for centuries. The Rabbis believed it did—hence this story, which served as a congratulatory reminder of just how much they had changed the Jewish conversation since the era of the Bible.

But who were "the Rabbis" (written with a capital "R," as opposed to "rabbis," the ordained officiants who represent Judaism today), and how did they come into existence?

We saw above how Alexander the Great brought Greek culture to the Land of Israel in the fourth century BCE, and how, in roughly 167 BCE, a Jewish dynasty of priests called the Hasmoneans (also known as the Maccabees) wrested independence from one of Alexander's distant successors. (The Jewish holiday of Hanukkah celebrates the revolt's success.) With the Hasmonean victory and its creation of a Second Jewish Commonwealth, new political groups came into being—most notably, the Sadducees (the priestly party) and the Pharisees (their rivals), whom a later group, the Rabbis, saw as their spiritual predecessors. In 70 CE, war with Rome reduced the Second Temple to rubble, erased the sacrificial cult that it had housed, and ended the era of the Sadducees and Pharisees.

The spiritual and political vacuum left by the destruction of the Temple was filled by a new scholarly class whom we call the Rabbis. We refer to them as scholars because central to their Judaism was an all-consuming concern for the study of Torah. Placing the story of Rabbi Akiba and Moses in a classroom is telling: the Rabbis were teachers—even the title "Rabbi" means "my teacher."

The Rabbis saw themselves as a continuation of the Pharisees, but the title "Rabbi" emerged only after 70 CE, when rabbinic ideals transformed Jews into a people centered on the study of Torah, the practice of prayer, and the performance of good deeds.

Of these three pillars—study, worship, and good deeds—study ranked highest, since only through study, the Rabbis held, could the details of what constitutes proper worship and true goodness be derived. Torah study, as the Rabbis understood it, presupposed the radical notion that in every era, the Bible (Written Torah) requires oral commentary (Oral Torah) to be brought up to date. The library of sacred texts that the Rabbis bequeathed to us as the written record of their conversations remains the very center of Jewish spiritual life to this day. Every Jewish innovation until modern times has been predicated on a thorough grounding in this absolutely essential rabbinic textual heritage.

Because the rabbinic period spans several centuries, it is best broken down into smaller periods of time, each with its own unique literature:

From 70 CE to ca. 200 CE, the Rabbis were known as *Tanna'im* (teachers). The tannaitic era ends with the *Mishnah*, a law code providing the basic outlines of the entire rabbinic way of life: how to pray, the rules of tithing, civil and criminal law, institutions of marriage and family life, what constitutes the sacred, and a whole lot more. The Mishnah represents the culmination of the tannaitic era and a bridge to the amoraic period that follows. The Tanna'im inhabited the Land of Israel, which the Romans had renamed Palaestina (from which we get "Palestine"). By 200 CE, however, rabbinic culture was spreading to

Babylonia (Iraq) as well. In both Palestine and Babylonia, therefore, a second wave of Jewish study developed, this one led by teachers called *Amora'im*—a word derived from the Hebrew *amar* (to speak), and emphasizing the oral transmission of tradition. The Amora'im provided the next, and largest, set of great rabbinic books, the *Talmud*—actually, two Talmuds: the Palestinian Talmud, which was promulgated around 400 CE, and the far more influential Babylonian Talmud, which was not finally redacted until sometime between 550 and 650 CE. The Talmuds are arranged as commentary on the Mishnah, although the Mishnah often serves as just a jumping-off point for much longer and deeper Talmudic conversations that take on an independence all their own. Sometimes, Talmud is called Gemara, an Aramaic equivalent— both *talmud* and *gemara* mean "learning."

The same Rabbis who gave us Mishnah and Talmud—which are largely legal in nature—invented yet another mode of discourse, elaborate and even fanciful commentaries on the Bible called *midrash*. Midrash arose as public exposition of Scripture in rabbinic study academies and in synagogues, where Rabbis pioneered the art form that we now call sermons. These midrashic expositions were then compiled in separate collections, many of which we now have extant.

By the seventh century CE, the next wave of rabbinic authorities, the *Ge'onim*, came to the fore in Babylonia, although it is hard to know precisely when. They probably emerged with the coming of Islam in the seventh century, but our first literary geonic record comes only with the move of the Muslim caliphate to Baghdad in 762 CE. Rabbinic authorities already there were renamed *Gaon* (plural: *Ge'onim*), a biblical word meaning, roughly, "Your Honor." They asserted authority over all Jews much as the caliph decided spiritual matters for all Muslims.

Palestinian Rabbis resisted their Babylonian counterparts' attempt to determine Jewish law worldwide, but over time, the geonic claim prevailed. By the end of the eleventh century, Jews everywhere began accepting geonic teaching as authoritative. The last great Gaon died in 1038.

By then Jews had spread far and wide throughout North Africa, Europe, and western Asia, and regularly wrote to the Gaon with questions about Jewish life and law. Ge'onim met the challenge by establishing a new literary format—legal discussions called *responsa* (singular: *responsum*) that incorporated precedents from prior rabbinic texts, especially the Babylonian Talmud. To this day, responsa remain the primary mode of Jewish decision making.

During the Middle Ages (see Part Three), the Jewish conversation branches out well beyond the Rabbis, whose legacy is discussed here. But the Rabbis are never left far behind. One cannot imagine Judaism, even today, without the rabbinic revolution that completely reformulated Judaism—by canonizing the final shape of the Hebrew Bible; by creating Mishnah, Talmud, midrash, and responsa; and by inventing the religious institutions we take for granted today: academies of study (the *yeshivot*); a way of life based on legal pronouncements; all of Jewish liturgy; the Jewish calendar and holiday cycle; and even synagogues as we know them.

From Politics to Piety
(1972)

Jacob Neusner (born 1932)

"They invested powerlessness with such meaning that ordinary folk, living everyday lives, might still regard themselves as a kingdom of priests and a holy people."

The patriarchs, prophets, priests, and kings of the biblical era were eventually replaced by the Rabbis, who traced their own roots to an influential group of Jews known as Pharisees. It is hard to know when, exactly, the Pharisees began, but a likely time is 167 BCE, as an outcome of the turbulent Hasmonean revolution. Since the Pharisees are central to the foundational narratives of both Jews and Christians, it is crucial to know just who they were.

That important question is the subject of this outstanding book by the most prolific and influential Jewish scholar of the late twentieth and early twenty-first centuries, Jacob Neusner. At last count, he had written or edited over eight hundred (!) books and thousands of articles. If anyone deserves an entry here, Neusner does—but how does one choose just one of over eight hundred options?

A good choice is *From Politics to Piety*, one of Neusner's earliest books and still one of his best. It is the sterling study of a question that has occupied scholars ever since modern scholarship began—in part, no doubt, because both Judaism and Christianity have a lot riding on the solution. For Jews, the Pharisees are the very foundation of rabbinic Judaism; their most notable founder, Hillel (a generation prior to Jesus), parallels Jesus in, for example, formulating his own version of the Golden Rule. The New Testament, by contrast, knows the Pharisees as self-righteous hypocrites. Where lies the truth?

Three sets of sources are relevant to the Pharisees: the Christian Gospels; the early rabbinic records (carried mostly in the Mishnah); and the work of Josephus, a Pharisee himself who retired to Rome after the Jewish-Roman War of 66–70 CE to write an account of the conflict. Josephus also composed a general history of the Jews, an autobiography, and a polemical response to an anti-Jewish diatribe based on calumnies leveled by various Hellenistic authors.

According to Josephus, the Pharisees were the equivalent of a modern ideology. Reflecting Greek categories of thought, he called them "a philosophy" that offered thoughtful positions on important issues of the time—a belief in an afterlife, for example, and the conviction that written sacred texts must be interpreted alongside oral traditions. As a political force, the Pharisees variously fought against or were supported by the Maccabean dynasty. Eventually, they were purged by a ruler known as Jannaeus, after which (says Neusner) Hillel withdrew the Pharisees from politics and transformed them into the more spiritual entity that rabbinic literature presupposes. No wonder Hillel ranks, in retrospect, not only as the most significant Pharisaic elder but also as the hero of the Rabbis and the putative father of the Jewish institution called the Patriarchate, through which a particular Rabbi, the patriarch (first among equals, as it were), came to represent the rabbinic community to Rome.

The Christian Gospels reflect the period after 70 CE, because even though they purport to be accounts of Jesus's own life, they were composed long after Jesus had died. The Gospel of Luke and its continuation, the Acts of the Apostles, portray the Pharisees as friends and even allies of Jesus. The other Gospel accounts, however, use the Pharisees (who no longer existed by the time they were written) as a convenient foil for Jesus—a benighted religious party better known for its hypocrisy than its religious scruples. But even when the Gospels are wrong—i.e., even when their authors use the Pharisees as convenient scapegoats—we can learn something about the very Pharisees they vilify.

Whenever the Gospels cite specific examples of Pharisaic practice, they fasten on issues of ritual purity around eating, the tithing of food, and rules about the people with whom one may eat. By the time of Jesus, therefore, this once political entity had become a spiritual religious sect emphasizing the belief that Jews are indeed (as the Bible has it) "a kingdom of priests and a holy people." Of first importance for the Pharisees, then, was the need to transfer rules of food, once followed only by priests, to everyone, as if even the average kitchen table were a continuation of the Temple altar. Hence the title of the book: *From Politics to Piety*.

With brilliant incisiveness, Neusner studies all of these sources to arrive at his conclusion. Neusner's account provides detailed textual analysis—which has become his hallmark—as well as a general picture of this all-important era. Readers will appreciate the author's sophisticated unraveling of ancient sources to unveil the truths they have to tell about this crucial period that gave us rabbinic Judaism and early Christianity.

Judaism is a religion of study, a tradition that prizes scholarship. *From Politics to Piety* stands high among exceptional scholarly works, a brilliant example of the kind of textually rooted research that Jews value so much, yet designed for the nonspecialist to read with enormous benefit. It is intriguing, informative, and inspiring—a paradigmatic example of how great scholarship really does make a difference.

The Mishnah: Pirkei Avot

(ca. second to third centuries CE)

"Turn it and turn it, for everything is in it."

Judaism is a religion of law, a continually evolving study of the multitudinous things one should or shouldn't do or be. But it bears hardly any resemblance to the way law is presented in the Hebrew Bible. The Bible would have us stone a stubborn and rebellious son; it urges vengeance on vast numbers of Israel's enemies; it requires "an eye for an eye, a tooth for a tooth." It presupposes a Temple and sacrifices, not a synagogue and prayer. It has no rabbis, only priests and Levites, who serve God in that Temple.

None of these examples of biblical law entered the Judaism of the Rabbis, the scholarly group that became dominant after 70 CE. Indeed, the Rabbis ignored or subverted it all. Sometimes they just outright admitted that the Bible's more draconian legislation had been intended only as a theoretical construct, not as an actual practice. In other cases, they relegated the Bible's laws to Temple times, knowing that the Second Temple had come to an end in the year 70 CE. Although the Rabbis prayed for the Temple's restoration, they made it virtually impossible for a rebuilding to occur: they banned human efforts to bring it about on the grounds that God alone would restore the Temple if and when God was ready. In the meanwhile, Jews should exercise patience.

Theologically, the Rabbis converted a God prone to occasional punishing anger into a God of continual loving pardon. "Happy are you, O Israel, for God loves you," went one rabbinic assurance, which continued, "Happier still are you, for you *know* God loves you." Consonant with that love, the most solemn day of the year, Yom Kippur, was outfitted with a set of confessions and the assurance that "God does not want the death of sinners, but their return to Him." The Rabbis cited the prophet Hosea's parable of a wayward wife whom the aggrieved husband welcomes back with love. The centerpiece of Jewish liturgy became the divine command to love God, preceded by the assurance that God loves Israel, too.

About the year 200 CE, these Rabbis promulgated a tersely written legal code in six volumes called the Mishnah. Most of the rabbinic legal revolution is readily apparent there, and the revolution was to continue in the monumental follow-up work, the Talmud.

As jurists, the Rabbis reached thoroughly innovative rulings while simultaneously maintaining that they were not actually novel. On the contrary, they held that the Bible was the inviolable divine constitution on which all of Judaism rests. In theory, God had dictated the written Torah to Moses on Mount Sinai, but only alongside an oral accompaniment that interpreted the true intent of the written word. This oral understanding, taught the Rabbis, had been passed down by word of mouth all the way from Moses to them, so that future generations could apply it whenever new times and challenges arose. The biblical books that followed the Torah were equally amenable to oral interpretation. So the Bible was foundational to Judaism, but only rabbinic interpretation could transform the foundation into a fully constructed edifice for Jewish living.

Most of the Mishnah is closely worded apodictic legal fiat, such as "The possibility that life might be endangered overrides Sabbath prohibitions regarding work" (i.e., the commandment to rest on the Sabbath should be broken in order to save human life); or, "If someone leaves a jug in the public domain, and someone else stumbles on it, breaking it, the person who fell is not liable for damages; if injury occurs, the jug's owner must pay damages to the injured party."

Like law in general, most of these decrees do not make for particularly interesting reading. In addition, the Mishnah's laconic wording demands that it be studied rather than read. Despite its absolute centrality in rabbinic Judaism, therefore, the Mishnah, as a whole, is not necessarily recommended for lay readers.

But there is an exception, an important one, a small portion of the Mishnah called *Pirkei Avot* (literally, Chapters of the Fathers). Except for the Bible and the prayer book, *Pirkei Avot* has probably been translated and printed more frequently than any other Jewish book in history.

Like the rest of the Mishnah, *Pirkei Avot* is attributed to Yehudah Hanasi (Judah the Prince), a name testifying to Judah's metaphoric stature in the chain of Jewish tradition. Its sixth and last chapter, however, was added anonymously sometime after Judah's death around 220 CE, possibly in order to have separate chapters to read during the six Sabbaths that occur between Passover and Shavuot (the holiday that marks the giving of the Torah on Mount Sinai). Most traditional prayer books customarily include *Pirkei Avot* as extra reading for those weeks. Some Jews read it at other times, as well—as spiritual preparation for the Jewish New Year, Rosh Hashanah, for example. It is readily available in many editions, therefore, sometimes with commentaries by this or that great rabbinic scholar from the Middle Ages or later.

Pirkei Avot comes with various English titles such as *Chapters of the Fathers* or *Ethics of the Fathers*. The "Fathers" are the generations from the first Pharisees (roughly 167 BCE) to the time of the Mishnah's promulgation around 200 CE.

Instead of conveying the usual technical legalities, *Pirkei Avot* provides ethical and commonsense maxims that form the Rabbis' underlying assumptions about God (theology), human nature (anthropology), and the universe (cosmology). It applauds a life of studying Torah— the Five Books of Moses, but by extension the Bible in its entirety, and all of Jewish learning as well. Since the Mishnah is a law code, *Pirkei Avot* emphasizes the ethics incumbent upon judges. But it also handles everyday advice for proper living, such as "Do not keep aloof from the community"; "Who is wise? One who learns from everyone. Who is strong? One who subdues the impulse to do evil. Who is rich? Those who are content with their lot. Who is honored? Those who honor others"; "Beloved is man, for we were created in the image of God"; "Where no one acts humanely, act humanely yourself"; or "Pray for the welfare of the government, for without it, people would swallow each other up alive."

At times, the advice in *Pirkei Avot* is opaque. What does it mean, for example, when it inquires, "If I am not for myself, who will be for me? Being for myself, what am I? And if not now, when?" How can it be that "Everything is foreseen, but freedom of choice is given"? This is a book that one reads again and again, going from commentary to commentary, to get ever deeper insight into the philosophy of being Jewish. That activity is exactly what the Rabbis meant by studying Torah. As *Pirkei Avot* itself says of Torah, "Turn it and turn it, for everything is in it."

The Babylonian Talmud
(ca. sixth to seventh centuries CE)

"The Talmud has no starting page. Every page assumes that you have read every other page except the one you are on" (anonymous axiom regarding Talmud study).

Most serious students of Judaism would say that if they had to be banished all alone for life to a desert island, and if they could take just one single book with them, they'd choose the Babylonian Talmud. The choice, they may say, is crystal clear; no other book, not even the Bible, comes close.

There is another Talmud, too, the Palestinian one. Together, they are products of Jewish minds from about the third to the sixth or seventh centuries CE. The Palestinian Talmud (created by Rabbis in Palestine) was codified about 400 CE; the Babylonian Talmud (created by Rabbis in Babylonia and very difficult to date) was redacted at least a century or two later. Since significantly more time went into its editing, the Babylonian Talmud shows more complex and sophisticated argumentation—and argumentation is what both Talmuds are all about. Ever since coming into being, it is the *Bavli* (Hebrew for "Babylonian") that has dominated Jewish life everywhere.

You do not *read* the Talmud so much as you *study* it, as a way to Jewish spirituality—a way, that is, to God. The ideal is a *daf yomi*, mastering one double-sided page of Talmud every single day, an impossibility for all but a few veteran students. Nonetheless, all over the world, thousands of Jews arise early enough each morning to master their page of intricately reasoned argumentation about arcane subjects that may have no immediate relevance to their lives; only then do they go to work.

The standard published version of the Babylonian Talmud contains twenty folio volumes, 2,717 double-sided pages in all. But the language is so terse and the logic so tight that the corresponding English version takes up over 8,000 double-sided pages—if you are studying a *daf yomi*, that amounts to about 3 double-sided pages in English of densely packed legal discussion a day. To make matters harder, the language of the Talmud is a succinct form of the rare and outdated Babylonian Aramaic dialect, printed without vowels or punctuation marks, and apt to mean many things, depending on whether you read a given sentence as a simple statement, a question, or an exclamation, for instance.

The Talmud purports to be a commentary on the Mishnah, the very first law code of the Rabbis. But most of it has nothing directly to do with the particular laws of the Mishnah that it comments upon. In form, it is sheer argumentation, the combined sayings of several centuries organized into two debating sides, as if generations of Rabbis spanning more than three hundred years had been summoned together for the occasion. Most of the arguments end without a decision being made for either side. It is perfectly normal to think your way through a closely contested argument that takes up several pages, only to find at the end that you still do not know the answer to the question that was propounded in the first place.

From the twelfth to the sixteenth centuries, extra-Talmudic writings codified one opinion or the other, but the Talmud remains blissfully unaware that the whole point of law is for it to be practiced. Real people in the real world need to know the complexities of civil rulings, religious edicts, and criminal law, all of which the Talmud discusses with incredible thoroughness. But generally speaking, the Talmud itself is not the place where you get those legal rulings. They appear only in the codes and responsa (see page 47), which sum up the law for practical purposes and apply it to real-life cases.

Talmud is to Jewish law what mathematics is to science and engineering. Mathematics has its practical side. But there is also pure mathematics that mathematicians study for its own sake. Discovering the equation that makes the numbers come out right can be a spiritually satisfying moment. Getting the Talmudic argument straight is a similar experience.

Pretty much any rabbi worth his salt (nowadays "her salt," as well) has written commentaries to the Talmud, or to already existing commentaries to the Talmud, or to commentaries to those commentaries. The most famous Talmudic commentators are Rashi and a group of Rashi's successors called the Tosafists, most of them stemming from medieval France and Germany. Rashi (1040–1105) is Judaism's most prolific commentator on both the Bible and the Talmud. The collective commentary written by the Tosafists—the school of thought begun by Rashi's grandsons, and lasting from the twelfth to the fourteenth centuries—is called Tosafot (meaning, "additional").

The Babylonian Talmud was first printed in sixteenth-century Italy, and ever since, it has featured the Talmudic text in the center of the page, Rashi's commentary on the inside margin, and the Tosafot on the outside. Since then, other commentaries have been added as well, some of them on margins farther out still, others as appendices to each of the volumes. The result is a layout that makes it more difficult still to cover the ideal "page per day," because once you have understood the original Talmud text, you still have Rashi and the Tosafot to work through. Rashi, at least, is primarily an explanatory commentary, helping you get through the original, but Tosafot is its own challenge, usually comparing a given passage in the page you are on with numerous parallel or related passages on other pages (that you are assumed to have read already), trying to iron out inconsistencies and conflicts.

Cultures invent their own favorite art forms, and then arrange them into hierarchies. In Western culture, for example, poetry is considered more artistic than prose, and the symphony outranks a march or waltz. Study of sacred text is the Jewish art form par excellence, and the height of such art is immersing oneself in Talmud.

Even as island castaways, with nothing to do but study Talmud their remaining lives, few students of Judaism could hope to rival the artistic mastery of the truly great Talmudists. But at least the castaway students wouldn't mind trying.

Midrash Rabbah ("The Great Midrash")
(ca. fifth to tenth centuries CE)

"Do not read the Bible literally; read it as if it means something else"
(anonymously given advice on the value of midrash).

Ever since the first and second centuries CE, when the Rabbis added the Prophets and the Writings to finalize the Hebrew Bible, Jews have read their Bible lovingly but not literally. Rabbinic doctrine taught that Moses received two things at Sinai—the written revelation on one hand and an oral accompaniment on the other. The former could be elucidated only alongside the latter.

In part, this oral tradition was indeed handed down through the generations—not all the way from Sinai, probably, but at least from the very first Rabbis to their successors throughout the chain of rabbinic tradition: and it grew with time, as each generation added to it. Today, no less than two thousand years ago, students of Torah arrive at their own new understandings that then become part of this authentic and ongoing oral tradition. Today's students, too, imagine, as it were, that whatever "novelties" they find in the biblical account have actually been there all along, just awaiting discovery. Ferreting out such ever new meanings—as if God were playing hide-and-seek with us, stashing away ideas that each generation is supposed to find—is an expression of Jewish spirituality.

Midrash is a particular genre of rabbinic literature designed to feature this vast body of oral tradition. Each midrashic book is arranged as a running commentary to the Five Books of Moses, in particular, but to some extent to the rest of the Bible as well. Midrash, in other words, is the written record of the Rabbis' creative reading of Scripture. For example, why did God punish the people who built the Tower of Babel? If we think we know, it is because a midrash reached us, since the Bible does not actually say. Most people think the builders were exercising the hubris of imagining they were like God. But maybe their sin lay also in caring more about stone and mortar than about people: when a person fell to his death from atop the tower, they called for a replacement; if a large chunk of stone fell, they mourned its loss, because the tower would have to be just that much smaller. That's a midrash.

The questions (and answers) are endless: What fruit did Eve offer to Adam? Contrary to popular opinion nowadays, it was *not* an apple. That idea came about because the Latin word for apple, *malum*, also means "evil"—and since the forbidden fruit came from the Tree of Good and Evil, readers of the Latin Bible assumed it was a *malum*, an apple. But the original Hebrew doesn't say what it was. So the midrash tries to identify the fruit. Granted, Adam and Eve were barred from tasting fruit from the tree of wisdom; but what other trees grew in Eden, trees from which they *could* eat? All kinds of trees, is one midrashic answer, including trees that grew bread, so they wouldn't have to work at making it.

To take another example, the Bible describes Noah as a good man "in his time"—but why the phrase "in his time"? A midrash says he was only relatively good, given how bad the rest of the people were in his day—but not as good as Abraham, who came later.

Jews look to the midrash for more than intellectual stimulation, however; every new interpretation has the potential for moral and spiritual insight. When we eat bread, we thank God for "bringing forth bread from the earth," because we look forward to the messianic day when God will provide food directly for all creatures by growing bread on trees again—which is to say, coming directly "from the earth." Noah might not have been perfect, but he was apparently good enough to warrant God's attention. So, too, we are expected to be good—but not perfect.

Sometimes the midrash is extended artistic embellishment. Deuteronomy doesn't say, for example, how Moses died, so the midrash fills in the blank: he died by a gentle kiss that God planted on his forehead, after Moses had made the rounds of the Israelite tents to say good-bye to all the people. When we read the story of Abraham carefully, we find that after Abraham tries to sacrifice Isaac, Sarah never talks to him again. Yes, says the midrash, Abraham must be the paragon of faith. But he should at least have talked the sacrifice over with Sarah before heading off on what she would surely have seen as a mission of madness. Sarah dies shortly after the incident. No coincidence, according to the midrash. She died of the shock; just imagining she might lose the son she had so devoutly prayed for gave her a heart attack.

Rabbis probably used midrash from the very beginning as raw material for sermons. Every week, Scripture was read formally in the synagogue—just as it is now—and the Rabbis spun together midrash after midrash, some of it inherited from other teachers, some of it altogether novel, a product of their own imagination. By the second century CE, collections began appearing. From the fifth to the tenth centuries, the largest collection, called *Midrash Rabbah*, was compiled by rabbinic teachers in Palestine. It is *rabbah*, "great," a multivolume reminder that the Bible contains endless depths of wisdom for each new generation to discover.

By the eleventh century, the great era of midrash collecting had ended. New midrashic readings of Scripture have continued to evolve, but they lack the authority of the midrash found in those classical collections.

The very first chapter of *Midrash Rabbah* sets the tone by asking how God constructed the universe. Like any other builder, God must have had some architectural plans to guide the actual construction. But what could God have created even before the physical universe, as the master plan for creation? The answer can only be "Torah." God created the world with Torah already in mind. More than just the Five Books of Moses and the oral traditions that expand upon them, Torah is a master plan for the life of everything God brought into being. Torah is the possibility for justice, love, hope, creativity, and the very laws of nature that amaze us whenever we look upward to the stars or inward to our souls. Every time we intuit a new midrashic insight into the workings of reality, we come one step closer to the fullness of divine wisdom that should guide us as we go about our earthly lives.

Aspects of Rabbinic Theology
(1909)

Solomon Schechter (1847–1915)

"The old Rabbis seem to have thought that the true health of a religion is to have a theology without being aware of it [. . .] With God as reality, revelation as a fact, the Torah as a rule of life, and the hope of redemption as a most vivid expectation, they felt no need to formulate their dogmas into a creed."

Solomon Schechter is one of the towering names in the pantheon of Jews in America. His fame as a scholar is international, since (among other things) he was one of the pioneer scholars studying the Genizah fragments—a cache of over 200,000 Jewish text fragments from the early and High Middle Ages that were discovered in a synagogue in old Cairo and that revolutionized our understanding of that period. But Schechter is of special importance to Jews on the American side of the Atlantic, since from 1902 to 1915 he served as the second president of the Jewish Theological Seminary of America, the educational institution of the North American Conservative movement founded in 1886. It was Schechter who shaped the seminary's character in its early years.

No collection of great Jewish writing would be complete without a text by Schechter, and fortunately he wrote not just for scholars but for laypeople, too. The most obvious, and best-known, example is a three-volume set of essays called *Studies in Judaism* (1896–1924), but the essays cover many topics, and not all of them have stood the test of time. His *Aspects of Rabbinic Theology* is a set of essays on classic Jewish theology that is worth reading today no less than when it first came out. It summarizes the worldview of the Rabbis who created the Mishnah, the Talmuds, and the midrash.

Quite remarkably, Schechter made absolutely no attempt to modernize the theological system he was describing. Without apology, he assembled what he took to be the primary theological concepts of rabbinic Judaism and let the sources speak for themselves, rather than refine their interpretation to make them more palatable for a modern audience. As he himself put it, "it would certainly not be an impossible task to draw such an ideal and noble picture of any of the great Rabbis, such as Hillel, R. Jochanan ben Zakkai, or R. Akiba, as would make us recognize a nineteenth-century altruist in them. Nor would it take much ingenuity to parade, for instance, R. Abuha as an accomplished geologist [. . .] But I have not the least desire to array the ancient Rabbis in the paraphernalia of modern fashion. The 'liberty of interpretation' in which so many theologians indulge seems to me only another word for the privilege of blunder and to deceive oneself and others."

What the reader finds here, then, is the unvarnished truth about what the Rabbis had to say about God, the human predicament, and the condition of the universe. Regardless of how these ancient lessons fall on modern ears, they do represent rabbinic thought, and two thousand years of Jewish history represent a running commentary on the teachings we can live by and the teachings we wish to reinterpret or do without.

Schechter was uniquely suited to his task. He had been born in Romania to a pious Hasidic family and attended a traditional yeshivah before going on to study Jewish tradition scientifically as well, in Vienna and Berlin. In the 1890s, he served as reader in Rabbinics at Cambridge University and as professor of Hebrew at University College, London. From there, he was recruited for the presidency of the Jewish Theological Seminary in New York. He was, therefore, perfectly capable of the kind of creative theological innovation that he intentionally omitted in the *Aspects*. A good example is his novel theological concept of "Catholic Israel." The word "catholic" means "universal"—the Roman Catholic Church, for example, understands itself to be universal—and Schechter conceived of the Jewish People likewise as a universal, or worldwide, entity that expresses itself through "the Synagogue": not individual synagogues, but a virtual gathering throughout time and space in which specific synagogues play a role.

Schechter considered the classical rabbinic doctrines described in the *Aspects* to be the spiritual legacy of this "Catholic Israel," and intended his book as the means to pass this legacy on to generations who would not be raised in the traditional milieu that he had known as a child.

The book begins with three chapters on God: "God and the World" elucidates the nature of God who is both transcendent (the God of creation) and immanent (the God who hears prayer); the next two chapters, "God and Israel" and "The Election of Israel," present what the Rabbis took to be the uniquely intimate relationship that God had established with the Jewish People—either because Israel was specially deserving, or as "a mere act of grace on the part of God" (the interpretation Schechter preferred).

The next several chapters define the Rabbis' central doctrine of God's sovereignty both on high and in this world, where we human beings are given the task of making that sovereignty real by fighting and ending evil. The precise means by which Jews understand that charge is the Torah in its larger sense (Schechter calls it "the Law"), the study of which is the most quintessential Jewish act of all. The end of the book traces Jewish concepts of sin and punishment, the relative goodness of human nature, the need for repentance, and the guarantee of forgiveness (another act of God's grace).

Readers will be amazed to find that Schechter translates the rabbinic concepts with theological terms that seem, at first, to be plainly Christian—"grace" being the best example. He is intent on showing that even though these terms are widely associated with Christian theology, they are really Jewish to their core. Traditionally, Jews have studied "the Law," not "theology"; they therefore have no ready words of their own to correspond to the theological terms that Christians have coined. Schechter sought to outfit Jews with at least the basics of rabbinic thought in order to claim the standard theological terms that he considered authentically Jewish.

Today's readers of *Aspects of Rabbinic Theology* will find the style somewhat dated, since its essays were written over a hundred years ago. But Schechter's concepts are eternal.

As a Driven Leaf
(1939)

Milton Steinberg (1903–1950)

"There is no justice and there is no Judge."

In Judaism, nothing is as sacrosanct as justice: not faith, nor even love, since the greatest love of all, the purest grace that God can grant, is the gift of Torah—and the Torah is, overall, a legal document demanding justice. The worst heresy a Jew can utter, therefore, is the conviction that there is no justice, and, if no justice, no divine Judge, either. The Babylonian Talmud records the apostasy of such a man, a scholar "gone bad": Elisha ben Abuya. When this man saw the enormity of evil that befalls good people, he denounced God the Judge and (implicitly) the Judaism of the Rabbis.

Nowadays, Judaism allows freedom of speech on matters of faith; except for a small band of ultra-Orthodox Jews, rabbis have neither the desire nor the power to excommunicate even the most dyed-in-the-wool "heretic." At times in Jewish history, however, excommunication was both real and powerful, and the excommunicant faced isolation from even friends and family. In the premodern world of tightly knit communities, it was virtually a sentence of death by suicide.

Elisha ben Abuya was a historical figure in the first century CE whom the Talmud charges with denying divine justice. His crime was so heinous that he has been known ever since as *Acher* (The Other One). *As a Driven Leaf*, which traces Elisha's path to his excommunication and beyond, is a terrific story by a master author—and possibly the most widely read Jewish novel of all time.

From the moment of Elisha's birth in Palestine to his growth into a freethinking Jewish patrician, the die is cast. At first, when his father dies unexpectedly, little Elisha is bundled off to Rabbi Joshua and given an Orthodox Jewish education that propels him to fame as a judge on the Jewish High Court. Following Talmudic legend, Steinberg has him join three other sages whose curiosity about the universe leads them to experiment with what the Rabbis considered dangerous teachings known ironically as "the garden" (in Hebrew, *PaRDeS*)—a "PaRaDiSe" of thought beyond the capacity of most human beings to comprehend.

It is like the forbidden tree of knowledge from the Garden of Eden, but growing wild! Only one of the four sages emerges safely; the others become addicted to the garden's temptations. One goes mad, the next one dies, and Elisha becomes an apostate to Greco-Roman culture and knowledge.

For the first half of the book, Elisha masters, accepts, but then wrestles with rabbinic doctrine. When a plague claims the lives of a fellow Rabbi's baby twins, Elisha's faith is shaken. The breaking point comes somewhat later, when he hears a father instruct his son to climb a tree and remove some eggs from a bird's nest, being careful to first send the bird mother away, in accordance with Deuteronomy 22:6 ("If you chance upon a bird's nest with the mother sitting over the fledglings or the eggs, do not take the mother together with her young. Let the mother go and take only the young in order that you may fare well and have a long life").

"The boy will live long," says a passerby, "for observe, in one act, he is fulfilling two commandments," sending the mother bird away and obeying his parents, both of which (according to the Bible) promise long life. When the child falls from the tree to his death, Elisha snaps. Other Rabbis accept the boy's fate as God's inscrutable will, and "drone on" with their lessons. But "revulsion swept Elisha. 'It's all a lie,' he said. 'There is no justice and no Judge, for there is no God.'" Unwilling to recant, Elisha is excommunicated by his rabbinic peers. He leaves for Antioch, the most cosmopolitan Greco-Roman city in Asia Minor.

The rest of the book features Elisha the Roman, not Elisha the Jew. In short order, he masters Hellenistic literature and ideas, falls in love with Roman justice, and tastes the life of upper-class Roman men who enjoy having servants, dine well each night, and philosophize in their spare time. But eventually, he sees the underbelly of Roman civilization: the wantonness of its night life, the ubiquity of its slavery, and the cruelty of its gladiatorial games. Unable to be fully a Jew, he is equally unable to be fully a Roman.

As a Driven Leaf weaves an adept tapestry of the Greco-Roman classics and Talmudic lore against the swirling backdrop of the early second century. It culminates in the major Jewish revolt against Rome in 132–135 CE and the resulting devastation of the Land of Israel, including Jerusalem. Jewish accounts picture a horrific end, with countless Jews massacred and a number of Rabbis tortured to death. The final scenes of the book place Elisha in the midst of all this, debating his place in history: an apostate who repents at the scene of his friends' slow death, or a confirmed Roman? Does he return to—or turn against—his people? The one thing Elisha knows is that he has no serenity either way.

Milton Steinberg was a disciple of Mordecai Kaplan (see page 263). Kaplan was deemed a heretic by some Orthodox Jews in the United States, who actually consigned his writings to fire in 1945. Steinberg promulgated Kaplan's message: the redefinition of God, no longer as a supernatural deity, but instead as an impersonal natural force for human goodness and satisfaction. Second-century Elisha is, in actuality, twentieth-century Kaplan, or, we might suspect, even Steinberg himself. Not just historical, then, this novel is a somewhat autobiographical account of the inner turmoil that the author suspects he would have encountered had he lived when rabbinic Judaism was just taking shape.

Many Jews encounter *As a Driven Leaf* in their teenage years. Others get to it in college or beyond. Either way, it is a page-turner, steeped in the sources of the Rabbis and the Greco-Roman philosophers, and appreciative of both. It illustrates not just a struggle of faith that marked thoughtful men and women in antiquity, but also the dilemma of modern Jews who emerged from the medieval ghettos and discovered the Enlightenment. The novel's continuing relevance is obvious to anyone who straddles the particularism of a single religious tradition and the universalism of secular modernity.

The Responsa Literature
(1955)

Solomon B. Freehof (1892–1990)

"It is doubtful whether any other historic literature has ever called forth so much mental energy in as large a percentage of its people as Talmudic literature has produced in this small fragment of humanity."

Every legal system establishes a mechanism for applying the law to novel circumstances. In the United States, for example, the Supreme Court has ultimate interpretive authority. But the final right to interpret the law is not necessarily lodged in a court. In ancient Rome, it was the emperor; and for Judaism, it is rabbis. Local rabbis are required to make rulings in everyday circumstances, but important questions that lack obvious solutions find their way to higher authorities, rabbis who become famous for their mastery of Jewish law. Orthodox Jews look to individual rabbis who are known for such legal acumen. Non-Orthodox Jewish movements tend nowadays to rely on a committee of such rabbis. The committee scrutinizes the same legal literature that Orthodox experts consult, but applies different criteria to it—the force of historical change, for example—and may end up rejecting old rulings that run counter to contemporary conscience.

Whether from individuals or committees, rabbinic decisions are framed as *responsa*, "answers" to questions that people raise. Like the American Supreme Court, Jewish responsa address actual matters, not hypothetical ones. Unlike the Supreme Court, however, Jewish law does not know the concept of moot cases, i.e., no case is deemed irrelevant because it has already been decided by the passing of time.

Another difference between the Jewish and the American legal systems is the fact that Americans can change a law by congressional fiat, and can even alter the Constitution, the ultimate arbiter of positions that jurists take. In Judaism neither method works. Jews have no ultimate voting body like the American Congress or British Parliament, and the closest thing there is to a constitution, the Bible, is treated as if it has been given directly by God—and can therefore not be amended by humans. But while responsa cannot change the "biblical constitution," they can interpret it in different ways.

47

The Bible is rarely adequate for deciding actual cases. That is why the Rabbis established the principle that the written law (the Bible) had to be interpreted with an accompanying oral law in mind, the oral law being the force of rabbinic tradition that, in theory, goes back to Mount Sinai. As we saw above, around 200 CE, the Mishnah—a determinative body of oral law—was promulgated; and some centuries later, much fuller (some would say, exhaustive) discussions of oral principle and precedent became available in the Talmud.

Responsa are the legal rulings based on the Talmud but promulgated separately from it. Over time, the number of responsa has grown exponentially, since any given issue is likely to attract separate responses from many rabbinic scholars, each of whom makes rulings independently of the others. As the mountain of rulings grows, so, too, does the sheer magnitude of cases that later generations of rabbis must work through as precedential evidence for subsequent decisions. They also depend on extensive medieval law codes—compilations of legal conclusions separate from the responsa, but taking the responsa into account—that attracted commentaries, then commentaries to the commentaries, and then commentaries to the commentaries to the commentaries—ad infinitum.

Nowadays, computer databases make comprehensive searches through Jewish legal precedent fairly easy and fast. But for most of Jewish history, rabbinic respondents used no index at all. The Talmuds and codes have various cross-reference devices, but they are paltry compared to the literature as a whole. Even today, it is not unusual to find Jewish legal experts who simply study constantly, memorize what they can, and then access their memory to decide where to start looking when any new case arises.

The Responsa Literature is a popular and altogether wonderful guide through this labyrinth of Jewish law, written by a brilliant jurist, Solomon B. Freehof. His interest in Jewish law was sparked during World War I by a stint as a Jewish chaplain in Iceland. With American Jewish soldiers stationed in a part of the world where night lasts several months, Freehof had to decide when "sunset" was and when, therefore, the required evening worship should be scheduled. (His decision was that "sunset" would be the same time as in New York.) Thereafter, for seventy-five years (he lived to be ninety-seven), he wrote virtually all the responsa of the Reform movement in North America, and when he died, an entire committee was needed to take his place. Freehof also wrote hundreds of articles, popular and scholarly, on aspects of

Jewish law. In this book, Freehof explains the responsa in ways that even a beginner can read and appreciate.

The chapters rival each other for interest. After short discussions on what responsa are, Freehof draws thumbnail sketches of the greatest rabbinic respondents from the Middle Ages on. Later chapters cite responsa that sparked widespread debate, how responsa address modern inventions, and some just downright curious responsa that history has bequeathed us.

When fifteenth-century Jews in Regensburg, Germany, were falsely jailed, for example, the neighboring Jews of Nuremberg sought to raise funds to "buy back" the prisoners. Worried about the large sum necessary, they asked an Italian rabbi, Joseph Colon, if a community may coerce its members into giving charity for people living elsewhere. Using a Talmudic analogy that permits forcing a city downriver to help a neighboring city upriver clean up the common waterway, Colon ruled in the affirmative.

Can a person sell his share of the reward in paradise that righteous people believe they will obtain? No, said twentieth-century New York rabbi Aaron Gordon, since by selling it, the seller indicates that he is not truly righteous and, therefore, has nothing to sell.

Can Jews pray in a church? Yes, said nineteenth-century respondent Saul Nathanson, as long as no blatant symbols of Christianity are displayed at the time.

Freehof's small volume is a gem. Judaism is, indeed, a religion of law. But law need not prove cold, dispassionate, zealous, and loveless. *The Responsa Literature* shows precisely how law can be wise, sympathetic, loving, and kind. Responsa of that sort are what makes the Jewish world go round.

Modern Jews Engage the New Testament
(2008)

Michael J. Cook (born 1943)

> "Modern Jews need to exchange their sense of victimization by the New
> Testament for confidence that they now knowledgably control this litera-
> ture and are thereby free from it."

This extraordinary book opens with a plea for Jews to renounce
"intentional ignorance" toward the New Testament, and promises
an engagement with Christian Scripture: "The Jewish People, in their
effort to comprehend their own history, need access to the New Testament because it has directed so much of it."

Michael Cook is an established Jewish scholar of the New Testament—still a relatively rare specialty for Jewish academics to pursue.
His teacher Samuel Sandmel (1911–1979) first pioneered this field,
which Cook has continued as its primary advocate, succeeding Sandmel as professor of Judaeo-Christian Studies at Hebrew Union College–
Jewish Institute of Religion in Cincinnati. Cook has written both scholarly and popular articles, intended for Jews and for Christians alike,
but here he challenges Jews in particular to conquer their antipathy to
New Testament study. *Modern Jews Engage the New Testament* is not an
easy book—it must be studied through, not read through. But Cook
is a master teacher who has organized the book like a series of popular
lectures, complete with charts, graphs, timelines, and chapter synopses.
At the heart of his narrative is standard biblical scholarship that sees the
New Testament as a canonical collection of books composed in the first
two centuries CE.

The New Testament—which is much shorter than the Hebrew
Bible that constitutes the "Old Testament" for Christians—contains
three parts: the four Gospels and the book of Acts; the Epistles (letters), mostly attributed to Paul; and the book of Revelation. Despite
traditions that place their authors in Jesus's day, all four Gospels were
anonymously composed well after the early thirties CE, when Jesus
died. It is hard to know for sure when they came into being—scholarly
views differ by a few years here or there—but Cook dates the Gospel
of Mark about 73 CE; the Gospel of Matthew in 85 CE; the Gospel of

Luke sometime after 94 CE; and the Gospel of John between 100 and 120 CE. The writer of Luke also composed Acts, chronicling the early church during the lifetime of its chief architect, Paul, who died around 64 CE. The earliest New Testament writings are therefore not the Gospels (even though they are the first four books in the New Testament) but the letters of Paul, which describe the situation that the book of Acts only examines in retrospect. The book of Revelation is altogether different, an apocalyptic vision composed around 95 CE, in response to the persecution of Christians under the Roman emperor Domitian.

Cook examines all of this from the perspective of the concerns that have dominated Jewish consciousness over the centuries. Who were the "scribes" and "Pharisees"? How Jewish was Jesus, anyway? Was the Last Supper a Passover seder? Were Jewish authorities involved in Jesus's crucifixion? To answer these and other questions, he compares New Testament passages, sometime verse by verse, to elicit contradictions, enigmas, and information gaps; he then applies history to decide what parts of the Gospels are true and what theological issues lie behind those parts that are not.

The authors of the Gospels were historians, but historians in antiquity took liberties with their subject matter that would be unthinkable today. It was commonplace to make up speeches that the historical figures did not actually say, but might have, had they acted as their biographers wished. And when the Gospel authors copied earlier accounts, they adjusted them to suit their own ends. The Gospel of Mark, for example, reports a scribe who asks for the most important Jewish commandment, and Jesus replies, "Hear O Israel, the Lord our God, the Lord is One," followed by, "You shall love the Lord your God with all your heart, with all your soul, and with all your might." Jews will readily recognize these lines as the Jewish affirmation of faith called the *Sh'ma*, a likely response by Jesus, who was a Jew.

The author of Matthew, however, who lived later, noticed that almost all the Christians in his community had begun as pagan Greeks, not as Jews. Wanting to blame Jews themselves for the church's "failure" to attract them, he subtly altered Mark's account. He supplied the gratuitous comment that the questioner only wanted "to test" Jesus; and he omitted Mark's conclusion, where the questioner commends Jesus on his answer and receives from Jesus the guarantee that he is not far from the kingdom of heaven.

The Gospel authors believed in Hebrew Scripture, and they shaped their histories as much by what they thought Hebrew Scripture had prophesied as by what had actually occurred. The account of Jesus's death, for example, is based not just on what really transpired but on an extended prophetic narrative drawn from a close reading of Jeremiah.

As its title implies, *Modern Jews Engage the New Testament* is not just an introduction to Christian Scriptures. It is an *engagement* by Jews *today* with the way those Scriptures have shaped Christian consciousness. An obvious interest is the anti-Semitism that the Gospel portrayal of Jews has occasioned over the centuries. But so, too, is the contemporary renewal of evangelical Christianity that is based on the book of Revelation. What do Christians mean by such terms as rapture and premillennialism? Why do Christian fundamentalists support a State of Israel? What role do Jews play in the end-of-history scenario preached by conservative Christians?

Jewish readers will not find the usual bromides here. The author explains and acknowledges the problems that the New Testament caused Jews in the Middle Ages. But this is not the Middle Ages anymore. After centuries of diatribe and disputation, the path of genuine theological and interfaith dialogue has been open now for almost half a century—ever since the Vatican's 1965 declaration *Nostra Aetate* (In Our Time), which laid to rest the false accusation that Jews had rejected Christ and killed him. *Modern Jews Engage the New Testament* equips Jews with the scriptural depth necessary to dialogue with Christians about both faiths.

3

The Middle Ages
The Conversation Broadens

꿍

For the first nine hundred years of the Common Era, Jewish life was still largely concentrated in Palestine and Babylonia (current-day Iraq), with outposts in important ports or cities elsewhere in the Mediterranean, especially in Italy and Spain. By the tenth century, Spanish Jews were well on their way to a golden age, and a hundred years later, Jews from Italy had crossed the Alps and founded centers of Jewish learning in the German Rhineland. The Spanish Jews are called Sephardi, and the Jews in Germany, Ashkenazi, after the Hebrew names for both countries.

Jews prospered in Spain, first under the Muslims, who arrived in the early eighth century, and then, with the centuries-long Christian reconquest, under Christian monarchs as well. Jewish well-being was shattered, however, by a series of anti-Jewish riots in 1381. Then, in 1480, King Ferdinand of Aragon and Queen Isabella of Castile—the Catholic kings—introduced the Inquisition in order to unify the populations of their respective realms, with loyalty to the church as their common banner. In 1492, Spain expelled its Jews, and five years later, Portugal followed suit. Most Sephardi exiles settled in the eastern

Mediterranean, which was undergoing a renaissance under Turkish Ottoman rule, especially during the reign of Suleiman the Magnificent (r. 1520–1566). Others remained in Spain or its imperial holdings as *conversos*—"converts" to Christianity in public, but practicing their Jewish faith in secret. (The old name "marrano" is generally avoided nowadays, because its original connotation was negative. Jews who converted were regarded as "new Christians" by the "old Christian population" of Castile, who called them "marranos," from the Castilian word for pig.)

When present-day Holland broke free of Spanish rule and declared its independence as a Protestant state in the 1580s, its conversos began practicing Judaism publicly. From Holland, Jews were readmitted into England in 1655, after having been expelled from there in 1290. From Holland also, Jews began to settle in parts of the Americas that were under Dutch rule.

Because of their geographical position in Europe, Spanish Jews of the eleventh and twelfth centuries were spared the wrath of the Crusaders. But the Jews in Germany were decimated by a populist army of the First Crusade that left France in 1096, then bivouacked in the Rhineland and slaughtered the Jewish communities there. As a result, the intellectual and cultural center of Ashkenazi Jewry moved to France, where the great commentator Rashi and the great Talmudic school of thought, the Tosafot, flourished. By 1305, however, Jews were undergoing the first of several expulsions from France, as well, and from the fourteenth to the sixteenth centuries a genuine dark age descended, as Ashkenazi Jews were blamed for the Black Death, accused of killing Christian children to use their blood at Passover, taxed by avaricious monarchs, persecuted by the church, and hounded from place to place.

By the sixteenth century, Ashkenazi Jews were moving east into Renaissance Poland (the golden age of Copernicus and the Jagiello kings in Cracow), where they established their own golden age of Talmudic study. Most Polish Jews remained poor, however, and in 1648, peasants and Cossacks in what is now Ukraine revolted against the local Polish landed gentry and murdered much of the Jewish population.

The Jewish conversation proliferated in the Middle Ages to meet this panoramic sweep of countries and cultures. It came to include biblical commentary and pietistic treatises on character, a wealth of philosophy and mysticism, Jewish travelogues, personal diaries, and responses to charges against Judaism generated by medieval Christianity and Islam. Early on (ca. 860 CE), the Jewish prayer book (the Siddur) came into being—and then grew through the addition of prayers, poetry, and meditations that were evoked by persecutions and peaceful times alike. The creative age of midrash had passed, but new collections of older material continued to appear, and the creative reading of Scripture did not cease—it was simply funneled into different literary forms: commentaries, arranged verse by verse to accompany the biblical text; scriptural interpretations, to be used when forced into disputations with Christian preachers; and justification for creative readings of Jewish law. Jews learned to speak new languages: the vernacular of the countries they inhabited (German, French, English, Spanish, etc.), but also their own internal languages—Yiddish in Germanic countries and eastern Europe; and Ladino in Spain, Portugal, and areas that Spanish émigrés populated. Yet through it all, Jews remained a single people with a singular conversation, carried more and more by a literary output of enormous proportions.

The Rabbinic Bible (Mikra'ot G'dolot)

"'These are the names of the sons of Israel' (Exodus 1:1). Rashi comments: 'Even though the Torah listed them by name during their lifetimes (Genesis 46:8–27), it lists them again after their deaths to show God's love for them.' Nahmanides comments: 'The unifying theme of the Book of Exodus is the first exile—the one decreed in Genesis 15:13—and of the redemption from that exile [. . .] It begins with a recapitulation of the names and number of those who came down into Egypt, even though this had already been detailed in Genesis 46:8–27, since their descent there was actually the beginning of the exile.'"

Jews are taught not to read the Bible just by itself. They read it together with commentaries that ferret out the multitude of meanings that the biblical account can be led to reveal. As we have seen, the search for those meanings began in the rabbinic period, with the Talmud and midrash. But it reached its height in the Middle Ages.

For the Jewish mind, all sacred wisdom exists simultaneously, going back (as it were) to Sinai. In science, new discoveries render old ones irrelevant. But in the realm of the sacred, later discoveries do not replace earlier ones. They just mutually enrich each other. To be sure, successive generations of interpreters unearth new biblical insights—called *chiddushim,* meaning, "novelties" (singular: *chiddush*). But medieval minds thought of such insights as having always been there, hidden away by God for us to find. And once found, they were added to the multitude of meanings already collected, part of the ever-expanding canon of interpretation for future generations to ponder.

The page layout of Jewish texts is therefore designed to facilitate an ongoing conversation across the centuries of interpretation. In the case of the Bible, the relevant biblical passage is centered on the page and surrounded in the margins with commentaries going back as far as the Middle Ages. The reader's eyes move back and forth from any given biblical verse to the multitude of opinions on what the verse might mean.

Presented that way, the Bible is called *Mikra'ot G'dolot* (literally, "The Great Scriptures"); in English it is commonly referred to as a Rabbinic Bible. Serious students of Torah routinely pore over the weekly synagogue reading as it appears in their Rabbinic Bible, and then meet on Sabbath mornings to argue the meaning of the text.

The most famous commentator was Solomon ben Isaac (1040–1105), of France, more usually called Rashi, an acronym of his Hebrew name, R[abbi] SH[lomo ben] Y[itzchak] = RaSHY. Other great commentators were Rashi's grandson Samuel ben Meir, known as Rashbam (ca. 1085–ca. 1174); Abraham Ibn Ezra (ca. 1089–1164), of Spain; and another Spaniard, Moses ben Nahman, also called Nahmanides (1194–1270). Different editions of *Mikra'ot G'dolot* make their own choices of which commentators to include—not always just the four mentioned here. A full set of *Mikra'ot G'dolot* covers all the books of the Hebrew Bible. Some commentators (Rashi in particular) wrote commentaries to most of them. Other commentators specialized in one biblical book or another.

Until recently, *Mikra'ot G'dolot* has been a closed book to anyone unfamiliar with medieval Hebrew. But in 2005, the Jewish Publication Society published an English version of the commentaries to Exodus, titled *The Commentators' Bible* (*Exodus*), edited by Michael Carasik, a professor of Bible at the University of Pennsylvania and the Reconstructionist Rabbinical College in greater Philadelphia. Four years later, the second volume, on Leviticus, appeared, also edited by Michael Carasik. The other three Torah volumes are expected to follow. For the first time, the world of medieval biblical interpretation is now open to English-language readers! Only the main four commentaries (Rashi, Rashbam, Ibn Ezra, and Nahmanides) are provided in detail, but others are synopsized whenever the editor found them especially enlightening.

The commentators read each biblical verse very, very closely, comparing it to other passages elsewhere in Scripture and referring back to earlier interpretations drawn from Talmud and midrash. Take, for example, the Bible's assertion (Exod. 13:18) that the Israelites left Egypt "armed" and headed toward the Red Sea and a roundabout route to the Promised Land. Why were they "armed"? And why didn't they take the direct route hugging the southern shore of the Mediterranean? Rashi connects these two pieces of information. God, he says, knew Israel would require weaponry when they encountered the peoples of Canaan. Had they taken the direct route, they would have packed lightly, leaving their arms back in Egypt. But knowing they would have to traverse an entire desert, they packed "everything they could think of," including weapons. Not so, argues Ibn Ezra. Exodus 12:39 says they didn't even have basic provisions for the journey; how, then, could they have taken "everything they could think of"? The only reason to mention weapons, he says, is to continue the theme of the previous verse, where

God expressly warned them that they would encounter war; so they left behind everything except weapons.

But Ibn Ezra isn't finished yet. He knows of another interpretation derived from the fact that "armed" in Hebrew is similar to the word "five." Some unknown commentator had translated "armed" as "fifthed," implying that only one-fifth of the Israelites made it out of Egypt safely—as if to say, "They left *fifthed*," and not "They left *armed*." But that solution would entail other difficulties. Since, according to the biblical account, only 55 males went down to Egypt originally, some medieval Muslim commentators had been deriding the Bible's insistence that the number of males leaving was 600,000 (Exod. 12:37). How could the number rise from 55 to 600,000, even if (as the Bible says) Jews spent four hundred years in Egypt?

Elsewhere, Ibn Ezra had answered that criticism by dividing the years of slavery into generational periods, figuring out how many male children each generation had, and, by exponential calculation, coming up with the requisite number of 600,000. But if it were true that only one-fifth of that total left, the number of male Israelites leaving would have been only 120,000. So, clearly, the word could not mean "fifthed." It indeed had to mean "armed."

Nahmanides here prefers a metaphoric meaning with spiritual significance: calling the Israelites "armed," he says, means that "they left Egypt defiantly, thinking themselves redeemed, rather than like fleeing slaves."

At stake, quite frequently, is a commentator's philosophy of interpretation. Rashi does draw on midrash, for example, but he often prefers literal meanings of the biblical text before him. Quite frequently, he also appends Hebrew-letter transliterations of medieval French equivalents for biblical words that his French-Jewish readers are unlikely to know. Ibn Ezra prefers a more scientific approach. Occasionally, he even suggests what was unthinkable during his time—that Moses did not write the *entire* Torah! Deuteronomy 34:10 says of Moses, "No prophet equal to Moses has arisen *until this very day*"—a day sometime after Moses died, obviously. How could Moses have described a time period after his death? Joshua must have composed that line.

Nahmanides often contends against both Rashi and Ibn Ezra. At times, he adopts metaphysical interpretations from the Kabbalah, the medieval Jewish mystical system that he was among the first to master.

Now that we have at least two volumes of *Mikra'ot G'dolot* available in English, everyone can study Torah alongside its centuries of interpretations, thus letting the Bible come alive as never before.

The Jewish Prayer Book (Siddur)

"Of all the books that line the shelves of a Jewish library, it is the Siddur, not the Talmud and not even the Bible, that Jews know best. The prayer book is our Jewish diary of the centuries, a collection of prayers composed by genera-tions of those who came before us, as they endeavored to express the meaning of their lives" (Lawrence A. Hoffman, editor, *My People's Prayer Book*).

Walk into any synagogue, and someone will hand you a Jewish prayer book (the Siddur, from the Hebrew root *s.d.r*, meaning, order)—a book so commonplace that it is taken for granted. Over the centuries, most Jews were too poor to devote the time necessary to become knowledgeable in all the Jewish classics. Out of daily habit, however, they could virtually memorize a prayer book, and after print-ing was invented, they could even own one. (While not all editions of the prayer book are exactly alike, they all follow the same underlying pattern and contain pretty much the same basic material.)

To know the history of the prayer book is to be in touch with the soul of the Jewish People as it has evolved through persecutions, golden ages, and everything in between. For everything is expressed within the covers of the Siddur: it is an encounter with three thousand years of fate and fortune, the essence of the Jewish spirit captured through the power of liturgy.

Unlike a conventional diary, however, the Siddur's pages follow no chronological order. A symphony is not organized by the dates dur-ing which the composer penciled in the particular notes and musical themes; it obeys a master plan of symphonic structure. So, too, the Siddur is artistically arranged to provide the symphonic message of the Jewish People's march through time. Recognizing the themes of Jewish history requires an unraveling of the liturgy's structure and a sense of how and why new prayers have come into being over the centuries.

Although many of the prayers are ancient—some of them going back to the Bible itself—our first extant Siddur came into being only about 860 CE, in Babylonia, and some of the most familiar prayers today were added later still. For example, the concluding daily prayer, the *Alenu*, although composed by the third century CE, was not added to the daily regimen until about the year 1400. Two standard hymns, *Adon Olam* and *Yigdal*, were created in the Middle Ages, the former by an unknown poet at an unknown time, the latter in the fourteenth century by followers of Moses Maimonides (see page 71) in Rome. They wrote a poetic version of Maimonides's principles to assert their allegiance in a time when their master's thought was being pilloried by others. Some prayers reflect the slaughter of German Jews by eleventh-century Crusaders; others celebrate freedom: a prayer for the government, for example, that became standard when sixteenth-century Holland broke free from Spanish rule and declared itself Protestant, allowing Jews to practice their faith openly once again. Most striking of all, perhaps, is the entire service that welcomes the Sabbath (*Kabbalat Shabbat*)—a creation of sixteenth-century mystics in the Land of Israel.

The most comprehensive way to approach the Siddur is through *My People's Prayer Book* (1997–2007), a series of ten volumes that covers all of the Jewish prayers, for weekday and Sabbath worship. As we saw above, Jewish sacred texts are traditionally laid out with the text in the center and commentaries around the edges. *My People's Prayer Book* follows that model, arraying each prayer side by side with commentaries relevant to it. These help the reader situate the prayers in their original context while relating them to the life of Jews today. The commentaries are modern, by scholars in Bible, Talmud, theology, Jewish history, and other specialized disciplines. Alongside the original Hebrew is a scientific translation with a commentary by the translator. Readers can approach the liturgy by following the course of one commentator rather than another, or by going through a combination of commentaries to get several perspectives on what just a single prayer has to offer.

The editor provides the history of each prayer. The commentators explain how the prayer in question utilizes the Bible, how medieval rabbis thought about it, what Judaism's mystical tradition has to say, or the prescribed way in which Jewish law (*halakhah*) asks that the prayer be said. Theology gets its place here not only through a standard theological outlook, but from a distinctively feminist point of view as well. The commentators represent the gamut of Jewish commitment: the four major Jewish denominations; men and women; scholars from North America and from Israel.

Modern Jews, especially liberal ones, have stripped the Siddur of medievalisms that they find offending, or have added new compositions to reflect contemporary circumstances. Thus one commentator provides the permutations that modern editions of the prayer book demonstrate, explaining the rationale for each one. Conservative, Reform, and Reconstructionist Jews can see why their prayer books differ from the Orthodox version, and they can trace their movements' alterations through time, from the birth of the modern era to our own day.

Each volume of *My People's Prayer Book* provides introductory essays, as well: how the prayer book came into being in the first place; the role of psalms in Jewish liturgy; the impact of mysticism; a Jewish approach to prayers of petition; the magic of nighttime liturgy; the spirit of Shabbat; and a great deal more. Taken as a whole, the set provides an encyclopedic insight into pretty much anything one might want to know about Jewish prayer.

Duties of the Heart
(ca. 1080)

Bachya ibn Pakuda (ca. second half of the eleventh century)

"I examined human behavior throughout history as recorded in books, and I found that, except for the more motivated and ascetic among them, most people were far removed from these types of mitzvot [commandments] and had to be encouraged and instructed in them. That goes all the more so for the majority of the people in our generation who scoff at most of the physical commandments, let alone the duties of the heart."

It is commonplace today to castigate ourselves for falling short of the virtue we attribute to generations past. In the Jewish case, we suppose that not so long ago, people customarily observed Shabbat, kept kosher, and led lives that were, in general, ritually and morally superior to our own. The culprit is said to be "the times," infected with every ignoble vice from rampant individualism to downright hedonism. It was never like that "back then," we claim, believing that people didn't lock their doors, children played in safety, and everybody was nice to each other.

But the existence of a great number of people who fall short of their responsibilities is nothing new. Take the eleventh century, for example, when Bachya ibn Pakuda, a Spanish Jew about whom we know very little, wrote *Duties of the Heart*. He penned it in Arabic, and it was translated into Hebrew in 1161. Bachya thought it human nature to ignore a particular type of virtue: duties of the heart, as opposed to duties of the body. Not that the people he observed were overly punctilious about the latter, either, but the former were hardly observed at all. Duties of the heart "seemed somehow abandoned [. . .] a field left fallow."

The Hebrew word *lev* (heart) can mean several things. In the Bible, it denotes the mind, the seat of reason. Eventually, it came to mean the place of emotion. For Bachya, it has yet a third meaning, a dimension we might call human interiority, the point of spiritual connectedness beyond both thought and feeling. *Duties of the Heart* is a book on Jewish spirituality.

By duties of the body, Bachya means *physical* commandments, like eating unleavened bread on Passover and hearing the sound of the shofar on the New Year. But he also includes as physical the giving of charity, which we might more readily associate with the heart—we even call it "heartfelt giving." Not so for Bachya. Duties of the heart, he contends, have nothing to do with emotional responses like loving a stranger and showing compassion for the homeless. These emotive states may just be the necessary condition for further *physical* acts (such as reaching into your pocket and giving the charity). The "heart" is something much deeper: it is the spiritual state of the *soul*.

Duties of the heart are neither actions nor feelings—they are contemplative and mystical, such as "believing the world has a Creator who created it from nothing and who is incomparable; accepting His oneness [. . .] reflecting on His marvelous creations which serve as signs of His presence, trusting Him, [and] surrendering yourself to Him [. . .] *all of which are unapparent from the outside.*" Duties of the heart are not our outer behavior (which can be seen) but our inner soul life (which cannot be seen). To be sure, they cover attitudes toward other human beings as well, not just toward God: the refusal to carry a grudge, for example, or to desire revenge. These, too, are duties of the heart, says Bachya, because whatever negative behavior they may prompt (such as the wish for revenge), they are signs of what we might call soul-sickness. With *Duties of the Heart*, he sought to nurture the soul lest it fall prey to soul-sickness.

In Bachya's time, Muslim and Jewish philosophers alike combined wisdom from their own religious traditions with teachings they inherited from Greek and Roman antiquity. Sometimes these were in conflict: Aristotle thought matter was eternal, for example, while Judaism believed it had been created by God. But other concepts were more easily harmonized, such as views about the soul. Both Judaism and Neoplatonism held that the universe had begun with an absolute Unity (Jews called it God). Judaism could easily adopt the further Neoplatonic idea that creation implied a series of emanations, through which the universe of material plurality had come into being. While the body is part of that material world, the soul is not. Matter is impure and unlasting—even our bodies become dust after we are gone. By contrast, Jewish prayer proclaims each morning, "The soul that You gave me, God, came pure from You."

Bachya's book is divided into a series of ten mystical gates (*sh'arim*, in Hebrew) that lead, by progression, from true belief in God to gratitude, trust, sincerity, humility, repentance, and even a sort of asceticism—not complete abstinence of pleasure but total devotion to God, all the while living out one's role in the world. Bachya warns against the life of a recluse, selfishly concerned for one's own soul alone. We are here on earth not just for ourselves, but to lead others also to soulful love of God.

Duties of the heart are no less commanded than the physical duties that we must fulfill out of responsibility, whether we like them or not. It is incumbent upon us to attain our own absorption with God, first by intellectual understanding, but then, in a deeper way, by attuning our soul to God's will. Trying to grasp God through reason alone is like looking too closely at the sun—instead of knowing the sun better, we go blind; and rather than grasping God more fully, we impair our rational capacity. Only the soul, which comes from God and which is by nature divine, can thoroughly know God at all.

We cannot totally do without our sensual selves, either, but we dare not abandon the deeper impulse to nurture our nonmaterial souls. Obsession with bodily needs alone promotes habits detrimental to the soul. The path of the soul, by contrast, leads to a state of seeing without eyes, hearing without ears, even thinking beyond reason, and attuning ourselves to divine beauties and mysteries that only the soul is able to perceive.

As we would expect of such a thoroughly spiritual account, the popularity of Bachya's thought has ebbed and flowed through time. It has most often been seen as a mere appendage to Bachya's duties of the body and the study of Talmudic tradition, which so glorifies and defines these duties. In nineteenth-century eastern Europe, however, a movement known as Musar accused Talmudic academicism of sterility without an inner life supporting it. Among Musar followers, Bachya attained renewed appreciation. So, too, in our own time, where a spiritual dimension to life is so highly sought, *Duties of the Heart* will inspire us. True, it is a lengthy treatise, and distinctively medieval in tone. But it need not be read from beginning to end, and virtually every page contains passages that genuinely move the soul.

The Kuzari

(ca. 1140)

Judah Halevi (ca. 1075–1141)

"I was asked to provide arguments and rejoinders against the attacks of phi-losophers and adherents of other religions—and also against Jewish sectar-ians—who attack the rest of Israel. This reminded me of something I had heard regarding arguments delivered by a Rabbi to the king of the Khazars."

Both philosophers and mystics seek God, but in different ways: phi-losophers seek *knowledge of* God, while mystics seek *communion with* God. Philosophy is intellectual; mysticism is experiential. Human beings have a natural leaning toward one or the other—we like arguing our way to reality, or we prefer experiencing it directly.

But these two poles are not absolute. Philosophers can value experi-ence, and mystics may philosophize about it, so there is indeed a middle ground. Judah Halevi's lasting appeal is that he occupied this middle ground. We know the divine, he insisted, not because our minds man-age somehow to grasp it through argument, but because of the human capacity to access God directly. This experience of knowing God directly is called revelation. Israel experienced it at Mount Sinai, and Jewish prophets have encountered it ever since. But both Israel and the prophets had to be open to revelation, and that openness has nothing to do with education or logic. It is more like the capacity to fall in love. We either have it or we don't.

Medieval philosophers were influenced by the great Greek thinkers of antiquity, especially Plato and Aristotle. Plato's thoughts, however, were often filtered through the teachings of Plotinus (ca. 205–270 CE), the founder of Neoplatonism. As Plato saw it, the world of our senses is a pale reflection of a higher world of ideas or forms. We recog-nize a triangle, for example, because we have an idea of "triangle-ness" that informs our sensory experience. Plotinus added the question, How does the world of ideas become a world of the senses to begin with? The sensual world, he concluded, is the result of a series of emanations from the ideal world, like the emanations of light from a candle: the light that we see is real enough, but hardly as real as the essence of candle-light from which it derives, and which we can never approach enough to experience directly. All we can know is this emanated copy of the true essence.

Judaism's two most paradigmatic philosophers are Maimonides and Halevi. Maimonides followed Aristotelian thought, which had no room for a higher order of reality called ideas, much less emanations from on high. Halevi, on the other hand, was the consummate medieval Neoplatonist.

In Halevi's view, God operates through emanated revelation to prophets, and not just the biblical prophets but also the entire people of Israel whom God met at Mount Sinai. Jews, he firmly believed, have a natural capacity for prophecy.

You can hardly reason your way to that kind of privileged divine communication, however, so its only proof is the power of historical experience—and for Halevi, this was the experience of the 600,000 male Israelites whom the Bible records as standing at Mount Sinai and whose account had been passed down faithfully, generation by generation, ever since. Indeed, he argued, Judaism is superior to Christianity and to Islam because these faiths accepted the Jewish People's testimony, while their own accounts were not shared by others.

Following Plato, Halevi framed his philosophy as a work of fiction, which he wrote in Arabic: the conversation between a rabbi and the king of the medieval Khazar nation. The Khazars—the Hebrew pronunciation is "Kuzars"—were a Turkic people who established a powerful independent territory in eastern Europe from the seventh to the tenth centuries CE, and who were believed to have converted to Judaism. Halevi portrayed the Kuzari king as conducting interviews about their faiths with an Aristotelian, a Christian, a Muslim, and finally a rabbi, who convinces the king of Judaism's validity.

Prophecy is given only to Jews, Halevi held, because Jews are like the heart of humanity; prophecy comes only in the Land of Israel, which is the geographical heart of the world; prophecy uses the Hebrew language, which is the heart, so to speak, of all other languages. In other words, according to Halevi, prophecy arrives in the Jewish tongue, in a Jewish land, and for Jews, because Jews alone have the capacity for it.

Halevi's obvious polemical intent is hardly appealing today. One might even go so far as to say that his proof for Jewish truth is racist. We can, however, pardon Halevi for wanting to demonstrate Jewish superiority in a medieval world where both Christianity and Islam dismissed Judaism as inferior and where Jews had neither the power nor the right to answer their accusers. The Kuzari king himself throws the dismissal of Judaism in the rabbi's face: if Judaism is true, he asks, how could Jews have fallen to such a low state?

The Kuzari belongs here because it is much more than one medieval man's justification of Judaism. It is a passionate outcry for the role of faith beyond reason, yet not an outright abandonment of reason as a way to appreciate that faith; and it glorifies religious tradition as a source of truth that reflects the experience of those who came before.

Halevi urges piety on very Jewish terms—not otherworldly, that is, but here on earth in the nitty-gritty of reality. "The servant of God does not withdraw himself from secular contact lest he be a burden to the world and the world to him [. . .] he loves this world and a long life." Prayer is more than a list of petitions; it "extends our consciousness of the Creator and creation." As such, it should not be pro forma: "The tongue does not talk idly nor speak in an automatic way like the starling or parrot [. . .] This hour of divine service constitutes the maturity and essence of time." What "strengthens and enhances joy" is "the duty of saying blessings for all we enjoy or suffer in the world."

A member of a wealthy family and a businessman in his own right, Halevi spent his early adult years traveling throughout Spain and expanding his education to include the best of Muslim thought and culture, not just traditional Jewish law and lore. He was as much poet as philosopher, known for secular and romantic poetry as well as for his pious poetic compositions. Of special interest is his collection of poetry called "Songs of Zion," an ode to his rhapsodic love affair with the Land of Israel that he held so sacred. At the end of his life, he set sail to live out his final days in Jerusalem, but was held up in Alexandria, awaiting favorable weather. He probably died there, without ever completing his voyage. Legend, however, could not abide the idea that this passionate romantic was denied his lifelong goal of inhabiting the Land. People came to believe that he somehow reached Jerusalem, kneeled to kiss the holy earth, and was trampled to death by an Arab horseman. That this incident never actually happened matters little. The legend is its own testimony to the love affair Halevi had with his Land and his People— and the love future generations of that People showered back on him.

The Itinerary of Benjamin of Tudela
(ca. 1173)

Benjamin of Tudela (ca. twelfth century)

"[Santa Sophia] is the seat of the pope of the Greeks [. . .] Close to the wall of the palace is the Hippodrome and every year on the anniversary of Jesus, the king gives a great entertainment there. And in that place, men from all the races of the world come before the king and queen with jugglery."

It is hard for us today to comprehend the difficulty of travel in medieval times: the roads were few and often bad, the lodgings were mostly primitive, and safety was a constant concern. The majority of people never left home their entire lives. But still, some were surprisingly mobile, especially once the Crusades had opened trade routes and pilgrimage destinations. Riches brought to Europe from Asia encouraged adventurous souls to see the world. One of those adventurers, long before Ibn Battuta and Marco Polo, was the Spanish Jew Benjamin of Tudela, whose travelogue (written in Hebrew) provides firsthand knowledge of twelfth-century geography and culture. Historians differ on his date of departure (1159 or 1167); but either way, he first headed north to Provence, and then traveled through the Mediterranean and beyond, getting as far as Persia in the east and Egypt in the south before returning home in 1172.

Sometimes translations of historical texts give us an insight into the translator's mind and motivation as well. That is certainly true of Benjamin's *Itinerary*, which was first published in 1840, then republished in 1907, together with an English translation. The editor in 1840, Abraham [Adolf] Asher, was a German bibliophile who contributed to the golden age of early modern Jewish scholarship. In the era when Jews were desperately seeking civil rights, Asher and his scholarly collaborators pointed to Benjamin's diary as a demonstration of the Jewish contribution to European civilization. The 1907 edition was the work of Marcus N. Adler, the scholarly son of the chief rabbi of Great Britain, at a time when the British Empire was establishing colonial outposts throughout the Middle East, precisely the area that Benjamin had described. Adler, therefore, provided a historical commentary in terms of Islamic dynasties and rivalries. The most recent edition of the *Itinerary*, from 1983, features the introductions from 1840 and 1907 and an invaluable discussion by Michael A. Signer, an outstanding Jewish medievalist who died before his time in 2009. He had taught for many years at Hebrew Union College–Jewish Institute of Religion in Los Angeles, and then at the University of Notre Dame.

Benjamin of Tudela lived in a time of transition. Christian Spaniards were fighting to retake Muslim Spain from the north, while Berbers were invading from Africa. Spanish Jews had reason to worry about their future under both. They had prospered in Muslim Spain, because Spain's Umayyad rulers generally allowed Jews to live peacefully alongside the Muslim majority. Recognized as monotheists, Jews were not forced to choose between conversion and death. The Berbers, too, were Muslim, but not as tolerant; they gave no special privileges to any unbelievers, not even Jews. As for the Christians, Christian theology saw Jews as a despised people who had rejected, and even killed, Christ.

Why did Benjamin undertake his outstanding journey? Prior to Signer's edition, three motivations had been offered, and Signer reviews them all. First, Benjamin was a pilgrim, but an unusual one, because he extended his journey to see more than just the holy sites in Palestine. Second, he may also have been hoping to expand his business by scouting out new trading partners. Third, given the political instability in Spain caused by both Christians and Berbers, he may have wanted to investigate potential havens to which Jews might flee, should they be persecuted. Signer adds a fourth motivation: "Jewish consolation."

The Christian and Berber conquests of Spain confronted Jews with a religious crisis, not just a political one. True, since the Roman destruction of their Temple in 70 CE, Jews had been in exile, but only, they believed, temporarily. Abraham's covenant with God had made them a chosen people, and God would someday restore them to their homeland of Israel with a messianic ruler descended from King David.

As the centuries dragged on, however, that hope was becoming harder and harder to sustain. If Jewish exile was intended to be temporary, why was it lasting more than a thousand years? Citing Genesis 49:10, "The scepter shall not depart from Judah," Christians pointed out that Jews no longer had a king; so the scepter must have been transferred to a new Judah—the kings of Christianity. The cultural brilliance of Muslim civilization, too, threatened Jewish self-esteem, since it far exceeded whatever Jews had produced in recent memory.

Benjamin sought to convince his readers that regardless of their condition in Spain, Jews elsewhere still appeared to be the chosen people. He reported that "the Pope had a Jewish bailiff; in Syria, a Jew served as the astronomer to King Nur-el-din; the [Jewish] 'Prince of Princes' in Cairo had a seat in the royal palace." Most of all, in Babylonia, the head of the Jewish community (the exilarch) lived like a king—just as the Bible had promised. He was "borne through the streets in great pomp, venerated by Jew and non-Jew alike." Clearly, contrary to the Christian interpretation of Genesis 49:10, Jews still had a ruler—in Babylonia. Moreover, Jews in Palestine were praying, fasting, and studying day and night to hasten redemption. Thus Jews in Spain should take comfort: exile would soon end.

But Benjamin's travels are intriguing in their own right. Rome, he exclaims, has "remarkable sights beyond enumeration [. . .] the coliseum [for example, where] battles were fought in ancient times and more than 100,000 men were slain." Also, "wealth like that of Constantinople is not to be found in the whole world." In Palestine, he finds biblical Samaritans still offering sacrifices. Near Baghdad is an island called Khuzistan, where merchants come from as far away as India to trade with the West. Jews are glassworkers in Aleppo, tanners in Constantinople, and silk weavers in Thebes. The various European nations all have fortifications, as if continually preparing for war. Genoa and Pisa are at each other's throats, and in Jerusalem, Jews choose to live near the Tower of David, where the protective walls are thickest.

Benjamin traveled both as a European and as a Jew: he was interested in everything he saw, but he sought out Jews wherever he went—not just the scholars and saints, but the everyday Jews who kept the Sabbath, believed in God, supported synagogues, and went about their business earning a living and raising families just as Jews do today. He confabulates some things, shows typical medieval biases in others, and reports ancient tales of wonder incredulously. But he is also a wonderful and objective source for medieval life—among the finest we have.

Guide for the Perplexed
(ca. 1200)

Moses Maimonides (1135–1204)

"The object of the enumeration of God's thirteen attributes is the lesson that we should acquire similar attributes and act accordingly [. . .] Human beings will then be determined always to seek loving kindness, justice and righteousness, and thus to imitate the ways of God."

Moses Maimonides (Moses ben Maimon) is one of the most towering intellectual figures of the Middle Ages. Although born in Spain, he lived much of his life in Egypt, where he served as court physician to the Muslim rulers. He established his stature through a great commentary to the Mishnah (in which he also formulated thirteen principles of faith for Jews; see page 74) and a brilliantly composed and organized code of Jewish law called *Mishneh Torah*. The philosophy that would make him more famous still was implicit in the introduction to his law code, but it came to fruition only with his *Guide for the Perplexed*, a presentation of his philosophical beliefs that he wrote in Arabic, in the literary form of an extensive letter (in three parts) to a disciple. It appeared around 1200, only four years before he died.

By then, Maimonides had become embroiled in one controversy after another. His law code, detractors said, had been intended to replace the Talmud, not just augment it. Jewish traditionalists attacked his philosophy as heretical, and as a Jew in Egypt, he contended with the Jewish authorities in Babylonia for the right to interpret Judaism for all Jews. Already in 1188, Maimonides had been accused of denying the traditional Jewish doctrine of resurrection. After his death, his philosophy came under even more fire, and for good reason. Even though the *Guide for the Perplexed* is replete with pious quotations from the Bible and Talmud, Maimonides questioned received Jewish doctrine. Most significantly, he held that God is beyond all anthropomorphism (having human form) and anthropopathism (having human feelings). He thereby attacked the literal reading of Scripture, explaining away a good deal of the biblical narrative as having only allegoric or metaphoric significance. Maimonides was the consummate rationalist, intent on harmonizing Jewish teaching with Aristotelian thought, a goal that his Jewish opponents found appalling.

Philosophers prior to Maimonides had attempted to prove creation and then to argue from creation to the need for a divine creator. Maimonides, however, rejected any possibility of proving creation, since it seemed to him equally possible that (as Aristotle had said) matter was eternal. So he began his analysis in the *Guide* with Aristotle's assumption —just for the sake of argument, he claimed. The existence and unity of God would have to be proven on their own ground, as would God's incorporeality (i.e., that God has no body). Imagine, Maimonides said, a stone being moved in front of a hole to block a draft of air. The stone has been moved by a stick, the stick by a hand, and so on. Similarly, the air moves by some higher principle of nature, which, in turn, must be set into motion by something higher still. The only way to avoid an infinite regress is to imagine a single entity that moves everything else, but that, by definition, is itself moved by nothing. That entity is God. Such a God can hardly be responsive to prayer, however, so instead of being petitionary, prayer becomes a means toward attaining higher knowledge of God.

Opponents also accused Maimonides of denying miracles. Nature must be miraculous, they held, not just a matter of scientific law. For Maimonides, by contrast, nothing was more demonstrably divine than the rational—we would say, scientific—workings of the universe, as described primarily in Aristotle's *Physics*—God being the ultimate, albeit rational, cause of it all. Even prophecy is thus a natural phenomenon. Still following Aristotle, Maimonides held that the human soul contains a rational faculty that can connect to the equally rational aspect of God called the active intellect. It is through such connection with the divine that prophecy occurs. Prophets thereby achieve knowledge of the divine laws on which human happiness depends. Moses is the greatest prophet, because he received God's law at Sinai directly.

God can have neither body nor feelings, since feelings imply want— if God felt happiness, after all, God could equally feel unhappiness, in which case God would not be perfect. Similarly God must be changeless, because change implies a defect at some point in time—and besides, the only way change can occur is through the chain of cause and effect of which God is, by definition, the unmoved mover that initiates all change but is itself beyond it.

Sometimes Maimonides's arguments are so mired in medieval assumptions about reality that they seem wanting today. But even when some of his proofs appear dubious, Maimonides's conclusions tend to strike modern readers quite positively. Those who find it hard to believe in a biblical God, for example, learn that they need not take biblical language about God literally. The only way to talk about God, Maimonides insists, is through negative attributes. When we say God is kind, we mean God is *not* unkind; living means *not* dead, and eternal means *not* limited. God may still have qualities of some sort, but not in a way that we can imagine them or speak about them.

Ethically, too, Maimonides appeals to modern consciousness. Vice, he says, is not ingrained in us; it is inculcated through childhood upbringing and habit. As such, education can correct it. Regarding human behavior, he accepts the Aristotelian notion of the golden mean: character flaws are like bodily disorders, which occur through an imbalance caused by inordinate growth of an organ or element within us; doctors simply restore equilibrium. By analogy, arrogant people need merely practice exceptional humility, until eventually the proper balance between pride and modesty sets in.

It is hard to overstate Maimonides's influence on later Judaism. For modern Jews, he epitomizes the Enlightenment ideal—centuries before the modern Enlightenment unfolded! He also greatly influenced the non-Jewish world. Thomas Aquinas is unthinkable without Maimonides as his guide, and Thomist philosophy governed Catholic thought for centuries.

Ironically, Maimonides may have been even more heretical than his opponents at the time charged. A substantial number of interpreters believe he spoke in veiled language, using traditional formulations to mask bold deviations from that very tradition. The leading advocate of this position was Leo Strauss (1899–1973), a philosopher and prominent Maimonidean interpreter who taught at the University of Chicago from 1949 to 1969. There may or may not be such an esoteric side to Maimonides, but it is altogether certain that Maimonides wrote for the "perplexed," and that ever since the *Guide* appeared, thoughtful men and women have been devouring it for guidance.

Principles of the Jewish Faith
(1964)

Louis Jacobs (1920–2006)

"The non-fundamentalist is inspired to investigate the facts and make the necessary adjustments, in the firm belief that it is this which his faith would have him do, since the God he worships is the God of truth."

A s they grow up, many Jews are told that "Judaism is deed, not creed." They find it puzzling that Christians have creeds, and that over the centuries, many individuals (and even whole groups) within Christianity have been excommunicated for questioning what seem, to Jews, to be relatively inconsequential aspects of one doctrine or another. One reason is that Christianity was formulated under the influence of the Hellenistic concept of religion as a philosophy rooted in doctrinal definitions; rabbinic Judaism, on the other hand, was not.

Eventually, however, these same Jews discover that even though Judaism worries more about what one does than about what one believes, Judaism *does* have creeds—but they are *guides to* belief, not *dogmas of* belief. From time to time, very important Jewish authorities have tried to codify what Judaism's most important principles are.

As early as 200 CE, the Mishnah affirmed the necessary belief in resurrection of the dead and revelation of Torah directly from God on Mount Sinai. Other tenets might just as easily have been included: faith in a messiah, for example, and in divine providence (God rewards good and punishes evil). The Mishnah omitted these because it was not trying to lay down a systematic set of beliefs, but rather a set of legal principles for leading a decent human life. In the Middle Ages, as Jews found it necessary to enter into dialogue with Muslim and Christian theologians, the requirements changed.

The most famous set of principles was adduced by Moses Maimonides. In his famous commentary to the Mishnah (completed in 1168), he formulated the following thirteen tenets of faith: (1) God exists; (2) God is one; (3) God is incorporeal; (4) God is eternal; (5) God alone is the proper object of worship; (6) God provides prophecy; (7) Moses was the greatest and final prophet; (8) the Torah was given to Moses by God; (9) the Torah is immutable; (10) God knows the thoughts and deeds of human beings; (11) God rewards and punishes; (12) God will send a messiah; (13) God will resurrect the dead.

Over the centuries, other Jewish philosophers followed, each with his own set of principles, but usually complicating matters because they did not just separate out certain basics (like Maimonides); they then also divided them further into subcategories. None of these alternatives lasted anywhere near as long as Maimonides's list did, no doubt because of the illustrious reputation of its author, but also because Maimonides was at the center of doctrinal controversies that rocked the rabbinic world from the twelfth to the fourteenth centuries. Ironically enough, medieval attempts to defame Maimonides merely added to his fame in the long run. Among other things, anonymous writers twice reformulated his principles as prayers, to make them accessible to average Jews: the better known example is the prayer *Yigdal* (meaning, "Exalted [be the living God]"), now a staple in every morning service. The other prayer, *Ani Ma'amin* (meaning, "I believe"), is also in the traditional prayer book, but is usually treated as optional. But one of its lines—faith in a messiah—has been set to music and is regularly sung, especially on occasions that memorialize the Holocaust and champion the age-old Jewish assurance of better days to come.

Because Maimonides lived in a Muslim world, first in Spain, then in Egypt, he focused on the Jewish approach to tenets of faith that Muslims emphasized, especially those that Judaism questioned. Maimonides agreed that Judaism is firmly and absolutely monotheistic, for example; but for him, the greatest and final prophet was Moses, not Muhammad.

Taken together, the thirteen principles of Maimonides are as fine a list of Jewish essentials as any. Modern Jews are likely to have trouble subscribing to some of them, but they allow considerable latitude—as we would expect from a set of beliefs that have weathered countless intellectual and spiritual storms. How does God reward and punish? What exactly is prophecy? And how is the messiah defined? These and other serious questions rightly occur to anybody who wants to understand what Jews believe.

Fortunately, an absolutely splendid modern book explores all this. Its author, Louis Jacobs, was an extraordinarily learned man whom *The Jewish Chronicle* (England's best-known Jewish newspaper) has called "the greatest British Jew of all time." In the 1960s, he almost became England's chief rabbi (the Jewish equivalent of the archbishop of Canterbury), but was denied the position by fundamentalists who were appalled at his support for the scientific view of the Bible's origins. He persevered in following his own path, and was instrumental in founding Britain's Masorti movement (meaning, "traditional")—loosely equivalent to North America's Conservative Judaism.

Louis Jacobs wrote over fifty books, but none better than this one, an in-depth, yet widely accessible, analysis of Maimonides's thirteen principles. It takes readers step by step through each one of them, stopping regularly to provide lengthy excurses on issues that the principles raise. Jacobs cites everyone, it seems: secular philosophers, sociologists, historians, his rabbinic contemporaries, and the great thinkers of Jewish tradition, all of whose thought he knows exceedingly well.

Principles of the Jewish Faith is perhaps the finest single treatment of Jewish belief over time. It spans all of rabbinic Judaism, a tradition going back two thousand years, so the fact that Jacobs wrote it half a century ago isn't terribly significant. There are few books to which readers interested in Jewish belief return as frequently as they do to this one.

The Zohar
(ca. 1287)

Moses de Leon (ca. 1250–1305)

"A spark of impenetrable darkness flashed within the concealed of the con-
cealed from the head of Infinity [. . .] Under the impact of splitting, a single,
concealed, supernal point shone. Beyond that point, nothing is known."

Mystical traditions are deeply embedded in the very fabric of rab-binic thought and practice. Medieval Judaism therefore inherited not just the classic texts of the Rabbis (Mishnah, Talmud, midrash, and early responsa) but an ongoing thread of mystical probing as well. Certain lesser-known midrashic recollections describe mystical trances by devotees who travel beyond the realm of worldly senses to encoun-ter God directly. A work from late antiquity called *Sefer Yetsirah* (The Book of Creation) accents the creative, and even magical, power of the Hebrew alphabet. These and other sources were explored further by twelfth- and thirteenth-century adepts in Germany, intent on a pietistic revival that included asceticism in practice and intense speculation on how a hidden God could become manifest to human beings.

When people today speak of Jewish mysticism, however, they usu-ally have in mind something else: Kabbalah, a catchall phrase for a set of doctrines and practices that first emerged in twelfth-century Provence. A century later, kabbalistic beliefs crossed the Pyrenees into Spain, where they found their most formative expression in the *Zohar*, ostensibly a midrash in form, but a highly fanciful one, filled with esoteric allusions below the obvious meaning of the sentences that constitute it.

Medieval legend deemed the *Zohar* an authentic revelation granted to Shimon bar Yochai, a second-century CE teacher in Palestine, but it is actually a combination of separate works created in medieval Spain. The *Zohar*'s most significant author, Moses de Leon, a Castilian scholar and mystic, wrote it in a concocted version of second-century Aramaic in order to attribute it to Shimon bar Yochai; it purports to be a record of conversations Shimon had with rabbinic colleagues over the secret meaning of Torah. With this approach, Moses de Leon did not have to admit that he had composed such a revolutionary mystical text all on his own. It was, so to speak, a pious forgery, not an unusual practice among authors of late antiquity and medieval times.

Central to Zoharic mysticism is a philosophical assumption rooted in the Neoplatonic doctrine of divine emanation: the universe as we experience it is not separate from, but an extension of, God. Its creation corresponds to the inner life of God, unfolding through stages of luminous evolution. Each stage is called a *s'firah* (plural: *s'firot*). This fragmentation of God into separate s'firot that began as divine self-expression ends in a plenitude of being that overflows into time and space to create our physical world. Along the way, forces of evil alienate the divine fragments from each other, a situation that must be corrected by human effort here on earth. Religious life, therefore, especially prayer, works in the human realm but also in the divine realm of the s'firot, unifying the fragmented parts of God. This esoteric understanding of the universe revealed through hidden scriptural meanings is the *Zohar's* overall topic.

Jews expelled from Spain in 1492 carried kabbalistic teaching throughout the Mediterranean, especially to the northern Palestinian city of Safed, tucked away in the Galilean hills. Kabbalistic writers then benefited from the invention of the printing press, which allowed large-scale production of their work to circulate quickly all over Europe. Before long, the *Zohar* had entered the pantheon of great books that are taken for granted as part and parcel of Jewish life.

The *Zohar's* doctrines reflect the historical milieu in which they were composed. The dominant Jewish philosophy of the time had been formulated by Moses Maimonides, who had combined classical rabbinic thought with Aristotelian philosophy. The Maimonidean God was perfect—and therefore incapable of change. It followed that prayer could hardly change God's mind. Neither could God be said to need prayer, since having a need would be an imperfection. So prayer must just be an exercise in intellectual well-being, a means to prepare worshippers for ultimate insight into truth. Most rabbis in Muslim countries found nothing terribly shocking in Maimonides's philosophy. But conservative rabbis who had been influenced by Christian thought attacked the Maimonideans in print, and even burned their master's writings.

Implicitly, the Jewish mystics answered this Maimonidean "threat" by asserting a more literal reading of Scripture, and a God who does indeed change. These mystics understood God's entire essence as the various stages of s'firot—nothing but change, in fact. Furthermore, they believed, God requires our prayers, since prayer unites the s'firot, making God whole.

By the time of de Leon, Christians had successfully wrested Castile from Muslim control. Enlightened rulers still granted Jews religious freedom, but pressure to convert was ubiquitous. Among other things, Jews were forced to attend sermons explaining baptism as the next, the natural, and the necessary step for Jews to take. As a counterforce, the *Zohar* personalized God as a deity who needed Jews to remain true to Jewish tradition, in order to end divine fragmentation and cure the world of its woes.

From its inception, the *Zohar* has proved contentious. Even people who accepted the account of its ancient origins considered it a fanciful elaboration of biblical teachings. From time to time, Jewish pretenders to messianic standing used it to support their claims, giving it a reputation for being heretically revolutionary. Rationalists, on the other hand, denounced its "irrationality"—its patent dependence on angels, for example, its blatant anthropomorphism, and its picture of a God who had relegated the most important divine messages to esoteric textual allusions that no one other than mystical adepts could understand. Scientific Jewish scholarship that arose in the nineteenth century denounced the *Zohar* as a medieval fraud and treated its imaginative presentation of Jewish truths with derision.

But with the revival of spirituality in the later twentieth century, people began revisiting mystical texts in the great religious traditions, with newfound appreciation for what these texts could teach. The *Zohar*—and the many mystical books and commentaries it has spawned over time—have become the avid topic of study, even in scientifically oriented seminaries that had once removed Jewish mysticism from their curricula. Today, study of the *Zohar* is intense and widespread.

Ultimately, the *Zohar* is a record of, and an invitation to, the sacred. If how we live has an esoteric divine complement, the *Zohar*'s content is not just a philosophical doctrine, however deep and interesting that may be. To translate the mundane, and even the ordinarily holy, into s'firotic language is nothing less than to participate in the divine.

Hebrew Ethical Wills
(1926)

Israel Abrahams (1858–1924) (editor)

"All the honor I desire is to be remembered for good because of you [. . .]
that those who see you may exclaim, 'Blessed be he who begat this one; blessed
be he who reared him'" (from the will of Judah ibn Tibbon, twelfth
century CE).

What parents do not worry about the values they have inculcated in their children? Wouldn't we all die happier knowing for sure we had outfitted them with sound advice to see them through life after we are gone? Israel Abrahams, the editor of this magnificent book, cites John Keats, who pondered, "What shall he murmur with his latest breath, / When his proud eye looks through the film of death?"

What indeed would be our final words to our children as they hold our hands and help us close our eyes forever? Rather than any material advice, we are much more likely to try one last time to outfit them for goodness, happiness, and success beyond monetary gain. And that concern goes back at least to biblical times. At the end of Genesis, Jacob blesses each of his children. King David passes on final words of wisdom to his son Solomon. And by the twelfth century CE, Jews of letters were writing ethical wills to their children.

As of 1926, when *Hebrew Ethical Wills* was first published (posthumously), some three hundred such wills had come to light. The number has grown by now, some of them by men and women just recently deceased, who were moved by this lovely tradition to write one themselves. The Abrahams volume contains the best-known classics, by such historically significant personalities as Judah ibn Tibbon (1120–ca. 1190), a physician and translator of medieval philosophical texts from Arabic into Hebrew, and Glückel of Hameln (ca. 1645/46–1724; see page 88), the remarkable mother, businesswoman, and diarist who had so much to say about Jewish life in her time.

Not knowing when they would die, parents frequently began their wills when their children were young or even barely born, and added to them as they grew older. Mothers wrote them, too, but as we would expect in a literary tradition passed down by men, most of the wills we possess come from fathers, and learned ones at that. Still, since throughout Jewish tradition nothing has mattered as deeply as learning, more individuals than we might imagine were literate. Abrahams explains that even average Jews in medieval days "spoke Bible," having memorized verse after verse as a matter of course while growing up. And most of the people represented in his book did more than just grow up with Scripture. They virtually mastered it, along with the Talmud and rabbinic tradition besides, all of which they bent to their own uses as they argued, pleaded, cajoled, and reminded their children to live the good life.

Side by side with impressive learning, we get gross medieval superstition. But even superstition is sometimes just a way to exercise good lawyerly practice. When a man is dying, says the kabbalist Shabbetai Horowitz (1561–1619), "Satan stands by his side tempting him. Who knows what a dying father might say at such a time?" So Horowitz concludes, "I solemnly swear that if at that time, I say anything improper, heaven forbid, what I say then is null and void. Only what I say now is binding."

Some things never change. Parents today who have supported their children through college may hear their own voice in twelfth-century Judah ibn Tibbon's words to his son Samuel: "I spent myself in educating and protecting you [. . .] These twelve years, I have denied myself the usual pleasures and relaxations for your sake." Apparently, however, young Samuel, the graduate, has been sowing his wild oats instead of studying, so Judah grumbles, "Alas, you did not choose to employ your abilities, hiding yourself from your books, not caring to know them or even their titles. If you had seen your own books in the hands of others, you wouldn't have known them."

Jews in Muslim Spain who wrote philosophical works used their native Arabic, and Judah ibn Tibbon is best known for translating these classics into Hebrew. Elsewhere in his will, therefore, he advises Samuel that he must learn to write well, being careful "in the use of conjunctions and adverbs, and how you apply them and how they harmonize with the verbs." Had Judah lived to see Samuel as an adult, he would have saved himself worry: the great Maimonides himself complimented Samuel on his Arabic, as Samuel translated the master's *Guide for the Perplexed* from the original Arabic into Hebrew.

Contrary to many negative stereotypes about medieval family life, writes Lawrence Fine in his introduction to the 2006 edition of the book, the wills often display "gentleness, tenderness, intimacy, and love." Fourteenth-century Eleazer of Mainz, for example, wants to be buried "at the right hand of my father. But if the space be a little narrow, I am sure that he loves me well enough to make room for me."

These scholarly men worry most about their sons. But daughters are addressed, too. Shabbetai Horowitz tells his daughters, "If your husbands are angry, leave them, and after the time of wrath has passed, rebuke them for their conduct." Eleazer of Mainz, whom Abrahams calls "an average man," instructs his daughters to "respect their husbands and be amiable to them." His sons, too, however, should "honor their wives more than themselves and treat them with tender consideration." Both sons and daughters should study and give charity.

By the eighteenth century, the wills do not just offer advice. They supply actual statements of faith to guide the lives of the writers' children. Most interesting, perhaps, is David Friesenhausen (ca. 1750–1828), who says, "I believe with perfect faith that the whole human race, Jew or Gentile, wise or ignorant, righteous or wicked, will enjoy felicity at the end, after bearing the punishment due to each according to his acts."

It is hard to read *Hebrew Ethical Wills* without wanting to write one yourself. In the meantime, you might want to ponder this extract from the 1733 will by Joel ben Abraham Shemariah of Vilna. He felt faint while taking a bath one morning. Taking the event as a possible omen of premature death, he wrote the following to his children: "To be at peace with all the world, with Jew and Gentile, must be your foremost aim in this terrestrial life. Contend with no one. In the first instance, your home must be the abode of quietude and happiness; no harsh word must be heard there; rather, over all must reign love, amity, modesty, and a spirit of gentleness and reverence. This spirit must not end with your home, however. In your dealings with the world, you must allow neither money nor ambition to disturb you."

4

Enlightenment, Emancipation, and Traditionalism

The Conversation Explodes

֍

For Europe's Jews, the nineteenth century was radically different from everything that had gone before. Nothing like it had been seen since the arrival of the Rabbis on the scene some two millennia earlier. The Rabbis had transformed the Jewish understanding of the Bible to the point where its literal meaning in Jewish life became obsolete; and what the Rabbis did to the Bible, the nineteenth century did to the Rabbis. The Rabbis had responded to the advanced Hellenistic civilization of the Roman Empire. The nineteenth-century crisis arrived with the pervasive triumph of science and modernity.

It all began with Napoleon, who freed Jews in western Europe from their ghettos. The intellectual Enlightenment of the 1700s had given rise to political emancipation a hundred years later. The Enlightenment gave Jews access to the modern world of liberal political thought and scientific learning; emancipation awarded them civil rights as citizens of nation-states. It is impossible to understand modern Judaism without coming to terms with these two phenomena.

During the eighteenth century, despite liberal Enlightenment theories, Jews still suffered from limitations on their civic freedoms carried over from medieval times. In Prussia, for example, Jews were officially excluded from citizenship, and could not even reside in such growing urban centers as Berlin. There were exceptions, however, primarily the so-called Court Jews, wealthy individuals who facilitated loans and business agreements for their royal patrons, or other "tolerated" individuals whose benefit to the ruling classes could not easily be overlooked. The German-Jewish philosopher Moses Mendelssohn was such a "tolerated" person in Berlin. The situation changed with Napoleon, who gave the right of citizenship to all Jews, not just the "tolerated" variety.

A product of the French Revolution, Napoleon Bonaparte (1769–1821) heralded "liberty, equality, fraternity," the threefold battle cry of the republic that proclaimed everyone—at least in theory—a free and equal member of human society. Wherever Napoleon went, he found Jews relegated to the squalor of ghetto existence, from which he promised to emancipate them.

To be sure, after Napoleon's final defeat in 1815, Europe's reactionary monarchs rolled back Jewish rights (and civic rights in general) wherever they could—but the ideals of the Enlightenment and the liberties of emancipation refused to die. The rest of the nineteenth century consolidated Jewish gains, and motivated Jews to experiment with religious reform (not altogether unlike the Protestant Reformation three centuries earlier). Regularly, however, the conservative rulers tried to restrict religious and civic freedom. Especially after the abortive revolution of 1848, many liberal-minded western Europeans—both Jews and non-Jews—headed to America, hoping for better.

Many of the Jews who remained in the Old World prospered, only to discover that anti-Judaism (hatred of Jews because of their religious beliefs) was being replaced with anti-Semitism (hatred of Jews on ethnic grounds), a far more damning ideology, since even conversion to Christianity could not save Jews from being seen by anti-Semites as inferior.

In the Americas, Jews had long been establishing their presence. Some had arrived with the explorers, possibly as early as Columbus. But the Inquisition in both Spain and Portugal prevented Jews in Latin America from proclaiming their Jewish identity, so it is hard to say how many Jews actually lived in these New World colonies. Patently obvious Jewish settlements arose only after 1630, with the arrival of the Dutch, who had broken free of the Spanish empire and had begun building their own colonial outposts for worldwide trade—including the Brazilian port city of Recife, which travelers described in 1642 as being no less than two-thirds (!) Jewish. One of these visitors testified, "Among the free inhabitants of Brazil the Jews are most considerable in number; they have a vast traffic, beyond all the rest; they purchased sugar-mills and bought stately houses."

By 1645, however, the Portuguese reconquest was well under way. Jews watched warily, for, as one observer put it, "They were sure to be massacred without mercy during the insurrection, or roasted without mercy if the insurgents should prove successful." A year later, amid ongoing fighting between Dutch and Portuguese, Recife's Jews returned to Amsterdam or left for other New World territories such as Suriname (also owned by the Dutch) or the island of Guadeloupe, which was French. Yet another group of Jews from Recife arrived in New Amsterdam (later renamed New York) in 1654, thus inaugurating Jewish life in North America.

Over the following decades, Jews began to settle in towns along the East Coast, including Savannah, Charleston, Baltimore, Philadelphia, New York, and Newport. By the early nineteenth century, the number of Ashkenazi immigrants from Europe had overtaken the earlier Sephardi settlers. In 1846, Isaac Mayer Wise, who would become the most influential rabbi of his time in America, arrived in New York. He was taken aback by the Jewish liturgical practices he encountered, but inspired by the promise of religious freedom he found. He took note of the rise of the varied Protestant denominations along the ever-widening frontier, and decided to establish a liberal Jewish equivalent that later became known as the Reform movement in North America. At roughly the same time, modern Jewish Orthodoxy was evolving as well, and by the end of the century, with the arrival of increasing numbers of Jews from eastern Europe, the Conservative movement came into being. (Reconstructionist Judaism was developed only in the mid-twentieth century.)

The Jewish narrative was more tortuous in eastern Europe, where there was more uncertainty as to what exactly Judaism was. Without having experienced Napoleon, no one in the East thought to call it a religion. "Peoplehood" still seemed apt, since the czar never did manage to consolidate the ethnic hodgepodge of peoples that were eventually brought together (by force) in the Union of Soviet Socialist Republics. But a conversation on Jewish identity could not fully arise as long as premodern thinking prevailed even *within* Jewish circles. In most cases,

Jews conceived of themselves as a people constrained by Talmudic law, a way of life with God at the center and rabbis as its interpreters. The pinnacle of Talmudic interpretation emerged from Lithuanian academies called yeshivot (singular: yeshivah; see page 118).

The iron rule of the yeshivot and their representatives had come under attack by eighteenth-century Hasidism, a popular romantic-mystical movement in southern Poland and Ukraine embraced by the poverty-stricken Jewish peasantry. Hasidism was hardly modern, however. It quickly petrified into its own brand of orthodoxy. Despite Napoleon's policy of freeing Jews—indeed, precisely because of it—Hasidic leaders supported anti-Napoleonic forces and were thrilled when he was defeated. The last thing they wanted was the Enlightenment and emancipation. Supporters of the Jewish Enlightenment movement (known as Haskalah) in the East opposed Hasidism, but without much success.

Jews had been invited to Poland as part of the sixteenth-century Polish Renaissance. But in a series of "partitions" (1772, 1793, and 1795), Poland was divided among the three great European powers on its borders: Prussia, Austria, and Russia. By the 1800s, therefore, the majority of eastern European Jews inhabited areas governed by Russia, whose czars vacillated on their Jewish policy. In 1881, Alexander III came to power, determined to eliminate the Jews under his rule altogether—a policy that was formally inaugurated by legislation announced in May 1882 and known as the May Laws. Under Russian rule, Jews had already been restricted to live in an area known as the Pale of Settlement (which included Lithuania, Belarus, and Ukraine). The May Laws shrank their rights of domicile even further, forcing the already impoverished population into even more severe penury.

To be sure, a privileged class of Jewish artisans and merchants had been allowed to reside in Russia's interior, but now, even that opportunity was curtailed. On Passover of 1881 (a year before the May Laws were proclaimed!), Moscow's Jews were driven westward into the Pale.

By the end of the nineteenth century, the czarist regime began to crumble, and so, too, did the traditional understandings of Judaism. In short order, a variety of Jewish alternatives weighed in. The Musar movement tried to remake tradition by applying a pietist approach to moralism, while the Haskalah movement promoted the intellectual and cultural ideals of the Enlightenment. A spectrum of takes on socialism emerged. The Bund was a moderate approach, with Jewish peoplehood at its center. A universalistic (even radical) brand sought to merge Jewish peoplehood into a classless society. Most lasting, perhaps, was

Jewish nationalism—in the form of Zionism, the hope for an independent Jewish state in Palestine. A similar ideology (that failed utterly) was Territorialism, the belief that Jews might have their own republic, but not necessarily in Palestine.

In the 1880s, all these alternative concepts were growing, even though most Jews in the East were not actively involved in any of them, being too poor to care. The lucky ones left eastern Europe, usually for America, where they arrived just in time to participate in the growth of the cities, the factories, and the banking industry so typical of the gilded era that produced the twentieth century.

The Jewish population everywhere rose sharply throughout the nineteenth century. While exact numbers are hard to come by, the *Jewish Encyclopedia* of 1901–1906 gives the following Jewish population figures, gathered between 1897 and 1901: Russia: 3,972,625; Poland (under Russian control): 1,316,776; Austria (including the formerly Polish province of Galicia): 1,224,899; Hungary: 851,378; Turkey: 282,277; Romania: 269,015; United Kingdom: 250,000; other European countries, combined: 312,863; and North and South America: 1,549,621.

Between 1881 and 1924, an estimated 2 million Jews, mostly from eastern Europe, arrived in the New World. Many others migrated to western Europe and to what would one day be known as Israel. Hitler eventually killed most of the Jews who stayed behind.

The Life of Glückel of Hameln
(1690s)

Glückel of Hameln (ca. 1645/46–1724)

*"There are people who say, 'Why should I always worry about my children?
Isn't it enough that I saw to them when they were young?' This is quite right
when children are in a good position and all goes well with them. But if, God
forbid, things go badly, would anyone with feelings not bear the burden of her
children and friends?"*

The year 1648 is best known for the end of the Thirty Years War,
which had embroiled most of Europe, leaving tens of thousands
dead and many more starving. Destruction was especially severe in Germany, Alsace Lorraine, and the Netherlands. To the east, a series of populist uprisings against the Polish nobility decimated Polish and Ukrainian
Jews along the way. Also in 1648, Shabbetai Tzvi, the most infamous
false messiah in Jewish history, announced himself. Eventually, in 1666,
he converted to Islam rather than face execution by suspicious authorities in Constantinople, but in his heyday, entire Jewish communities
were split on the question of whether God was finally sending redemption to his suffering people. In retrospect, we can see that the year 1648
was an in-between time that looked backward upon the death throes of
the Middle Ages and ahead to the birth pangs of modernity.

Glückel of Hameln came into this world just a few years earlier and
witnessed the gruesome aftermath of the war around Hamburg, the
city of her birth. Despite the official Peace of Westphalia, the fighting
dragged on, here and there, as an everyday event. Glückel does not
mention the Polish pogroms, but she met plenty of Jewish refugees
fleeing from the East, as well as Jews from the Spanish Empire trickling
over the border into the Protestant Netherlands, where they hoped
to escape the Inquisition and reclaim their Jewish identity openly.
In the wake of Shabbetai Tzvi, she watched deluded Jews abandon
property they were sure they wouldn't need after being carried away
at last to Jerusalem by the messiah. Glückel herself prayed regularly
for redemption, even ending her chronicle with the report of the sky
opening like a curtain to display heavenly wonders—a sign, perhaps,
that deliverance was at hand.

But Glückel was no ethereal mystic; her piety left room for her to run a family and a business, the details of which she chronicled in memoirs (written in Yiddish) from 1691 to 1699. She died in 1724—the year that Immanuel Kant was born, and five years before Moses Mendelssohn's birth—after a long and utterly remarkable life.

"Every two years I had a child," she writes, "and suffered much, as is natural when there is a household of small children. I often thought that no one had such a heavy burden as I [. . .] but I, foolish one, did not know how well things were with me, when my children were like olive branches around my table." She had twelve children in all, some of whom died of ordinary sickness or extraordinary plague. Those who survived had to be married off to someone with an appropriate family background, wealth, and reputation for Jewish learning. People married young—Glückel had been only about fourteen, and began having children shortly thereafter. About the same time Glückel became pregnant with one of her later children, one of her older daughters became pregnant, too, and people took bets on who would deliver first.

How Glückel had time for anything beyond raising children is difficult to fathom, but she managed to become a learned Jew and accomplished businesswoman. Like many Jews of the time, her first husband, who stemmed from Hameln, bought and sold gems—a risky enterprise, given the epidemic of highway robbery and war. (According to Glückel, one young man, Mordecai, unwisely took to the roads alone and was summarily shot by a drunkard seeking to rob him.) To avoid carrying too much cash, Jews developed trading routes and used each other as bankers along the way. Not that all Jews were honest—Glückel's husband was almost ruined by a con man pretending to be a business partner. But overall, the business system worked. Wealthy Jews married into each other's families, thus developing a complex web of family interdependence that lessened the likelihood of outright theft, fraud, and double-dealing.

When Glückel's first husband died of an accident in 1689, she waited out the required month of mourning, and then examined the books, took over the business, and became a successful trader, investor, and banker in her own right. She attended fairs, negotiated business deals, and regularly came to the aid of one or more of her offspring who needed bridge loans and more. While her husband was still alive, it was Glückel who drew up the complex partnership agreement that her husband and a newfound business acquaintance signed.

Jews lived precariously, always at the mercy of various authorities in the hodgepodge of countless larger and smaller states that did not become a united Germany until the 1870s. In Hamburg, for instance, only "tolerated" Jews were allowed residency, although many more lived there illegally. Jews were on sufficiently good terms with the authorities to allow Glückel's husband to hire an army colonel as protection. But they handled quarrels internally, knowing that gentile courts used torture as an everyday means of interrogation. Once, Glückel tells us, two Jews were caught stealing from a third; one of them was imprisoned, tortured on the rack, and hanged; the other escaped by agreeing to be baptized.

Glückel knew the Bible, Talmudic tales, and popular literature, which she put to good use as a magnificent moralist. She saw her memoir as an ethical tract—a warning, actually—to keep her children on the straight and narrow. She attended synagogue, at least from time to time; sometimes fasted twice a week as personal penance; and supported Talmud students as a demonstration of charitable piety. She hoped it would all influence God for the better, but at the same time she was a fatalist, believing literally in the liturgy's claim that God seals every person's fate on the High Holy Days of Rosh Hashanah and Yom Kippur. She prayed for her son Mordecai's success, but added, "What does it help? God has already decided what will be."

Glückel's memoir is a gold mine of information on everyday Jewish life in the years leading up to the Enlightenment, at least among the wealthy: She employs barber-surgeons to determine whether to lance a boil under her daughter's arm. Jewish communities regularly house Jewish wayfarers and pay for their upkeep from charity chests. Traders room in inns that use random piles of hay for beds. Women who attend synagogue sit either in a separate section behind the men or in a gallery overlooking them. At Jewish marriages, wedding rings are weighed to establish their worth—a pro forma bow to Talmudic law that treats marriage as a business contract. Men belong to groups called *chevras*, which meet for daily study both before and after business hours. Life is hard but enjoyable, especially at the ubiquitous weddings where one child after another is launched into early adulthood.

Glückel left her mark on the world as a competent businesswoman, a loving mother, a pious woman, a wise advisor, and an ordinary person who laughed, suffered, played, and worried—like all of us, even today. We could do worse than live our lives governed by the personal motto she left us: "Stinginess does not enrich; charity does not impoverish."

Jerusalem
(1783)

Moses Mendelssohn (1729–1786)

"Let everyone be permitted to speak as he thinks, to invoke God after his own manner or that of his fathers, and to seek eternal salvation where he thinks he may find it, as long as he does not disturb public felicity and acts honestly toward the civil laws, toward you and toward his fellow creatures."

Jerusalem is a revolutionary document, even for an age of revolution. Mendelssohn wrote it, in German, in 1783, roughly halfway between the American and the French revolutions. Both raised issues of church and state, and while France never fully dismantled religious power, America did—but not decisively until Madison's presidency in the 1810s. By that time (though probably unknown to Madison), Mendelssohn had long argued America's case.

To be sure, the American situation was far from Mendelssohn's mind. His concern was the civil condition of Jews in Europe, especially in Germany, where Mendelssohn himself had led the way, ever since being admitted into Berlin in 1743 as one of the few Jews "tolerated" in the Prussian capital. He taught himself German, Greek, and Latin, and achieved an international reputation as the very epitome of Enlightenment culture. In 1781, Christian Wilhelm Dohm argued the Jews' case in a tract titled *On the Civil Improvement of the Jews*. Mendelssohn composed *Jerusalem* just two years later.

Mendelssohn received the attention he did because he was far more than an ivory-tower philosopher. He knew Immanuel Kant (1724–1804), Europe's leading thinker of the time, and was a close friend of the playwright and literary critic Gotthold Ephraim Lessing (1729–1781), who had himself supported integration of Jews into Western society and who encouraged Mendelssohn's philosophical writing. The lead character of Lessing's famous Enlightenment play *Nathan the Wise* (1779) was modeled after Mendelssohn. From modest beginnings as a tutor to wealthy families, Mendelssohn rose to business prominence as partner in a silk factory and was awarded special status as "Jew under extraordinary protection" by the Prussian king Frederick the Great (1712–1786).

Jerusalem was not Mendelssohn's first public appeal. Writing from Holland in 1656, Rabbi Manasseh ben Israel had petitioned Oliver Cromwell to readmit Jews to England, from which they had been expelled in 1290. In 1782, Mendelssohn had supplied an introduction to a German translation of ben Israel's famous petition.

Jerusalem continued the argument. It is divided into two parts: a philosophical treatise on politics and religion in general, followed by a description of Judaism as a religion consistent with the first part's ideal. In part 1, Mendelssohn takes up the philosophical notion of a social contract, along the lines of the seventeenth-century British philosophers Thomas Hobbes and John Locke, both of whom he cites. Central to the Age of Reason was the belief that, from the time of creation, human beings had been endowed with the faculty of reason and certain intrinsic rights. Locke called them "life, liberty, and the pursuit of property." Thomas Jefferson changed "property" to "happiness," and Mendelssohn, too, emphasized happiness.

As most people saw it, the state of nature was not all "Garden of Eden." Hobbes had viewed it most negatively, as "solitary, poor, nasty, brutish, and short." Mendelssohn was less gloomy. It was hardly a war of "all against all," as Hobbes would have it, but it did hamper the search for happiness, since the absence of government meant an absence of laws, and without laws, people could make no contracts with one another. But contracts are central to human life because we cannot get very far without exchanging goods and services, and such exchange is, at least implicitly, contractual. States arise to enforce contracts, in the interests of the individuals who have ceded some of their natural rights to the state toward that very end.

But happiness, in Mendelssohn's view, also depends on convictions—hence the need for the institution of religion, what Mendelssohn calls a "church." The state governs our actions; the church inculcates true beliefs. Not that human beings need special revelation of these beliefs—our rational faculty alone would eventually arrive at them. But the church helps us along. Membership in the state is an arrangement that individuals freely accept in order to have an institution that governs their contractual relationships with each other; the church addresses our relationship to God, something altogether different. The most important issue for Mendelssohn is to distinguish the power that state and church have in their respective fields of influence—and then to keep them altogether separate.

All of Mendelssohn's philosophy follows from his understanding of the need for contracts, which he limits to actions that produce harmonious workings among people. When we left the state of nature, he says, we gave the state the right to make rules and enforce them—all for the sake of our individual happiness. "The state is viewed as a moral person [. . .] it can give and take, prescribe and prohibit according to law"—unlike the church, with whom we made no contract in the first place, since contracts are limited to the disposition of goods, not beliefs. "The only rights possessed by the church are to admonish, to instruct, to fortify and to comfort."

To this day, Mendelssohn's philosophy deserves attention on its own grounds, even aside from Jewish interests. But Mendelssohn did argue it on behalf of Jewish civil rights. Jews do indeed have their own peculiar beliefs, yet no one can prohibit their entering the body politic just because of those beliefs—not the state, which governs actions, but cannot legislate beliefs; and not the church, which addresses beliefs, but has no power to enforce them.

In the second part of *Jerusalem*, we learn that Judaism is consistent with this model. True, the Bible is a blueprint for a commonwealth run by priests, but in Mendelssohn's view that was temporary. It ceased many centuries ago. Judaism's revelation since then carried three sets of truths: *universal truths*, available to everyone through the faculty of reason; *historical truths* that we take on faith from people who came before us; and *Jewish law*, which functions symbolically to retain the purity of Judaism's truths. These truths are entirely in keeping with reason, so are not Judaism's alone. But history shows how true beliefs can deteriorate into superstition and error. God therefore chose the Jewish People to guard the purity of the eternal truths that reason endorses and that are held by *all* reasonable people.

In its time, *Jerusalem* was not generally received positively: it threatened the church's influence upon state policy; argued against Christian attempts to convert Jews; held up Judaism as the more reasonable religion of the two; claimed Jesus as a Jew who would have retained Jewish law, were he still alive; and limited the power of rabbis. The book did, however, evoke praise from none other than Immanuel Kant, who saw in Mendelssohn an ally for his own position on religion, and judged that *Jerusalem* had "ingeniously" denied Christians the right to "demand of a son of Israel that he change his religion."

Mendelssohn has worn well. His concerns are no less relevant now than they were in 1783. He was an early and powerful advocate for the separation of church and state. He emphasized the faculty of reason that ought to unite all people, regardless of race, creed, and nationality. He called for education as the only means to arrive at a just and beneficent citizenry. And he prohibited persecution of religious minorities.

Tormented Master
(1979)

Arthur Green (born 1942)

> "This image of dependency and passivity on the part of the disciples was also sometimes depicted in terms of the 'holy union' of matrimony. Receiving advice from the tzaddik is like receiving his seed; the intimacy of that moment between master and disciple may only be compared to the intimacy of union between man and wife."

Tormented Master is Arthur Green's magisterial biography of Nahman of Bratslav (1772–1810), one of the best known, but perhaps also the most controversial, of the Hasidic masters. During his later years especially, Nahman composed brilliant parables that are still widely cited for their wisdom. But there was another side to him. He was, as Green makes clear, a "rather troubled person."

Hasidism arose in eighteenth-century Ukraine, the revolutionary creation of Israel ben Eliezer (ca. 1698–1760), who became known as the Baal Shem Tov (or Besht, the acronym of Baal SHem Tov), meaning, "master of the good name," an allusion to his proficiency in using God's name for theurgic purposes. Although incredibly complex, his doctrine, in simplified form, appealed to huge numbers of destitute Jews in eastern Europe for whom the vaunted ideal of Talmudic study was an economic impossibility. More than God wants learning, the Besht taught, God wants the heart. He was equally at home, however, in the deep mystical doctrines of Kabbalah, which attracted an intellectual elite to his circle. Hasidism thus balanced a populist message with an intellectual one. Hasidic masters spoke to the reality of the poverty-stricken Jewish condition but also generated an internal dialogue balancing Talmudic study with mystical insight.

Hasidism's natural opponent was the Yeshivot, the established Talmudic academies in Lithuania. At first, this Talmudic elite fought Hasidism bitterly. By 1800, however, the movement had emerged triumphant among the majority of Jews in the East, and various Hasidic groups competed with each other, each group led by a charismatic leader called a *tzaddik* (meaning, "righteous one"; plural: *tzaddikim*), also known as the *rebbe*. They presided over so-called courts, where followers brought gifts to the rebbes, who were adored as miracle workers, personal guides, and intercessors with God. With time, Hasidism's revolutionary zeal devolved into ultraconservativism, protecting medieval consciousness from Haskalah, the brand of intellectual and scientific rationalism that enlightened Jews of eastern Europe had embraced.

Rationalists despised what they saw as a reversion to patent superstition alongside the practically idolatrous veneration of the tzaddik. In the nineteenth century, German-Jewish immigrants to America brought that negative view with them. Eastern European Jews, by contrast, part of the great migration of 1881 and beyond, arrived with fondness for at least popular Hasidism—its stories, melodies, and legends. And the twentieth century has been divided in its judgment of Hasidism. On the one hand, after World War II, Hasidic emigrants from eastern Europe came to North America, Israel, and western Europe still passionately allied to their leaders, more conservative than ever in reaction to the rampant secularism they encountered in their new surroundings, and committed to isolationism from all things modern. On the other hand, most modern Jews have managed to overlook the movement's passionate medievalism and concentrate instead on popularized Hasidic lore that emphasizes joy, celebration, and a set of Zen-like anecdotes that convey a sense of deep mystical insight. Philosophically, none other than Martin Buber (see page 269) compiled two widely read volumes of Hasidic tales (as he had heard them), and Abraham Joshua Heschel (himself a scion of a famous tzaddik family; see page 266) popularized Hasidism in compelling poetic prose.

No one personifies Hasidism's complexity better than Nahman of Bratslav. Although Arthur Green does not insist on the term, his description leaves little doubt that Nahman suffered from what we now call bipolar disorder. At times he sank into depression so serious that he tried every which way to commit suicide, literally starving himself to the point of near-death, or rowing alone into the middle of a lake and allowing the boat almost to capsize. Reflecting their master's agony, his disciples became "an elite of sufferers and strugglers." But Nahman was equally known for moving his disciples to manic celebration. He danced frenetically, and clapped his hands during prayer with the certainty that he was thereby able to evoke God's creative power. "The world," he boasted, "has not yet tasted of me at all. If they were to hear but a single one of my teachings with its melody and dance, they would simply pass out."

A great-grandson of the Baal Shem Tov, Nahman grew up in Ukraine. As a young man, he internalized the conviction of his own sinfulness, struggling especially against sexual urgency that haunted him throughout his life. As a tzaddik, he demanded that his followers compose penitential prayers regarding their own sexual desires, and personally heard their intimate confessions.

At the height of his life, he imagined himself as not just another tzaddik, but as *the* tzaddik of his generation, even (at times) the *only* true tzaddik. He became convinced that he was a reincarnation of the soul given to Abraham and then Moses, and as such, was the precursor of the final messiah—or even the actual final messiah himself.

Nahman himself sometimes admitted to being a madman. But from the very depths of madness, he saw what others could not. Hence our fascination with him—not as a study of mental disorder, but as a foray into spiritual genius. While the first Hasidic masters had described the absence of God as pure illusion, Nahman faced its agonizing reality squarely, thereby giving suffering its due—all the while teaching, as if with wisdom more associated with Buddhism than with Judaism, that "this world does not exist at all." In the end, God could be found through ultimate loneliness, what Nahman called *hitbod'dut*, there being nothing as real as God, perhaps even nothing real other than God. His understanding of the power inherent in verbal confession prefigured insights by Freud; his emphasis on face-to-face relationship anticipated the theology that we associate with Buber.

Arthur Green is unmatched for brilliance in interpreting Jewish mysticism. He is also a majestically influential figure in contemporary North American Jewish life and thought. In the 1960s, he pioneered the countercultural Chavurah movement that challenged staid and suburban Jews to open themselves to greater literacy and Jewish competence. In 1986, he became president of the Reconstructionist Rabbinical College (RRC), thereby wedding Chavurah Judaism to the ultra-rationalistic ideology of the founder of Reconstructionism, Mordecai Kaplan. In 1993, Green returned to his native Boston as a professor of Jewish philosophy at Brandeis University, and in 2003, he became the founding dean and guiding rabbinic voice at a new nondenominational seminary nearby known as Hebrew College. Green's understanding of Jewish mysticism, generally, and its Hasidic varieties, in particular, is formidable—and his *Tormented Master* is a historical, psychological, and spiritual masterpiece.

An Autobiography
(1793)

Solomon Maimon (ca. 1753–1800)

"My religion enjoins me to believe nothing, but to think the truth and to practice goodness."

Solomon Maimon: married at twelve; rabbi at thirteen; father at fourteen; abandons wife and child at twenty-two; spends twenty-five years as self-centered heretic, intellectual seeker, and dissolute epicurean; masters German, French, Latin, mathematics, physics, pharmaceutics, and philosophy; writes commentary to Kant's philosophy that surprises even Kant for its erudition; dies alone of alcoholism.

So goes a hypothetical biographical sketch of Judaism's most infamous rogue who, come what may, single-mindedly devoted his life to the Enlightenment ideal of universal reason and, in the process, wrote (in German) what is probably the most colorful autobiography in all of Jewish literature. This is as honest as any exposé gets: a mere 110 pages in length, but packed with insights into Maimon's life and times, including the lurid conditions of premodern Jewry that made Jewish emancipation nothing short of redemptive.

Maimon's grandfather was among the small minority of Polish Jews who escaped extreme poverty by managing the estates of Polish counts. The family fortune was eventually lost, however, and Maimon was subjected to all the miseries of traditional Jewish schooling, which he pillories as "an inferno" to which "children are damned in the bloom of their youth." It is commonplace to celebrate the Jewish thirst for knowledge, but that celebration is tarnished by Maimon's recollections of the system that provided it: children beaten by teachers, indescribably filthy classrooms, and a benighted curriculum that Maimon describes as "mind-killing" attempts "to create meaning where none existed." Even allowing for Maimon's bias, this is quite a stark description!

He grew up in what is today Belarus, and exposed the underbelly of Polish Hasidism as (in his view) the province of crooked and calculating leaders who pretend to divine insight into their followers' private affairs but get their information by posting informants among them. At one point (to illustrate the virtue of joyousness before God), the group's leader, the tzaddik, provokes his followers into sadistically whipping a man because his wife gave birth to a daughter instead of a son. Other Hasidic pietists preach repentance but practice bodily mortification to the point of killing themselves.

Jewish entrepreneurs could escape from this religious bipolarity of mania at one extreme and misery at the other by working their way into the corrupt economic system of the Polish gentry (as Maimon's grandfather had done)—but with the likelihood that either their mercurial masters or the oppressed peasants, allied with brutal and ignorant local church authorities, would eventually turn on their Jews with revenge. Alternatively, great minds might persevere through the Jewish school system and become famous rabbis, for whom doors would open everywhere by dint of their superior Talmudic reputation. As a child prodigy, Maimon chose the latter, but was too driven by intellectual curiosity to remain within it for very long.

As a child, he had tasted the fruit of secular wisdom by secretly constructing a model of the solar system to understand the heavens in ways that left biblical explanations far behind. Eventually, he abandoned his child bride and son in search of Enlightenment knowledge in the West, teaching himself European and classic languages along the way. From then on, he read incessantly, becoming something of a polymath.

Maimon's early years overlapped with Moses Mendelssohn's rise to fame as master of Enlightenment wisdom, so Maimon headed for Berlin in the hope of becoming Mendelssohn's student. His journey there was plagued by wretched poverty, and when he finally arrived, the Berlin authorities regarded him as a freeloading beggar, not as the kind of Jew who deserved the right of residency in the city. To be sure, he was eventually admitted, and impressed Mendelssohn's circle with his unadulterated quest for universal reason. But alongside Maimon's prodigious genius went a corresponding impatience with Judaism, which he saw increasingly as superstitious nonsense. Before long, he became what he called a committed Epicurean, devoted only to maximizing pleasure and minimizing pain. Having already cut his ties with Jewish traditionalism, he proceeded next to alienate the Berlin Jewish rationalists, who were shocked at his dissolute living patterns. In despair, he tried to convert to Christianity, but even the pastor rejected him because of his refusal to compromise his Enlightenment persuasion that denied Christian truths as much as it did Jewish ones.

Intellectually, however, his credentials were impeccable. Among other things, he had mastered Kant's *Critique of Pure Reason* (1781) and sent its author a massive commentary on the work; Kant read enough of it to testify that "none of my opponents have understood me and the main problem so well as Herr Maimon."

Solomon Maimon spent the greater part of his life shuttling back and forth from one European city to another (Königsberg, Breslau, Hamburg, Darmstadt, Amsterdam, Berlin) in a restless search for recognition without ever finding happiness. At the end of his *Autobiography*, he confesses, "I have not yet reached the haven of rest." For seven more years, he contributed learned articles to a variety of publications, Jewish and general, but died, all alone, when he was not even fifty.

No other book sheds such firsthand light on conditions among Jews on either side of the Enlightenment divide. No doubt, Maimon wrote selectively, highlighting conditions that would justify his checkered career, but he did not wholly invent them. The seamy side of Polish Jewish piety, the extremes of poverty in which average Jews pursued what lives they had, the system of elite Talmudism that opened doors for the Jewish scholarly class—all of this is chronicled in Maimon's frank and detailed account. We also see the courage it took for Jews to abandon their medieval presuppositions and the difficulty entailed in obtaining the secular wisdom that small-minded rabbinic authorities considered heretical.

It is hard to summon up much personal sympathy for Maimon, who alienated everyone he encountered, and who made his abandoned wife chase him all across Europe to get a divorce. But it is hard also to dismiss his uncompromising intellect, and the mental cost it exacted from him on a day-by-day basis. In the end he was a tortured soul, fated to die an intellectual recluse.

His *Autobiography* is colorful enough to make you want to finish it in a single sitting. Its impact on our understanding of the Jewish condition as the Enlightenment blossomed will remain with you much longer.

The Nineteen Letters
(1836)

Samson Raphael Hirsch (1808–1888)

"Dear friend, forget whatever you have known of Judaism heretofore; listen as though you had never heard anything concerning its teachings, and you will not only be reconciled to the Law, but you will be genuinely filled with love for it."

Nowhere in the nineteenth century was the Jewish battle for modern religious identity waged more ferociously than in the many individual states that eventually became a unified Germany. As the 1800s progressed, western European Jews began attending universities and joining the body politic as modern human beings worthy of inclusion in civic affairs. But emancipation came slowly, and until it did, "too much Jewishness" marred one's chances for career advancement. The great German-Jewish poet Heinrich Heine (1797–1856), for example, believed nothing of Christianity, but converted to it because he saw it as his "ticket of admission into European culture."

Heine never ceased *feeling* Jewish, but whatever inner conflict conversion might have entailed for him was mitigated by the fact that he had already abandoned much of Jewish religion—and in that regard, he typified many in the rising Jewish middle class of western Europe. He was not alone in leaving Judaism for Christianity, not because Christianity was so appealing but because the premodern Jewish option seemed no better, and joining the church was understood to be a necessary prelude to becoming fully European. Liberal rabbis reacted with concerted efforts to make Judaism consistent with modern culture.

Jewish religious reform had begun with laypeople—most notably, Israel Jacobson (1768–1828), who modernized Jewish worship and education, first in the Napoleonic kingdom of Westphalia (where Jews had been liberated from ghetto life), and then in Berlin. Jewish lay reformers were eventually joined by rabbis throughout Germany—such as Zacharias Frankel, Abraham Geiger, and Samuel Holdheim—who had attended universities, adapted Jewish theology to European rationalism, and applied the nineteenth century's fascination with history and evolution to Jewish tradition. By no means was there yet a "Reform movement," but there were independent efforts at reform that ranged from moderate to radical, with representatives of all positions applying their views in local German synagogues where they had authority.

Religious change was difficult to achieve, however. Among the mixture of political entities that later became Germany there were some free cities, such as Hamburg, where a Reform synagogue could be established as early as 1818. But in most places, the law classified Jews as members of communities that they could not leave without simultaneously leaving Judaism as well. A single synagogue was supposed to represent them all. At first, that worked against reform. Unable by law to erect synagogues of their own, would-be reformers had to work from within the established synagogues, which were controlled by traditionalists and supported by reactionary German rulers who looked askance at any kind of liberalization, the Jewish variety included. But as more and more Jews were (or threatened to be) baptized, reform took stronger and stronger hold in German synagogues, and in 1876 it was the Orthodox who appealed, successfully, for governmental permission to establish their own places of worship.

But not all Orthodox rabbis were recalcitrant traditionalists. Some attempted to combine traditional Judaism with modern thought, and no one more so than Samson Raphael Hirsch, whose approach to Orthodoxy was in many ways as "enlightened" as anything the reformers were offering.

Hirsch had attended the University of Bonn, where he befriended Abraham Geiger, one of the key critics of Talmudic tradition (later the two men would become bitter opponents). From 1830 to 1846, Hirsch served as the governmentally appointed chief rabbi in two northern German districts before moving on to Moravia (today part of the Czech Republic) and then Frankfurt am Main. While in Moravia, he participated in the abortive revolution of 1848, and his enlightened brand of Orthodoxy won him enemies among both the liberal Jewish reformers and the more traditional Orthodox. Hirsch's Judaism, too, was a modern survival strategy for emancipated Jews, but unlike the reformers who measured Talmudic law by the standards of modernity, Hirsch saw everything good about modernity already embedded in the Talmud, which he insisted on retaining in its totality. In 1836, Hirsch expounded his position in a set of *Nineteen Letters*, composed in German and addressed to an imaginary critic by the name of Benjamin.

This fictional opponent is an intellectual who criticizes traditional Judaism by citing "the mechanical practices of parental customs, a few fragments of Bible and Talmud [that were] taught me in an old-fashioned *cheder*" (the dismal religious school classes to which children were subjected). Religion should help us attain "happiness and perfection," Benjamin holds, whereas "the Jewish People remain poor in everything that makes human beings great and noble and that beautifies and dignifies their life." Indeed, "[Jewish] law itself prohibits all enjoyment," while "Jewish lore only perverts the mind by cramming it with petty subtleties," so that "the broad principles of universal morality are narrowed into anxious worry about insignificant trifles." Judaism has become an "embarrassment in our associations with Gentiles [and created] difficulties in business."

Hirsch's own position in the *Letters* is expressed by his fictional hero Naphtali, a rabbi, who justifies Jewish tradition exactly as the reformers did: with the claim that God had charged Jews with a mission. He is particularly eloquent when he cautions that "the earth is not yours." Human beings are "given to the earth, to respect it as divine soil," and be "the administrator of the whole divine estate." That holy task requires God's "great truths," the spreading of which is Israel's historical charge. In what sounds as anti-Zionist as anything the reformers might have said, Naphtali (Hirsch) claims, "The independent national life of Israel was never the essence or purpose of our existence as a nation, but only a means of fulfilling our spiritual mission." He finds purpose even in exile, which teaches Israel to eschew earthly power in order to perfect its faithfulness to God instead; and he goes so far as to welcome Christianity as Judaism's ally in bringing "the tidings and existence of the All-One, of the brotherhood of man."

But the Jewish mission that Hirsch intends transcends the narrow purview of those who would sacrifice Jewish law to achieve it. Reform may be "well intentioned," he has Naphtali say, but by changing or abolishing Talmudic law, it has become "the evil of our time." A fresh study of Jewish texts will reveal purpose behind every Jewish obligation, a most compelling example being Sabbath rest, which he defines as our opportunity to "return the borrowed world to its Maker." The entire legislation (even the seemingly arcane) is justified, as admonitions to universal justice, for example, and symbolic reminders of great truths.

The Nineteen Letters is essential reading for anyone serious about understanding the nineteenth-century fight for the Jewish religious soul. Hirsch is passionate, brilliant, and sometimes even poetic. He inspired entire generations of German Orthodoxy, and is considered by many—even today—to be the founder of modern Orthodoxy.

Reminiscences
(1901)

Isaac Mayer Wise (1819–1900)

"The reforming spirit was innate in me; it was my foremost characteristic. In addition to this, I was an enthusiast on the subjects of America and freedom [. . .] Consequently, I could begin at once to reform and improve the world."

These are the words of the most influential American Jew of the nineteenth century, Isaac Mayer Wise, in his memoir, *Reminiscences*. He appreciated the New World greatly, because unlike so many Jews in western Europe, who felt they had to convert to Christianity as an entryway into society, Jews in the United States could be Jewish *and* American at the same time. "I began to Americanize with all my might," he wrote.

American Judaism was still in its infancy in the mid-1800s, when Wise arrived in New York. The total Jewish population of the United States had not yet reached 50,000, and was concentrated in a few cities on the East Coast and in the Midwest; because most Jewish leaders knew one another, at least by reputation, it was not difficult for Wise's mercurial personality to leave its mark on almost everything Jewish at the time. His diary entries abound in bouts of vacillating elation and depression. On the one hand, he thought of himself as "the spoiled darling of American Jewry," working "for the good of humanity" and "composing hymns," because "in my soaring imagination, I saw American Judaism proceed to a glorious future and become a mighty intellectual and moral influence in this country." On the other, he suffered from hypochondria, withdrew from the world, and retreated into books or travel. At one point, he almost despaired of the rabbinate and took up law.

His life was never dull. Even discounting the overblown rhetoric in *Reminiscences* as the fruit of his manic moments, one has to be impressed by just the cast of characters with whom Wise hobnobbed over the years, including the most famous senator of his day, Daniel Webster; newspaper magnate Horace Greeley; and even three United States presidents (James Knox Polk, Zachary Taylor, and Millard Fillmore).

Born in Bohemia, where he had studied to become a rabbi, Wise immigrated to the United States in 1846. On July 23, 1846, "I landed in New York with wife and child and two dollars in my pocket. I had grown heartily weary of Europe." But when he walked the streets of Manhattan, still nothing but "a large village" in his eyes, he found few synagogues, fewer rabbis, and little thirst for Judaism. Liturgically especially, Wise was aghast. Contrary to the decorous worship Wise envisioned, he found congregations "as ill behaved as in Europe," and cantors "who trilled like a mock nightingale and leaped about like a hooked fish." Everything was for sale: the best sanctuary seats, the honor of being called to the Torah, even a prayer for the sick. An exception to this sad state of affairs was the Munich-born Max Lilienthal, a reformer like Wise, who had arrived in New York two years earlier. But Wise was shocked to hear even Lilienthal deliver a sermon mourning the loss of the ancient Temple in Jerusalem; he walked away committed to speeding up the eradication of "Polish-cabbalistical rabbinism and supernaturalism" that still held so many Jews—including even Lilienthal, apparently—in thrall.

That very fall, Wise accepted an invitation to serve as rabbi in a congregation in Albany, where he promptly reformed the liturgy. Rabbis had yet to attain the respect they would enjoy later, and when the president of the Albany synagogue—angered by Wise's reforms—forbade him to appear on the pulpit, he went anyway; an actual fistfight between the two men ensued. Soon after, Wise's followers built their own competing synagogue where reform would not encounter such resistance.

In 1854, Wise was called to a congregation in Cincinnati, then known as the Queen City and a candidate to become one of the greatest Jewish cities in the country. Having global aspirations, Wise left pastoral and managerial duties to others, while he spent weeks at a time as an itinerant preacher—not just back east, but from St. Louis to Chicago and all points in between, founding or strengthening synagogues along the way. In addition, he wrote one of the two most popular prayer books of his day (titled *Minhag America*), edited two newspapers (one in English, the other in German), and engineered what would become the Reform movement in North America.

Isaac Mayer Wise perceived himself as the savior of all Jews in the New World. Protestant churches were at that time dispatching missionaries to fight the evils of frontier life, and Wise fought those who targeted Jews. As a Jewish reformer, he laid claim to being a centrist, appealing to moderately Orthodox voices on the right and more radical reformers on the left. But ritually, Wise was adamantly progressive: he replaced the Old Country prayer style called *davening*—which he found cacophonous—with a choir of men and women, vernacular readings in English and in German, and suit-and-tie attire instead of traditional worship garb (i.e., the prayer shawl called *tallit*; the head covering called *yarmulke*; and *tefillin*, the phylacteries). Unsurprisingly, he ran afoul of great Orthodox voices such as Morris Jacob Raphall and Bernard Illowy, who had arrived more recently from Europe; but he also faced opposition from the great Isaac Leeser, who was gamely trying to wed Orthodoxy to modernism in Philadelphia.

Socially speaking, it was gentlemen's lodges, not synagogues, that attracted Jewish men at the time. B'nai B'rith, the most famous and lasting of these, had just come into being, and Wise joined it—but at the same time, he was a Mason, an Odd Fellow, and, as he puts it, a member of "the Druids, Harugari, and I know not what other orders." These lodges were secret societies that mostly featured rituals to initiate members into ever higher levels of standing, but they also functioned socially as meeting places for men of influence to discuss business and community matters.

Wise's *Reminiscences* covers only the opening years of his career in America, from 1846 to 1857 (it was first published in 1874/75, in America's leading German-Jewish newspaper at the time, *Die Deborah*). It therefore antedates Wise's founding of the major national Jewish institutions for which he became famous—the seminary, congregational organization, and rabbinic association that became the pillars of North American Reform Judaism. No matter: it is a fascinating window into nineteenth-century America, as well as an unabashedly self-aggrandizing chronicle by one of the most colorful personalities in American Jewish history. The pages testify to a time when railroads were just beginning, "world wars" were unknown, Germany was the cultural ideal, and eastern European Jewish migration was not even a thought. Despite the paucity of Jewish numbers, education, means, and influence that Wise found when he arrived, he never doubted the potential for Jewish American success, and more than anyone else, he became the master architect who proved himself correct.

Tevye the Dairyman
(1894–1916)

Sholem Aleichem (1859–1916)

"Go have children; suffer humiliation; sacrifice for them; work night and day; and for what?"

The explosion of options for Jewish identity in nineteenth-century eastern Europe is evident in the rise of Hebrew and Yiddish literature, particularly in the city of Odessa, the Ukrainian center of culture and the arts on the northern coast of the Black Sea. It is hard to say when the first Jews arrived there—indeed, the historian Jacob Rader Marcus once famously said that no Jew ever arrives first anywhere; there is always another Jew who came earlier. By the 1890s, however, the city had become a magnet for Jewish authors and poets, all of whom were well versed in the traditional world of the Talmud, midrash, and subsequent rabbinic literature. Equally attracted to modern culture, however, they spoke Russian among themselves, and nursed a love-hate relationship with the language of the Jewish street: Yiddish.

Yiddish is the outgrowth of a medieval German dialect spoken in the Rhineland, intermixed with classical Hebrew vocabulary and written in Hebrew characters. By the sixteenth century, it was carried eastward into Poland and Russia, where it incorporated Slavic loan words as well. Nineteenth-century Jewish elitists deemed it an unruly jargon, unworthy of literary expression. In 1881, Sholem Yankev Abramovitch (1836–1917) moved to Odessa and established himself as a breakthrough writer who dared to elevate Yiddish from sociolect to literature, partially because other than his fellow literati, few people had been able to read his early work written in modern Hebrew. Abramovitch became famous under his Yiddish pseudonym Mendele Mocher Sforim (Mendele the Bookseller), and is today celebrated as one of the founders of both Yiddish and modern Hebrew literature.

In 1890, Abramovitch was joined in Odessa by the man destined to become the most famous Yiddish writer of all, Sholem Aleichem. His pen name was the Yiddishized version of *shalom aleichem*, the standard Hebrew expression of greeting that means "Peace be unto you." Sholem Aleichem was born Shalom Rabinovitz, to a moderately wealthy family in Ukraine. He suffered poverty, however, when his father's business failed; and when his mother died of cholera shortly thereafter, he was bundled off with his sisters and brothers to stay with grandparents. As a young man, Rabinovitz wrote stories in Hebrew, but eventually turned to Yiddish, adopting his pen name (he later said) to hide his identity from his father—whose support of Haskalah led him to oppose the renaissance of Yiddish, which he associated with the traditional Jewish lifestyle that he hoped modernity would correct.

Biographers describe Sholem Aleichem as frenetically creative, able to write standing up, sitting down, and lying in bed—even drowning the sorrow of his eldest son's sudden death by closeting himself away at his writing desk. He was a master of literary caricature, in love with the Jewish people whom he described, and on fire with the subtleties of their language. Early on, he put together a list of his stepmother's favorite insults and curse words. Years later, he created Tevye the Dairyman, arguably the most famous character in all of Jewish literature, and universally familiar now from his stage and screen presence in *Fiddler on the Roof.*

Actually a set of stories composed between 1894 and 1916, the Tevye chronicle foreshadows the doom of the old order. The Industrial Revolution has brought socialism, and with it the demise of the old class structure rooted in wealth and mastery of Torah. One of the Tevye tales (written in 1899) establishes a running theme through its very title: "Children, Nowadays." "Go have children; suffer humiliation; sacrifice for them; work night and day; and for what?" shouts Tevye in an admission of defeat. In subsequent Tevye stories, one of his daughters, Shaytle, shuns the old-time matchmaking tradition that would have landed her the wealthy (but unlearned and middle-aged) town butcher as her husband. She has the audacity, instead, to fall in love—a new idea to Tevye, and therefore, bad enough in itself! To make matters worse, Shaytle chooses as her fiancé a local yokel; and finally—and worst of all—she announces her engagement, without apparent regard for what her father even thinks! A second daughter, Hovel, runs off with her freethinking socialist tutor. And a third daughter, Chava, falls in love with a Russian Cossack, gets married in a church, and leaves Judaism altogether.

By Sholem Aleichem's day, many Jews in eastern Europe had moved to large cities such as Odessa, Warsaw, and Lodz, where the acid of modernity was rapidly corroding the authority of Jewish tradition. Tevye, however, still inhabits a *shtetl*, a tiny rural village where tradition lasts a bit longer. Jews and Eastern Orthodox peasants—in equal numbers—have lived there together in uneasy rapprochement, holding fast to their own versions of an old-time world that will soon be history. Tevye is the Jewish everyman of the shtetl, who cannot open his mouth without citing some biblical or rabbinic aphorism, but often in garbled or misapplied form, a sign of tradition's eroding authority. And Tevye knows the rabbinic jig is up. He manages both Shaytle's refusal to abide by the marriage he has arranged and Hovel's insistence on marrying a freethinking socialist. But even Tevye has his limits: he observes the traditional mourning customs for Chava, who has married outside of Judaism; following Jewish tradition, her grieving father is obliged to count her as if she were dead.

Despite his literary fame, Sholem Aleichem spent much of his life in poverty. He moved frequently, settling with his large family in America in 1906, but returning to Europe a year later when two plays he had written in New York turned out to be failures. In 1915, he migrated again to New York, and died the following year. Most of the sweatshops on the Lower East Side closed so that hundreds of thousands could attend his funeral.

Fiddler on the Roof came out as a Broadway musical in 1964. By then, most Jews had celebrated the post–World War II euphoria by buying homes in what became wryly known as "gilded ghettos" of the suburbs. Like Tevye, they, too, had daughters (and sons) who were challenging traditional realities. Away at college, they were marching against a war, discovering free love, experimenting with drugs, and falling in love with non-Jewish partners. These suburban parents were hardly able to cite Jewish proof texts for what they believed, but they did remember the "good old days" when living Jewishly was simply taken for granted. The shtetl had become the idyllic subject of romanticized nostalgia.

What they saw on the Broadway stage was their own lives writ large— a generation of children threatening everything their parents stood for. Their Shaytles would abandon marriages with hometown boys and go off as flower children in faraway communes. Their Hovels were joining the new left, burning draft cards, and fighting police in protests against the Vietnam War. They had few Chavas who married out of Judaism altogether—but that would come just a little bit later. Today's Chavas who marry gentiles do not necessarily leave Judaism, however, and their Tevye fathers do not mourn their symbolic deaths.

Sholem Aleichem's world has become our own, saturated with nostalgia, but all too real. We laugh and cry with Tevye, who is still everyman, as his wife, Sarah, is our everywoman. How do we hold on to the past while inhabiting the present? The times have changed—but the question hasn't.

Stories
(ca. 1889–1915)
Isaac Loeb Peretz (1851/52–1915)

"It was toward the end of the good times and the beginning of the bad times [. . .] The nineteenth century in its old age appeared to have caught cold and to be running a slight fever [. . .] Nobody foresaw that the world's soul would grow dark and its body convulsed [. . .] None of this distracted from the need to get to know ordinary Jewish life—to see what was going on in the shtetls."

Isaac Loeb Peretz was a storyteller's storyteller, whose tales of happiness, fear, horror, and pure, sheer amazement have become the stuff of Jewish folklore. Many a child has been raised on them as if they go back to the Talmud, rather than being the solitary imagination of one great writer. At the heart of Peretz's tales is a commitment to intellectual honesty on one hand and a passion for "the values to which we may legitimately attach our lives," according to Maurice Samuel, who was himself a spectacular storyteller and a great admirer of Peretz. And the scholar Ruth R. Wisse (see page 121) calls Peretz "arguably the most important figure in the development of modern Jewish culture."

Peretz came from a pious traditionalist family in Zamosc, a town in southeast Poland that was under Russian rule at the time and known as a beacon of the Jewish Enlightenment. Young Peretz was thus exposed not just to the Talmud but to general culture as well. Unable to afford books of his own, he convinced a local bookseller to give him a key to his library of literature, philosophy, poetry, and political theory—in French, English, German, and Polish. "There were so many books!" he recalled. "I determined to read them all, starting from the first straight through to the last."

For a number of years, Peretz practiced law by day and wrote poetry by night, but in 1887, for reasons unknown to us, the Russian government suspended his legal license. Thrust back into poverty, he decided to move to Warsaw. For the rest of his life, he worked as a civil servant to the Jewish community there, poorly paid but with time to write (in Hebrew and Yiddish) and to encourage other Jewish artists.

By the 1890s, Peretz became enamored of socialism, but grew distrustful of its doctrinaire ideology, which seemed overly simplistic to him. He saw no reason why class conflict would necessarily grow into a revolution, and he suspected that the revolutionaries, once in power, would be no better than the old order that they had replaced. He also worried that a socialist society would have no room for Jewish identity and culture, a suspicion enhanced by the views of the Polish-German socialist leader Rosa Luxemburg (1870/71–1919). Luxemburg had co-founded the Polish Socialist Party and made clear her intent to separate from the Jewish tradition in which she had been raised. (Peretz probably knew her, since her family came from Zamosc as well.)

As we have seen, another Jewish strategy for political success at the turn of the twentieth century was Jewish nationalism. Peretz rejected Zionism in favor of its rival, Territorialism, which envisioned a Yiddish-speaking Jewish republic within Russia. The Yiddish republic never materialized.

Unlike the republic he championed, Peretz's stories will live forever, collected in a number of anthologies and translations. One of them, *Prince of the Ghetto* (1948), by Maurice Samuel (1895–1972), has become a classic. More recently, Yiddishist Ruth R. Wisse published *The I. L. Peretz Reader* (1990), which includes not just his stories but also a drama, unfinished memoirs, and more.

Beyond just enchanting, Peretz's stories are sometimes even haunting. In "Devotion unto Death," for example, we are introduced to a magical garden, "a paradise in which bloomed the tree of life and the tree of knowledge of good and evil. Wide upon the landscape shone the light of the original seven days, pouring out gold on branches and leaves and blossoms: a multitude of birds played among the trees, and there was a universal singing and burgeoning and unfolding of life [. . .] The soul of the world was speaking."

The Garden of Eden, surely! But more beautiful than the Bible ever imagined it, and at the same time more deadly, too, for the story's title foreshadows a tale on the age-old topic of good and evil. Peretz had been consumed by the theme of sin since youth, even wracked with grief over the state of the world.

But Peretz was much more than just another moralist. His tales reverberate with the fabulous: the billy goat whose magic horns unfurl at night to reach the Milky Way, where the stars are really jewels that the horns extract and bring back to earth to buy food for the hungry; a Job-like saint "whose thoughts wander about in the upper world, while his feet wander about in the lower"; a virtuous woman who saves her husband from a snake bite by putting herself in the way, but since she knows she died unjustly, she serves as her own defense attorney on high and convinces the heavenly tribunal to restore her to life.

Peretz specialized in unforgettable characters. Yochanan the water carrier recites psalms poorly—"he could not say two lines without three mistakes." The pious but poor Reb Yechiel, whose "door is practically off the hinges," is consumed by worry—not that a thief will break in, but that if a break-in occurs, he, Reb Yechiel—because of his own carelessness in not fixing his door—will be guilty of having tempted the thief to sin. The cantor of Lahadam has his voice stolen by Satan because his singing is so beautiful that every Jew who hears it is automatically moved to repentance—and what future can hell have, if no one dies with unrepentant sin?

Some of these characters have become the stuff of legend, like the rabbi who is so pious he is even said to be permitted to visit heaven on occasion. When he skips High Holy Day services, a doubter follows him to see where he is going, only to find the rabbi dressing up like a peasant to cut firewood for an elderly woman shivering in the cold. When the rabbi's disciples insist again that he must be in heaven, the doubter acknowledges, "If not higher!"

Peretz's best-known character is probably Bontsche Schweig (Bontsche the Silent), a poverty-stricken simpleton who never complains. When God promises him whatever he wishes, poor Bontsche can think of nothing better than a hot buttered roll. Bontsche is no hero for Peretz, who loved the shtetl types he made famous but nursed a love-hate relationship with the conditions that produced them. He embraced the Jewish love of learning, but he condemned the persistent Jewish quietude in the face of oppression.

Peretz wielded a revolutionary pen, telling delightful stories but charging his very heroes with inconsequence and worse. Take Mendel, an altogether prayerful scholar whose wife, Bryna, works herself to death while he buries his nose in the good books and rests on Shabbat, just as Jewish law demands. When Bryna finally dies of overwork and malnutrition, Peretz observes, "She who had attracted no notice in life was hardly visible on her deathbed. She was so thin!"

No one remembers the legal cases Peretz worked on in his days as a lawyer. But the world of the shtetl that he memorialized and told about is—thanks to him—forever unforgettable.

The Wise Men of Helm and Their Merry Tales
(1942)

Solomon Simon (1895–1970)

"A Helmite was going to Warsaw, when his wagon died, his horse fell apart, and his whip became lame in one leg."

It was commonplace once for every Jewish child to be regaled with stories about the shtetl, one of those tiny tucked-away Jewish-Yiddish villages in eastern Europe prior to their destruction by the Nazis. The shtetls were inevitably filled with unfortunate souls who existed—one could hardly say "lived"—there. They were tragically poor, personified sometimes by what the Yiddish language calls a *schl'miel*, someone who does everything wrong, or a *schl'maz'l*, someone whose luck must have run out the day he was born. A schl'miel is the guy who always spills his coffee; a schl'maz'l is the guy on whom it inevitably spills.

Such people apparently really existed. Some of the stories may have been stretched, or even fabulated, but the characters were real. We do not see them quite as much anymore, because modern society tends to institutionalize them. The shtetl had to let them roam the streets. But it did not on that account let them starve. However inept these individuals were, they were also made in God's image and deserved being watched over by their more fortunate neighbors. No doubt, the stories idealize the picture somewhat—but not that much. Taught from birth to care for the unfortunate in their midst, real-life shtetl Jews arrived in western Europe or the Americas as liberals or even socialists, and the second generation in the United States went on to become Roosevelt Democrats. They remembered the lesson of shtetl poverty—*and* of shtetl compassion.

What kept the memory green was the humorous telling and retelling of tales about these societal unfortunates, often lumping them together in an imaginary village called Helm (taking its name from the real-life town of Helm, or Chelm, in eastern Poland). Countless children—and adults as well—have laughed themselves silly over the town's nonsensical adventures, some of which have been collected in this slim but classic children's book, *The Wise Men of Helm and Their Merry Tales*, first published in Yiddish as *Di Helden fun Khelem* (The Heroes of Helm).

Its author, Solomon Simon, was a distinguished Yiddishist dedicated to making Jewish folktales available to children who, he feared, would otherwise forget their Jewish heritage. He was born in a shtetl in eastern Europe, attended a yeshivah, and migrated to America in 1913, where he became a dentist. But his passion remained the Yiddish language and culture.

These "wise men" are anything but wise. To call them fools is to be kind. They do, however, mirror a jaundiced yet idealized view of shtetl life at its worst and, simultaneously, at its best, depending on one's point of view. There is Mottel the mayor; Tevya the tailor; Berel the beadle (the town crier); Gimpel, the "wisest" of them all; and the ubiquitous rabbi, to whom the citizens turn when only Talmudic insight will explain life's challenges. Wisdom flows freely here—witness Gimpel's observation that summer days are long and winter days short, because days expand with heat and contract with cold.

The sorry lot of all these Helmites is the unfortunate result of a struggling angel carrying souls in a sack. Everyone knows, of course, that differences in character, personality, and mental acumen derive from the nature of our souls, which God supplies when we are born. Alas, an angel carrying a supply of foolish souls once flew too close to a mountain crag, which ripped open the bag, letting its souls fall to earth in the valley below, the very valley where Helm is located.

The real-life poverty of the shtetl comes through in the Helmites' utter lack of anything but the legendary potatoes and beets that eastern Europeans harvested for winter food. But do not think these poor souls lazy! They were always coming up with schemes to reverse their fortune—like the night they decided to kidnap the moon. To maximize their capture, they waited for it to be full, then collected its reflection in a tub of beet soup (borscht), and covered the tub before it escaped. One dark night, when the moon was but a sliver in the sky, and the market for moonlight correspondingly inflated, they removed the cover, only to find their moon missing. To no avail, they poured out the borscht, hoping the moon was hiding in the bottom. When it wasn't there, Gimpel explained that it must have melted in the borscht, and sure enough, here and there, using what little light there was, he found little bits of melted moonlight wherever the borscht had spilled.

The Wise Men of Helm and Their Merry Tales would warrant inclusion here just because it is a famous sample of Jewish humor rooted in shtetl folklore. But the stories are also wry reflections on the human condition. When one of the Helmite schemes actually pays off—albeit only briefly—"the rich got richer and the poor got worries. And as always happens, the poor came to be jealous of the rich and the rich came to fear the poor. That was the way of the world."

The characters are loveable, their stupidity is pardonable, and their motives are exemplary. Below the foolishness, we get true Jewish wisdom, the set of humane values that are supposed to govern the not-so-humane conditions that shtetl dwellers knew all too well—like the day Mottel the mayor was found crawling around the floor because he saw "that everyone had lost heart, and he decided to find it"; or when, poor as they are, the Helmites insist on supplying their synagogue with an alms box to collect charity, since even the poorest are expected to give to people poorer still. When thieves make off with the box, the villagers insist on replacing it, because "What kind of synagogue would it be without an alms box!" They foil the thieves by placing it up high where no one can get to it, but then have to construct a ladder to reach it themselves. What good is a charity box that no one can put charity in? They forget that thieves, too, can climb a ladder. But it is better to give and have the charity stolen than not to give at all.

The stories collected here are just a sample of the many tales left to us about the magnificently poor but good citizens of Helm, and collections other than Simon's are available (*The Fools of Chelm and Their History* by Nobel Prize winner Isaac Bashevis Singer, for example). But Simon's is a classic that is lovingly told with a rapt audience of children in mind.

To this day, the number of Helmite stories continues to grow, as ever new anecdotes are invented and summarily assigned to—where else?— Helm. They warm the depths of our souls, as all heroic acts of kindness do when we hear of them. If the Helmites lack wisdom, the stories do not. They display Jewish humor at its best: self-effacing, poking fun at even grim reality, admitting our inability sometimes to make things right, but hoping anyhow for justice, love, and goodness—eventually.

In My Father's Court
(1966)

Isaac Bashevis Singer (1904–1991)

"[As a child] I stood on the balcony and gazed about me. How vast was this world and how rich in all kinds of people and strange happenings! And how high was the sky above the treetops! And how deep the earth beneath the flagstones! And why did men and women love each other? And where was God, who was constantly spoken of in our house? I was amazed, delighted, entranced. I felt that I must solve this riddle."

As a practical joke, a young Jewish man in Warsaw sends his girlfriend a dead mouse wrapped in an expensive jewelry box. Responding in kind, the young woman sends back a freshly baked cupcake filled with excrement. Each side sues the other in a court of Jewish law presided over by Isaac Bashevis Singer's father. The court is an ordinary room in the rabbi's modest Warsaw home, where Isaac grows up as a veteran observer, sometimes serving as volunteer bailiff besides. "There are in this world," he concludes, "some strange individuals, whose thoughts are even stranger than they are."

In My Father's Court relives a series of such cases as a prism through which we can view the inner life of the traditionalist Jewish community where Singer was raised. It is autobiographical, covering (among other things) the traumatic years of World War I, when Jews were caught between the warring Russian and German armies. The chapters first appeared in New York City's Yiddish newspaper *The Forward* (*Forverts*), but by the time of their translation and publication in book form in 1966, Singer was well along the way to becoming the celebrated author of novels, short stories, memoirs, children's tales, and plays. He had begun his literary career as a translator of German thrillers into Yiddish—which remained his literary language of choice. In 1935, he fled Poland and the specter of rising anti-Semitism and went to the United States, leaving behind his wife and son, who preferred moving to Moscow, and later, Palestine. In 1978, Singer received the Nobel Prize in Literature, which cited his "impassioned narrative art," rooted "in Polish-Jewish cultural tradition," but "bringing universal human conditions to life."

Rabbi Singer (Isaac's father) was a Hasidic Jew, pious and zealous for justice, who walked about as if the whole weight of God's world rested on his shoulders. "Nothing but the Talmud and eternal questions interested him," Isaac recalls. So unworldly was he that "more than once he could not find his way home from the study house. And since he never looked at a woman [. . .] he might easily have mistaken grandmother or a sister-in-law for his wife." He never even called his wife by name!

Far from being naive, however, Isaac's father was positively Solomonic, and if, by chance, God really had entrusted the world to anyone, there could surely have been found no one finer: he immersed himself daily not just in legal niceties, but in the spirit behind a law designed to celebrate God's grace and presence in human affairs. "Shame!" he shouts, in the case of the mouse and cupcake. "It is a violation of the law, 'Ye shall not make your souls abominable' [. . .] First, it was impious; second, it was loathsome; third, such acts lead to anger, gossip, slander, and discord. It was also dangerous, for the victim, overcome by nausea, could have become seriously ill. And the defilement of edibles, the food that God had created to still man's hunger and over which benedictions were recited, was itself a sacrilege [. . .] And here, instead of thanking and praising the Almighty [. . .] men had taken this gift and used it to provoke their neighbors—had defiled what God had created."

Stung by the rabbi's remarks, the litigants withdraw their case and the rabbi forfeits the fee they would otherwise have paid him. But no matter. Money merely feeds the body, and to Rabbi Singer, "The body was mere appendage to the soul."

Singer does not romanticize eastern European slums. We hear of a man who asks Isaac's father if Jewish law allows him to sleep next to his recently deceased wife—not out of ghoulish desire, but because she is awaiting burial the next day and there is no place for him to rest the body other than in his one-room hovel, where rats scurry endlessly on the floor. Refusing to subject either himself or his wife's body to hungry rodents, he wants them both to lie that night on the only narrow bed he owns. From the already close-to-destitute Jewish community, Isaac's father collects contributions to rescue the situation and provide for the indigent man who has so little.

The Jews whom Singer describes are never far above the poverty line. Even his own family shares with the rest of the building's inhabitants a single outhouse infested "with rats and mice everywhere, overhead as well as on the floor." Children customarily prefer using the stairwell as a toilet—and housewives use it as their garbage dump.

Through it all, however, one gets not just the poverty and pathos but the dignity and duty that shored up Jewish life in eastern Europe. We would hardly want to return to this world of premodern superstition that believed in "souls reincarnated as animals, houses inhabited by hobgoblins, and cellars haunted by demons"; where Jews lived in constant fear of gentile violence; and where women were of decidedly second-rate status. But young Isaac was not unusual in mastering early literacy; and how can we not admire the moment when he abandoned a game of cops and robbers because, as he was about to hide in a cellar, he remembered his father saying, "We are all the children of God. In every one of us, dwells a soul [. . .] There are divine sparks even in mud!"

In My Father's Court is more than a chronicle of the poor and the pious seeking Old Country justice under Talmudic law, and more also than a reminiscence of the author's ascetic and scholarly father. It is a first-rate story of the whole Singer family, with its impressive pedigree going back to rabbinic worthies on both his father's and his mother's sides.

By the end, the family is split in many directions: Isaac's famous older brother, Israel Joshua (see page 155), turns into a freethinker and socialist who falls afoul of his pious father, then barely survives World War I conscription in the Russian army, and becomes an acclaimed writer. Almost everyone in this large extended family will eventually be murdered in Nazi death camps. Isaac will escape to America, but remember enough of his childhood to give us this sensitive account of the good and the bad in a world that is now long gone.

The Yeshiva
(1967/68)

Chaim Grade (1910–1982)

*"He was a recluse, but unwillingly and without joy. He thought of Reb Israel
Salanter, the founder of the Musar movement. Reb Israel's big, innocent,
melancholy eyes had seen Hell, and he wanted to save Jews from its torments.
Hence he wrote in his Musar epistle, 'Man will be whipped in Hell. He will
have to give an account of his deeds in the next world.'"*

Except for the synagogue, no institution has influenced Jewish life
more than the yeshivah (plural: yeshivot, sometimes translated as
"academies"), the institution dedicated to producing masters of the Talmud. Until the nineteenth-century emergence of liberal Judaism and
university-like institutions for rabbinic study, the only way to become
a rabbi was to study privately or to attend a yeshivah, where Talmud
dominated the curriculum to the point of being the only thing that
mattered. Every rabbi was necessarily a Talmudist.

The Talmud itself records the institution of the *m'tivta*, the Aramaic equivalent of the Hebrew *yeshivah*, "[a place of] sitting," with the
purpose of studying. From the eighth century CE on, we find yeshivot throughout the Mediterranean. Two centuries later, they came to
western Europe; and as Jews moved into eastern Europe, the institution
of the yeshivah traveled there as well. The most famous yeshivot, and
the ones honored most by Jews today, were established in nineteenth-
century Lithuania and Russia, beginning with Volozhin, a town near
Vilna (Vilnius), in 1802. Others followed by the mid- to late nineteenth
century, in such famous Jewish centers as Mir (Minsk), Slobodka, and
Telz (Telsiai).

Perhaps no one knew the reality of yeshivah life more intimately than
Chaim Grade, himself a product of one, before moving on to become
a famous Yiddish writer and poet. He spent the first part of his life in
Vilna, fled from the Nazis, lived temporarily deep in the Soviet Union,
and migrated to New York in 1948. His oeuvre includes novels (*The
Agunah* [1961] and *The Yeshiva*), novellas, and the memoir *My Mother's
Sabbath Days* (1955).

We think of the classic Lithuanian yeshivah as a placid and orderly center of study where students immersed themselves in timeless texts, far from the madding crowd. But just the opposite was the case. As long as rabbinic Judaism enjoyed unrivaled authority, the yeshivot that trained rabbis were centers of enormous power. Once that authority was questioned, however, they became lightning rods of controversy.

A first wave of criticism arose when eighteenth-century Hasidic leaders in Poland and Ukraine challenged the claim that yeshivah scholarship was the only criterion for Jewish authenticity. In its place, they championed religion of the heart, not just the mind. And that earlier divide was nothing compared to the nineteenth-century opposition that charged both yeshivah society and Hasidic life with recalcitrance, intransigence, and irrelevance. This time, the condemnation came from a variety of modernists, who objected to each other as well: Zionists, socialists, religious reformers, and *maskilim*, i.e., the followers of Haskalah. The last-named even established an alternative Jewish school system with the support of the czarist government, which hoped thereby to eradicate Jewish "obscurantism."

At the same time that they were attacked from the outside, the world of the yeshivot suffered internal fractures as well, particularly with the moderating influence of the Musar movement, the creation of Israel Salanter (1810–1883), of Lithuania. Instead of ever more emphasis on the complexities of Talmudic logic, Musar promoted the building of character through intense personal humility, devout religious fervor, and the study of pietistic classics such as Bachya ibn Pakuda's *Duties of the Heart*. A particularly extreme form of Musar was practiced in Novaredok (present-day Novogrudok, in Belarus). The Novaredok yeshivah where Chaim Grade studied is the setting for his sweeping novel *The Yeshiva*, originally composed in Yiddish.

Grade portrays himself as student Chaikl Vilner, a boy practically stolen from home by the central character, Tzemach Atlas, a Novaredok enthusiast who travels from city to city, building an entire network of Novaredok-style yeshivot and populating them with children smuggled out of Russia. The book follows the intersecting paths of several sets of characters engaged in separate story lines that coalesce at the end. The question throughout is the nature of Jewish identity in a world where the authority of the Talmud is no longer taken for granted.

Few of the Novaredok characters are likeable, and some are downright obnoxious—the opposite of what Salanter expected his Musar movement to produce. As Grade tells it, the Novaredok variety was extremist in its pietistic demands. Novaredok lore pictures its founder

Yosef Yoizel Horowitz (1848–1919) studying eighteen hours a day while standing up almost all the time, and never handling money except for the coin he paid the attendant at the ritual bathhouse where he went daily to rid himself of his sins. In the novel, Musar students pray with Pentecostal fervor, "breaking all the benches and the prayer stand." It is sinful to enjoy even ordinary marital sex. The *musarniks* (followers of Musar) suspect even their own good deeds of being motivated by the evil impulse.

Never out of sight is the background squalor of Jewish life in the shtetls. Chaikl (like Grade in real life) is the son of an impoverished family supported by his mother, Vella, a fruit peddler. Too poor to feed him, Vella virtually gives him away to a drunken fanatic who pays for his education, but beats him, until eventually, Tzemach Atlas rescues him for a yeshivah future. Chaikl's fellow yeshivah students are in constant competition, to the point where one of them commits suicide, and another one tries but fails. When Tzemach hears that yeshivah students are reading Enlightenment books, he colludes with a known Jewish mafioso to have the entire library burned.

Women are particularly pauperized. If they are old, they barely subsist. If young, they scheme endlessly to find a budding yeshivah scholar to marry, in the hope of sharing the prestige that their scholarly husband will accrue through his Talmudic acumen. There are some heroes: a non-Novaredok Talmudist who embodies dignity, learning, and compassion, to whom the novel's characters go for advice. Chaikl himself is thrown into inner turmoil when Tzemach's ex-wife shows up and rouses the sexual stirrings he never knew he had. In the end, he leaves the yeshivah for secular Judaism—as Chaim Grade himself did.

The Yeshiva might not be an easy read. As in so many Russian novels, the characters in Grade's literary masterpiece are legion, and their names alone are a challenge to remember. But it is worth slogging through: it is written very well, and the reader's "slog" befits the plot, where characters slog through lives of hopelessness. One reaches the end of it with a sigh of relief that the vaunted ghettos of eastern Europe are gone.

The Penguin Book of Modern Yiddish Verse
(1987)

Irving Howe (1920–1993), Ruth R. Wisse (born 1936), Khone Shmeruk (1921–1997) (editors)

"The shtetl slid into a period of economic disintegration and social decomposition. Yet it also flickered with a late brilliance [. . .] another instance of the capacity Jewish life has shown through the centuries for spiritual self-renewal."

Sometimes the introduction to a book is as good as the book itself. That certainly is the case with this marvelous collection of poetry, presented here in the original Yiddish and in English translation. After you have read the introduction, you feel as if you have been reading Yiddish poetry all your life, and cannot wait to meet up with old friends whose work the introduction celebrates.

Better than any historians, these poets lay bare the culture that bore them: a century or so of Yiddish life in Russia, Poland, and the United States—one major upheaval after another: czarist persecution beginning in 1881; the Russian Revolution of 1917 and the Stalinist purges of the 1930s and 1950s; mass migration to America, particularly New York's Lower East Side—in some ways, one gigantic sweatshop of immigrants crowded together in almost inhuman living conditions; World War I, with Jews caught between two warring armies—Russians and Germans—and then suffering further persecution by nationalist Poles, Czechs, and others; and the ultimate horror—the Holocaust. Any single one of these traumas should have been enough to stifle a people's genius.

Yet just the opposite occurred. Yiddish, just barely a literary language until the middle of the nineteenth century, came alive in a flurry of writings that absorbed, and then expressed, the impact of each and every one of these historic upheavals. Through it all, Jews responded actively, both politically and culturally—itself a remarkable turnaround from medieval times, when passivity had prevailed.

The rise of Yiddish literature began around 1850 or 1860, ran its remarkable course in Europe and America, and ended around 1950. The entire sweep of this grand Yiddish century comes through in this monumental collection of poetry.

The book begins with "Monish," a semiautobiographical account by Isaac Loeb Peretz composed over a period of twenty years (1888–1908). It reflects the demise of the traditional world in which Yiddish writing emerged. Monish is a Talmudic child prodigy who "laps up Torah like a sponge / His mind is lightning." Fearful that such intense Talmudic study will bring the messiah, Satan sends Lilith disguised as a beautiful temptress. (Lilith is a fictitious character of Jewish folklore, the first wife of Adam who ever after besieges Adam's pious male offspring who try to do God's will.) Modernity thus arrives for Monish in the form of romantic love. He abandons the ascetic life of a Torah scholar—and all hope for an early arrival of the messiah—"for a girl."

The period when Jews left Russia in droves is reflected by Zishe Landau (1889–1937), who came to America when he was seventeen. He "weeps and mourns [. . .] for everything that was ours," which "now vanishes with the smoke."

The Nazi nightmare is much addressed in these pages, nowhere better than in the challenge to God by Jacob Glatstein (1896–1971). "Without Jews," Glatstein promises, there is "no Jewish God." If this is "the Jews' last hour," then it is God's eclipse as well. But what can God do? Drawing on the traditional view of a God who could not prevent the Temple's destruction and the ensuing exile, and who therefore settled for going into exile with the Jewish People, Glatstein calls God "my wandering brother" who "sits with me, my friend, clasping me, and sharing his last bite."

So monumental was the Holocaust that it left little room in modern Jewish consciousness for a proper appreciation of the Stalinist trauma. Stalin's victims were often intellectuals who had hoped for acceptance of Yiddish as one of the many licit languages of cultural expression in the Soviet Union. At the same time, they were universalists, anxious to leave behind the worn-out poetic themes of ghetto culture—its Talmudic scholars and fiddlers on the roof. Even before the Russian Revolution, Dovid Hofshteyn (1889–1952), from Kiev, for example, was exploring the utter solitude of "Russian fields on winter evenings [. . .] Where can one be more lonely?" He would later continue his meditation on loneliness in "City," a poem that saw the modern metropolis as a ship carrying emigrants from field to factory, but a "ship of loneliness" equally as desolate as the vast Russian countryside left behind.

As Stalinist censors tightened their cultural noose, Hofshteyn found himself trapped by a governmental campaign to "rid Yiddish of 'the Hebrew component.'" In one of his poems, for example, he had to change the Yiddish word for sunset, *shkiye,* to the Russian term *ovnt-randn*—in the eyes of this volume's editors "decidedly not an improvement." Hofshteyn hailed the founding of the State of Israel, and was thereupon rounded up by Stalin, imprisoned, and shot in 1952.

Yiddish flowered in the New World as well, especially on New York's Lower East Side. There, too, many poets abandoned Old Country obsessions—the "shtetl stories" and "Diaspora themes" driven by nostalgia. "I am bored," the poet H. Leivick (i.e., Leivick Halpern [1888–1962]) declared, "by Hasidic tunes [and] folksy sing-songs." But equally, he and several like-minded poets (including Zishe Landau) who called themselves *Di Yunge* (The Young) set out in the 1910s to be more than "the rhyme department of the Jewish Labor Movement." They sought to illuminate telling details of daily life. Mani Leyb (1883–1953), for example, explored "the bonfire of my Indian Summer," where "crickets are playing sadness on my soul" and "trees—blue wax—glow in cold nudity." But the Yiddish renaissance faltered in America, too—not through persecution but through acculturation. No amount of stunning poetry could rescue Yiddish from being seen as the immigrant language that Jews in North America were intent on dropping as soon as they could set foot outside the inner-city Jewish neighborhoods where they had grown up.

The Penguin Book of Modern Yiddish Verse includes the Yiddish equivalents of romanticism, modernism, expressionism, symbolism, and all the other Western literary styles that challenged the disappearing past as the nineteenth century slid into the twentieth. But each poem has a specifically Jewish flavor, created by the color and cadence of the Yiddish language. Readers of Yiddish poetry say frequently that its appeal to Jewish consciousness has yet to be matched, even by modern Hebrew.

The editors here are exceptionally well known for their expertise in the field of Yiddish language and literature. Irving Howe was part of the remarkable cadre of 1950s New York Jewish intellectuals described by Alfred Kazin (see page 254). Ruth Wisse has helped establish Yiddish as an academic discipline in North America, first at Montreal's McGill University, and then at Harvard University. Khone Shmeruk fled Poland during the Hitler era, then moved to Israel; he died back home in his native Warsaw and was eulogized in London's *Times* as "the world's foremost scholar of Yiddish literature and folklore."

The final verdict of these three distinguished editors adjudges Yiddish poetry as "a poetry of homelessness and dislocation [. . .] In Yiddish writing, the shadow of history falls heavily."

The Pity of It All
(2002)

Amos Elon (1926–2009)

"In the eighteenth century, there can hardly have been more than sixty thousand Jews in the German states [. . .] When, in 1870, more than thirty independent German states consolidated to establish a united Reich, Jews were still an insignificant minority of slightly more than 1 percent. Sixty years later, on the eve of the Nazi takeover [. . .] the relative number of Jews had dropped to 0.8 percent. One wonders how so small a presence, even indirectly, could have triggered such vast enmity."

The story is told of an American professor of Judaica in the 1970s, who, as he was interviewing potential doctoral candidates, inquired, "Are you at home in the holy tongue?" When assured of the student's Hebrew competence, he would respond, not altogether in jest, "Actually, I meant German." He had escaped Nazi Germany and felt completely at home in America, but he never gave up on German as the true language of Jewish culture.

Given the Nazi nightmare that ended it all, it is hard to imagine the extent of this great Jewish love affair with Germany. Nowadays, Jews hardly remember it and have trouble believing it—even though, arguably, no group of people has contributed more to modern German greatness than did its Jews, who (until Hitler) considered their contribution fully rewarded by the country they were happy to call home.

Amos Elon was a famous Israeli journalist, essayist, and author of several highly acclaimed nonfiction books, including *The Israelis* (1971) and *Herzl* (1975). Born in Vienna, he came with his parents to Palestine in 1933. For *The Pity of It All*, he combed through hundreds of books, letters, news accounts, and diaries to illuminate two centuries of German-Jewish greatness—from 1743, when Moses Mendelssohn was admitted to Berlin as a specially "privileged" Jew, until 1933, when Hitler came to power. The book ends with another famous German-Jewish philosopher, Hannah Arendt (see page 201), departing Berlin on the eve of the Holocaust, after a brief interlude in a Gestapo prison. "A circle was closing," Elon remarks. "Arendt's train out of Berlin sped south [. . .] in the opposite direction taken two centuries earlier by the boy Moses Mendelssohn, on foot."

There was no unified Germany until the 1870s, when Prussia's Otto von Bismarck hammered it together with "blood and iron." And Germanism extended beyond Germany's borders into the Habsburg Empire, especially its capital, Vienna. By then, the list of prominent Jews in both realms was well established. The Viennese side of the story is just touched on in Elon's book, but is readily available in the biographies of such famous Jews as Sigmund Freud (see page 140), Gustav Mahler, and Theodor Herzl (see page 131). It is the less well-known side of Jewish life in Germany proper that Elon chronicles.

Elon's history is especially rich in biographical vignettes of the many outstanding personalities through whose eyes we watch history unfold: the abortive revolutions of 1830 and 1848; Bismarck's reactionary absolutism; the fortunes of German socialism; the economic panic of 1873; the two world wars; and the Weimar interlude. Through it all, there runs the extended career of one outstanding German Jew after another: industrialists, scientists, artists, scholars, musicians, journalists, politicians, publishers, and writers. Heinrich Heine became Germany's foremost romantic poet, and a grandson of Moses Mendelssohn was the great composer Felix. Already in the late 1700s, a daughter of Mendelssohn, Dorothea, and another patron of high culture, Rahel Varnhagen, held living room salons that attracted the likes of philosopher Friedrich Schleiermacher and all-around genius Friedrich Schlegel (he was a philosopher, linguist, writer, and critic, and eventually married Dorothea, who left Judaism for Catholicism). Bismarck's unification of Germany was financed by the banker Gerson Bleichröder. Gabriel Riesser, vice president of the Frankfurt National Assembly after the 1848 revolution, was a member of the delegation that offered the German imperial crown to King Frederick William IV of Prussia. Abraham Geiger, Zacharias Frankel, and Samson Raphael Hirsch pioneered what we now call Reform, Conservative, and modern Orthodox Judaism. Never mind more familiar names such as Martin Buber and Albert Einstein. The list goes on and on.

But we get so much more than names here. Elon's account sweeps across the full panorama of German-Jewish life, and addresses specifically the ambivalence of Jews who assimilated in record numbers (perhaps half of Berlin Jewry, according to the historian Heinrich Graetz, who watched it happen). Throughout the nineteenth century, conversion to Christianity was common among Jews across Europe who sought advancement—as nominal Christians, they qualified for university and government posts.

The dark side of Elon's story is the ever-increasing anti-Semitism, advocated by German artists and intellectuals such as the composer Richard Wagner and the historian-politician Heinrich von Treitschke. It surfaced early, in the 1819 pogroms in Germany called *Hep! Hep!* riots, then again during the 1848 revolution, and later still, as Jews were blamed for the 1873 economic panic. The term "anti-Semitism" was first coined in the 1850s by a French count, Joseph Arthur de Gobineau. He was a proponent of social Darwinism, according to which higher orders of human culture had the right to destroy lower orders out of which they had emerged. Jews, he believed, were among these lower orders that should be left behind. The specifically German version of the theory, which targeted Jews in particular, can be seen in the infamous work *The Foundations of the Nineteenth Century* (1899) by Houston Stewart Chamberlain, Richard Wagner's son-in-law. Chamberlain argued that "Aryans" had evolved with their own "race-soul," marked by honesty and loyalty, whereas "Semites," he held, were by nature immoral and greedy. Anti-*Jewish* sentiment had been an ugly part of European history for many centuries—but anti-*Semitism*, by contrast, was new; its focus was not religion but "race," a category from which it is impossible to escape.

In retrospect, as the title proclaims, *The Pity of It All* reads like a real-life Greek tragedy—we know what happens in the end. The Jewish fatal "flaw" was unrestrained worship of German culture despite the realities of xenophobic racism and the sweep of German nationalism that eventually became the Third Reich. But in its time, Jews had reason to believe that Germany was their home, and German the holy tongue.

5

Turn of the Century

The Conversation Divides

๏

In eastern Europe, the death knell of premodern Jewish traditionalism was equally an announcement of birth—of twins, in fact, two modern ideologies that fought to fill the religious vacuum: Jewish nationalism (Zionism) and Jewish socialism (the Bund). Both were great movements of human aspiration that can be seen as Jewish to their core—secular, to be sure, but secularized versions of the age-old Jewish messianism that Jews had carried ever since their exile to Babylonia. They shared a distaste for the traditionalist religious authorities (who urged pious passivity instead of political activism) and, therefore, a disdain for Judaism as a religion. Western European Jews, too, embraced these two political strategies—indeed, Zionism's great hero is Theodor Herzl, a fully Westernized Jew from Austria. But overall, western Europe's Jews focused on religious reform; Herzl's Zionism succeeded only because Jews in the East—who were focused on political, not religious, change—insisted on it.

Despite the rise in anti-Semitism as the nineteenth century wore on, Jews in countries such as Germany or France believed that university education and modernized religion would earn them acceptance as German or French citizens of Jewish religious persuasion. Ever since

Moses Mendelssohn in the eighteenth century, that had been the claim of the Western Enlightenment. Eastern Europe was altogether different. To begin with, the Eastern Orthodox churches had never gone through a reformation; religion in the East, therefore, went hand in hand with the ultraconservative state—neither of which had room for Jews. In addition, Jews were confronted with Slavic nationalism, which had been growing since 1856, when Russia's defeat in the Crimean War led it to abandon rapprochement with the West and turn inward (and backward) instead. Despite some false dawns of promise earlier in the century, it had become clear by the 1880s that Jews had no role in a czarist state. For most Jews, the question then became whether to abandon Russia for a state of their own (Zionism)—or to foment revolution from within (the socialist Bund).

Zionism was the Jewish version of the nationalistic fervor that swept through all of Europe in the mid- to late nineteenth century, producing, among other things, the unified nations of Germany and Italy. An early Zionist theorist, Moses Hess (see page 134), was an avid reader of Giuseppe Mazzini (1805–1872), who had argued the case for the uniqueness of the Italian national character; surely, Hess reasoned, the Jewish People was equally singular. The 1861 proclamation of Rome as the capital of a newly united Italy led Hess to suggest a similar Jewish state, with Jerusalem as its capital. His book *Rome and Jerusalem* was published in Germany in 1862.

Zionism as a concrete political movement, however, is generally dated only to 1882, when the first wave of some 7,000 eastern European romantics—who called themselves *Hovevei Zion* (Lovers of Zion)—left czarist Russia for Palestine. Zionism's prophetic voice came with Theodor Herzl (1860–1904), an acculturated Viennese journalist who became convinced that anti-Semitism was endemic to Europe, and that only a Jewish state could save the Jewish People from destruction.

Jewish socialism as a political movement also responded to anti-Semitism and the debilitating Jewish condition under the czars. But unlike Zionism, it sought a classless society for everyone, not an independent nationalist Jewish state in Palestine. Jews had long been attracted to the moderate form of socialism that urged evolutionary, not revolutionary, means of achieving economic and political reforms. In 1895/1896, however, Jewish workers in Vilna went on strike, and in 1897 (the same year that saw Herzl's First Zionist Congress), fifteen Jewish socialists in Vilna declared a Jewish workers' society that became known as the Bund. In the few years leading up to the 1905 Russian

Revolution, the Bund organized massive strikes in the heavily Jewish industrial centers of Lodz and Bialystok, but after 1905, its strength dissipated under pressure from more radical Jewish socialists who sided with the Bolsheviks and rejected the idea of a specifically Jewish identity in the international socialist society that they hoped to found.

In 1917, Zionists claimed their first step to victory when Britain's foreign secretary, Lord Balfour, promised his government's support of a Jewish state—should the allies win the Great War. That same year, the Russian Revolution reached fruition with the Bolshevik accession to power. For two years, civil war embroiled Lenin's Bolsheviks (the Reds) and the rival Mensheviks (the Whites) in a protracted struggle that continued with war against Poland and the eventual establishment of the Soviet Union in 1922. With Jews targeted for destruction by all parties—the Reds, the Whites, and Polish nationalists—Zionism flourished, prompting further waves of emigration to Palestine, each one called an *aliyah* (a "going up" or "ascent").

Anti-Semitism within socialist ranks completed the rout of the overtly Jewish Bund, as Jews who opposed Bolshevik extremism were simply eliminated. Other Jews, however, abandoned Judaism and played significant roles in the Russian communist state that was coming into being. The best such example may be Lev Davidovich Bronstein (1879–1940), better known as Leon Trotsky, Lenin's right-hand man. Trotsky began as the commissar for foreign affairs, but quickly moved up the ranks to command the Red Army and forge the Bolshevik victory in the Russian civil war.

In 1929, however, Lenin's successor, Joseph Stalin, expelled Trotsky and initiated a hunt for Jewish party members, especially in his Great Purge of the 1930s and an anti-Semitic campaign in 1952 (motivated by Stalin's claim of a "doctors' plot" to kill Soviet officials). The generation of Jewish socialists in America that had come of age by then was shocked to discover the depths to which Stalinist communism had sunk, compared to the revolutionary dreams that Jewish socialists had hoped to realize.

Jewish socialism, therefore, proved a dead end, while Jewish nationalism did not. The two ideologies were combined, however, in the State of Israel, where most of the founders were socialists who sought to instill socialist ideals within the Jewish society they were establishing. Other amalgams of once warring opposites occurred as well—for example, Jewish religionists who had opposed Zionism came to embrace it, founding Zionist parties themselves. Zionism thus eventually incorporated all the available interpretations of what a Jewish state should look like.

Zionism and socialism, and the politics and economics they stand for, are at the core of Jewish modernity. Alongside the intellectual Enlightenment, these two activist ideologies pushed the Jewish conversation far beyond the religious boundaries that had defined it ever since its biblical and rabbinic origins. With the onset of modernity, Jewish writers have not necessarily been rabbis, and many have had only passing familiarity with the Bible and rabbinic classics. But as Jewish conversationalists, they care deeply for the past and future of the Jewish People, identify proudly as Jews, claim historical continuity with the Jewish story across the centuries, and may still have Zionist or even socialist aspirations. Other modern Jewish writers, of course, are religious to their core. Although not necessarily traditionalists, they, too, have assimilated the lessons of the past two centuries, which juxtaposed Judaism as a religion with the chief secular ideologies of the time, nationalism and socialism. Ever since then, the Jewish conversation has not been the same!

The Diaries
(1922–1923)

Theodor Herzl (1860–1904)

"We shall build houses, palaces, workingmen's homes, schools, theatres, museums, government buildings, prisons, hospitals, asylums—in short, cities—and make the country so fertile that it will have earned its title, The Promised Land."

In the nineteenth century, the sprawling Austro-Hungarian Empire held over 50 million subjects, not just in Austria but also in what is now Italy, the Czech Republic, Slovakia, Hungary, Serbia, Bosnia, Croatia, Romania, and parts of Poland and Germany. Not just a political capital, Vienna was a cultural magnet as well. Throughout the 1800s, imperial citizens from the East increasingly flocked to Vienna to make their fortunes and pass as bona fide German speakers, rather than ethnic outliers of lesser status.

Theodor Herzl's family moved from Budapest to Vienna in 1878, when Theodor was eighteen years old. He was so successfully assimilated that he joined a *Burschenschaft*, a student fraternity dedicated to furthering the development of a pan-German state. He studied law in Vienna, but ended up as a playwright and journalist, and became a correspondent, and then literary editor, of a leading Austrian newspaper, *Neue Freie Presse*. Among the stories he covered was the 1894 trial in Paris of Captain Alfred Dreyfus, a French Jew who was falsely accused of treason. Herzl later claimed that hearing Parisian mobs threaten "Death to the Jews" awakened him to "the emptiness and futility of trying to 'combat' anti-Semitism."

In fact, the Dreyfus affair only strengthened a conviction that had seized him earlier. In Vienna, he had attended a performance of an opera by the outspoken anti-Semite and German arch-nationalist Richard Wagner, and returned home on fire with the idea of *Jewish* nationalism. That very night, he began writing *The Jewish State* (*Der Judenstaat*), a work dedicated to resolving the much-debated "Jewish question," which he was certain would "persist wherever Jews live in appreciable numbers. Wherever it does not exist, it is a necessary consequence of Jewish immigration. We are naturally drawn into those places where we are not persecuted, and our appearance there gives rise to persecution." Only an independent Jewish state would make Jews immune to ever-worsening Jew-hatred "even in highly civilized countries." The book was published in Vienna in early 1896.

He died only eight years later, something of a broken man, having taken upon himself the establishment of a real Jewish state—somewhere. He had worn himself out visiting Europe's various potentates to find powerful backers for his dream. His natural charisma proved attractive—Martin Buber described him as "a countenance lit with the glance of the Messiah"—as did his reputation as an accomplished journalist and de facto representative of the Jewish People. It is amazing that any of these emperors, kings, and politicians received Herzl at all, and in the end, nothing came of it. They temporized, misled with promises, lied outright, or used him for their own purposes.

If the sole measure of Herzl's success were the actual achievement of a Jewish state, his frenetic years of shuttling back and forth among the rulers of Europe would have to be judged a failure. Typical of his missions to various governments was a hearing by the Russian interior minister, Vyacheslav von Plehve, in 1903, which Herzl's admirer and fellow Zionist Shmarya Levin dismissed as "inadvisable, simply because the most solemn promise of von Plehve was utterly without value." The grand duke of Baden said that he "would like to see it [the Zionist plan] come about," but practically speaking, Baden—a small German state—was in no position to champion it; the grand duke suggested that Herzl should try the Habsburg emperor in Vienna. On another occasion, Herzl hoped the German emperor would sponsor a Jewish settlement in Palestine, while intervening with the Turkish sultan to admit more Jews into what was still Ottoman territory. The emperor never did. When Herzl finally got to the Ottoman capital, the sultan would not see him, explaining privately, "I would rather have my flesh be cut up than cut out Palestine from the Muslim land."

But for all that, Herzl was a herculean man with equally herculean achievements. More than anyone else, he put the Jewish People on the map. He brought Jews together from across the globe in search of a common political destiny—announced publicly at the First Zionist Congress in 1897, in Basel, Switzerland. After his death, the Zionist organization he had built became a Jewish government in exile, an address to which Jewish representatives from every country came for further biennial deliberations.

To the eastern European masses of Jews who heard of him, Herzl was a modern-day Jewish king, but in retrospect, he seems more like a prophet, alternately worshiped and reviled—especially when, no matter what he did or with whom he met, a Jewish homeland in Palestine seemed far from realization. At times, he was offered some other solution—a tract of land in present-day Uganda, for example, or a settlement at El Arish on the southern shore of the Mediterranean.

The issue, for Herzl, was immediate and critical: how to advance a Jewish state somewhere—anywhere—so that Jews might live safely beyond the reaches of anti-Semitic violence. To most Jews, however, nothing short of the Land of Israel would do. The fact that Herzl would not hold out for Palestine sometimes alienated fellow Zionists, and he was at times suspicious himself of what he was accomplishing—how could he not be? In a moment of personal candor, he wondered in his diaries whether, perhaps, he was only "a creditable Talmudic scholar who wanders from town to town and whom rabbis and rich men ply with free meals."

In addition to the world's political leaders, he had to deal with wealthy Jewish magnates from whom he hoped to receive funding—such as Baron Maurice de Hirsch (1831–1896), the industrialist and philanthropist in Paris who financed Jewish agricultural settlements as far away as the United States and Argentina; and the Rothschilds themselves, Europe's leading banking family with offices in London and Paris. Thoroughly acculturated in their European estates, however, they were hardly willing to concede that Jews required a homeland somewhere else. When, at one point, Herzl's advisors suggested he should send advance letters to wealthy Jews to get their support, he reacted with a diatribe in his diary: "This is a cause that belongs to the poor Jews, not the rich. The protest of the latter is null, void, and worthless." Two days later, he came down with a bronchial infection. "A prophet must have healthy lungs," he was told.

Dreamer, madman, savior, and prophet, Herzl died of heart failure when he was only forty-four. The London *Times* supplied a eulogy, announcing that he had been buried simply (no flowers or speeches), in Vienna, as he had requested. He had further asked "to be buried in the vault beside my father, and to lie there until the Jewish People shall take my remains to Palestine." In 1949, they did just that, naming his burial place in Jerusalem Mount Herzl.

Herzl's diaries, which cover the years 1895 to 1904, are an invaluable source for understanding their writer's greatness. His foibles and failures are there to see as well, but overall, one finishes the diaries finding it hard to believe that one man did so much. They remain Herzl's real last will and testament to the Jewish People whom he loved.

The Zionist Idea
(1959)

Arthur Hertzberg (1921–2006)

"What marks Zionism as a fresh beginning in Jewish history is that its ultimate values derive from the general milieu. The Messiah is now identified with the dream of an age of individual liberty, national freedom, and economic and social justice—i.e., with the progressive faith of the nineteenth century."

The great modern Jewish movement we call Zionism was in large part directed against the rabbinic religious ideals that had governed Jewish assumptions for nearly two millennia—since the tragedy of 137 CE, when the last gasp of Jewish revolt against Rome was punished by the brutal execution of its leaders and the renaming of Jerusalem as a pagan city off-limits to Jews. Preferring the safety of passivity to the pain of self-assertion, the Rabbis had declared the era from the fall of the Temple to the coming of the messiah an age of passive loyalty to God, who alone would bring redemption when the time was ripe. Zionism decided the time had already ripened long ago.

A powerful testimony to the Zionist story is Arthur Hertzberg's classic collection of essays written by the greatest Zionist thinkers of all time. The gamut of entries includes such famous names as Theodor Herzl, Ahad Ha-am (see page 137), and David Ben-Gurion (Israel's founding prime minister); but also lesser-known, albeit influential, personalities such as the Serbian mystic Judah Alkalai (1798–1878) and the German socialist and philosopher Moses Hess (1812–1875). As early as 1874, Alkalai argued that the messiah would arrive only after a cataclysmic eschatological war preordained by the Bible (Ezek. 38:2–3); the Zionist settlement of the Holy Land, he thought, would inaugurate that final historical battle.

Hess, a Western thinker who was poles apart from Alkalai's mystical traditionalism, reached a similar conclusion from a secular point of view. His socialist predilections had led him to replace religion with a more universalistic dream of human freedom. But as time went on, he saw that "nature does not produce flowers and fruits or plants and animals which are all alike." In history, too, nature produces distinctive peoples, each with its own role in the ongoing saga of redemption from servitude. True, "Judaism is the root of our whole contemporary universalist view of life," but the era when Jews were to spread God's word as a people dispersed throughout the nations had passed; given modern nationalism, it was time for Jews to attain the next stage in God's plan, regaining their homeland to become "the mediators between Europe and far Asia."

Hess's idea of the inherent disparity that separates one ethnic group from another illustrates a larger trend in nineteenth-century thought. The previous century had inaugurated the Enlightenment, whose advocates assumed that all human beings were essentially equal, despite their surface differences. The Age of Reason culminated in the French Revolution's call for universal "liberty, equality, fraternity." In reaction to that revolution, however, nineteenth-century conservative monarchs turned the philosophy of romanticism into an ideology of nationalism, and propagated ethnic and cultural differences—hence the rabid anti-Semitism that plagued the last half of the century.

This ballooning anti-Semitism gave Zionism traction. After the czarist May Laws of 1882, which called for an end of Jewish existence in Russian territory one way or another, it became impossible to imagine anymore that "Jew hatred was merely a hang-over from the medieval past." Leon Pinsker (1821–1891), another early Zionist from the East (and the founder of the Hovevei Zion movement), anticipated Herzl by recognizing anti-Semitism as "a thoroughly modern phenomenon, beyond the reach of any future triumphs of humanity and the Enlightenment in society as a whole." Jews would either attain their own land or remain forever subject to perennial persecution. The May Laws reverberated mostly in the East, however; assimilated western Jews (such as Herzl himself) were converted to the cause only as the blatantly anti-Semitic Dreyfus Affair unfolded in France in the 1890s.

Arthur Hertzberg's long introduction to *The Zionist Idea* is as masterful a summary of Zionist thought as one is likely to find; and reading the essays and excerpts themselves is like tuning into an extended conversation among all the Zionist greats. A. D. Gordon, Zionism's secular mystic and saint, called on Jews to work the land as "zealots of labor," since "when, O Man, you return to Nature [. . .] you will know that you have returned to Yourself." Ahad Ha-am visited Israel, but lived outside of it for virtually his entire life, because he thought "the real and only basis of Zionism is [. . .] spiritual." The philosopher Martin Buber, too, thought the problem spiritual, but while Ahad Ha-am identified "spiritual" as a renaissance of Jewish culture, Buber had in mind the core universal values of Judaism—not just "egoistic nationalism," but "Hebrew humanism." Eliezer Ben-Yehuda, the father of modern Hebrew, who had moved from Paris to Jerusalem in 1881, predicted, "Today we may be moribund, but tomorrow we will surely awaken to life; today we may be speaking alien tongues, but tomorrow, we shall speak Hebrew."

When a British commission virtually cut off Jewish immigration to Palestine in 1939, Chaim Weizmann (who would become Israel's first president) actually sobbed as he reminded his audience, "I, for twenty years, have made it my lifework to explain the Jewish People to the British, and the British People to the Jews [. . .] The British—that mighty empire—must not commit this sin against the People of the Book."

Arthur Hertzberg was one of the great Jewish American voices of the twentieth century. He became a Zionist activist in the 1940s, and in 1963 he accompanied Martin Luther King, Jr. on his March on Washington. Despite his commitment as a historian to preserve the Jewish past, another one of his books, *The Jews in America* (1989), warns that "a community cannot survive on what it remembers; it will persist only because of what it affirms and believes." Appropriately, he concludes *The Zionist Idea* by anticipating the Jewish dilemma of the twenty-first century, when Judaism becomes entirely an identity of choice. "What I have been describing here," he says, "is, of course, what Jean-Paul Sartre has called 'the situation of the Jew.' [. . .] The Jew is not almost solely, as Sartre would have it, a creation of anti-Semitism [. . .] I believe it is basic that the Jew creates himself, by his choice of his own identity." The Zionist legacy is a clarion call to that choice.

Selected Essays
(1912)
Ahad Ha-am (1856–1927)

*"I try to give my weary eyes a rest from the scene of ignorance, of degrada-
tion, of unutterable poverty that confronts me here in Russia, and find comfort by looking across the border [into Germany]. Do I envy these fellow Jews
of mine their emancipation? No! A thousand times No! The privileges are
not worth the price! I may not be emancipated, but at least I have not sold my
soul for emancipation."*

Only rarely do people nowadays either read or write essays, and
the very word "essay" commonly means nothing more than what
one attaches to a college application. That is unfortunate. The essay is
a short, manageable, and compelling way to make one's voice heard on
a subject of importance. As far back as Roman times, Cicero left one
on old age, for instance, as Seneca did on anger. It was the sixteenth-
century French courtier Michel de Montaigne who brought the genre
to perfection, and thereafter, essays became a powerful literary weapon
with which to fight causes. The founders of America regularly argued
their case through essays.

Judaism has its own master essay writers, among whom there is
none better than Ukrainian-born Asher Hirsch Ginsberg, who chose
to be called Ahad Ha-am (One of the People). He received a traditional
Jewish education from his father, and then turned to Jewish philosophy,
as well as to works by Haskalah Enlightenment authors who were
experimenting with Hebrew as a living tongue. Along the way, he
studied French, English, Latin, and Russian. In 1894, he moved to
Odessa, then the cultural capital of modern Jewish thought and letters,
where he encountered Leon Pinsker and the Hovevei Zion movement.
By 1889, he began the essay writing that would make him famous. His
lifelong cause would be Zionism.

Today, we think of Zionism mostly as a political movement—which
it was, under its founder, Theodor Herzl. Ahad Ha-am, however,
argued for a long-range view that addressed the internal paralysis of
the Jewish spirit, not just the external emergencies that threatened
Jewish lives. Simultaneously, in what would prove prophetic, he foresaw

138 ᕽ One Hundred Great Jewish Books

conflict breaking out between Jews returning to Palestine and Arabs already living there. Herzl had imagined that Arabs and Jews would live happily side by side, since Westernized Jewish immigrants, with modern education and skills, would raise living standards for everyone; by contrast, Ahad Ha-am predicted an ongoing struggle about the ownership of the land that both groups claimed as their patrimony.

Ahad Ha-am still championed the Jewish People's right and necessity to return home to Zion. But he opposed immediate emigration to populate the land. Jews were not ready, he insisted. Proper groundwork had to be laid. The issue was not simply saving Jews: it was saving Judaism, or, as Ahad Ha-am thought of it, Hebrew culture. Uprooting whole populations prematurely to settle Palestine would not guarantee the successful flowering of the ideals and purpose that are the essence of the Jewish spirit. Zionism would ultimately require a Jewish homeland, but land alone would not suffice. Jews would need to prepare for their eventual return by mustering all their cultural power to do so as Jews in spirit. Israel would be a "spiritual" center for a Jewish cultural renaissance.

Over the course of three decades, he made his case, largely through essays on Jewish history. As history, they fail—they are far from accurate—but as ideology they are spectacular. As Ahad Ha-am saw it, Hebrew culture had reached its zenith in the biblical prophets' uncompromising vision of a people devoted to universal righteousness. The Rabbis of the early centuries CE had compromised that vision: when they lost their independence to Rome, they had settled for what Rome would offer—Jewish religion as a subject people. Medieval penury kept Jews in that sorry state: spiritually enriched, perhaps, but ghettoized.

Now, however, Jews had a choice. The most obvious option was acculturation with the West. For Ahad Ha-am, that amounted to slavish imitation of the host culture: Jews in different lands would engage in "competitive imitation," instead of remaining true to their own authentic cultural past—and without the cultural past, they would forget their prophetic purpose. A similar fate would befall Zionists who made it to Israel, but made no effort to retain the Jewish spiritual legacy without which Jews would survive but Judaism would be dead. The heritage without a state in which to reside is a disembodied soul. Zion resettled is the body with which the soul can unite. Free to let Hebrew culture flourish, a Jewish state would water even the arid landscape of the Diaspora.

Ahad Ha-am became the most influential Zionist voice for Jews remaining in the Diaspora. It was possible, he showed, to be a true

Zionist without having to move to Israel, because one could support the Jewish state as a center for Jewish culture from abroad. Ahad Ha-am certainly did not oppose immigration to what would become a Jewish state. His resistance was to the *haste* with which that state was coming about—a function, he thought, of the zeal which always attends messianic movements, since the Jewish determination to return to the land of the Bible was just that—Jewish messianism, in modern secularized form. To be sure, the onslaught of the Nazis made such theoretical concepts inapplicable—Jews had to be saved, during the war if at all possible, and certainly after it, for there were Jews still interred in displaced persons' camps across Europe, with no home to return to.

Ahad Ha-am visited Israel several times, but lived mostly in London, where he wrote avidly while lending his voice to internal Zionist debates from afar. Following the 1903 mass murder of Jews in Kishinev, for example, Herzl argued for an immediate establishment of a Jewish state in Uganda, which the British government offered in place of Palestine. In keeping with his emphasis on the continuity of Jewish history and culture, Ahad Ha-am decried the plan. In 1917, he played a role in obtaining the Balfour Declaration, but was not as enthusiastic about it as his more politically minded Zionist opponents were.

Eventually, Ahad Ha-am decided the time had finally arrived for him, too, to return home. So in 1922, he left London for Palestine, and died there just five years later.

Nowadays, Ahad Ha-am's cultural Judaism is regularly revisited, and the State of Israel has overall indeed become the cultural center of which Ahad Ha-am had dreamed. Hebrew newspapers, music, books, learning, and research are everywhere. Hebrew is spoken on the streets. Whether the larger goal of furthering the Jewish prophetic purpose has yet come about is another matter. But Ahad Ha-am always advocated patience—and the story isn't over yet.

Moses and Monotheism
(1939)

Sigmund Freud (1856–1939)

*"In a new transport of moral asceticism the Jews imposed on themselves con-
stantly increasing instinctual renunciation, and thereby reached [. . .] ethical heights that had remained inaccessible to the other peoples of antiquity.
Many Jews regard these achievements as the second main characteristic, and
the second great achievement, of their religion. Our investigation is intended
to show how it is connected with the first one, the conception of the one and
only God."*

On his thirty-fifth birthday, in 1891, Sigmund Freud received
a surprise gift from his father, Jakob: the Bible that Freud had
studied as a child, newly bound in leather and outfitted with a Hebrew
inscription calling on him to open its pages and rediscover its "wellsprings of understanding, knowledge and wisdom." His birthday Bible
languished unread until 1934, when Freud finally took up his father's
challenge to open it again, possibly because Hitler's accession to power
a year earlier had moved him to confront his Jewish identity anew. The
literary result was *Moses and Monotheism*, Freud's only ostensibly Jewish
book. Its first two parts, "Moses an Egyptian" and "If Moses Was an
Egyptian," appeared in 1937. But the third and last—and most controversial—part, "Moses, His People, and Monotheistic Religion," was
withheld from publication for fear that the powerful Austrian Catholic
Church would take umbrage at its irreligious audacity and manage to
get it banned. In 1938, Freud was forced to flee Austria because of the
Nazi annexation, and sought refuge in England. The next year, already
terminally ill with cancer, he added this third part and published the
work as a whole. He died later that year.

It was hardly what Jakob Freud had had in mind, however. Rather
than being nourished by the Bible's own "wellsprings," *Moses and Monotheism* applied Freud's earlier theory of religion in general to Judaism in
particular—with shocking results.

In an earlier book, *The Future of an Illusion* (1927), Freud had
already analyzed religion as a consequence of the human need to control our instinctual drives: unable to provide immediate gratification,

we divert our energy into artistic and cultural constructs that provide at least narcissistic satisfaction. Religion further provides an ethical construct to justify our instinctual self-denial, largely through the illusion of an omnipotent God who punishes us for moral lapses. Such an image of God would never have occurred to us, Freud was certain, had we not experienced a potentially tyrannical father in our infancy— making religion not just an illusion but a childish one at that. Religion is doomed in the long run, because we cannot help but grow up and discover that good people suffer, evildoers prosper, and there simply is no all-powerful God taking care of us.

Freud's reference to the childhood origin of religious belief harks back to two of his earlier works, the 1907 monograph "Obsessive Actions and Religious Practices" that compares religion to an obsessive-compulsive neurosis, and an expansion on that theme, *Totem and Taboo* (1913). Freud had read Darwin's description of the dawn of the human species in a primeval horde (not unlike a wolf pack). He was also familiar with anthropological studies of totemistic tribes who claimed descent from an animal ancestor and erected taboos against sexual relations with anyone in their tribe. They never ate the animal corresponding to their mythological animal ancestor, except on rare occasions when they had a feast specifically dedicated to it.

With all of this in mind, Freud described his original notion of the Oedipal complex not simply as a feature of individual human psychology, but as the primal event in the formation of the human species. He pictured the chief male of the original human horde as contending with his sons for sexual favors from the females. The sons eventually murdered and ate their father, but overcome with guilt, they then projected the love for their father onto a putative animal ancestor, which they worshipped and obsessively avoided eating—except at religious feasts that replicated the primal sin of consuming the real father.

God is the *human* projection of the father we once ate, said Freud, outfitted with appropriate anger and punishing power. Ethics are the means by which we avoid succumbing to basic instincts. Religious ritual channels base desires into acceptable avenues of expression—a religious feast, say, instead of patricide. "God" is an illusion; and religion is saturated with obsessive-compulsive behavior, for which we ought to seek a psychological cure.

Freud presupposed all of this in his final major work, on Moses. He marveled at the obsessive preservation of Judaism, despite centuries of persecution. The secret, he thought, must lie in its religious essence—

religion as an obsessive reaction to the primal sin of patricide. It followed that Moses must have been such a primal father, slain by his people, who then passed on their guilt from generation to generation. As an avid reader of everything scientific, Freud had also studied Christian scholarship that attributed monotheism not to Moses but to the Jewish prophets who lived several centuries later. In Freud's understanding, by the time of the prophets, the accumulated burden of patricide guilt must have become too much to bear. The prophetic insistence on a single, all-powerful, and jealous God must have arisen out of the repressed memory of having murdered Moses, the primal father of the Jewish People.

Moses and Monotheism is bad history and questionable psychology. It has exercised no influence on Jews, most of whom have never even read it. But it stands out as a singular statement about Judaism by one of the supreme geniuses of modern times, a striking example of the Jewish ambivalence shared by many intellectual figures of the time. Like so many accomplished Jews, Freud had achieved intellectual fame, but anti-Semitism prevented his being accepted as a social equal among his cultural and scientific peers. In addition, Freud worried about the future of the science he had invented, psychoanalysis. Almost all its practitioners, and even most of its patients, were Jews. He was therefore concerned that it would be ignored in the broader scientific community because it would be pigeonholed (anti-Semitically) as a "Jewish science." So he regularly downplayed his own Jewishness.

But Freud was more Jewish than he let on. In his masterful study *Freud's Moses*, historian Yosef Yerushalmi demonstrates that Freud knew enough Hebrew to be able to read the flowery inscription that his father had written in his Bible. He even gave his dog a Hebrew name. His social circle in Vienna was almost entirely Jewish, and he belonged to B'nai B'rith, the Jewish men's club that had been established in 1843.

Sigmund Freud remains an enigma: a debunker of Jewish faith and practice, but a proud Jew nonetheless. In a preface added to the 1930 Hebrew translation of *Totem and Taboo*, he confessed to being "an author who is [. . .] completely estranged from the religion of his fathers [. . .] but who has yet never repudiated his people, who feels that he is in his essential nature a Jew and who has no desire to alter that nature." He continues to turn up regularly in Jewish conversation, and remains among the plethora of geniuses whom Judaism has bequeathed to the world.

My Life as a Radical Jewish Woman
(1954)

Puah Rakovsky (1865–1955)

"On the Days of Awe, I went to the women's shul, where I was accepted as a firzogerin [a prayer leader] for the women who couldn't read by themselves. At that time, when I was thirteen, an absurd idea suddenly was born in me: is there a God or not? That is what I wanted to find out, no more no less."

Imagine a woman raised in practically medieval conditions in Poland—a "simple Jewish girl from a good Jewish home" (as Paula Hyman, the editor of *My Life*, describes her) "whose one and only function was to sit and wait for a bridegroom." She somehow breaks free and fights for women's rights decades before the word "feminism" is even invented. She creates the first "revolution" on the "Jewish street," founding a Jewish girls' school in Warsaw and a national Jewish women's organization, while becoming a committed Zionist and socialist. After experiencing the worst anti-Jewish riots of eastern Europe, however—first the aftermath of World War I, and then the violence associated with Hitler's accession to power—she moves to Palestine in 1935, and dies there twenty years later, when she is ninety. Imagine all that, and you have the life of Puah Rakovsky.

Rakovsky's recollections are worth reading just for her account of the traditional Jewish shackles against which modern Jews in eastern Europe rebelled. Here was a world where girls were married off at age thirteen or fourteen and had children a year or two later; where, as late as 1897, about 60 percent of Jewish women in Russia were illiterate; and where mothers bore children every other year for two decades or more, so that grandchildren might easily be older than their own uncles and aunts.

That was the case with fourteen-year old Puah, whose family could look back on over thirty generations of rabbis! She fell in love with her uncle, who was barely older than her, but she had already been promised (without her knowledge) to a stranger. As she put it, "The atavism of enslaved Jewish women had its effect upon me." Forced into marriage, she had the temerity to demand a divorce—something women never did. When her husband refused to grant it, even her own parents supported his decision.

In classical Jewish law, women who cannot obtain a divorce from their recalcitrant husbands may never marry again. For many Jews nowadays, Jewish legal practice manages to get around all this, but in Puah's time, there was no way out. So she makes the ultimate threat: if she is not divorced, she will renounce her faith, taking her children with her. Now her husband relents, but she still cannot marry her uncle, because he is a *kohen*, a descendant of biblical priests, and the Bible forbids marriage between a kohen and a divorcee! Her uncle tires of challenging public mores and marries someone else.

By then, however, Rakovsky has moved on. As a teenager, she has already "come to the conclusion that God does not exist [. . .] and stopped praying three times a day." With time, "I had become a terrible heretic, had thrown away my wig [married women were forbidden to show their hair in public], and had a non-kosher kitchen." She is a freethinker who, everyone suspects, will soon leave Judaism altogether.

Rakovsky was hardly abandoning Judaism, however, much less the Jewish People, whose cause she would champion for the rest of her life. She had indeed left traditionalist Judaism behind, but only to personify the stormy world of modern Judaism in search of itself.

Much of Poland was then part of czarist Russia, which had established public schools to which Jews were admitted, in the hope that they might become assimilated. Rakovsky became a teacher for such a school, and, for the rest of her life, remained a passionate educator. As one would expect, she read widely—she was thoroughly familiar with Marx and Freud, for example, and was at home not just in Yiddish, Polish, Russian, and Hebrew, but also in French and German.

Puah Rakovsky was not the only woman in her family to become a professional—two of her sisters became dentists (which was surprisingly commonplace for women then). Nor was she the only female socialist voice in a movement that prided itself on classlessness. But no one yet imagined women among the pioneers of Jewish Palestine. Leadership in early settlement movements, according to Rakovsky, was actually "closed to women." But she broke through the barriers even there. She attended annual Zionist congresses, and she provided personal observations about their founders: Herzl, for example, was so inherently shy that at gatherings he sometimes "simply escaped and hid."

No one rivals Rakovsky's personal prophetic vision and projects designed to raise the status of other women. She cannot abide the "Jewish girls" who "sit and wait for a bridegroom," or the prevailing bourgeois notion that working women are an embarrassment. A common couplet of the time typified this chauvinistic attitude: "The nursery rhyme, 'Who will sew?' / Sarahke the seamstress, lower than the low."

Through it all, Rakovsky never forgets that she is a mother, grand-mother, sister, and daughter. She worries endlessly about family mat-ters, especially keeping her children with her as her career advances. A sister commits suicide, and when one of her own daughters dies in childbirth, she accepts the "new obligation to take care of three orphan" grandchildren. When her son insists on settling in the newly created Soviet Union, she visits him, and reports positively on what she finds there. Those are, of course, the years before Stalin, who later bans her from revisiting the Soviet Union because she translates Trotsky's *Life* into Yiddish. She is cut off even from receiving letters from her aspiring communist son.

Paula Hyman, a superb scholar of modern Jewish history, provides a wonderful introduction to Rakovsky's life. "The Jewish population [of Russia] had mushroomed from 1.6 million in 1825 to more than 5 million in 1897, even though almost half a million Jews had left czarist Russia in the last three decades of the century." In the Bialystok of Puah's birth, "Jews accounted for more than 2/3 of its population of some 14,000. As the city industrialized and grew to having a population of close to 70,000 by the end of the century, Jews maintained their proportion of the total." In retrospect, Jewish life was about to shrink dramatically, of course. Czarist persecution, World War I and its anti-Semitic aftermath, the Russian Revolution, Stalinist purges, Jewish emigration, and Hitler's "Final Solution" all contributed to relegating eastern European Jewry to a set of memories.

It is hard to imagine circumstances where it might have worked out differently. But Puah Rakovsky prefigured what Jewish life might become despite the Nazi devastation, for people like Puah would persist in dreaming a better future. She embodied the Jewish faith in education, advancement, and freedom. She personified the accomplishment of women in particular. And she pushed the Jewish conversation in ways that never could have been imagined before her.

Poems
(1891–1934)

Hayyim Nahman Bialik (1873–1934)

"The sun has disappeared from behind the treetops. / Come, let us go to meet the Sabbath Queen. / For she is descending, holy and blessed, / Accompanied by angels of peace and of rest."

When it comes to modern Hebrew poets, it has been said that there is Bialik, and then there is everyone else. Not that "everyone else" wouldn't include other fine poets. But for insight, artistry, and influence, no one matches Hayyim Nahman Bialik, who bridged the critical years between the dying traditional world of the eastern European ghetto and the birth of a modern Jewish state. His poetry has since proven timeless.

Bialik was born in a corner of the Old World, the poor Polish province of Volhynia (then part of Russia), where Hasidic masters spoke Yiddish and reserved Hebrew for prayer; but he made his way to a new world, the future State of Israel, where Hebrew would become the national language, and Bialik the Jewish People's unofficial poet laureate.

Bialik's father, an impoverished barkeeper, died when Hayyim was six, and his mother, too poor to keep him, handed him over to his paternal grandfather. Early years were spent in traditional yeshivah studies, but in 1891 he moved to Odessa, the hub of modern Jewish writing at the time. At first, he says, "Starved and tormented, I lived in cellars with victims of tuberculosis." But his reputation grew, and eventually he encountered Ahad Ha-am, whose prophetic demand for a revival of Jewish creativity became Bialik's lifetime calling. He lived for a while in Warsaw, spent some time in Berlin (where he cofounded a publishing company), and moved to Palestine in 1924.

Bialik internalized his era's passionate debate over the Jewish future, becoming the poetic voice of all its aspects. His earliest Hebrew poem, "To the Bird" (1891), announced his generation's yearning to settle in the Land of Israel. "Do you bring news of peace from the land's great bounty, / From the plains, from the valleys, from the hills, from the caves? / Has God shown His mercy and comforted Zion? / Or is she abandoned and still filled with graves?"

Two years before he died, he composed "To Work," a paean to the Zionist faith in labor—draining swamps, clearing fields, and planting gardens of plenty. "Who planted trees on the plains / For fruit and for shade again and again, / And in the fields sowed grain? / Whom to thank? Whom to bless? / Work and industriousness!"

Even though Bialik lived and breathed the hope for a Jewish cultural renaissance in the Land of Israel, he was also an appreciative witness to the traditional world that he had grown up in. He memorialized the shtetls of eastern Europe, for example, where kabbalists rose at midnight to pray for redemption. But his recollections could be devastating as well. From his own youth, he knew the life of the yeshivah student, shut away from the sun, steeped in holy texts not only as if nothing else mattered but as if nothing else even existed. His picture of a *matmid* (meaning, "perpetual"), the perpetual student of Torah, captures perfectly the way Talmudic excellence was then assumed to demand sacrifice of all that is normal in human life—family, love, nature, everything that others take for granted. Contemplating that world's sense of complete dependency, as opposed to the Zionists' emphasis on taking charge of their own affairs, he proclaimed, "We are heroes! / The last generation of slaves, the first to be free."

Bialik is especially known as the poetic voice that memorialized the 1903 pogrom in the city of Kishinev, not far from Odessa. Violence erupted at Easter time, when a Christian child was found murdered. It later turned out that the culprit was a family member, but the first and automatic response was the ancient so-called blood libel—the claim that Jews would kill Christian children to use their blood for Passover. A *New York Times* correspondent described the 1903 carnage that, to Bialik, epitomized Jewish helplessness: "The anti-Jewish riots in Kishinev, Bessarabia, are worse than the censor will permit to publish. There was a well laid-out plan for the general massacre of Jews on the day following the Russian Easter. The mob was led by priests, and the general cry, 'Kill the Jews,' was taken up all over the city. The Jews were taken wholly unaware and were slaughtered like sheep. The dead number 120 and the injured about 500. The scenes of horror attending this massacre are beyond description. Babes were literally torn to pieces by the frenzied and bloodthirsty mob. The local police made no attempt to check the reign of terror."

Bialik responded with two of his most famous Hebrew poems, "On the Slaughter" and "In the City of Slaughter." In the first, he addresses heaven, charging, "O Heaven, beg mercy on my behalf. / Is God among you, and are you around Him? / For I have not found Him [. . .] In eternal wickedness let Heaven rot." In the second poem, he turns his attention to the limitations of Old World Jewish culture that allowed Jews to go to their slaughter so easily. "Your slain were slain for nothing," he contends, "Your deaths devoid of purpose, and devoid of purpose your lives, too."

Bialik wrote his own epitaph in 1904: "After my death say this of me: / There was a man—and look! He is no more. / He died before his time, this man, / His life's music and verse cut short. / A pity! He had one more song. / And now that song is lost forever, / Forever lost." Indeed, Bialik's lifetime poetic output, though substantial, was not enormous. Yet he wrote enough to testify to the many sides of the Jewish soul that he loved so much.

In 1908, his love for tradition even drew him back to his youthful days in a traditional yeshivah, where he had mastered the vast corpus of rabbinic law and lore. Anxious to guarantee its availability to generations of readers who would never have access to rabbinic sources directly, he coedited *Sefer Ha-aggadah* (*The Book of Legends*), a magisterial compendium of Talmudic and midrashic tales.

Still, it is Bialik the poet whom Jews remember most. Like no one else, he gave poetic voice to the aspirations of the Jewish People arising out of its age-old history on one hand and the persecutions of Bialik's time on the other. Yet his poems speak to more than Jews alone, for they testify to the ordinary love that every human being is capable of, the universal heartbeat of the soul that poets have eternalized from the beginning of time.

Why I Am a Jew
(1927)

Edmond Fleg (1874–1963)

"As for me, my child, who have so long sought for the evidence of the existence of God, I have found it in the existence of Israel."

Few people felt the pulse of the late nineteenth and early twentieth centuries more than Edmond Fleg. According to Stephen S. Wise, one of the great leaders of American Judaism and of the Zionist cause in the first half of the twentieth century, Fleg epitomized "Westernized, de-ghettoized Jews who think as humans, philosophize as Westerners, [and] feel as Jews."

Fleg was all of that. Born Edmond Flegenheimer in Geneva, he grew up as an assimilated Swiss-French intellectual—with a bent toward humanism at the expense of a Jewish identity so attenuated as to be all but invisible. He had been raised in a Jewish home where "the blessing after meals seemed as much a necessity as the meal itself," and where the meal was "altogether kosher"—but in public, the Fleg family ate non-kosher food, and eventually, Jewish observance at home slipped away, too.

While attending university in Geneva, the breadth and depth of Western civilization convinced young Edmond of Judaism's irrelevance. His father actually read and understood Hebrew, calling it "a beautiful language"—in Edmond's view an absurd judgment, given the magisterial complexity of Latin. It also didn't help that his rabbi doubled as professor of comparative philology at the university, preferring his academic over his spiritual calling. Nor was Fleg impressed by the "grotesque pictures" provided by iconoclastic Jewish humor, such as the story of Moses playing cards with the Almighty and pleading, "Please, God, no miracles."

Before long, Fleg became entranced by the Gospels, which he welcomed as a profound "revelation of suffering." He would have converted to Christianity, had he been able to embrace the doctrine of God becoming human. Unable to do so, but equally alienated from the Judaism of his youth, he took his intellectual doubts directly to God. He discovered that in "my nightly conversations with God [. . .] the words, 'Reveal Thyself if Thou art,' which I formerly repeated in my agony, were no longer a prayer; they were a summons [. . .] Then, giving up the effort to obtain speech from the non-existent, I abandoned Him." Proud of his philosophical knowledge, ashamed of his Jewishness, but too "rational" to be a Christian, Fleg settled for a philosophical potpourri of deistic universalism, which gradually deteriorated into the skeptical nihilism typical of the aesthetic movement at the time, an intellectual trend that abandoned certitude of knowledge and even of ethics. He later castigated his certainty that there were no certainties, calling it philosophical "dilettantism" designed to indulge his chief pleasure, "to admire myself." But that judgment came only when the forces of history had awakened Fleg, the adult, to the realization that he had rejected God and allowed "the inmost voice of my people to grow silent within me."

Despite his foray into aestheticism, Fleg was attracted to liberal universalism, the assumption that the world would move steadily toward peace and justice for all. This love affair with liberalism was part and parcel of the times. Following Napoleon, France had gone through a dizzying spiral of republics, monarchies, and even empires, culminating in yet another republic (the third) as a reaction to the Prussian occupation of Paris in 1871. Its liberalism tempted not just Fleg, but Jewish intellectuals in general, the most famous being Émile Durkheim (1858–1917), a founder of modern sociology.

This liberal reverie was shattered in 1894, when, as we saw, the French Jew and army officer Captain Alfred Dreyfus (1859–1935) was tried on the trumped-up charge of treason. Despite ample evidence of his innocence, Dreyfus was pronounced guilty and locked away in a cell on Devil's Island (French Guiana), where he almost died. Anti-Dreyfus—anti-Semitic—demonstrators charged Jews with plotting every tragic defeat in the story of Christian Europe.

Dreyfus was the pawn in a much larger political chess game: an alliance of reactionary monarchists, the military, and the Catholic Church to reinstate old values. When liberal forces finally prevailed, and Dreyfus was released from prison in 1899, Durkheim returned to his university classroom as if nothing had happened. Fleg, however, judged the vaunted French liberalism a farce.

Awakened now to his Jewish identity, Fleg met "the beacon light" of Zionism and its "new prophet," Theodor Herzl. "I admired in these Zionists what I wished I could admire in myself," Fleg wrote, "fidelity to an ancestral soil that had endured two thousand years." Attending the

Third Zionist Congress, in Basel, in 1899, Fleg became convinced that he "was a Jew, essentially a Jew." But knowing himself as well to be "of France, a Frenchman," he sought the secret to living proudly as a Jew in the Diaspora.

For the next three years, he abandoned his growing career as an author and playwright, and turned to the study of Hebrew and Jewish texts—not just the Bible and the Talmud, but medieval philosophy and Kabbalah, too. "Monotheism and messianism" became the dual watchwords of his rediscovered faith. Proudly Jewish but no less a universalist than ever, Fleg saw it as his destiny to "unite my race with all humanity."

He fought in the trenches of the Great War and came to see "the wandering Jew" as symbolic of the pain and tragedy that the war had meted out to mothers of sons on both sides of the battlefield. Anti-Semitic outbreaks in newly nationalized countries like Poland and Romania only furthered Fleg's belief that Jews were somehow meant to mark the premessianic era by symptomatic wandering and persecution. But more and more, Israel's eternal message was being carried also by other civilized peoples, who, together with the Jewish People, would realize the world's messianic destiny.

Fleg's book ends with a litany of affirmations that have proved so moving through the years that they tend to be repeated not just in literary anthologies but even in prayer books, where they are recited as virtual creeds of Jewish faith. "I am a Jew," he says, "because the faith of Israel requires of me all the devotion of my heart. I am a Jew because in every place where suffering weeps, the Jew weeps. I am a Jew because at every time when despair cries out, the Jew hopes." These, and similar sentiments, are what Fleg is best known for. But they are only a tiny part of a much larger work, one of the most compelling accounts we have of an alienated Jew's thought-provoking return to Jewish tradition.

Fleg dedicated *Why I Am a Jew* "to you, my grandson who are not yet born," still a fiction of his imagination, since his sons at the time were only nineteen and fourteen. He wondered, therefore, "When will you be born? In ten years, perhaps fifteen . . . When will you read what I here set down?" Did he even have grandchildren who read, valued, and saved their grandfather's account, committed to passing it on to *their* grandchildren as an everlasting legacy from generation to generation? We do not know—Fleg's biographers do not tell us. What we can say, however, is that Fleg's *literary* legacy has been adopted by the entire Jewish People, and is well incorporated, by now, into the Jewish conversation of the ages.

The Jewish Gauchos of the Pampas
(1910)

Alberto Gerchunoff (1883–1950)

"There are fierce arrogant Gauchos, wife-stealers, and Camachos, as well as the most learned of rabbinic scholars in the little Jewish colony where I learned to love the Argentine sky and felt a part of its wonderful earth. The story I've told—with more detail than art—is a true one."

This lyric and at times messianic collection of short stories opens with Rabbi Jehuda Anakroi's stirring words to the Jews in Tulchin, a shtetl in czarist Russia—and the town where Alberto Gerchunoff was born, which he still remembers as having "a permanent cover of snow and an equally permanent program of harassment by the neighboring Cossacks."

"You'll see! You'll see!" Anakroi promises, "All of you! It's a country where everyone works the land where the Christians will not hate us, because there the sky is bright and clear, and under its lights only mercy and justice can thrive." He does not mean the Land of Israel, however, but Argentina, the locus of an ambitious settlement program designed by the philanthropist Baron Maurice de Hirsch of Paris. Baron de Hirsch, however, was just half of the equation. The other half was the welcome proffered by the Argentine government, which had plenty of empty land to fill and a constitution that guaranteed religious freedom. The Argentine offer coincided with the czarist land restrictions under the May Laws of 1882.

And that is how Gerchunoff's Jews remember arriving in Argentina. With 250,000 Jews, the country today has the third-largest Jewish population in the Americas, behind the United States and Canada.

We are familiar with the classic tales of cowboys who roamed the American Wild West. The Argentine grasslands, known as the pampas (plains), had their own version: the gauchos. By 1889, when the Jews of Gerchunoff's narrative began arriving, the classic gaucho was disappearing, as the pampas were increasingly parceled into "neat little farms." Many gauchos were forced to seek work as farmhands, or as independent farmers alongside their Jewish neighbors. In the book, Don Remigio, a member of this dying gaucho breed, tells stories of the old days "bursting with life and danger," when a man could even "engage in a little bit of crime." Gerchunoff sought, through his literature, to cloak Argentinian Jews in the idealized mantle of the gaucho persona that he was hearing so much about.

Gerchunoff had left Russia as a child, and his family settled in the Argentine province of Entre Rios (north of Buenos Aires), first in Moisesville, a farm colony named after Baron de Hirsch's son, in gratitude to the great man who had made the Argentine "Palestine" possible—for that is how the Jewish settlers thought of it: their own Zion. While still a boy, Gerchunoff's family moved to a second settlement nearby, Rajil, where the action of *The Jewish Gauchos* takes place.

But "action" may be too strong a word. Stylistically, Gerchunoff is a modernist for whom plot is secondary to ambience, a feel for the colony's cast of characters, whose interior life comes alive in the series of vignettes that constitute the book's successive chapters. Favel Duglach, for example, is the resident poet "who never missed a rodeo"; and Dr. Yarcho mesmerizes his patients' imagination with wisdom he never learned in medical school. "Does the moon ever fall?" asks fifteen-year-old Jacobo, the orphan boy of the colony. "It falls into the Parana every morning," the doctor explains, "and just before the stars come out at night, the Fisherman upstairs picks it out and rolls it into the sky."

The gauchos whom the Jews encounter specialize in "country aphorisms [and] properly vulgar curses." They chew tobacco, live mostly in the saddle, and use their knives to fight duels. But their "valiant barbarous spirit" comes with "tenderness of love"—an attractive combination for young Jewish women who find life with them an alternative to the traditionalist female role that the colonies seek to retain. Having known nothing of romance from the Old Country, Jewish parents still try to arrange marriages for their daughters—as if this is still Russia! Miryam, the daughter of Don Jacobo, runs off with Rogelio Miguez, because "they could understand each other in song"—Rogelio's "thrilling vidalitas" (Argentine folk songs) and Miryam's Jewish responses.

The cult of the gaucho attracts Jewish boys, too: Jacobo wears "wide gaucho trousers [. . .] a shining dagger, and a small lead-weighted boleadoras, the native lariat." His grandmother despairs: "Look at him! The complete Gaucho—those awful pants, the belt, the knife, and even those little lead things to kill partridges with."

Jacobo is playacting. For the Jews in Argentina, gauchoism is just symbolic of the need to acculturate and belong—the exact opposite of the persecution that characterized Jewish life in eastern Europe.

Even soothing memories of the golden age of Spanish Jewry are denied these Spanish-speaking Argentinian Jews, because of the Inquisition that ended Jewish life there. "May Spain sink into the sea," says Rabbi Anakroi. "May she break into pieces [. . .] as a punishment for having tortured our brothers and burned our rabbis."

Looking for heroes, the Jews of Argentina hark anxiously back to the biblical days of David and Solomon. But they also embrace the gauchos. As Duglach, the poet, puts it, "I admire the Gauchos as much as I admire the ancient Hebrews. The Gauchos are patriarchal and noble."

But the admiration for the gauchos is not altogether shared. Miryam, after all, rode off with one, as did an unnamed daughter of Reb Ismael. The first generation of settlers may have become farmers, but they still work at being Jewish—they keep Shabbat, attend synagogue, and honor Jewish tradition. It is the second generation that falls in love with the gaucho alternative. The Jewish parents are caught in a bind. Having adopted their beloved Argentina as a new Zion, they cannot easily dismiss the idealized gaucho tradition—yet they would never want to lead a gaucho's life. The problem is their children would.

Immigrant groups rarely rejoice in their children's wholesale rejection of the Old World in favor of models drawn from the new land that promises freedom. But does that freedom ever really pan out? For Jews in Argentina, it has been a mixed story so far. In 1919, a government-backed pogrom erupted in Buenos Aires, and during the presidency of Juan Perón (1946–1955), Argentina became a favorite hideaway for Nazis escaping arrest by the allies (Adolf Eichmann, for example; see page 201). In the 1950s and 1960s, fascist street fighters vandalized Argentinian Jewish cemeteries and synagogues, and from 1976 to 1983, a ruling military junta targeted some 2,000 Jews for arrest and torture. With the return to democracy under President Carlos Menem in 1989, security for Argentine Jews returned, but these Jews are ardent Zionists who remain on guard and who hold strongly to the ideal of aliyah to Israel.

The Brothers Ashkenazi
(1936)
Israel Joshua Singer (1893–1944)

"A thick mist had descended from the skies over Lodz. A wind rose and blew the dust of the cemetery in the eyes of the mourners. Heavily and slowly, like the rolling mists above them, they turned back to the desolate city. 'Sand,' they muttered, covering their eyes with their hands. 'Everything we have built we built on sand.'"

In the end, eastern European Jews were murdered by Hitler. But the Jewish *society* called Eastern European Jewry did not have to wait that long. It had been under attack for almost half a century before Hitler arrived on the scene. Who was the culprit? The czars? The communists who replaced them? The Great War? Post–World War I nationalism? Just plain poverty and disease?

Tragically, the answer is "all of the above," each one intricately intertwined with the larger history of eastern Europe that was one major, protracted conflict for territory, prestige, and power. The battle centered on greater Poland, which found itself wedged between European superpowers, and between medievalism and modernity, still fighting it out for dominance.

No single work illustrates this enormous tension better than Israel Joshua Singer's *The Brothers Ashkenazi*, a novel of Tolstoyan majesty written originally in Yiddish. Its focus is the city of Lodz, which the Industrial Revolution had made into the textile capital of eastern Europe. From a population of 13,000 in 1840, Lodz grew to 500,000 in 1914; by then, some 40 percent of the city's inhabitants were Jews, most of them impoverished workers.

The central protagonists of the novel, which spans the late nineteenth and early twentieth centuries, are the twin brothers Simcha and Jacob Ashkenazi, modern stand-ins for the Bible's Jacob and Esau. The biblical Jacob was the quiet one—a scholar, in rabbinic lore; but also the conniver and business genius who stole Esau's birthright and blessing. Esau was the handsome, virile hunter whose physical endowment won him his fortune. Instead of Jacob, *The Brothers Ashkenazi* gives us modern-day Simcha Meyer Ashkenazi, the scholar turned capitalist; and in place of

Esau, we get (ironically) Jacob Bunim Ashkenazi, graced only with good looks and enough sheer luck to attract the love of the city's wealthiest eligible daughter. Simcha, by contrast, makes his money the hard way, marrying the daughter of the pious Reb Abraham Hirsch, then working his way up the ladder of Reb Abraham's textile factory—until he cuts corners and eventually steals the plant from his unsuspecting father-in-law, whom he puts out to pasture. Known now as Max (a Europeanized version of the traditional Hebrew name), Simcha Meyer abandons his studies and his morals, wishing only to make a killing in the marketplace.

The Jewish workers whom Max exploits are "pious people, convinced of their own unimportance," and the system that enmeshes them is insidious. "The more skillful workers bullied the weaker ones, the accepted weavers tormented the apprentices [. . .] Every worker who had passed through the hell of an apprenticeship relished the idea of inflicting these sufferings on another." These, moreover, are the handloom workers, all of them about to be displaced by the advent of factories with steam-powered looms and a workweek that includes the Sabbath—conditions that further dismantle the old religious way of life.

Revolution arrives in the form of two traditionalists turned socialists, Nissan and Tevyeh, who are workers themselves and champions of the proletariat. When Max cuts worker salaries to maximize profit by a few more kopecks, Tevyeh quotes chapter and verse to convince his fellow workers of the justice of their cause. "Stand together," he pleads. "Bring them [the owners] to their knees, the dirty thieves." Max consults with Lippe Chalfan, a Lithuanian Jew who had "worked his way in among lower Russian officials and found out who took graft easiest and where it went furthest." Lippe reports the socialist troublemakers to the authorities, and in time, Nissan is carried off to a Siberian prison. But he returns—with a vengeance, at a time when Max has practically left Judaism altogether, and settled in the interior of Russia as a privileged Jewish industrial magnate.

Israel Joshua Singer's major preoccupation was the class struggle with which he personally engaged for most of his life. His better-known younger brother, Isaac Bashevis Singer, retained affection for the religious milieu in which he was raised. Israel, by contrast, could not bring himself to romanticize "the stench of religion," as he remembered it. After turning first to the Haskalah movement, he embraced hopes for a proletarian revolution. By 1922, however, his observation of the early Bolshevik state purged him of the belief that a socialist society would herald good news for modern Jews.

The Brothers Ashkenazi is both historical and autobiographical fiction. It chronicles its author's disgust with traditionalist religion that held Jews back from enjoying what modernity had to offer—and his equal antipathy to the socialist reality that took its place. None of the characters here are happy; and few of them are likeable. The most appealing turns out to be Jacob Bunim, also known as Yakob. Compared to Max, we hear little of Yakob, who turns up mostly as a profligate libertine, cheating on his wife and mishandling his business. But he is spared the pain of being a disillusioned ideologue! When Max is jailed inside Russia as a capitalist speculator and left to die in prison, "muttering the Psalms to himself, remembering them out of his boyhood years," Yakob emerges out of nowhere to save him. "For the first time in his life, Max felt the sensation of shame [. . .] All his life he had foolishly considered Yakob a brainless, feckless, incompetent trifler. He saw before him a man of character, imagination and daring."

But Singer's pessimism about any Jewish future in either nationalist Poland or communist Russia is eventually projected onto Yakob, who escapes the communists with Max only to be accosted by a Polish gendarme who taunts the two brothers to yell, "To Hell with the Yids," and orders them to "give us a little dance and song to entertain our soldier boys here." Max is a survivor; he obeys, "twisting and turning until he collapsed on the floor covered with perspiration." Not so Yakob, whom the gendarme kills. Ever the industrialist, Max rebuilds his factory, although joylessly, and dies penniless in the Great Depression, reading the biblical book of Job and recalling how Job "cursed the day he was born."

The Jewish future, in any case, lies elsewhere, we are led to believe—maybe in Palestine, where the Zionists have headed. But the novel came out in 1936, when a Jewish state was still, at best, an idealist's dream. Singer himself migrated in 1933 to America, not to Palestine. Perhaps he had encountered enough failed idealism in his day to be suspicious of anything wrapped in glory for the future. He lived long enough to see Hitler; but not long enough to see the State of Israel demonstrate that some dreams can actually come true.

The Complete Works of Isaac Babel

(2002)

Isaac Babel (1894–1940)

"I have a family: a wife and daughter [. . .] They must remain here [in Paris]
in freedom. But what about myself? Should I stay here and become [a] taxi
driver? [. . .] Should I return to our proletarian revolution? Revolution
indeed! It's disappeared! The proletariat? It flew off, like an old buggy with
a leaky roof, that's lost its wheels [. . .] Here a taxi driver has more freedom
than the rector of a Soviet university."

These are Isaac Babel's words from a conversation he had in 1932 in Paris with a friend, Yuri Annenkov, who had left the fledgling USSR in 1924. Babel had traveled from Moscow to Paris to visit his first wife and daughter, who, like Annenkov, had settled there, but shortly thereafter Babel returned to Russia, telling Annenkov that he had been called back "in the most dramatic conditions and no money and a lot of debts everywhere." Still, he insisted, "I'm glad that I am going to Moscow," even though "all the rest is bitter and uncertain." In 1939, Babel disappeared, a Stalinist secret, blotted out of official memory until 1954, when it was revealed that he had been arrested as part of Stalin's Great Purge.

Babel was but one of Stalin's Jewish victims. A host of Soviet-Jewish writers were killed from the mid-1930s to the 1950s, including Pinchus Kahanovich (1884–1950), a novelist trained in Kabbalah who went by the Yiddish pen name Der Nister (The Hidden One); the poet-playwright Peretz Markish (1895–1952), who had once been in political favor and won the coveted Stalin Prize for literature; and the novelist-essayist David Bergelson (1884–1952).

The purge began in 1936, by which time Stalin's criteria for literary excellence had no room for anything other than "socialist realism," portraits of the world that honey-coated his own leadership. Troublemaking, truth-telling Isaac Babel was a natural target. Born in Odessa, he moved to St. Petersburg in 1916, and joined the communist cause— serving as a military correspondent in the Russian civil war between Bolsheviks (the Reds) and Mensheviks (the Whites) in 1919, and the war with Poland the year after. But he always lived on the edge. His fictionalized account of the fighting, *The Red Cavalry Stories* (1926), which made him famous, included the actual names of the Soviet military commanders Budyonny and Timoshenko, who later achieved positions of power and were not thrilled to read what Babel had written about them. He was able to survive this first bout with authority just by publishing an official apology, because his literary hero and protector, Maxim Gorky, came to his defense. But Gorky himself died under suspicious circumstances in 1936; and three years later, Babel was arrested, imprisoned, tortured, and eventually executed.

The *Red Cavalry Stories* were based on Babel's wartime diary, and then supplemented by additional stories titled *The Red Cavalry Cycle* and *The Red Cavalryman: Articles*. The collection mixes the twisted fantasy of wartime humor with graphic descriptions of wartime cruelty. One of the articles, "Murderers Who Have Yet to Be Clubbed to Death," is an eyewitness account of what remained after an organized slaughter of Jews by the Whites: "Seventy-year-old men with crushed skulls lay naked in pools of blood, infants, often still alive, with fingers hacked off, and old women, raped, their stomachs slashed open, crouched in corners." Even "our [own] soldiers, who have seen a thing or two in their time and have been known to chop off quite a few heads, staggered in horror at what they saw."

This is not Babel's only reference to the victimization of Jews, whom Whites suspected of being accomplices of the Reds, and whom Poles treated as alien threats to the purity of Polish nationalism. In the first of the *Red Cavalry Stories*, a Jewish woman in Novograd points to her murdered father, whose "gullet has been ripped out, his face hacked in two," explaining, "the Poles were hacking him to death and he kept begging them, 'Kill me in the backyard so my daughter won't see me die!' But they wouldn't inconvenience themselves. He died in this room, thinking of me."

It is hard to say which trauma the Jews found worst: to die just by inhabiting the frontier between Russia and Germany and their back-and-forth troop movements from 1914 to 1917; to be slaughtered by the Whites after 1917, for supposedly siding with the Reds; to be murdered after 1918 by Polish nationalists; or, if they really were indeed Reds, to be turned upon by Stalin in 1936 and after.

Babel was far from being a Jewish parochial, however. Although he received a traditional Jewish education in Talmud, the Jewish intellectual life of Odessa—where he studied music, literature, and finance—made him a true universalist. His fictionalized stories, written in Russian—

better described as vignettes, some of them just one or two pages long—reflect his real-life experience on the front, where cruelty disguised as heroism affected everyone in sight, not just Jews. Anelya, a nurse, offers herself as a prostitute to an anarchist militia, since "I have three children to feed; it's not like I'm a virgin or something." A White soldier "hacks" his son to pieces because he has sided with the Reds. Babel's own army specializes in "making mincemeat of the Poles." These are horrific accounts that inscribe themselves on a reader's conscience.

Even though the *Red Cavalry Stories* are Babel's best-known work, he wrote much more than that. If his war stories picture Jews as victims, his *Odessa Stories* give us Benya Krik, a Jewish gangster worthy of Damon Runyon, and a supporting cast that includes people with unlikely names such as Tartakovsky the "Yid-and-a-Half." When an anti-Semitic gang of Odessa thugs beats up on Jews, the followers of Tartakovsky pretend to bury him in a local cemetery. The casket is really filled with machine guns, which they turn on the unsuspecting thugs.

What makes this volume especially moving is that it was edited by Babel's daughter Nathalie (1929–2005), who remained in Paris with her mother when her father returned to the Soviet Union, and who later found her way to America. Her Afterword describes her life through the Nazi era as a Russian citizen in Vichy France. "Being Russian, French, American and Jewish," she finally decided, "meant that wherever I am, part of me could be somewhere else." But "New York became a good place to put my confusions to good use," so she moved there and, as a student at Columbia University, fought the academic bureaucracy in a way that would have made her father proud. When she angered a professor of Italian Renaissance by suggesting she might know something about "his sacred field," he "countered with an eight-page single-spaced mandatory reading list." Fortunately for us, Nathalie "countered with hysterics in the office of the department chairman," allowing her eventually to graduate, and, later, to edit her father's literary legacy. And what a legacy it is!

From Berlin to Jerusalem
(1977)
Gershom Scholem (1897–1982)

*"The reason I embraced Zionism was not that the establishment of a Jewish
state seemed urgent. For me, as for many others, this aspect of the movement
played only a secondary role, or none at all, until Hitler's destruction of the
Jews [. . .] Of greater influence were the tendencies that promoted the redis-
covery by the Jews of their own selves and their history, as well as a possible
spiritual, cultural, and, above all, social rebirth."*

Until Gershom Scholem, Jewish mysticism was studied by a core of
true believers, and considered "utter nonsense" by most academics. It took a self-taught genius like Scholem to crack open its complexity and reveal its wisdom even for the uninitiated. He burst on the scene
in 1941, with a famous set of lectures published as *Major Trends in Jewish Mysticism.* His writings thereafter span the entire history of Jewish
mystical writings, covering just about everything, it seems: hidden doctrines of God, the symbolism of the Star of David, false messiahs, and
even the mystical roots of rationalistic German Reform Judaism.

Scholem's scholarly contribution alone would merit his inclusion
here, but in addition, he was one of the most fascinating and influential
characters in modern Jewish history, an intellectual of towering proportion, and an argumentative personality with strong feelings on issues
large and small.

He grew up in Berlin which, in the early 1800s, had finally opened
its gates to large numbers of Jews, but only on condition that they
change their names. Until then known by their first names in combination with "son or daughter of" ("Isaac, son of Abraham," for example),
Jews were obliged to adopt German family names, so as to facilitate
official record keeping for public tax purposes. Among the new Berlin
settlers, one family chose Scholem, a Yiddishized version of the Hebrew
shalom (peace). Four generations later, parents on their way to becoming thoroughly Germanized had a son whom they named Gershom.

The original Gershom had been the son of the biblical Moses. *Gershom*
means "stranger there," an indication of the status of the Hebrews in
Egypt. As it turned out, Scholem was well named, since he believed

that full integration of Jews into European culture was impossible. Jews would always be "strangers there." The very culture that Jews hoped to enter was rife with rising anti-Semitism.

As a child in Berlin, Scholem had been educated in the best of Western culture: everything from Latin to German romantic poetry. At home, Jewish practices attenuated to the point of being ludicrous: the Scholems kindled Sabbath candles, but lit after-dinner cigarettes from the flames; they celebrated Christmas by playing "Silent Night" on the piano.

The internal dissolution of the Scholem family mirrors the ideological warfare that defined Jewish identity for much of the twentieth century. Gershom's father was a businessman who wanted mostly to be left alone as a fully German Jew: Jewish by birth and ethnicity, but nothing more. One of his sons flirted with right-wing German nationalism, another became a communist, and Gershom completed the picture, studying Jewish history, teaching himself Hebrew, and joining the Zionists. When the communist son, Werner, was arrested for treason, Gershom the Zionist was expelled from home alongside Werner, because their disappointed father was equally enraged at them both.

Scholem's recollections, subtitled *Memories of My Youth*, illuminate the tiny, even parochial, life of German-Jewish intellectuals. He knew them all, it seems: the philosopher-theologians Martin Buber and Franz Rosenzweig; the political activist Zalman Rubashov (who became the third president of Israel under the name Zalman Shazar); the writer and future Nobel Prize winner S. Y. Agnon; the mathematician and logician Gottlob Frege; Walter Benjamin, the philosopher; Erich Fromm, the psychologist; and others. One wonders what would have happened if they had been allowed to live out their natural lives at German universities, instead of having to flee from the Nazis or being murdered by them.

The final chapter of his memoir brings us to Scholem's adopted home, Jerusalem, where he moved in 1923, soon after graduating from the University of Munich. He had chosen Jerusalem not for its religious significance but because it was the epicenter of historic Jewish consciousness, and the natural place to settle if one was not intent on building a kibbutz or otherwise settling the land (farming was the last thing most of these intellectuals had on their minds).

But nurturing and harvesting Jewish scholarship was as much a chapter in the Zionist Jewish narrative as the better-known story of working the actual land. By the time Scholem arrived in Palestine in the early 1920s, Jerusalem already contained the seeds of a national library that would eventually come to house either the original or a copy of every available book and manuscript ever produced by Jews. Two years later, Scholem attended the inauguration ceremony of Hebrew University, to this day the academic center of Jewish studies worldwide. He described the ceremony, with a panoply of scholars, writers, and politicians being addressed by England's Lord Balfour, the signer of the 1917 document that had promised the founding of a Jewish state. Jerusalem still had "no running water, electricity, or telephone." But there was a university!

There was also hope, support, and community. "It was years," Scholem wrote, "before I became accustomed to staying in a hotel occasionally. Wherever you went you found a place to sleep. Everyone visited everyone [. . .] When you went out, you left your house open. It did not occur to us that there might be a theft. There was, in fact, no stealing, but when we returned, someone was often lying in our bed."

Scholem personified the modern Jewish dilemma: to give up Judaism as irreclaimable, or to reshape it as something old yet renewable. Scholem's Zionism was a response to the threat of losing Judaism to assimilationists on one hand and traditionalists on the other, neither of whom he could tolerate. In those days, he explained, "we did not know that Hitler was going to come, but we did know that, in view of the task of a radical renewal of Judaism and Jewish society, Germany was a vacuum in which we would choke."

Through the scholarly erudition of his books as well as his own towering personality, Gershom Scholem helped to compensate for the vacuum in Germany by instilling a fullness of Jewish learning in Israel, and from Israel back to Germany and throughout the world. Scholem's personal contribution was the application of scientific study to Jewish mystical literature, a field that he himself invented, pioneered, and dominated until the day he died. Scholem demonstrated its genius, even to the point of drawing from it a theory of Jewish history. As a founding father of the Jewish state, he also managed to weigh in on pretty much every issue of Israel and the Jewish People until his death in 1982. *From Berlin to Jerusalem* is his fascinating firsthand account of how he and others like him got it all started.

6

The American Experience
to World War II

The Conversation Expands

〰️

The founding father of American Jewish institutional life was Isaac Mayer Wise, who emigrated from Bohemia to New York in 1846. The poverty and ignorance of the backpacking Jewish street vendors whom he met appalled him. But in defiance of what he observed, he projected a bold vision of a Diaspora community in America whose greatness would dwarf every similar experiment in Jewish life that had gone before. In his own words, "I painted the future in golden hues." Most observers looking back from today's vantage point would credit him with prescience bordering on prophecy.

Jewish and American cultures have seemed destined to be partners in history. The pioneering eighteenth-century German-Jewish philosopher Moses Mendelssohn spent a lifetime arguing for the separation of church and state, but in Europe, it did not happen, while in America, it did. Centuries of persecution coupled with the love of learning had fostered a culture of Jewish entrepreneurialism—and America rewarded entrepreneurs. Jews did poorly where privileged classes squelched the promises of equality—but more than any country Jews had known, America was the land of equal opportunity. As a legal culture, Judaism values justice— and American courts presented a juridical system that the Talmud would have applauded. This did not all happen overnight, but it *did* happen, and over time, as America thrived, so, too, did American Jews.

Jews arrived in America in several waves of immigration. As early as 1654, a boatload of Sephardi Jews arrived in New Amsterdam (later renamed New York) from Recife, Brazil. Its inhabitants had lived happily under Dutch rule there, but were fleeing now because newly arrived Portuguese conquerors were bringing the dreaded Inquisition with them. By the time of the American Revolution, these Sephardi Jews had spread along the Atlantic seaboard, establishing communities in such places as Savannah, Charleston, Philadelphia, New York, and Newport. They were joined by Ashkenazi Jews from central Europe, a wave that picked up force in the nineteenth century, particularly after the failure of the 1848 revolutions in Europe. By far the largest wave, however, was the Jewish mass migration from eastern Europe between 1881 and 1924, when more than 2 million individuals left the Old World in hope of a better life. Most of them passed through Ellis Island and settled on New York's Lower East Side.

By 1900, the Lower East Side was already teeming with recent immigrants, but still only beginning to achieve its reputation as the most crowded American neighborhood in history. Just three years later, a tenement house survey found over 2,200 people living within just two acres—the equivalent of 700,000 people per square mile (compared to today's average of "only" 65,000 people per square mile across Manhattan). And it would get much worse—immigration had not yet peaked.

The Lower East Side was both a great melting pot and a colorful mosaic, full of unique individuals but also certain "types": the ghetto child fighting the ties of greenhorn parents, the strong-willed Jewish mother, the pushcart peddler and the sweatshop worker who barely eked out a living. There were traditionalist rabbis, too, but they wielded relatively little influence in a community that was Jewish by ethnicity and culture more than by religion. To be sure, newcomers were not slow in establishing synagogues, but most of them were tiny and did not outlast the first generation that founded them. Jews in the American ghetto were much more apt to drop religious sentiment and concentrate instead on working hard to amass the savings necessary to move up and out.

Although poor in capital, they were rich in spirit. Jews with little money for food still bought one or more of seven Jewish daily newspapers. Three Yiddish theaters on just one street (the Bowery) packed in crowds every Friday, Saturday, and Sunday night, where attendees received programs that featured poetry to read in between acts. One theater offered a Yiddish version of *Hamlet* ("translated and improved"), featuring Hamlet's uncle as a small-town rabbi in Russia and Hamlet as a student in rabbinic school. Poets and essayists were everywhere, and so were cafés and clubs: debating clubs, socialist clubs, English clubs, Zionist clubs, anarchist clubs, and more, all of them stages for vociferous political debate.

Jews brought their traditional love of learning to American shores. At an elementary level, parents insisted on educating their children to ensure their future beyond the ghettolike conditions where they were being raised. Harry Golden (1902–1981), who made his name editing the *Carolina Israelite* in Charlotte, North Carolina, recalled mothers who were unable to speak a word of English, but who unfailingly outfitted their children with library cards and insisted (in Yiddish): "Go; go and learn; go now." On a more advanced level, the maturation of eastern European immigrants coincided with the expansion of universities in America, which Jews attended with a passion.

Anti-Semitism grew as second-generation Jews in the New World left the ghettos to claim their share of the American dream. By the 1920s, universities were erecting informal Jewish quotas; businesses honored restrictive covenants; cities excluded Jews from desirable residential areas; and hospitals refused attending privileges to Jewish doctors. In 1915, B'nai B'rith leader Leo Frank had been lynched in Georgia; by 1920, Henry Ford was publishing anti-Jewish invective in his weekly *Dearborn Independent*; with the 1930s, "radio priest" Charles Coughlin added fuel to the anti-Semitic fire; and from 1939 to 1941, a German American Bund in the United States blamed Jews for having started World War II for their own financial interests.

In response to being denied opportunities in America's social and economic system, Jews developed their own Jewish resorts and hospitals. As Ivy League universities closed their doors to them (from 1920 to 1940, the Jewish student body of Columbia University Medical School dropped from 50 percent to 7 percent, for instance), Jews flocked to New York's City College, which came to be known as the "Jewish Harvard." Only later, with the recognition after World War II of what anti-Semitism in Europe had led to, did anti-Semitism in the United States lose traction; and only then did Jews join other Americans as equals in what became a postwar economic and religious boom.

With universities now once more open to them, Jews reasserted their commitment to higher education, a trend that has continued ever since. (In the year 2000, 55 percent of all Jewish adults in the United States had graduated from college, and 25 percent had earned a graduate degree; comparable figures for Americans in general were 29 percent and 6 percent.)

Jews had been adept at business from their very arrival in the New World. Peter Stuyvesant, the governor of New Amsterdam, reluctantly accepted the 1654 shipload of Jews, on condition that they not become public wards—a problem he need not have worried about, as the Recife arrivals were overwhelmingly successful entrepreneurs, some of them with mercantile connections to the Dutch West India Company. Ashkenazi Jews, too, created American business empires—banking and investment firms including Kuhn, Loeb & Co.; Lehman Brothers; Goldman Sachs; and department stores like R. H. Macy and Company and Bloomingdale's. Financial giants such as the Schiffs, Seligmans, and Warburgs were names to conjure with in New York society. Out west, Levi Strauss joined the California Gold Rush, and alongside Jacob Davis in Reno, Nevada, he received patent number 139121 for the process of using copper rivets to reinforce work pants—jeans!

At the same time, eastern European Jews had brought socialist sympathies with them, with the result that in America, Jews often represented both business and labor at negotiating tables. The American Federation of Labor (AFL) was founded by Samuel Gompers (1850–1924). Emma Goldman (1869–1940) was a well-known communist and even an anarchist, but also an early champion of birth control. (She was deported to Russia in 1919, but left for western Europe two years later when she came to see that the reality of a communist state ran completely counter to her championship of individual human rights.)

Jews were also prominent in America's burgeoning entertainment industry: Irving Berlin (1888–1989), one of the greatest popular composers and lyricists, wrote over 1,000 songs, including "White Christmas" and "Easter Parade." Other Jewish American composers and lyricists include George (1898–1937) and Ira (1896–1983) Gershwin, Jerome Kern (1885–1945), Oscar Hammerstein II (1895–1960), Aaron Copland (1900–1990), and Leonard Bernstein (1918–1990). In musical theater alone, these artists gave us *Show Boat, Annie Get Your Gun, Oklahoma!, South Pacific, The King and I, West Side Story*, and *The Sound of Music*. American television was largely pioneered by Jews, and Hollywood would be unthinkable without impresarios such as Louis

B. Mayer (Metro-Goldwyn-Mayer) and Harry, Jack, Sam, and Albert Warner (Warner Bros.).

These various developments that went into the American Jewish success story expanded the Jewish conversation well beyond religion. To this day, Jews debate the extent to which Jewish identity is definable in terms of Jewish culture, music, and universalistic ideals that arise from the Jewish experience through history.

This is not to say that Jewish religion was dormant during the period of American growth leading up to World War II. With the unfolding of eastern European immigration, the American Jews of German descent were drawn to Isaac Mayer Wise's legacy that so valued Enlightenment thinking and Western cultural aesthetics. These Reform Jews, as they were increasingly called, included the bankers and retailers who established Conservative Judaism also, not for themselves, but as an alternative route to Americanization for the eastern European newcomers. In the 1930s and 1940s, a Conservative rabbi, Mordecai Kaplan (1881–1983), developed yet a third denomination, Jewish Reconstructionism. Orthodoxy remained an option throughout the period, not so much as a particular denomination but as a spectrum of alternatives that held fast to a stricter reading of tradition in the face of American acculturation—especially under the guidance of Bernard Revel (1885–1940), who served as the first president of Yeshiva University in New York. Revel converted it from an American version of a Lithuanian yeshivah to a modern American university dedicated to producing learned Orthodox rabbis for the North American milieu.

The secular Jewish conversation spawned by eastern European Jews who saw Judaism primarily in ethnic and cultural terms was, therefore, matched by a religious debate that expressed the various shades of Jewish denominationalism. Zionism, too, was gaining ground throughout the years prior to World War II, giving Jews the opportunity to develop Jewish debates on Jewish nationalism as well.

From America's revolution in 1776 to Israel's birth in 1948, the Jewish story has been the steady weakening of European Jewry—until its near demise under Hitler—paired with the equally steady growth of American Jews to a position of influence among Jews worldwide that no one could have imagined even a hundred years ago. After 1948, with the existence of a Jewish state, the story has changed somewhat. But without American support there would be no Israel, and the Jewish future continues to be driven by the creativity of Jews on both sides of the Atlantic.

American Judaism
(2004)

Jonathan D. Sarna (born 1955)

"'A nation dying for thousands of years,' the great Jewish philosopher Simon Rawidowicz once observed, 'means a living nation [. . .] If we are the last— let us be the last as our fathers and forefathers were. Let us prepare the ground for the last Jews who will come after us, and for the last Jews who will rise after them, and so on until the end of days.'"

The study of American Judaism owes much to Jacob Rader Marcus (1896–1995), a professor at Hebrew Union College, who shaped it. Under the traumatic impact of the Holocaust, he abandoned his original field of expertise, German-Jewish history, and took up the story of Jews in America, which, he was sure, would replace Germany as the greatest Jewish Diaspora community in the world. Ever since 586 BCE, when Babylonian invaders destroyed the Temple of King Solomon and carried Jewish leaders into captivity, Jews have built Diaspora communities, which have achieved ever new heights in Jewish creativity. But Marcus was right. By most standards—religious creativity; advanced Jewish studies; publishing output; Jewish economic well-being; Jews in politics, the arts and sciences; the Jewish contribution to social justice—it can probably be said that no other Diaspora matches the one we call America.

In 2004, Jews in North America celebrated their 350th anniversary, and paused to take stock. American Jewry had burgeoned into the largest, wealthiest, freest, and most educated Jewish community the world had ever seen. In 1790, George Washington himself had promised the Jews of Newport, Rhode Island, that the government of the United States "gives to bigotry no sanction, to persecution no assistance." And Abraham Lincoln reaffirmed Jewish rights in 1863, after General Ulysses S. Grant tried to expel Jews from areas under his command because he mistakenly thought them responsible for war profiteering. (On display at the National Museum of American Jewish History in Philadelphia are two prayers of gratitude composed by Jews on both of these occasions, utilizing biblical verses whose initial Hebrew letters spell "Vashington" and "Linkolen," the Yiddishized spellings of the presidential names in question.)

As we saw in the introduction to this Part Six, Jewish history in America is traditionally divided into chapters that correspond to different waves of immigration: a Sephardi wave beginning with the arrival of Jews from Brazil in 1654; a central European (usually called German) wave in the nineteenth century; and an eastern European wave that crossed the Atlantic from the 1880s to 1924. (So large was this third wave that American isolationists, protectionists, and anti-Semites joined forces to convince the U.S. Congress to end it through the Emergency Quota Act of 1921 and the Immigration Act of 1924.) A fourth wave of Jews—survivors of the Nazi persecution—arrived after the end of the war, and a fifth wave of Jews came from the former Soviet Union, following the fall of the iron curtain in 1989.

Each successive wave adapted to the economic and social conditions that it found upon arriving. The Sephardi Jews settled along the Atlantic coast, as part of colonial America, building synagogues that exemplify the neoclassical architecture of the era, in such places as Newport, Savannah, and Charleston. German Jews who arrived as part of the Industrial Revolution, especially in the postbellum American North, discovered the advent of the railroad, which allowed them to settle the Midwest. During the Gold Rush, some Jewish forty-niners found their way overland to California, where they encountered fellow Jews who had sailed into Pacific ports. (These West Coast arrivals are not well represented in the standard historical scheme that focuses almost exclusively on the Atlantic ports of entry.) Eastern European Jews at the turn of the twentieth century fueled the growth of New York, especially, but also made their way to most other urban centers, where they endured harsh conditions before making their way up the social ladder and out into the suburbs. The last two sets of immigrants—survivors of the Nazi regime and of the Soviet system, respectively—also overwhelmingly settled in urban centers, where existing Jewish communities galvanized efforts to welcome them. (In 1820, the American Jewish population stood at barely 3,000. By 1877, the central European influx had boosted the number to a quarter million. By 1930, eastern European immigration had brought it close to 4.4 million.)

Describing Jewish American history according to immigration patterns has its benefits. But it overlooks the larger pattern of Jewish identity that is determined by the grander sweep of American history itself. *American Judaism* chronicles the Jewish story as just such an ongoing American phenomenon, and thereby avoids what Jonathan Sarna claims to be the major fault of many histories written earlier: their "haunting fear that Judaism in the new world will wither away." He chronicles instead "a much more dynamic story of people struggling to be Americans and Jews, a story of people who lost their faith and a story of people who regain their faith, a story of assimilation, to be sure, but also a story of revitalization."

Perhaps no one is better able to bring this story to life than Sarna, a professor of American Jewish history at Brandeis University and chief historian of the National Museum of American Jewish History. Sarna has written, edited, or coedited more than twenty books, and this one may be his best—it won the Jewish Book Council's Jewish Book of the Year Award in 2004, and was praised as being "the single best description of American Judaism during its 350 years on American soil."

American Judaism is indeed a treat: it makes for easy reading, it is thoughtfully presented, and it is filled with tidbits of information that beg to be shared with a friend. It is particularly detailed regarding Jewish Orthodoxy, but does ample justice to all streams of Jewish thought and practice. The first two chapters provide an excellent treatment of the Colonial and Revolutionary eras. The next chapters take us through the Civil War and postwar reconstruction—the period of German-Jewish dominance and the beginnings of Reform Judaism.

Especially fascinating are the ensuing chapters that describe the arrival of eastern European Jews and the spiritual crisis that set in when these Jews came to realize that alongside newfound religious freedom came the opportunity to reject affiliation with anything Jewish at all. In 1916, fewer than 12 percent of America's Jews belonged to synagogues. Most Jews no longer kept kosher, and many had abandoned their faith for a combination of socialism and *Yiddishkeit*, an ethnic-cultural celebration that sometimes went no deeper than preferring Jewish friends to gentiles, partly a reaction to nativist anti-Semitism at the time.

In his Conclusion, Sarna analyzes "American Judaism at a Crossroads." In these illuminating pages, we understand the issues that thoughtful Jews worry about today, in an age in which President Washington's Newport assurance has prevailed, but where old-style ethnic Judaism is insufficient to claim Jewish loyalty. With the numbers of Americans born Jewish and still identifying as Jews dropping, and with intermarriage on the rise, Jews wonder what their future will be. Sarna's own assessment is inspired by the quotation that opens this entry: an ever-dying people doesn't really die. It doesn't even fade away. There is no reason to believe that American Jewry, already a Diaspora without equal, cannot continue to grow in greatness.

The Promised City
(1962)

Moses Rischin (born 1925)

"The most rapid and the most revolutionary transformation in the millennial history of the Jewish People."

S omewhere on the map of eternity, there is a pantheon of great Jewish cities: foremost among them Jerusalem, of course, but also Diaspora centers where echoes of greatness even now seem to reverberate in the air. The great synagogue of Cordoba still stands, in a Jewish quarter where Moses Maimonides was born. Among the jumble of tilted gravestones in Cracow's Jewish cemetery lies one with the name of Moses Isserles, a sixteenth-century master codifier of Jewish law. Rembrandt himself memorialized the old Jewish quarter of Amsterdam.

When the titular father of American Judaism, Isaac Mayer Wise, landed in New York in 1846, he found relatively few Jews—and many of them were peddlers. But that was before the Civil War and the ensuing economic boom that made New York City the nation's economic capital, its busiest port, and an industrial center specializing in light manufacturing—precisely at a time when the necessary workforce arrived from eastern and southern Europe. Among the new arrivals were Jews who headed to Manhattan's Lower East Side, where they transformed the face of America's greatest city.

The Lower East Side is a tract of land ballooning out over the East River, roughly fifteen by twenty-three city blocks in size. "In 1870, the Jews of New York were estimated at 80,000, or less than 9% of the city's inhabitants. By 1915, they totaled close to 1,400,000 persons (nearly 28%), a number higher than the city's total population in 1870." And more Jewish immigrants kept on coming—until 1924, when Congress voted to limit new arrivals, partly influenced by a "racial hygiene" theory that feared the submergence of "superior" Nordic races, and partly to appease labor unions by reducing competition for jobs.

Remnants of the great Jewish Lower East Side exist to this day. Still standing on East Broadway is the building that housed *The Forward* (*Forverts*), once the city's most influential socialist newspaper. New York's most famous Jewish settlement house, the Educational

Alliance, also on East Broadway, is now serving ethnic minorities who have taken the place of the Jews. The Alliance and its branches once attracted some 37,000 adults and youngsters, nearly all of them Jewish, every single week.

It is hard to overstate the role of the Lower East Side in the elemental consciousness of today's American Jews. Most of the books that exemplify the era are novels or firsthand memoirs. *The Promised City* is a history book. It is, moreover, a history book composed by the superb historian Moses Rischin, now an emeritus professor of history at San Francisco State University and an authority on ethnic history generally in America.

True to his reputation, Rischin provides a detailed, comprehensive, but readable chronicle of the teeming streets, the tenements and sweatshops, and the culture of politics and learning that allowed most of the population to escape eventually, with nostalgic memories of the good old days there—even if they were not always so good. Take the utterly overcrowded tenements: the area had originally been zoned for private homes on lots 25 feet wide and 100 feet deep. With the mass immigration, they were converted into five- to six-story walk-ups holding a total of twenty or more families, in two- or three-bedroom flats, with one bedroom in each flat probably rented out to an additional four or five boarders. The lucky ones had indoor plumbing and a shared single bathroom for two such "family" units. Garbage was habitually thrown over the landings or out the window. In the short term, everyone's goal was to buy food and pay the rent; in the long term, residents plotted to get out.

Although it was a slum, the school absentee rate among Jews was a mere 8 percent, caused almost entirely by sickness—Jews insisted on schooling. Fortunately, despite the fetid living conditions, sickness was rare, since Jewish law had accustomed even freethinkers to practice hygiene. Education served political ends, as Jews devoured journals, attended lectures, and followed newspaper accounts of the unfolding Russian Revolution. There was no shortage of Old World Orthodoxy, but the widely embraced beliefs were "socialism and anarchism, positivism and the religions of humanity, Ethical Culture, and a medley of social ideals that promised a key to the universe."

Rischin places this story within the larger tale of the evolving American ethos. Philanthropic help to immigrants, for example, was part and parcel of the Social Gospel movement, Protestantism's activist response to poverty in the late nineteenth and early twentieth centuries. It also played into the religious struggles of well-off Jews in uptown Manhattan. One of social welfare's strongest Jewish advocates, Felix Adler (1851–1933), once slated to follow his father as rabbi at the flagship Reform synagogue, Temple Emanu-El, left it in 1876 in order to launch the nonsectarian (and rival) New York Society for Ethical Culture. The Lower East Side presented precisely the great misery that adherents of Ethical Culture sought to remedy.

Another powerful Jewish presence on Manhattan's Lower East Side was the American labor movement. The area had always known political socialism—immigrants brought that with them. Russian-born newspaper editor, poet, and anarchist David Edelstadt (1866–1892), for instance, promised that "Lasalle [and] Marx will deliver us from the Diaspora." But the successful unionization of labor was something new, and Jews excelled at it. One of the earliest unions in America was the United Hebrew Trades founded in 1888, and Jewish labor organizer Samuel Gompers became the first president of the American Federation of Labor (AFL). As labor's influence expanded, the unions' Labor Day replaced the socialists' May Day as the most important day on the calendar for workers.

But as the Jews moved out of the Lower East Side, they were increasingly less likely to be laborers. By 1914, old-timers mourned the loss of Yiddish at AFL meetings. "The Jews were fairly ravenous for education," Rischin writes, quoting Gompers. "Industrial work was merely a stepping-stone to professional or managerial positions." Nevertheless, to this day Jews are inordinately supportive of the liberal causes that socialism, and then labor, put on the American agenda. And it all originated on Manhattan's Lower East Side.

Bread Givers
(1925)

Anzia Yezierska (ca. 1880–1970)

"Worse than being an outcast, I simply didn't belong [. . .] Even in college, I had not escaped from the ghetto."

Anzia Yezierska was a heroic, troubled, and tragic woman. She arrived as an immigrant child from Poland and grew up alongside eight siblings on New York's Lower East Side. While her father escaped responsibility under the pretense of being a student of Talmud, her mother raised the family by working at whatever she could find. At age seventeen, Yezierska left home with the dream of becoming a teacher.

At first, she rented a succession of tiny, dreary rooms while working in sweatshops and laundries and learning elementary English from a janitor's daughter. Eventually, she attained a scholarship to Columbia University's Teachers College, graduated in 1905, taught school for a brief period, and then turned to writing.

Yezierska's personal life reads like a soap opera. Her marriage in 1910 to her first husband, Jacob Gordon, lasted less than a year, after which she married his friend (and the man she had loved to begin with) Arnold Levitas. Their daughter Louise was born in 1912. Two years later, she left Levitas and moved with Louise to San Francisco, where she tried her hand at becoming a social worker. Unable to support herself, she conceded child custody to Levitas and returned to New York, where she developed a love affair with philosopher and educator John Dewey, who had been her professor at Columbia. Looking back, years later, she described her life as perennial loneliness punctuated by skepticism.

Yezierska's writing career was likewise a somewhat sorry tale, in that her books were barely read—in part, perhaps, because they focused so exclusively on the very poverty of the ghetto that would-be readers were anxious to forget. Her luck promised to improve in 1922, when Samuel Goldwyn filmed a silent movie based on her 1920 novel, *Hungry Hearts*, and three years later Sidney Olcott did the same with her 1923 book, *Salome of the Tenements*. Goldwyn even brought her out to Hollywood for a brief stint as a screenwriter. But she missed New York, turned down a lucrative contract to remain in Los Angeles, and returned to the city she loved to write about. She survived the Great Depression through a government grant in support of writers that saw her cataloging trees in Central Park, and by the 1950s, although still a writer who had yet to be fully "discovered," she was at least writing reviews for *The New York Times*.

Bread Givers is Yezierska's semiautobiographical novel. Its heroine, Sara Smolinsky, is a fiercely independent woman ahead of her time, scarred by the traditional world of the Lower East Side she spurns, without social support for the alternative way of life she seeks, and continually beset by conflict and doubt.

Haunting almost every page of *Bread Givers* is Sara's father, a domineering man who rigidly controls his wife and four daughters, making them support the family while he pursues a parasitic life that he claims to be consistent with religion and Talmud study. In fact, he is rarely true to either. He never cites tradition's many compliments to women, preferring instead a steady barrage of "pseudo-Talmudic" quotes demeaning women, generally manufactured by himself.

He naturally laments the passing of European Talmudic culture, but tries to reproduce it anyway by investing little time with family, but a lot with other men in synagogue, the study halls, and lodges, where he spends inordinate amounts on charity, as (he claims) befits his scholarly pretensions. Whether he believes it or not, his own family starves, while he urges faith in God. "That is why I am so deeply buried in the ground by you," shouts Sara's mother. "You turn all your worries on to God!"

As if still living in Poland, he forces his daughters to accept less than satisfactory marriages contracted through matchmakers, thereby foiling their hopes for marriages of love. Much of the novel's conflict revolves around the question of whether the Smolinsky women will declare freedom from this patriarchal tyrant. They do—and yet they don't. Sara's mother is verbally defiant yet submissive in the end, leading Sara to wonder about both her parents: "Here, in America, where girls pick out for themselves the men they want for husbands, how grand it would be if the children also could pick out their fathers and mothers."

Like the author herself, Sara is the only persistent escapee, abandoning her home with her mother's tacit assistance, then living in squalor while somehow becoming a *teacherin* (a Yiddishized Anglicism meaning, female teacher). At last she can fall in love, and she does, but with uncertain consequences—and in the end, her father comes back to haunt her. Her mother has died in the interim, and he has married again, having had an affair (we suspect) with this second wife-to-be even while his devoted first wife was dying. He was only planning, he later explains, to have another female in the house to cook and clean for him. The second wife, it turns out, has married for her own selfish reasons—to guarantee the presence of a man to provide for her. For a while, her new husband has been bringing in death benefits from his first marriage, but they are gone now, and the two of them have been reduced to poverty. Conveniently for them both, Sara just then resurfaces as a successful *teacherin*, and her father takes up his perennial claim that the purpose of daughters is to care for their fathers. The climax of the book narrates how Sara navigates the restatement of these demands, precisely as her own life is on the brink of independence.

Yezierska writes like a literary primitivist; there are no subtleties here. But she thereby lays bare the equally unsubtle realities of Sara's attempted escape from immigrant culture. "What's all this physical education nonsense?" she asks her dean at Columbia. "I came to college to learn something." She is equally amazed at the "spick-and-span cleanliness" of her newfound college classmates, which she expresses in a reversion to Yiddishized syntax: "It smelled from them, the soap and the bathing." She is enthralled by discovering birthday parties, because "I never knew that there were people glad enough of life to celebrate the day they were born."

Sara does graduate. In a chapter entitled "My Honeymoon with Myself," she recognizes that with graduation, "I had fought my way up into the sunshine of plenty." Finally a college grad and, therefore, truly arrived in America, she approaches a realty office where "a polite agent greeted me with businesslike courtesy." But shortly thereafter her father reappears to remind her that she is indeed a stranger in a strange land: a downtown immigrant in uptown America, a Jew among WASPs, and a woman in a man's world.

Bread Givers is not a pretty story. Offering a woman's view of the Lower East Side, it is a devastating account of Old World Talmudic patriarchs, the women they tyrannized, and the psychic cost of one woman's efforts to seek the kind of independence that we take almost for granted today.

Jews Without Money
(1930)
Michael Gold (1893–1967)

"I was first proud of my book when I visited Germany in 1931 and found that the radicals [German socialists] were translating it and were spreading it widely as a form of propaganda against the Nazi anti-Semites."

S oon after Hitler had come to power in 1933, Nazis broke into the dwelling of a German friend of Michael Gold's who happened to be translating a chapter of *Jews Without Money*. "The officer picked up some sheets of [the] manuscript [. . .] 'Ho, ho, ho!' he roared. 'So there are Jews without money!'"

Michael Gold (the pseudonym of Itzok Isaac Granich), a passionate left-wing political activist and proletarian writer, had chosen this provocative title specifically to show that "the great mass of Jews in the world today are not millionaire bankers, but paupers and workers"— a painful lesson he had learned growing up on Manhattan's Lower East Side, "a block from the notorious Bowery, a tenement canyon hung with fire-escapes, bed-clothing, and faces. Always these faces at the tenement windows."

Gold's memoir of his childhood ends with the image of "a man on an East Side soap-box" proclaiming "that out of the despair, melancholy and helpless rage of millions, a world movement had been born to abolish poverty." Although still just a teenager at the time, Gold listened intently because he had already bottomed out in life. Filled with despair after having moved from one hellhole of a job to the next, he had variously signed on with a gang leader and with religion, hoping either to rob or to pray his way to deliverance. Ringing in his ears was his father's own ill-fated life: "Twenty years in America, and poorer than when I came. A suspender shop I had, and it was stolen from me by a villain [his partner]. A house painter foreman I became, and fell off a scaffold. Now bananas [from a pushcart] I sell, and even at that I am a failure." So Gold listened to the soapbox prophet and concluded, "O workers' Revolution, you brought hope to me, a lonely, suicidal boy. You are the true Messiah. You will destroy the East Side when you come, and build there a garden for the human spirit."

To be sure, Gold's decision to record his jaundiced memoir of life in society's gutters was colored by his radicalism, but the radicalism had nothing to do with the culture of the Lower East Side of which Jews are justly proud: its libraries and cafés, educational classes and theater. These Gold never mentions. His Lower East Side was a father he idolized, a mother who worked for pennies when his father couldn't, and a world of victims rather than heroes.

There is not a lot of analysis here; Gold was not an intellectual. But he was passionate, and his passion saturates the pages of *Jews Without Money*. Here are the prostitutes and small-time gangsters who are conveniently missing from the rosy memories of Jews whose parents exchanged poverty for addresses uptown or in Brooklyn, and who later, as suburbanites, made visits to old East Side haunts that started looking good through nostalgic lenses.

Gold, by contrast, remembered "pimps, gamblers, and red-nosed bums" on their way in and out of "Jake Wolf's saloon." At age five, he figured out what the many "girls [. . .] naked under flowery kimonos" were selling. "Earth's trees, grass, flowers could not grow on my street; but the rose of syphilis bloomed by night and by day." Kid Louis ran a boys' gang that specialized in the "popular sport" of raping girls. Masha, the blind Russian girl, worked for Harry the pimp. Gold himself was more mischievous than criminal, but the leader of his gang ended up in prison.

Even though most of Gold's neighbors were Jewish, he knew also the Italians, Poles, Irish, and Chinese, some of whom had flats in his own tenement. When an adult street bum tried to seduce Gold's little boyhood friend, Joey, Italian laborers in the vicinity practically beat the man to death with their shovels. But overall, ethnic groups lived in uneasy tension and distrust. Gold's mother "was opposed to the Italians, Irish, Germans and every other variety of Christian with whom we were surrounded. 'May eight and eighty black years fall on these *goys*!' she said [. . .] 'They hate and kill Jews [. . .] I have seen them in Hungary.'" Gold grew up hearing how "Christians loved to kidnap Jewish children," how "they also cut off children's ears, and made a kind of soup."

But even behind his mother's harsh words, there is goodness. Mrs. O'Brien is an Irish woman upstairs whose drunken husband beats her. "Their boy has been sick for years," explains Gold's mother. "All their money goes for doctors. That's why he drinks and beats her." When Mrs. O'Brien offers a whole nickel to any child who will play with her bedridden son, Mrs. Gold tells Michael to visit the child for free." It will be a good deed," she says. "The Christian child is lonely. Nothing can happen to you."

Tammany Hall, the political machine of Manhattan's Democrats at the time, looms large in *Jews Without Money*—again, not as a matter of history, but in the raw immediacy of Gold's recollection. Tammany ward boss Baruch Goldfarb made Gold's father an overnight American citizen, and then took him to three different polling places to vote in every one of them. "All you do is mark a cross under the star. Under the star, remember!" Later, Gold's father joined a Democratic lodge for ritualized fun such as "secret passwords, the gold and purple sashes and white gloves, the theatrical ceremonies."

Gold might have lacked sophistication, and he was an ideologue bent on showing the evils of capitalism. But the particular brand of capitalism that Gold had experienced as a child *was* evil, and what he lacked in formal learning he made up in observations that the homeless usually record: the cold winter, for example, when "we boys dug out a litter of frozen kittens and their mother. The little ones were still blind. They had been born into it, but had never seen our world."

And Gold was an excellent streetwise philosopher. Remembering that even before the Dutch, the English, the Irish, and the Jews, "the red Indians once inhabited the East Side," he points out that "each group left its deposits, as in geology." When the kindly owner of a grocery store gives away so much food that she cannot pay her rent, he thinks, "Kindness is a form of suicide in a world based on the law of competition."

Looking back on his childhood, he concludes, "Jewish bankers are fascists; Jewish workers are radicals; the historic class division is true among the Jews as with any other race." That universal necessity of class conflict seems an unlikely conclusion to draw today. But the conditions that drove Gold to it are certainly worth reading, and Gold is right about one thing: poverty and cruelty, but sometimes also heroism, were part of human life even in New York's famous Jewish Lower East Side.

Awake and Sing!
(1935)
Clifford Odets (1906–1963)

"This is what I tell you [. . .] DO! Do what is in your heart and you carry in yourself a revolution. Not like me. A man who had golden opportunities but drank instead a glass tea. "

Clifford Odets's father, Louis, had followed the usual course of first-generation Jews, becoming a peddler upon arriving in America—in his case it was Philadelphia—from eastern Europe, and then working hard to get his family out of the ghetto. The Odetses moved to the Bronx in 1908, where Louis owned and managed a printing plant and became vice president of a boiler company. In good Jewish fashion, he taught Clifford commitment to the Jewish family on one hand and the universal human family on the other. The first made Clifford a conscious Jew; the latter made him a socialist who even joined the communist party very briefly.

That was enough, in 1952, for the U.S. government's House Un-American Activities Committee to summon Odets to testify in its Cold War witch hunt for communists. By then, he had written a number of dramatic successes—four of them once played on Broadway at the same time—and had been living in Hollywood for twelve years, writing screenplays and collecting modern art, a distinctly bourgeois life for which his leftist friends never forgave him. He died of cancer eleven years later.

Awake and Sing! is Clifford Odets's first full-length play and a moving memorial to the Great Depression and the Jewish family. It features the Bergers, crowded into a tiny Depression-era apartment in the Bronx. Mother Bessie, strong to the point of being coldly unfeeling, holds the family together, while Myron, her ineffectual husband ("a born follower" who went to law school, but never even got close to becoming a lawyer), voices an independent opinion on rare occasions, but has learned, over the years, that it is better to go along with whatever Bessie says. He "likes people, likes everything," but from Bessie's perspective, barely copes. "If I didn't worry about the family," she shouts, "who would? [. . .] Here without a dollar you don't look the world in the eye [. . .] this is life in America."

Their son Ralph is in love with a woman we never meet: Bessie rejects her because she is too poor to lift Ralph out of his economic hopelessness. Poor Ralph. "Mom, I love the girl," he pleads. "I want you to let her live here for a while." "I could die from shame," Bessie retorts in a bitter aside. "A year already he runs around with her." And then, to Ralph: "Maybe you wanted me to give up twenty years ago. Where would you be now? You'll excuse my expression—a bum in the park."

Their daughter Hennie is pregnant but unmarried. She will have to trade in her dreams of marrying "a millionaire with a mansion on Riverside Drive" for "a poor foreigner," the only slouch around whom Bessie can convince to marry Hennie while being led to believe that he somehow fathered Hennie's child.

Much of the play revolves around two characters who are polar opposites: Bessie's father, Jacob, and her brother Morty. Jacob links the first and second Jewish generations in America. He must have arrived from the Old World, then moved to the Bronx—just as Louis Odets did in real life—but there the parallels end, for Jacob is a would-be Marxist and dreamer, bitter about the American obsession with money. "In my day," he says, "propaganda was for God. Now it's about success." Morty is the epitome of that success: crass, unfeeling, a lover of expensive cigars and of his penthouse, which he leaves on occasion to go slumming at his sister's.

Jacob's patriarchal ambitions, if he ever had any, have long been usurped by daughter Bessie's pragmatism. He is largely relegated to taking the family poodle, Tootsie, for walks on the roof. Unlike his children, however, he was raised with at least a modicum of Jewish knowledge. Bessie inherited nothing but the accent, the Yiddishized English that early generations of immigrant Jews struggled to abandon. Jacob is at least ineptly prophetic. He combines the rabbinic hope for resurrection with the American hope of success (helped along, he wishes, by a Marxist corrective). Neither one of these visions looks especially promising at the time. But ever passionate for a better future, Jacob supplies the double entendre that gives the play its title: "Awake and sing, ye that dwell in the dust, and the earth shall cast out the dead" (Isa. 26:19). Lacking Jacob's European childhood, his children and grandchildren cannot even recognize it as a quote from the Bible—but if they had, they might more easily have sympathized with the verse that comes immediately beforehand: "It is as though we had given birth to wind; we have won no victory on earth."

The importance of *Awake and Sing!* is its bold presentation of Jewish American life in the 1930s, hardly a pretty picture and something

American Jews today would rather overlook. This is *not* the rags-to-riches theme, the "up from poverty by hard work and enterprise" motto, the indomitable Jewish spirit, and all that. The Berger family has none of it. The fabled generations of the Lower East Side were in truth miserably poor, and the Bergers, their Depression-era progeny, were no better off.

The Bergers of the world are the people history leaves behind. And they are everywhere. As the Rabbis put it, they are born "against their will" and will die likewise. They are not the completely disinherited on earth. They are just not the heroes of which myths are made. They are certainly far from the mythic stereotype of the Jews who vaulted in a single generation from Lower East Side poverty to the gilded ghettos of the suburbs. Yet they are equally as real. One meets them still as working-class Jews whom tabloids rarely feature.

What makes the Bergers stand out is their time and place: barely out of the ghetto, they have been hit by the Great Depression. But they, too, manage somehow, in the end, to voice the inveterate human optimism that rejects utter despair. The closing scene of *Awake and Sing!* pictures Ralph, bereft of his girlfriend and cheated by his own mother out of an inheritance that she will apply to keep the family afloat, rather than let the money lift at least her son out of poverty. Yet even Ralph, even then, vows, "Let me die like a dog if I can't get more out of life [. . .] right here in the house. My days won't be for nothing. Let Mom have the dough. I'm twenty-two and kickin'! I'll get along." And he remembers Grandpa Jacob's appeal to Isaiah: "'Awake and sing,' he said. Right here, he stood and said it."

Passage From Home
(1946)

Isaac Rosenfeld (1918–1956)

*"These trees had so much stronger and more ponderous a grasp of life than I.
A common life ran through all of us, but it was precisely that which was so
fearful. For if it was the same life, it was also the same blindness, the same
unconscious growing and reaching for the sun, and the same meaningless
non-being, counting for nothing [. . .] We would all die ignored."*

The Jewish American writer and critic Isaac Rosenfeld epitomized
alienation, in an era when alienation was a prerequisite to claiming
the title of "intellectual." As a philosophical concept, "alienation" has
quite a pedigree, beginning with Hegel's belief that human creativity
inevitably fashions a world that confronts its own makers as something
alien to them. Marx applied this Hegelian idea to the distantiation of
workers from the product of their labor, and in the twentieth century,
the term passed along to French existentialists (led by Jean-Paul Sartre)
and a coterie of New York Jewish writers and critics in the 1940s and
'50s. They had been raised as Marxists and, despite Stalin's purges of the
1930s, had yet to admit the full perversity of the Stalinist state.

Born in Chicago and a high school friend of the better-known writer
Saul Bellow, Rosenfeld moved temporarily to New York in 1941, where
he became a fellow traveler among its crowd of Jewish intellectuals.
When "Isaac," as everyone called him, died a sad death back in Chicago
in 1956, those intellectuals showed up in force at the funeral. Daniel
Bell observed, "He might have said, '*C'est la vie*,' and added, wryly, 'And
you call this a *vie*?'" His friend Alfred Kazin summed up his life: "He
lived not like a writer but like a character in search of a plot." And Irving
Howe called him the "golden boy" of the New York literary elite—"but
also a Wunderkind [who] died of lonely sloth." Tragically, for Rosenfeld
alienation was no mere intellectual concept. It was the caption to the
caricature that was his life.

Passage From Home, his only (and quite autobiographical) novel,
features fourteen-year-old Bernard (Bernie) Miller growing up in the
1930s in Chicago, a stand-in for American Jews in general, whose
"teenage" metamorphosis from immigrants to full-fledged Americans

was under way. These were the decades between the "heroic" era when eastern European Jews had arrived in America's cities, and their post–World War II exodus to the suburbs. The protagonist's parents and grandparents are still Old World characters in Chicago's immigrant Jewish ghetto, and they have names so Jewish that they sound like parodies. But people really had names like that! The neighborhood friend of Bernard's grandfather is still called Pinchus, but Grandpa himself has become Morris; Bernie's father is Harry, his stepmother is Bessie. His uncle Joe is married to Chiah Gitel, whose uneasy status between generations comes through in the English equivalent she chooses: Anita Gertrude. Gertrude was a common first-generation name; but Anita was still pretentious in the 1930s.

Joe and Anita have invested in orthodonture for their daughter Essie, who is in training to become the much caricatured postwar suburban JAP ("Jewish American Princess"). At a family get-together, "she flutters her eyelids and lets her lips part with ennui, thereby displaying her braces as well as her boredom."

Bernie is less precocious than Essie and still mostly at home among family—even though his is a dysfunctional family, toward which he feels acute ambivalence. "When they [the extended family] are all packed in, the house becomes a ship," he says. "You can feel it rocking under you; you think it has taken on an independent motion [. . .] hitting the family's course. Where they go, you go [. . .] for if you were to leap overboard or cut loose, and cast yourself adrift, there would be only the sea around you, and, unable to survive without them, you would drown."

The two other major characters in the novel are Bernie's bohemian aunt, Minna, and Willie, a non-Jew who was married to Bernie's deceased cousin Martha and who still frequents the family. Both of them are family outcasts: Minna because of her wild lifestyle and some secret event in her past (having something to do with Harry and his first wife); and Willie because he is a *goy*, the epithet used by immigrant Jewish culture not just to designate, but to define, the quintessential non-Jew as lesser than Jews in character and in aspiration. Willie fits the bill! He is an ex-sailor with a tattoo, unschooled, chronically out of work, and a denizen of bars; what money he makes he spends on fun instead of saving it to get ahead.

Fascinated by Willie and infatuated with Minna, Bernie introduces the two of them, who become live-in lovers. As an exercise in independence, Bernie leaves home to live with Willie and Minna, but then is caught in the middle of every family triangle imaginable.

Jewishly, too, Bernie finds himself in the middle. His grandmother still bakes *challah* and lights Sabbath candles, but his stepmother, Bessie, has given that up. She remembers her Zionist youth, when she "would dance the *hora*, sing Hebrew songs, and take courses in farming," but other than nostalgia, she has little Jewishness left in her. Nevertheless, when Bernie moves out, she sends him "an old prayer shawl [tallit] and set of phylacteries [tefillin]" together with a note: "You have forsaken your father; do not forsake your God." But it is too late. His grandfather had still used this prayer garb. "It was my inheritance from him," Bernie admits. But by the time he gets it, "it was vacant of God" already.

Passage From Home is realism without romance. If Bernie has jumped the ship of family, it is because the family is going down anyway. With nothing left but Jewish nostalgia and the certainty that they are different than Willie the goy, the characters are adrift from their Jewish moorings and headed for an uncertain landfall. Like Rosenfeld himself, Bernie will join the New York Jewish intelligentsia, where he will temporarily revive the best of Yiddish culture and enrich the world of American literature—a fitting contrast to his cousin Essie's empty version of next-generation Jewish life (as described, for example, by Philip Roth [see page 251], Rosenfeld's younger contemporary and prophet of the generation that Rosenfeld never lived to see).

But *Passage From Home* is also a lyrical and touching memoir of an in-between generation that gets little attention, especially compared to the singular eras before and after. Rosenfeld pictures it on its way to somewhere still unnamed. By way of contrast, the biblical Abraham comes to mind as he travels to a land that God will show him. Bernie, like Rosenfeld, has no God and, we suspect, no place to go. If the members of the in-between generation suffer alienation, it is because they will have to travel the journey to nowhere all on their own.

7

The Holocaust and Israel
The Conversation Is Focused

᠅

From the time of their occurrence in the mid-twentieth century all
the way to today, the Holocaust and the founding of the State of
Israel have dominated Jewish conversation like nothing before or since.
Jews call the Holocaust the *Sho'ah*, a Hebrew word used in the Bible
to denote cataclysm, catastrophe, or disaster. The independent State of
Israel that arose in 1948, just three years after the Holocaust ended,
is widely referred to as a miracle—even by Jews who do not believe
literally in miracles—because against all odds, and apparently out of
nowhere, just when Jewish existence seemed most tenuous, the age-old
Jewish hope for return to the land of the Bible was realized. Israel welcomed the devastated remnants of Jewish populations from Europe and
the Middle East, bringing the Zionist dream to fruition and guaranteeing a haven for Jews still locked away in ghettos and displaced persons'
camps because no one else would have them. The entries here elucidate
these two utterly singular events in all of Jewish history and the extraordinary role they play in the minds of Jews, who still live in their shadow.

It was hard to assimilate either event as real. It took Jews until
the 1960s to come to terms with the enormity of their European

victimization in the 1930s and 1940s. The birth of Israel was easier to understand, but not that much easier to believe. After the Second Jewish Commonwealth had ended in 70 CE, almost two thousand years needed to pass before another commonwealth could come into being.

In the interim, Jews had wandered the globe, settling here or there for greater or lesser periods of time, but never forgetting their ultimate goal: a return to the Holy Land. And now they had come home. At the very same time, not only were uncanny estimates of Jewish deaths under the Nazis still mounting, but to that unfathomable number, new deaths were being added every day as Holocaust survivors were murdered by nationalists and anti-Semites in the countries where they had once lived and to which they had hoped to return—only to find that they were still not wanted there.

Given the enormity of the Jewish population interned in displaced persons' camps after World War II, the very first piece of legislation passed by the new State of Israel was the Law of Return, the guarantee that every Jew has the inalienable right of refuge and citizenship in Israel—too late for the 6 million murdered by the Nazis, but not too late for the potential victims of whatever horrors the future might hold.

To be a Jew in the late 1940s and the 1950s was to have experienced history firsthand. Row after row of books sought to assess the sea change that had occurred. By now, the rows of books have become entire multimedia libraries, as the conversation continues unabated. What do we owe the victims who were shot, gassed, experimented upon, and otherwise tortured to death? Is Jewish suffering the essence of what Jewish history is all about? How "Jewish" should a Jewish state be? Should it follow Jewish law—and if so, whose interpretation of that law? Should it embody Jewish values—but if so, what exactly are those values?

More Jews now live in Israel than anywhere else in the world. But even the millions of Jews in the Diaspora, who have chosen to remain where they are, have not abandoned their claim to Israel as a Jewish homeland that is essential to their Jewish consciousness. What role, they ask, should *they* play in shaping and guaranteeing Israel's future? How do they respond to the policies of Israeli governments that they do not like? How can Diaspora and Israeli Jews build strong futures that respond to their own historical challenges—either within the Land of Israel or outside of it—while still ensuring a shared destiny as members of the Jewish People? More than half a century after the Jewish world changed forever, this remains a very current dilemma for Jews around the world.

We will return to some of these issues in the final part of this book, which brings the Jewish conversation to the present. For now, we turn to the momentous years when these questions were just taking shape, the era that gave us both the near destruction of the Jewish People and the miraculous resurrection of Jewish aspiration in the founding of the Jewish state we call Israel.

The War Against the Jews 1933–1945
(1975)

Lucy S. Dawidowicz (1915–1990)

"'The Final Solution of the Jewish Question' was the code name assigned by the German bureaucracy to the annihilation of the Jews [. . .] 'Final' means definitive, completed, perfected, ultimate. 'Final' reverberates with apocalyptic promise, bespeaking the Last Judgment, the End of Days, the last destruction before salvation, Armageddon. 'The Final Solution of the Jewish Question' in the National Socialist conception was not just another anti–Semitic undertaking, but a metahistorical program devised with an eschatological perspective. It was part of a salvationist ideology that envisaged the attainment of Heaven by bringing Hell on earth."

Hundreds of books now provide overviews of the enforced Jewish descent into the Nazi hell. Choosing a single representative title from among them is no easy task. But for over thirty-five years, *The War Against the Jews* has remained a justly popular choice as a work that is historically accurate, comprehensive in scope, and gripping in its page-by-page appeal. Perhaps no other single book better captures the facts of the horror, alongside the imponderable: how was it possible that human nature and civilized society let it happen?

Lucy Dawidowicz was a professor at Yeshiva University in New York, specializing in Holocaust Studies. In the immediate aftermath of the war, Dawidowicz had gone to Europe to help survivors redefine their lives, and in 1981, her book *The Holocaust and the Historians* attacked historians who saw Europe's Jews as too passive and therefore somehow complicit in their own destruction. *The War Against the Jews* shows that the Jews had absolutely no options open to them. From the beginning, Hitler saw his campaign against them as the centerpiece of his overall enterprise, not just as an added component that he might just as easily have abandoned in an effort to win the larger war. Eradicating Europe's Jews amounted to a separate fanatic war in and of itself, begun the day Hitler came to power and continuing to the very end. The Holocaust would have occurred even if World War II had not. Hitler lost the larger war. He very largely prevailed in this one.

Hitler became chancellor of Germany on January 30, 1933. Within weeks, there were boycotts of Jewish stores and organized violence against their owners. By March, Jews had been banned from government positions and the professions; by April, they were expelled from the civil service; in July, they lost their citizenship; in October, cultural and educational jobs were closed to them. The Nuremberg Laws of 1935 protected the "purity" of "German Blood and German Honor" by banning marriages and extramarital relations with Jews. Nor could Jews have "German" household servants. The year 1938 saw the systematic transfer of all Jewish business into "Aryan" hands.

On November 9, 1938, violence was ratcheted up. In what came to be called *Kristallnacht* (Night of [Broken] Glass), some 7,000 Jewish businesses and synagogues were smashed or torched, almost 100 Jews were killed, and untold thousands beaten and maimed. Within days, Jewish children were expelled from schools, adults were fired from whatever jobs they still had, and Jews of all ages were banned from public places. With Jews now stripped of any semblance of life, the Nazi government turned to the question of how to get rid of them altogether. Until 1938, the government had favored allowing Jews to emigrate while leaving their possessions behind. When too many Jews still remained, emigration became expulsion, and when that, too, failed, the "Final Solution" was hatched.

What impacted that "Solution" most was the German occupation of Poland after September 1939 (the beginning of World War II). Poland's western provinces were annexed to Germany proper. But the majority of Polish Jews lived in eastern Poland, a large land mass that the Nazis set aside administratively under the innocuous title *Generalgouvernement* (General Government), and to which the remaining million or so Jews in German-speaking Europe were expelled as well. Germany was finally free of its Jews: it was "*Judenrein.*"

Systematic murder was all that remained, and it was diabolically accomplished in highly bureaucratic and deviously clever ways. To begin with, as German troops expanded eastward into Russia in 1941, specially trained army and police units called *Einsatzgruppen* followed along, mopping up operations by shooting every Jew they found, and burying them in mass graves that the victims first had to dig themselves. In cities, where the population density made that policy unworkable (Warsaw and Cracow, for example), Jews were herded into ghettos to die of starvation and disease. And then there were the concentration camps.

Camps in Germany had been established as early as 1933, to serve as holding pens for several categories of the unwanted, including political opponents of the *Reich*. With the occupation of Poland, concentration camps were added there to hold the Jews transferred from western Europe, and simultaneously, to make slave labor available to German industry and the war effort. In 1941, camps were supplied with gas chambers and crematoria. Eventually, the ghettos were liquidated—and their few remaining Jews joined others from all over Europe, being dispatched in cattle cars where they were stuffed together to the point that many died of exhaustion, starvation, or asphyxiation before they even got to the death camps. Those who managed to arrive alive were selected out for immediate liquidation, or, if they still had some promise of labor left in them, were allowed to work until they dropped—or, more likely, became sick or weak enough to suggest that they, too, be gassed. Others were hanged, shot, or otherwise killed for minor infractions or for reasons of bureaucratic whim.

Others besides Jews were executed in the camps: some 250,000 Roma (Gypsies), for example, and tens of thousands of non-Jewish resisters. But the Nazi obsession was Jews. Even in the last years of the war, as the German armies retreated, they took Jews with them on a forced march westward, shooting the stragglers as they went. Such was the single-mindedness with which the war against the Jews was conducted. The final list of Jews murdered in the death camps alone reads, in part: Auschwitz, 2,000,000; Majdanek, 1,380,000; Treblinka, 800,000; Belzec, 600,000; Chelmno, 340,000; Sobibor, 250,000.

Lucy Dawidowicz describes all this in detail. For this alone, her book is required reading. But the facts of the Holocaust take up only a third of what is a much lengthier and deeper account. The chapter on living conditions in the ghettos is almost too painful to get through. Dawidowicz charts Jewish resistance, and raises (but rejects) the possibility of willing Jewish complicity. Yes, the Nazis established internal Jewish governing bodies to enforce legislation and, eventually, to select successive waves of deportees—but compliance was forced upon them. She also tracks the remarkable achievement of German Jews between both world wars, which all came to naught because of the virulence with which anti-Semitism had been carried like a deadly virus in German culture, waiting for the right moment to erupt.

Historians will differ on details such as the role of the Jewish governing bodies and the willingness of everyday Germans to go along with it all. But the enormity of the Holocaust can be denied as little as it can be grasped. It is too much to take in, and it becomes ever more unfathomable, the more we know of it. Yet nothing about Jews in the past half-century can be understood without it.

The Night Trilogy:
Night (1958); Dawn (1960); Day (1961)
Elie Wiesel (born 1928)

"Never shall I forget that night, the first night in camp, that turned my life into one long night seven times sealed [. . .] Never shall I forget those moments that murdered my God and my soul and turned my dreams to ashes."

Reading Elie Wiesel inevitably elicits acknowledgment of the miraculous, because there is no rational way to explain the fact that he is still alive. He is not the only Jew to have this dubious distinction. Like the others who somehow managed to resume their lives in the aftermath of suffering beyond measure, he bears an indelible testimonial to his tale in the number that the Nazis tattooed on his arm: Wiesel was Auschwitz prisoner No. A-7713.

It was spring 1944, when the Nazis finally added Hungary to the list of places whose Jews would be shot, hanged, gassed, buried alive, or cremated until no single Jew remained on earth. With the Russian front advancing and Hitler holed up in the Berlin headquarters to which he had retreated, the 15,000 or so Jews in Wiesel's Romanian town of Sighet imagined they would escape the agony of German occupation. Not that anyone could envision what that agony turned out to be. Even though Moishe the Beadle, a foreigner in town, had been deported early and then escaped to issue the warning, no one listened.

Elie Wiesel, who was fifteen at the time, was deeply immersed in a traditional Jewish life not far removed from what it would have been a century (or several centuries) earlier: studying Talmud by day and Kabbalah by night, punctuated with a three-times-daily regimen of prayer. What modernity could not interrupt, the Nazis did. Jews were herded into ghettos, "ruled by the delusion" (as Wiesel puts it) that God would somehow come to the rescue.

Wiesel would personally go through all the horrors of the Holocaust in record time: the deportation to Auschwitz in cattle cars with no food or drink for days on end, and people dying while crushed together standing in their own waste; the death of his sister and mother; the "selection" processes, where a flick of the commandant's hand sent you to the chimneys; the forced labor; the daily starvation and cold; and the beatings and public hangings, including a young boy who dangled in the air, writhing for half an hour, before he died. When Wiesel and the other inmates were forced to troop by and watch him, Wiesel concluded that God died there, too, hanging from that very gallows.

Wiesel was also part of the forced march west to another camp, Buchenwald, intended to ensure that no Jews were left for the advancing Russian army to liberate. Most died of hunger (they ate snow), exhaustion (they were already emaciated ghosts), freezing (it was winter and they had no coats), or "sport" (riddled with Nazi bullets). Wiesel somehow survived. Until the end of time, he says, he will remember watching his father die before his eyes. "I heard his voice, but I did not move [. . .] It had been his last wish to have me next to him in his agony at the moment his soul was tearing itself from his lacerated body [. . .] I was afraid. Afraid of the blows. That was why I remained deaf to his cries. Instead of sacrificing my miserable life and rushing to his side, reassuring him, showing him that he was not abandoned [. . .] I remained flat on my back, asking God to make my father stop calling out my name, to make him stop crying. So afraid was I to incur the wrath of the SS."

Jews who never had to go through it all can read and reread Wiesel, just because they feel responsible to hallow the memory of his father.

Elie Wiesel is a poet, a writer, and a thinker extraordinaire. Inevitably, one wonders how many other Wiesels went up in smoke, their stories untold. Wiesel writes for them all.

Night is the first of Wiesel's trilogy, his death camp memoir. The miracle of his survival increases severalfold with what follows. His two novels *Dawn* and *Day* detail the moral and experiential agony of knowing you are a survivor and do not merit being one. Perhaps "survival" is too strong a word. "Our dead take with them to the hereafter not only clothes and food, but also the future of their descendants." Can you be a survivor if your future already lies buried?

Dawn explores the moral dilemma of Elisha, the novel's protagonist, who has survived the Holocaust and made it to Palestine. While fighting the British to establish a free Jewish state, he has joined a small band of terrorists and is charged, as the novel opens, with his first execution. A randomly chosen British soldier has been kidnapped and will be shot in reprisal for a Jewish partisan whom the British are hanging. The *Dawn* of the title is the Jewish state in the making—but at what cost? Elisha has been recruited by Gad, the Hebrew namesake of a biblical prophet, but pronounced the same as the English "God." How can Elisha disobey a mandate from Gad? But how can he, once hunted by the powerful, now assassinate the innocent? Does he do it? "Hatred is never an answer; death nullifies all answers. There is nothing sacred, nothing uplifting, in hatred or in death," Wiesel writes—but that is after the fact.

Day somewhat mirrors Wiesel's own story. A young man who has survived and lives in Paris is struck by a taxi, and almost killed. The rest of the book follows his recuperation, as he balances between life and death—remembering. His name rarely occurs, as sometimes he does not even know who he is, for he has taken into himself all the horror of the characters in his concentration camp past: he is "the slaughterer," for instance, who strangled a baby, lest its crying give away the hiding place of the entire band of Jews seeking to evade their captors. He is "the smuggler" who smuggles into life the visage of normality, but cannot pass an innocent smokestack without shuddering. "Does life have meaning after Auschwitz?" That, says Wiesel, is what *Day* explores.

Perhaps no other writer has brought the horror and the message of the Holocaust home to millions of readers with the same profundity as Wiesel. He chaired the United States President's Commission on the Holocaust, responsible for the United States Holocaust Memorial Museum in Washington that opened in 1993. He has applied the lessons of the Holocaust to the fate of others, urging the world to come to their rescue: Muslims facing genocide in Bosnia, for example, and refugees in Darfur. Wiesel is the recipient of numerous honorary doctorates for his indefatigable work as a voice of conscience for humanity, and in 1986, he was awarded the Nobel Prize for Peace. He concluded his acceptance speech with the lesson, "A destruction only man can provoke, only man can prevent. Mankind must remember that peace is not God's gift to his creatures, it is our gift to each other."

No one else can point to the unfathomable and suggest the unimaginable with the poetic power that Wiesel manages on virtually every page. *The Night Trilogy* is not recommended for enjoyment. There are times when enjoyment is so completely not the point. It is simply required reading.

Survival in Auschwitz (1958); The Reawakening (1965)

Primo Levi (1919–1987)

"Driven by thirst, I eyed a fine icicle outside the window, within hand's reach. I opened the window and broke off the icicle but at once a large, heavy guard prowling outside brutally snatched it away from me. 'Warum?' I asked him in my poor German. 'Hier ist kein warum' (there is no why here), he replied. "

"**I** prefer the role of witness to that of judge," writes Primo Levi in the Afterword to his two-volume testimony to human survival: first as an inmate at a work camp in Auschwitz, and then as a survivor and displaced person, making his way through Russia back home to his native Italy. Not that he withholds judgment on those responsible for the ultimate mass-murder machine he has just narrowly escaped; but Levi's brilliance as a writer lies in his almost eerily dispassionate account of what he himself experienced and witnessed. It is as if he had been granted invisibility to roam the concentration camps in order to take notes and then sit down at a typewriter to achieve the stylistic elegance necessary to portray what cannot easily be imagined, let alone grasped, by an outsider.

Auschwitz, Levi reminds us, was not just one but some forty camps. Its administration capital alone ("Auschwitz Central") held 20,000 prisoners. Adjacent were "a set of three to five camps, depending on the period," known as Birkenau, which "grew to contain about 60,000 prisoners, 40,000 of them women, and in which the gas chambers and cremation furnaces functioned." Levi was *Häftling* (prisoner) No. 174517, one of 12,000 other slave laborers housed at Buna-Monowitz, the largest of many associated work camps. He survived, he says, "chiefly through good luck," living through the worst of the nightmare when the Nazis were losing the war, but redoubling their efforts to kill as many Jews as possible before the inevitable end—24,000 were murdered in Auschwitz alone on just one long August day of 1944.

Levi is most incisive when describing the ins and outs of the Auschwitz prisoner culture spawned by the camp's incessant terror. He puts us in the mind of a *Häftling*: Years after being liberated, you still walk with eyes obsessively focused on the ground, hoping to spy a piece of string. Someday, you will need the string to hold together a shoe, because without the shoe, you will develop infested sores that impede your walking; and if you are unable to march briskly to and from work, you will be summarily shot. Or, if you somehow escape that, on the next "selection" day ("*selekcja*"), when you must run naked through the winter cold to demonstrate your unhampered ability to work, you might limp, and then you will be "chosen" for imminent gassing. Even if your shoes hold together, you can always trade the string for food, the black-market commodity most in demand for people who must survive on a daily ration of a little bread and some watered-down soup. Sometimes, you have traded away your only shirt, for which you will be beaten, but you will be given another shirt—of sorts. No matter that it is falling apart; you have the string you hoarded, and you can use it to tie the shirt pieces together enough to remain on your body.

Levi's powerful prose paints an entire cast of concentration camp characters. The "guests" of the camp include "criminals, politicals, and Jews," each group marked by different, colored emblems (a triangle or Jewish Star) sewn on their jackets. A few SS men dot the landscape, but the average Jew's fate is in the hands of *Kapos* charged to oversee *Kommandos*, the worker teams. There are "prominents," too—"the aristocracy, the internees holding the highest posts." A "camp brothel composed of Polish *Häftling* girls is reserved for the *Reichsdeutsche* [the German citizens running the camp]." The wretched souls who cannot hack camp life and are doomed to crematoria are called "*musselmans*." In a way, however, there are "no criminals nor madmen, no criminals because there is no moral law to contravene, and no madmen because we are wholly devoid of free will, as our only action is, in time and place, the only conceivable one."

On January 27, 1945, the first Russian soldiers arrived in what was by then a ghost camp, stocked with shadows of those human beings who had been too sick to be taken on the Nazis' forced march westward, but who had somehow been overlooked by the German soldiers dispatched before their departure to murder anything moving. The Russians appeared over the horizon just as Levi (who had been holed up in the infirmary) was about to dump the body of a friend into a mass grave, to prevent it from freezing and someday rotting alongside the thousands of other corpses strewn everywhere in sight.

Soon he was to discover a second bureaucracy, this one charged not with his death, however, but his deliverance. "These Russians," he wrote, "were curiously sensitive to the fascination of red tape (of which, however, they wholly missed the ultimate rational significance)." As a result, he was transferred from one command to another, in a circuitous route across the Russian steppes and back, stopping off, with no purpose whatever, for days and even months, before moving on to some other wholly inexplicable stage of his journey home to Italy.

The Reawakening details all of this, including the immediate postwar horrors of continued hunger, the aftershock of having survived, and the persistent anti-Semitism (one infamous example is the 1946 pogrom in the Polish city of Kielce that killed 40 of the 200 Jewish Holocaust survivors there). But *The Reawakening* is surrealistically humorous, too. Levi teams up with a comedic team of survivors looking for home: Cesare, a wonderfully lovable rogue gifted with the black-market ability to trade anything for anything; a seventy-year-old bricklayer who knows how to curse, but not much else; and a "little old man from Trieste" with the curious name of Mr. Unverdorben. For no apparent reason, the train carrying this band of unlikelies to yet another camp for displaced persons breaks down at the village of Starye Dorogi, where they pantomime negotiations to get food from Russian peasants, but later dine on horsemeat courtesy of returning Russian troops trading in their worn-out horses.

At the end of *The Reawakening*, we have gone full circle, from a seemingly ordinary life in Italy to the hell of the Holocaust and back to Italy—but is such a return even possible? Did Primo Levi manage it? Perhaps he did—the very title of this book suggests that the long night of agony did indeed give way to the absurdities of Starye Dorogi and a journey back to his native Turin. But the title takes on ominous dimensions when the author associates it with his recurrent nightmare of being back in Auschwitz, dreading the inevitable daily summons in Polish, "*Wstawach!*"—"Wake up!" And then, there is the tragic way that Levi died: he fell to his death—perhaps deliberately—inside the apartment building in Turin where he lived.

He left behind a literary bequest to humanity, his own interrupted life and the detailed observations upon it: more than a dozen books, short stories, essays, and poems. Upon hearing of Levi's death, Elie Wiesel observed that "Primo Levi died at Auschwitz forty years earlier." Upon reading his testimony to future generations, we might say: Primo Levi remains alive even today. His insistent voice seems destined to remain forever.

Eichmann in Jerusalem
(1963)

Hannah Arendt (1906–1975)

"What for Hitler, the sole, lonely plotter of the Final Solution [. . .] was among the war's main objectives [. . .] and what for Eichmann was a job, with its daily routine, its ups and downs, was for the Jews quite literally the end of the world."

Jews who grew up in the immediacy of the Holocaust's long shadow often asked their parents why some new Jewish residents in town had numbers tattooed on their arms. Parents knew the answer, but had difficulty saying it. The children may have vaguely gotten the picture of lots of Jews having had something awful happen to them in some country far away. Whatever they were told by their parents, the hush in which it was conveyed warned them away from pursuing the topic any further.

This reticence typified the postwar Jewish response to the Holocaust. In part, perhaps, it was self-inflicted guilt (whether appropriate or not) about not having done more to save Europe's Jews. In part, it was the fact that no one yet had a vocabulary adequate to the task of grasping the enormity of the horror that was still sinking into our numbed collective consciousness. Then, too, albeit unconsciously, people might have wanted the whole thing to go away, so that they might take up their perfectly normal lives again as if nothing so radically evil had ever descended upon earth.

In 1961, this reticence (and certainly the option of "taking up perfectly normal lives again") vanished, for on April 11 of that year, Adolf Eichmann was put on trial in Jerusalem for crimes against the Jewish People and against humanity. He had been captured by Israeli agents in Argentina in 1960 and brought to Israel to stand trial. On May 31, 1962, he became the only person in the history of the State of Israel to be subjected to capital punishment.

During the fourteen weeks of his trial, reporters around the world wired home the shocking testimony provided by some ninety concentration camp survivors. Among the courtroom observers was Hannah Arendt, herself an escapee from the Nazis, who had fled to America in 1941 and was covering the trial for *The New Yorker*. Her dispatches were later published in book form as *Eichmann in Jerusalem*.

It is hard to find a more controversial book. Arendt was a gifted intellectual and celebrated political thinker, known for studying the phenomenon of totalitarianism and characterizing Jews historically as "a pariah people." Born in Hanover, Germany, she was no stranger to controversy: In the 1920s, she had a love affair with her university teacher Martin Heidegger, possibly the most influential German philosopher of her day, but a man who went on to support the Nazis briefly in 1933—without ever recanting his position after the war ended. She was an ardent Zionist who favored a two-state solution in the Middle East, warning (alongside Martin Buber) of the dire consequences that would follow from a vibrant Jewish state without a parallel national entity for the Palestinians. Arendt had studied with some of the most celebrated minds of the twentieth century—not just Heidegger, but also Edmund Husserl and Karl Jaspers. She served as visiting professor at several American universities before being appointed as full professor at Princeton University—the first woman to be so honored. But nothing prepared her for the uproar that would follow her account of the Eichmann trial.

The facts of the Nazi era were well known and largely unquestioned, even by Eichmann's lawyer. But what role did Eichmann actually play in the atrocities with which he was charged? Hitler's war against the Jews required their enforced transport to concentration camps where they were either worked to death or murdered. Eichmann, a Gestapo chief, directed that transport.

Most of the trial involved memories provided by Holocaust survivors. Arendt made no friends by judging them largely irrelevant to the trial, saying that witnesses were being allowed to take the stand even if their testimony could not be directly connected to the accused. She charged Israel's prime minister, David Ben-Gurion, with being "the invisible stage manager" of a trial designed not so much to bring Eichmann to justice as to let the world know what Jews had been subjected to, so that the world would never forget.

Arendt's well-known work on totalitarianism had already unmasked the "radical evil" of the Nazi and the communist regimes. Now she added to the lexicon of evil by accusing Eichmann not of ardent extremism, but of the "banality of evil." As a Nazi bureaucrat, his sin was the very crime he offered as his defense: he had simply followed orders. He demonstrated what ordinary people, not just demonically twisted minds, are capable of.

Needless to say, Arendt's judgment appalled concentration camp survivors. And to make matters worse, Arendt implicated Jews in their own destruction. Wherever they went, the Nazis had charged local Jewish leaders with all the little tasks that went into the destructive process—taking a Jewish census, listing Jewish holdings, and so on. The same leaders delivered quotas of Jews for the concentration camps, until at the end there was no one left to deliver but themselves. She seemed—in part, at least—to blame the victims, for agreeing "to walk to their doom on their own feet carrying their own little valises."

Still, it was not the Jews, but the Nazis who were the perpetrators, and within the Nazi system, it was all the little Eichmanns that made it work. "There existed not a single organization or public institution in Germany that did not become involved in criminal actions and transactions."

What bothered most critics of *Eichmann in Jerusalem* was its author's apparent attempt to distance herself from the victims, as if she herself had not been one of them. Gershom Scholem, the celebrated scholar who was also Arendt's mentor and friend, accused her of lacking elementary love for her fellow Jews. "In you, dear Hannah," he wrote to her, "I find little trace of this." But after the war, Arendt had opened her first lecture in Germany with the reminder "I am a German Jew driven from my homeland by the Nazis." If Arendt's coverage of the Eichmann trial did not overflow with her own appreciation of the victims whose words she reports, it was not because she lacked sympathy for their plight, but because she approached her task committed to a dispassionate evaluation of the judicial process that even Eichmann deserved. Arendt's reportage is required reading precisely because she wrote it that way, thereby presenting us with the trial's proceedings as if we had been there ourselves.

Eichmann in Jerusalem raises issues that are still being debated today. What is the nature of evil? How could a civilized culture like Germany have brought about such a diabolical end? What role, if any, did Jewish authorities unknowingly play in abetting Hitler's "Final Solution"?

Arendt's book is not easy to get through, precisely because these important issues are discussed with detail and the depth of thought that few observers other than Arendt could have managed. It is part history (What happened?), part political science (In what context was it possible?), and part theodicy (What is the origin of evil altogether?). Arendt pulls no punches, and in so doing, she gives us a dark drama of human nature, background politics, and even the judicial process. More than that, her book is a superb example of a great philosophical mind struggling with the moral dilemma of evil itself.

Badenheim 1939
(1979)

Aharon Appelfeld (born 1932)

"Train journeys are nice, aren't they?"

Badenheim *1939* is the literary equivalent of a horror film, where the characters awaken to a pleasant, sun-filled day with nothing untoward on the horizon, but then are met with the ghastly recognition that there is a monster on the loose. Here we are given a bucolic account of ordinary people in a fictitious Austrian spa town on their unsuspecting way to a horrible end. One is tempted to put the novel down and shout out warnings. Don't these people know this is Austria in 1939, and they are about to be swallowed up alive as early Jewish victims of the Holocaust? They don't, obviously. Retrospective omniscience is a luxury they will not have.

There is a difference, a crucial one, between horror films and Aharon Appelfeld's novel. *King Kong* and *The War of the Worlds* never happened, while the Holocaust did. There were countless real towns just like Badenheim, just as there really was a Hamburg, a Prague, a Warsaw, and a Vienna, each of them with Jews who could not foresee the story's tragic denouement.

Appelfeld lived through it. He grew up in the town of Czernowitz, Romania, now part of Ukraine. When he was only eight years old, the Nazis murdered his mother and sent him to a concentration camp. He escaped, went underground, later joined the Soviet army as a cook, and then languished in an Italian camp for displaced persons before finally making it to Palestine in 1946. In Israel, as an adult, he met his father, whom he hadn't seen since he was eight. He later recalled, "We were separated and I had not seen him for twenty years. He escaped, he was in Russia, and then after twenty years I met him, not knowing each other."

Until the Eichmann trial in 1961, Jews were reticent to face up to the enormity of the Holocaust. Aharon Appelfeld was one of the first authors to break the silence, and has since become internationally known for doing so.

The power of this novel is its extraordinary ordinariness. Throughout the book, characters seem to come and go, not by authorial device, but by chance, the way people really do drift in and out of locations and situations by their own machinations rather than by someone else's. It is set in Badenheim, a resort town with the usual vacation amenities, including a summer music festival that is being mounted by a regular guest and impresario, Dr. Pappenheim, the novel's main character.

Pappenheim appears at the vortex of the comings and goings of other summer guests: some identified only by their role (hotel manager, pastry shop owner, head waiter), others by name. Trude is a dying consumptive married to Martin, the town's pharmacist. Professor Fussholdt is a serious academician who does nothing but attend to some manuscript he has been working on. Karl is married to a woman who is "Prussian born and bred," and has children being raised in military school by their grandfather. Frau Zauberblit has married a German general, no less, but the couple is divorced, and their daughter frantically wants her Jewish mother to renounce all "maternal rights."

We know the end of this horror story. None of these people will be alive very much longer. Frau Zauberblit's daughter hopes to avoid classification as Jewish, but Hitler will have other ideas. Professor Fussholdt's manuscript will never see the light of day. When Mandelbaum, a famous singer touted by Pappenheim as the festival highlight, goes missing, Pappenheim is disappointed enough to conclude that "his life isn't worth living." The Nazis will agree—for reasons other than what Pappenheim imagines. Poor sick Trude has it right when she runs screaming onto the veranda, as if in a nightmare. Martin calms her with the innocent assurance "There are no wolves here." But there are!

The Nazi wolves are disguised not as sheep but as the workers of the sanitation department. When they register all Jews in town, Frau Zauberblit praises their "order and beauty." It turns out the sanitation department knows more about the Jews than the Jews know about themselves—even that the father of one of them "wrote a book about arithmetic in Hebrew." In short order, they seal off the town, cut off its mail, close off the water supply, and pass off Poland as a virtual spa where Jews will happily agree to be resettled. To the end, these assimilated Jews imagine the best. "'There is nothing to be afraid of,' says Pappenheim. 'In Poland, there are lots of Jews.'" Then, to everyone's surprise, cattle cars arrive instead of luxurious passenger accommodations.

Lurking below the surface is the ongoing disregard that "*echte*" ("real") Austrian-German Jews have toward their eastern European Jewish cousins, whom they see as embarrassingly unrefined. Leon Samitszky, for instance, is a Polish Jew whose parents moved west when he was a child, but who—not being "true" Westerners, and being "uncultured" by Western standards—"didn't give me any musical education." He asks Frau Zauberblit, "Do I have the honor of addressing an Austrian citizen of Jewish origin?" "You do, sir," she responds, condescendingly. As the Nazi net tightens, the Westerners are sure it is the fault of the eastern Jews, whom the sanitation department—"quite rightly," the Westerners would say—considers suspect. But we know, as they do not, that Hitler will lump all Jews altogether. As Samitzky tells Pappenheim, a Westerner, "Your nose testifies to the fact that you're no Austrian."

Badenheim 1939 was initially greeted with mixed reviews, not for its quality (everyone agreed on its brilliance) but for its message. Some thought it a Zionist tract, contending that Israel is the only safe place for Jews to live. Others condemned Appelfeld for blaming the victims who hadn't seen the Holocaust coming. That most did not, in fact, see it coming, is undeniable. But was Appelfeld saying they should have? Hardly. *Badenheim 1939* is a terse, absurd, and dreamlike tale of unimaginable horror. It is also a reflection on human, not just Jewish, nature, which makes us want to will away what is just not "willable." It acknowledges, but does not judge, existential reality.

Maus

(1986 and 1991)

Art Spiegelman (born 1948)

"My father bleeds history."

The time was the 1930s, and liberal hopes were hard to come by, given a world mired in economic hardship and on its way to fascism. Two American Jews, Jerry Siegel and Joe Shuster, hatched the notion of a superhero who would save humanity from such evil. Knowing something of the immigrant experience, they depicted their hero as an immigrant himself—albeit not just from a foreign country, but from a different planet. That is how, in 1938, Superman was born—and how comic books went mainstream in America.

It's a stretch to call *Superman* a Jewish comic book, but it is not too much to call American comic books a Jewish creation. Jerry Siegel and Joe Shuster were not the only Jews to leave their mark on the new medium. So, too, was Bob Kane, who invented *Batman* in 1939, and Joe Simon and Jack Kirby, the co-creators of *Captain America* (1941)—a hero who took an outright stand against Hitler and the Nazis. Simon worked for another Jew, Martin Goodman, who ran a publishing company later named Marvel Comics. Goodman's assistant, Stan Lee, revived *Captain America* and (together with Steve Ditko) gave us *Spiderman*, in the 1960s. In Europe, at the same time, René Goscinny, a Jew by descent and possibly the most brilliant European comic book creator, was authoring the hugely successful French comic book series *Astérix*. Goscinny had lived in New York in the 1950s and was friends with the creators of *MAD* magazine.

By the 1960s, some of these Jewish comic book artists were contributing to an underground genre that reflected the counterculture of the Vietnam years. One of them was Art Spiegelman, who later (in 1980), cofounded his own comic book publication, *Raw*. In *Raw* he previewed in serialized form what is certainly a Jewish work, and a work of genius at that: *Maus*, the story of his father's experience in the Holocaust. In 1986, the various strips were published as a graphic novel, and in 1991, a second volume was added. Volume 1 covers the period from the mid-1930s to 1944, with the heading "My Father Bleeds

History"; Volume 2 picks up in 1944 and is labeled "And Here My Troubles Began."

Maus is deceptively simple in form: a black-and-white comic strip, where Jews are portrayed as mice, the Nazis as cats. The Polish collaborators who worked in the concentration camps despite the barbarism of their task are presented as pigs, and the American liberators are featured as "man's best friend"—puppy dogs.

What makes *Maus* so daring is indicated in its subtitle: *A Survivor's Tale.* As much as it is indeed an illustrated depiction of life in the Nazi camps, it is even more a definitive look at the way the next Jewish generation relates to that experience. The author portrays what his father tells him, but, simultaneously, he supplies a story within a story—himself talking to his father to convince the father to tell him the story. *Maus* is therefore about Spiegelman's father, Vladek, but also about the son, Art, who depicts himself depicting himself. Early on, for example, he promises he will omit from the chronicle the embarrassing story of his father's early love affairs, but we know about the promise only because he puts the love affair in anyway, and then includes himself making the promise that he will not keep.

Maus unveils the horribly strained relationship that "the second generation" has with its "survivor parents." Like other children born to survivors after the war, Spiegelman knows something of his parents' past, but never enough—having been too frightened or confused as a child to ask questions and connect the dots. He knows that his mother, Anja (who escaped the Holocaust as well), committed suicide in America in 1968; he knows, too, that he lost a brother, Richieu, born in Europe and killed there as a child. In *Maus*, he makes his father, Vladek, tell him the rest: he and Anja had entrusted Richieu to a caretaker in hope of saving him; when Richieu was slated for Auschwitz anyway, the caretaker fed him poison—a better way to die; Vladek himself survived because of quick thinking and inventiveness—and a massive share of just plain luck.

Real-life Art Spiegelman grew up in New York, with nightmares of Nazis pulling him from his home. He used to wonder which of his parents he would have saved, had he been forced to choose just one of them. Now, as an adult, he wants to save at least their stories, but he feels "inadequate trying to reconstruct a reality that was worse than my darkest dreams [. . .] and trying to do it as a comic strip!" The first volume of *Maus* was a much celebrated success—something of a problem for a child of Holocaust victims, who scarcely wanted to benefit from the Holocaust in any way. In the second volume of *Maus*, therefore, Spiegelman agonizes over the problem that success has brought with it.

"Whatever I accomplish doesn't seem like much compared to surviving Auschwitz," he tells his therapist in the story. He lives less with guilt than with pervasive sadness, and often anger—at the picture of dead Richieu, for instance, whom his parents practically worship as the lost icon of their own lost European world. What frustrates him most is his father: clutching, demanding, suspicious, almost paranoid, and manipulative to the end, even with his son and daughter-in-law (who puts up with Vladek, and with her husband, Art—or Artie, as his father calls him—as well).

Vladek is haunted by a past that never truly passes. He remembers it all, and even relives it. Having known want, he lives cheaply now, in fear of losing everything again: from the restrooms of restaurants he takes home paper towels to use as napkins; pockets matchbooks from hotels; and picks up old telephone wire, just in case he should ever need it. He remarried after Anja's death, but constantly berates his new wife, who, he suspects, wants only his money, and who is "guilty" of oversights such as opening a new container of salt when there are two already opened. When he finds an open cereal box in his pantry, still filled with cereal, he glues it back together and pleads his Holocaust history to get the grocery-store manager to take it back.

The pathos of this father-son relationship becomes clear when Art requests some diaries that his mother, Anja, has apparently left behind. They are gone, Vladek says. Later, he "remembers" that he himself destroyed them in the depths of his depression. To be exact, he burned them, an ironic—albeit unconscious—reenactment of Nazi book burning. He adds salt to Art's wound by admitting to him that he read the diaries first and knew that Anja had said, "I wish my son, when he grows up, he will be interested in this." Art, who himself suffered a depression after his mother's suicide, calls Vladek a "murderer" who has killed off Art's only route to Anja's past.

It would be a serious mistake to lump together the experiences of all "second-generation" Jews in any single portrait. They *all* have stories of their own, of course, and the whole point is not to merge them into an undifferentiated whole that loses the specificity of the singular life that each one is. Many, however, do share the compulsion to pass their parents' horrific stories on: for the sake of their parents, who deserve at least that; for the sake of humanity; and for their own sake and the sake of their children.

Israel

(1998)

Martin Gilbert (born 1936)

"At five o'clock on the afternoon of 14 May 1948, in the main hall of the Tel Aviv Museum, a ceremony took place that inaugurated the State of Israel. The ceremony began with the singing of the Jewish anthem 'Hatikvah'. A few moments later David Ben-Gurion, as Prime Minister and Minister of Defence of the newly created provisional government, put his signature to Israel's Declaration of Independence."

By 2007, more Jews lived in Israel than in any other country on earth: 5,309,000, to be exact. Most had arrived as refugees escaping persecution. No one else would take them, and Israel actually wanted them. In 1945, the Jewish population in Palestine had numbered only 517,000. From 1948 to 1950, the first two years of statehood, 120,000 more people arrived from displaced persons' camps in Europe, where they had been interned at the end of World War II, awaiting a place to go. They were joined by Jews suffering oppression in Arab lands, 123,371 of them from Iraq alone. The announcement of a Jewish state had triggered anti-Jewish riots in Yemen, and over 45,000 Jewish victims were airlifted to Israel in "Operation Magic Carpet." By 1950, "Jewish immigration was so rapid that the figure became obsolete even as the counting was in progress. The 1948 census had given a Jewish population of 716,678 [. . .] The 1950 census gave 1,029,000 Jews."

Assimilating the newcomers to Israel was a great challenge, since they usually arrived penniless, spoke no Hebrew, and had no means of employment. Because of lack of permanent housing, they first lived in tent cities called *ma'abarot* (temporary quarters) that, however, disappeared within a decade.

In 1984 and 1991, other airlifts carried thousands of persecuted Ethiopian Jews to Israel, many of whom had never seen running water or electricity before. The largest new wave of immigrants came from the former Soviet Union—900,000 from 1989 to 2001—boosting the Israeli population by almost 20 percent.

Jews are intensely proud of these figures, testimony to the post-Holocaust Jewish vow of "Never again!" From an Ashkenazi, eastern

European enclave in Palestine, Israel had become a multiethnic and multicultural haven, on a fast track to becoming an agricultural, scientific, intellectual, economic, and artistic success story. The early settlers drained swamps, watered the desert, built roads, founded universities, planted forests, erected cities on sand dunes, and achieved universal suffrage. They also built a citizen army, because it all had to be done in the face of surrounding Arab powers that declared war on the nascent Jewish state in 1948, and have been launching terrorist attacks upon it ever since.

In 1956, Israel fought alongside England and France—in the so-called Sinai [Desert] campaign—to guarantee the free movement of ships through the Suez Canal. After capturing the Sinai, Israel withdrew on condition that a United Nations peacekeeping force would police the area separating Egypt from Israel. When Egypt expelled the United Nations forces in 1967 while mobilizing for yet another all-out war, Israel launched a preemptive attack that became the Six-Day War, an unmitigated Israeli victory that vastly expanded its territory, putting over a million Arab inhabitants under Israeli control.

That war and its aftermath changed everything, especially after the follow-up war of 1973, when Egypt and Syria jointly attacked, catching Israel unawares on Yom Kippur. Israel suffered heavy casualties but fought back, and after three weeks, a cease-fire was implemented.

Until then, Israel had been ruled by socialist moderates such as the founding prime minister, David Ben-Gurion, but the anxiety of having almost been massacred in 1973 led to the election of right-wing and hardline Menachem Begin as prime minister in 1977. During the old regime, General Moshe Dayan, hero of the 1967 Six-Day War, had sympathized with the Arabs under Israeli occupation, saying, "I want a policy whereby an Arab can be born, live and die in the West Bank without ever seeing an Israeli official." The new regime thought otherwise. Claiming Israel's right to the captured land, it joined forces with radical religious parties that interpreted the Bible as promising the land to Jews in perpetuity. In 1975, Gush Emunim ("Bloc of the Faithful"), an ultra-Orthodox movement, began erecting Jewish settlements in the very midst of the occupied Arab population. By 1982, continued shelling of Israeli settlements in the north prompted the Lebanon War, in which General Ariel Sharon surprised his own government by pushing as far as Beirut, and then closed his eyes as Arab Muslims in two refugee camps were massacred by rival Arab Christian militias—an action that Sharon aided and abetted by illuminating the camps with flares. The war ended badly; Israeli forces retreated; and Israel's days of innocence were forever over.

Peace between Israel and Egypt had arrived in 1979, and peace with Jordan followed in 1994, but in 1987, and again in 2000, popular uprisings called Intifada erupted in the West Bank and the Gaza Strip. At roughly the same time, Hezbollah and Hamas, terrorist political parties dedicated to destroying Israel, became established in Lebanon and in the Gaza Strip, respectively—making a final peace seem farther away than ever.

But the story of Israel is much more than a series of wars. It is the story of cultural transformation beyond anyone's wildest imagination. Education is universal and mandatory. Archeology is a national pastime. Museums are everywhere. Music festivals abound. The arts are thriving. It is a world leader in computers, high-tech innovation, breakthrough agribusiness, fashion and design.

Israel's history is also an unforgettable cast of characters who brought it all about and left memoirs that take one's breath away. When Golda Meir (prime minister from 1969 to 1974) visited Jews in Moscow, for instance, 50,000 of them turned out despite Soviet threats of reprisal for asserting their Jewish identity. Moved to tears, all she managed to say to them was a single sentence (in Yiddish): "Thank you for having remained Jews." Before statehood, Yitzhak Rabin (twice prime minister, in the 1970s and 1990s) was charged with rescuing illegal immigrants whom England would otherwise deport back to Europe. As he climbed the mountain ridge into Israel carrying "a terrified Jewish child—a child of the Holocaust," he reflected, "My shoulders bore the hopes of the Jewish people."

This great tapestry of Israel's past comes alive in an epic work, encyclopedic in its scope, by British master historian Sir Martin Gilbert, the official biographer of Winston Churchill and author of more than eighty books. His account captures it all—not just the intransigence of the surrounding Arab leaders who still refuse to recognize a Jewish state, but also the travesties committed by the Jewish side (yes, Arabs did needlessly flee their homes in the 1948 war, but yes, also, the Israeli army forced many of them out). In the end, Gilbert cites President Shimon Peres, whose 2007 inaugural address admitted that, as a nation, "we are flawed and have erred." But "there is no room for melancholy [. . .] If sometimes the atmosphere is autumnal [. . .] spring is waiting for us at the threshold. The spring will definitely come!"

Nothing evokes Jewish conversation the way Israel does, and Gilbert's history provides both its autumns and its springs—all that is needed to enter that conversation with facts, with perspective, and with hope that eventually, "the spring will definitely come!"

Only Yesterday
(1945)

Shmuel Yosef Agnon (1888–1970)

"The Land of Israel is not given to those who eat manna. I'm not a great scholar, but I do know that when the children of Israel entered the Land of Israel, the manna stopped."

Jews around the world have been raised on the myth of Zionist settlers building up a homeland by dint of sweat, adrenaline, and gallant dreaming: swamps drained, *kibbutzim* (farm collectives) established, and entire cities constructed. There is some truth to this: Jews in Palestine did all that. But it was not all dancing around a campfire singing pioneer songs.

Israel's history is conventionally divided according to waves of immigration, each one an *aliyah*, an "ascendance." The image derives from the rabbinic view of Israel as the heart, or center, of the universe, and Jerusalem as the center of the center. If the same idea is expressed vertically, immigration to Israel becomes a case of "ascending." The First Aliyah (1882–1903) was spurred by draconian restrictions on Jewish freedom in Russia. The Second Aliyah (1904–1914) responded to pogroms in Russia and Ukraine, especially the horrific events in Kishinev in 1903. Shmuel Yosef Agnon was part of that aliyah: he arrived in Israel in 1908.

Agnon was born Shmuel Yosef Czaczkes in Austro-Hungarian Galicia and received a traditional Jewish education, moderated by his mother's love of the Enlightenment. His first full-length book, *Agunot*, suggested the pen name Agnon. It is common to refer to him as Shy Agnon, "shy" being an acronym of his first initials SH[muel] Y[osef], and, at the same time, the Hebrew word for "gift." Agnon is a *shy*, a gift to the Jewish People.

Only Yesterday is Agnon's gifted tale of the way life really was back then for the early settlers. The novel's protagonist, Isaac Kumer, is a naive dreamer from Galicia who is dispatched to Palestine during the Second Aliyah by his father, who hopes that Isaac will amount to something there. But Isaac cannot even find a job. Eventually, by pure happenstance, he becomes a house painter in Jaffa, before the time when its sister city, Tel Aviv, was born (1909). The rest of the novel chronicles Isaac's peregrinations back and forth to Jerusalem and the various characters' psychological perspectives on the Jewish homeland in the making.

Modernist literature has been described as "the end of a story line," and *Only Yesterday* is quintessentially modernist. The plot is secondary to the narrator's panoramic stream of consciousness that meanders off into meticulously detailed tangents, each one the equivalent of a short-story gem unto itself. At one point, for instance, Isaac paints the word "crazy" on the back of a wild dog, after which the plot continues, in part, from the perspective of the dog, which is kicked around, unnoticed and powerless to affect its own destiny. The dog symbolizes the Jewish People, whom Zionists viewed as being kicked around and powerless through the ages of its "exile" from its land. In the end, the dog abandons its passivity and bites Isaac, the scourge who painted him in the first place. The dog's craziness turns out to be a self-fulfilling prophecy of the oppressor who painted it with the word "crazy"; the parallel craziness of the Zionists is their insistence on leaving the comforts of Europe to seek the harsh realities of Palestine—but that, too, was forced upon them by the oppressive majority who called Jews crazy for refusing to convert to Christianity and thereby assimilate into Western history.

The brilliance of *Only Yesterday* derives from Agnon's patented style and his empathy for the human condition, a gift wrapped in obsessive specificity and packaged with ironic humor and multiple allusions to rabbinic literature.

Jaffa and Jerusalem are polar opposites, the new and the old. The Jerusalemites have been there seemingly forever. As medieval religionists praying for the messiah, they despise the modern Jaffa secularists, who "come to the Land of Israel to anger the Creator in His own house." In return, one of Isaac's Jaffa friends predicts of the Jerusalemites, "If they won't go to hell for their idleness, they'll be sent back to this world to be workers and artisans so that in the next incarnation they can repair what they have damaged in this one."

The Jews in Jerusalem live off charity that is collected from Jews abroad. As for their piety, we get plenty of ascetics and saints, but also a preacher with the hilarious name Reb Grunam May-Salvation-Arise. He walks with "one eye turned down to hint to the Holy One how meek was that man and one eye turned up to see how many are those who wanted to hear him." He is "far from boasting and preaching in public, but since a commandment has come to be fulfilled," he relents. "Perhaps I'll say a word or two."

Then there is the fabled but real Ottoman bureaucracy. "Sending a letter through the Turkish post office is like throwing it into the Dead Sea." But even the Jewish clerks "are not wont to work too much, especially bank clerks, especially in the Land of Israel, where all their work is done in six or seven hours, and [. . .] between one hour and the next, they bring them a cup of coffee and between one coffee and the next, lemonade."

In this real world of real people, dreams are dashed and some settlers return to Europe. (Agnon himself returned there and lived in Germany from 1913 to 1924.) But heroism happens on the margins. As they dare to build the new city of Tel Aviv—on sand dunes, no less—"our comrades stand sunk in sand," until eventually, "a sort of road now sprouts from the sands and lets a person's feet stand firm, and men and women come from Jaffa and try out their feet on the road. Behold the wonder, the road doesn't sink and the foot doesn't drown in the sand."

Even the Jerusalemites have their day as they venture outside the old city to build what has since become the ultra-Orthodox neighborhood of Meah Shearim—a risky enterprise, without the Old City walls to protect them from violence and vandalism by those who opposed an expanded Jewish presence in the land. "Anyone who didn't worry about the poor worried about himself, for when the gates of the Old City were locked at night, everyone outside the wall was unprotected."

Agnon followed in the footsteps of Hayyim Nahman Bialik as Israel's leading literary figure. Agnon received the Nobel Prize in Literature in 1966 (together with another Jewish writer, Nelly Sachs), and his response offers a key to remember him: "As a result of the historic catastrophe in which Titus of Rome destroyed Jerusalem and Israel was exiled from its land, I was born in one of the cities of the Exile. But always I regarded myself as one who was born in Jerusalem."

Poetry and Stories
(1955–2000)

Yehuda Amichai (1924–2000)

"There was never enough peace in the country for me to return to reminisce in the places of war [. . .] All of us—the enemy and we ourselves—were terrible children who killed each other in our childishness."

German-born Yehuda Amichai first saw the light of day in 1924. His Orthodox parents, surnamed Pfeuffer, named him Ludwig. His grandfather was a farmer, his father a shopkeeper, and Ludwig became a writer. And what a writer he became!

He is known primarily for his poetry, but his short stories should not be overlooked. In one of them, "The Bar Mitzvah Party," he catches himself maligning a light switch that fails to ignite the electricity, and then remembers, "How can I complain? Even I only light up when switched on, and for some time, there's been no button in me to summon up a large and happy light." The cheery bar mitzvah boy whom he is visiting, by contrast, was a "young verse in the Bible of the world." Few writers match Amichai for his metaphoric sympathy with the way our lives are constructed.

In 1936, Ludwig's family fled the Nazis and moved to Palestine, where he changed his name to Yehuda Amichai (literally, Judah, "My-People-Lives"). He fought as a British soldier in World War II, then joined the Palmach, the strike force of the Haganah (the underground army of Jewish Palestine during the mandate period that led up to statehood). He saw action also in Israel's later wars, which recur in his writing with grim regularity. But so, too, do traditional Judaism's rituals, holidays, and sensibilities, which Amichai inherited from his Orthodox upbringing. Amichai thus embodies two diverse sides of modern Jewish identity: the reflective inheritor of Jewish tradition, and the secular warrior of the Jewish state. Throughout his writing, he infuses the former into the latter, championing the inherent heroism of the ordinary people who are neither: the people who wish mostly just to go through life holding hands, walking in the park, watching television on occasion, and raiding the refrigerator for food they don't need to eat.

The quotation with which this entry begins (from a short story titled "Dicky's Death") recalls such an ordinary man, Dicky, Amichai's gentle battalion commander and "the only mature one among us," whom war called away from home and who "walked two days before his death to see his new-born." But even the bar mitzvah boy would have predicted the probability of Dicky's dying on his way through enemy lines to get back home for the night. The children in the boy's class end up playing a game, and Amichai concludes, "All of life is played according to the rules of a game. Whoever is ignorant must put up collateral: Sometimes they give a watch or a handkerchief. Sometimes they give a heart, or a hand, or a leg, or life itself."

In his poem "Autobiography 1952," Amichai remembers how "My father built over me a worry as big as a shipyard." He became a champion of ordinary people not just in war, therefore, but in peacetime, too, as if each of their worries should be his own as well—a proper part of the "shipyard worry" that he had inherited. He had been raised on rabbinic writings that anticipated redemption coming in a grand sweep of God's hand, a miraculous arrival of a messiah. For Amichai, however, redemption is an altogether ordinary thing, a simple change of focus that occurred to him while watching tourists so fascinated with history that they ignored the men and women trying to eke out a living in history's shadow. Guides would point to real people only to use them as reference points for locating instances of historical ruin nearby. Amichai argued that redemption would arrive only when guides work the other way around—pointing to historical ruins to draw attention to ordinary passersby. A Roman arch would be less important than real-life people who pass under it to buy groceries for their families.

As a young man during the founding days of Israel, Amichai embraced the burgeoning modern Hebrew language. That Israel would be a Hebrew-speaking country was by no means a foregone conclusion. Originally the language of the Bible, Hebrew had become also the language of prayer and of some medieval secular poetry, but it was considered too holy for everyday human speech. The literature of rabbinic scholarship from Talmudic days onward was Babylonian Aramaic—a sister language to Hebrew. Ordinary Jewish life was conducted in the language of the host culture in which Jews found themselves (Greek, Arabic, French, German, and so on). When talking among themselves, Jews sometimes used a combination of the host language with Hebrew and Aramaic. For Jews who hailed from Spain, this was Ladino; for those whose home was central and eastern Europe, it was Yiddish.

That all changed because of Eliezer Ben-Yehuda (1858–1922), a linguistic "zealot" from Lithuania who had studied at the Sorbonne before he moved to Palestine in 1881 and decided to dedicate his life to reviving Hebrew. Undeterred by the fact that it had not been spoken for two millennia, he simply started speaking it, making up words as necessary and inflicting the language on his wife and children, because he refused to speak anything else. It worked. Hebrew is now the universally regarded language of Jewish peoplehood. Jews all over the world strive for at least some familiarity with Hebrew, not just the biblical variety but the fully modern idiom of Israeli streets and society.

By the time Amichai was born (two years after Ben-Yehuda's death), the revival of Hebrew was well under way, and Amichai's subject matter was the poetry of actual life. Never mind the vines and fig trees of the prophets, or even the stylized love of the biblical Song of Songs. Amichai's poems became a living laboratory for the many new words that had to be coined for a new land and a new era: jet planes and portholes for tanks, bank notes and housing projects, "ground breaking ceremonies [and] processions of black ants." He depicts the modern Jewish experience of Israelis who read, work, and play, but are called off to war on occasion to ensure a future where their children will likewise be able to read, work, and play.

Both Israeli and Jewish to his core, Amichai is equally a conscientious member of the human family across the globe, whose writing suggests that the humanity we share across battle lines will save us from ourselves. He writes about Yom Kippur, 1967, only a few months after the Six-Day War when Israelis regained access to the city of Jerusalem and found themselves able to traverse its ancient marketplace for the first time in twenty years. Leaving the synagogue briefly to take that walk, Amichai remembers the recent war while also anticipating the liturgy to which he will return, a final solemn Yom Kippur service that warns us to repent before the gates of heaven close.

Seeing an Arab store "with buttons and zippers and spools of thread," he remembers that his own father ran such a shop in Europe. Unburdening himself to the Arab shopkeeper, he sums up the centuries of complexity that comprise the Jewish story—how, in the end, his father was buried in Europe while he himself made aliyah to Israel. In perfect symmetry, Amichai returns to the "Closing of the Gates" liturgy while the Arab closes the gates to his shop—silent testimony, perhaps, to the dream that both sides will close the gates on their troublesome past and move forward together.

Letters to an American Jewish Friend
(1977)
Hillel Halkin (born 1939)

> *"Classical Zionism held that it is the fate of Diasporan Jewry in the modern world to be hopelessly trapped between the Scylla of assimilation and the Charybdis of anti-Semitism, the only escape from one being into the jaws of the other and vice versa [. . .] Jews as a people had a future in the modern world only as an autonomous community living in a land of their own [. . .] Only in such a state [. . .] could a secular Jewish culture develop to fill the void left in Jewish life by the decline of religion."*

There are few Jewish books more controversial than this one, written by a New Yorker who moved to Israel—he made aliyah—just after the Six-Day War of 1967, and who subsequently argued the moral necessity of his decision to a friend still living in the Diaspora. The subtitle says it all: *A Zionist's Polemic*. One is likely to approach the book as the author's "friend," convinced in advance, perhaps, how easy it will be to refute Halkin's arguments. But his case is so compelling, it becomes hard for a Jewish reader in the Diaspora *not* to embrace the Zionism Halkin espouses and make the move as well.

Four decades have passed since Halkin penned his letters. The world has vastly changed, and yet, quite amazingly, Jews are still debating the challenge he so deftly posed. His chain of arguments is not easily refuted:

(1) Until the Enlightenment, Jews were a religious people, convinced beyond a doubt that God (a real Being) had chosen them and revealed the Torah as the Jewish mandate throughout the centuries.

(2) The Enlightenment made it impossible for Jews to believe in such a God, let alone such religious particularity; and emancipation made them citizens of the world. In an instant, both the rationale and the necessity of being a Jew collapsed.

(3) But acceptance as citizens has proved illusory. Authoritarian nation-states use anti-Semitism as a tool to shut Jews out of positions of prominence, while simultaneously preventing them from becoming a viable cultural minority; democracies, by contrast, do grant Jews

freedom, but at the cost of the rationale for remaining Jewish in the first place. The result is assimilation, even in the United States, where Jewish numbers have been rapidly declining because of low Jewish birth rates and intermarriage.

(4) American Jews try to invent new rationales for their Jewish survival, usually the belief that Judaism is a universalist religion that will bring about a messianic future for all humanity. It would be more honest, however, to admit that traditional Judaism is parochial, concerned primarily with the survival of the Jewish People and only secondarily with the bettering of humanity—which, in any event, it has largely left to God rather than to undertake on its own.

(5) There is little reason, therefore, to retain this religion altogether. Attempts by Reform and Conservative Jews to make it over into a universalist, synagogue-based doctrine are dishonest and doomed to fail because, in the end, nobody believes in the God whose existence is necessary for the whole religious enterprise to make any sense in the first place. Only Jewish Orthodoxy—which still retains the medieval pottage of God, revelation, and chosenness—is valid, but it is doomed to be practiced by a tiny minority that, in any event, will thrive better in Israel than in the Diaspora.

(6) Israel provides an alternative to this futile vision of Judaism as a religion. As a secular Jewish state, Israel can nurture Judaism as a culture—not a high culture but the lived culture of a people's language, songs, jokes, pastimes, and "attitudes to such ordinary things as sex, age, wealth, work, [and] love"—the way French or German cultures are not just Voltaire and Goethe, but the everyday pulse and "feel" of the places we call Paris and Berlin.

(7) But given the constant warfare that such a Jewish state entails, why bother? "Why should Jews insist on existing?" Halkin asks, and answers, "Because we do." Secular Jewish culture can evolve into the next great chapter in the ongoing narrative of Jewish hopes and history, the way modern France and Germany are vivid continuations of the French and German stories. The time has come, therefore, for all Jews to abandon the Diaspora existence and move to Israel.

Serious thinkers have felt the necessity to address Halkin's beautifully argued statement of Zionism at its most extreme. Jewish fiction overwhelmingly explores the existential angst of living in the Diaspora.

Jewish nonfiction ponders the necessity of Halkin's claim and its obvious conclusion that Jews must inevitably move to Israel. Is the Jewish Diaspora really just an exercise in futility, even in the United States? Is Judaism as a liberal religion doomed? Alternatively, can Diaspora Judaism prove Halkin wrong by legitimately evolving a theological claim to being a modern and sophisticated religious approach to a better human destiny? Isn't there some transcendent—that is to say, "religious"—reason for remaining Jewish, even for liberal Jews, who do not believe literally in the Bible and in rabbinic paradigms of God and chosenness?

Clearly, Jews in free countries have not all given up on the Diaspora, and are unlikely ever to do so. As much as Israel is central to their consciousness, they continue to believe that they can lead fulfilling Jewish lives elsewhere. Indeed, by 2007, more Jews were leaving Israel than moving to it, so that even while Jews who faced persecution found a haven in the Jewish state, Jews in free democracies tended to remain where they were.

Halkin could still be right, of course. Diaspora communities may grow in numbers temporarily but still end up assimilating to the point of disappearance. So Jewish conversation in the Diaspora focuses more and more on the question of what a compelling modern theology would look like: Can a sophisticated liberal thinker in the Diaspora reimagine God and chosenness authentically? Is Judaism as a culture, not as a religion, itself a viable continuation of Judaism, even in Israel? Or will "cultural" Israelis stop, in some important way, to be continuers of Judaism? What, really, are the options for Jewish existence today, and what roles do Israel and the Diaspora play vis-à-vis each other, especially (for religious Jews) given the calculus of a God whom we have not given up on, and a history whose end remains inscrutably hidden from us?

Hillel Halkin was imbued with his love of Hebrew and Jewish culture by his father, a scholar in New York City. An author and translator in his own right, Hillel Halkin has rendered over fifty works of fiction, poetry, and drama from Hebrew and Yiddish into English, including what many consider the definitive translation of Sholem Aleichem's *Tevye the Dairyman*. But his reputation as a serious essayist and thinker comes through best in the timeless challenge posed by *Letters to an American Jewish Friend*. It is not an easy read, as his questions are not easy questions to answer. But in the several decades since Halkin framed them, his questions have not disappeared. On the contrary, with Jewish freedom increasing to the point where Jews can—if they wish—assimilate with ease, these questions become more important than ever.

From Beirut to Jerusalem
(1989)

Thomas L. Friedman (born 1953)

"American Jews are going to have to rethink some of their basic attitudes toward Israel [. . .] Israel is not a Jewish summer camp, where you come for a weekend and see that your kid is eating okay and then go home; Israel also isn't a coffee-table book [. . .] that you keep out in the living room and never read."

How is one to make sense of Israel and its neighbors today? To Jews who both idolized and idealized the Land of Israel, it once seemed clear: the Zionist dream come true; a military miracle at its founding; a social utopia in the making; a beacon of hope for the entire Middle East; the answer to the Holocaust; and a guarantee of "Never again!"

Those were the days when everything seemed obvious: the 1948 War of Independence had begun with an invasion by the surrounding Arab states; the 1956 Sinai campaign was a response to Arab aggression. The Six-Day War in 1967 was Israel's only option when Egyptian forces massed for attack. The almost catastrophic Yom Kippur War in 1973, launched by Egypt in the south and Syria in the north, demonstrated Israel's vulnerability despite its military supremacy. To this day, that does seem accurate.

But more recent historians, many of them Israelis, reveal another side to events like these. Even in the War of Independence, not all the Arabs who left their land just fled out of fear or in response to Arab overlords who urged them to do so. Some were displaced as part of Israel's military strategy. Even before the turn of events that unfolded with the changeover of the Israeli government following the Yom Kippur War, not all Arabs were evil, and not all Israelis were virtuous. The Ben-Gurion government had its share of scandals, Israel's socialism was faltering, and the Labor Party was fraught with dissension.

The changeover from the Labor legacy to Menachem Begin as the prime minister in the 1970s revealed the other side of Israel: a militant coalition of ultra-religious parties; claims that Israel had the right to all the territories conquered in 1967; and new Jewish settlements expanding deep into the West Bank and Gaza. Especially after the

1982 invasion of Lebanon and Israel's complicity in allowing Christian militias to massacre Muslim civilians in Lebanese refugee camps, it became impossible to see the Middle East the same way. The years of idolization and idealization were over.

How can a balanced observer navigate this metaphoric minefield of charges and countercharges by Arabs and Israelis, with a recognition that there must be some truth on both sides? Beginning in 1979, *New York Times* reporter Thomas L. Friedman undertook a journey of almost ten years to figure it all out. Beginning in Beirut, and ending in Jerusalem, he spoke to combatants on both sides and traced the ongoing conflict to much more than the simplified scenario of Arab versus Jew. *From Beirut to Jerusalem* is Friedman's detailed, sophisticated, and nonpartisan account of what was really going on.

His stays in both cities coincided with enormous change in the area. In 1975, civil war ripped apart Israel's northern neighbor, Lebanon, which ended up being virtually annexed by Syria. To protect its northern flank, Israel invaded Lebanon in the 1982 war. In 1985, Israel withdrew its troops unilaterally, and two years later, the West Bank and Gaza erupted in the Intifada. Friedman moved from Jerusalem back to America the year after.

Friedman places blame on both sides, offering us an account that is far from the simplistic story that so many people imagine it to be.

In Beirut, he sympathized with "the random, senseless death" of ordinary people falling prey to internecine rivalries among the historically hostile tribes that constituted Lebanon in the first place. He was introduced to Hezbollah, a violent faction that "knew more about kidnapping journalists than accrediting them." He observed the rising fortune of the Palestine Liberation Organization (PLO), which only pretended to be seeking peace, and he accused "the Western press," which "coddled the PLO and never judged it with anywhere near the scrutiny that it judged Israeli [. . .] behavior." In 1982, Syria put down an internal rebellion by massacring thousands of its own citizens, and then paving a layer of concrete over their bodies as if they had never existed. There are no heroes to this Byzantine maze of interconnected rivalries that defy logic, understanding, and forgiveness.

But Israel fares no better. Yes, it is at least a democracy, but a fractured one, in which right-wing interests have regularized the building of settlements in the West Bank, most of them by religious zealots or rampant adventurers or both. At the Lebanese refugee camps of Sabra and Shatila in 1982, Israel did indeed turn a blind eye, as its Lebanese

Christian allies took "groups of young men in their twenties and thirties [. . .] lined up against walls, tied by their hands and feet" and then "mowed [them] down gangland-style."

Once upon a time, Israelis had found a powerful symbol for their country by pointing to peaceful settlements created out of malaria-infested marshes or bottomless sand dunes. By the time Friedman arrived, they were pointing instead to Yad Vashem, the Holocaust memorial in Jerusalem.

This Holocaust-dominated thinking magnified Israel's victim mentality and made the whole country "Yad Vashem with an air force." Because secular Zionists "had not bothered to build an interpretation of Judaism that could live with the modern world," they abandoned the religious landscape to violence-prone ultra-Orthodox rabbis who made good use of Israel's democracy by controlling swing votes in a shaky electoral system and thereby obtaining the collusion of leaders who preferred politics to ethics.

Given all this, Friedman analyzes the love affair that links American Jews to Israel and wonders how long it will last. "Israelis were nurtured on the myth that the Diaspora does not count and that Jewish life there is not authentic," he writes, while Americans related to Israel as "a substitute religion." That two-way delusion is over, Friedman believes.

Arab-Israeli hostilities matter deeply in their own right. But they serve also as a challenge to the age-old dream that brought Israel into being in the first place. Jews within and outside of Israel should at least exchange myth with reality. Whether the Arab side will respond with a genuine desire for peace is not a Jewish question. But Israel's politics are!

In growing numbers, Jews in the Diaspora and in Israel itself have become troubled by Israel's policies in the territories won during the Six-Day War. Arab terrorist groups with power (Hezbollah and Hamas) still claim as their mission the destruction of the Jewish state. But multiplying Jewish settlements in Arab territories hardly seems the right response. Exactly what Israel should (or even can) do is not easily decided, however—certainly not by armchair intellectuals and pundits overseas.

True enough, much has happened since 1988 when Friedman left his post in the Middle East. But his book is by no means out of date. Perhaps better than any other, it provides a realistic view of the background that cannot be ignored if one is to make any sense at all of what is happening today in the Middle East. When it came out, *From Beirut to Jerusalem* unmasked both sides of the conflict, provoking uneasiness among moderates in both camps. The conflict continues. So does the uneasiness.

A Tale of Love and Darkness
(2003)

Amos Oz (born 1939)

"The one thing we had plenty of was books. They were everywhere: from wall to laden wall, in the passage and the kitchen and the entrance and on every windowsill. Thousands of books, in every corner of the apartment. I had the feeling that people might come and go, be born and die, but books went on forever. When I was little, my ambition was to grow up to be a book."

Israel is a small country, small enough for it not to be altogether unusual to run into someone whose grandfather knew the first prime minister, or whose second cousin once argued with the army chief of staff while picking apples together in a kibbutz. That intimacy was even more common when Amos Oz was growing up and Israel was more like a mom-and-pop store than a strong, sovereign commonwealth.

Israel today is a multicultural mixture with a Jewish population from all over the world. But prior to 1948, the Jewish population in Palestine came primarily from eastern Europe, giving the new settlements not just religious but ethnic homogeneity. Palestine's Jewish intellectuals, it seemed, had simply picked up their coffee tables and newspapers from the cafés and salons of Russia or Poland and moved them to similar haunts in Jerusalem or Tel Aviv, without even letting their conversations lapse.

Amos Oz grew up amid such pre-statehood intellectuals. His father read sixteen or seventeen languages, and spoke eleven; his mother, not far behind, read seven or eight and spoke four. His father took walks with little Amos, pointing out scholars here and there, the way boys in the Bronx must have been shown baseball legends, and little Los Angelenos, Hollywood stars.

Oz was born in Jerusalem, at metaphoric arm's length from the disaster that swept up his less fortunate relatives, like cousin "Daniel Klausner who would live for less than three years" because Nazis "would come to kill him to protect Europe from him." Oz remembered "a bookbinder with a nervous breakdown" who would scream from his balcony, "Jews, help, hurry, soon they'll burn us all." Hence Oz's ambition to "grow up to be a book." "Books are not difficult to burn, either," he concluded, "but if I grew up to be a book, there was a good chance that at least one copy might manage to survive."

In a way, Oz *did* grow up to be a book—this book, *A Tale of Love and Darkness*, which is his story, a profoundly moving account of a family history that includes his mother's depression, his father's stunted aspirations, and his own evolving artistry as a writer. Never far from power and fame himself, he was part of the larger narrative of Israel in the making.

Although just a child when the United Nations voted Israel into being on November 29, 1947, Oz remembers every detail of it: how for weeks and months prior, the adults sat up nightly, calculating the improbability of a Jewish state being born; and how even his emotionally distant and intellectually removed father broke into primal sobs of joy when the impossible actually occurred.

Israel's early years featured internal political battles between ideologically warring factions. Prime Minister David Ben-Gurion was a socialist intellectual. His nemesis was Menachem Begin, a follower of the militant Zionist leader Ze'ev Jabotinsky. Oz's father, who despised Ben-Gurion, used to take his son to hear Begin lecture every Saturday morning—an alternative Sabbath ritual for secular Israelis who did not go to synagogue. In those early years of Israel's history, the Hebrew revival was still very much in flux, and when Begin, at the climactic moment of his oratory, referred to armaments using an old Hebrew word that Amos Oz's generation associated with "penis," the boy was thrown into a fit of laughter. Discovering that his father's idol had clay feet was, he says, "the fall, my expulsion from paradise."

No longer enamored even of Begin, Oz entered his teenage years as an independent spirit, and at age fifteen joined a kibbutz, the equivalent, he tells us, of American Jews attending ashrams to escape their cloying parents—in Oz's case, his father's generation, "the gloomy refugee scholars of whom Jerusalem was full."

In his early years in the kibbutz, an older farm worker passed on an image of Israel's reality that Oz would never forget. "What do you expect from them?" the man asked, referring to Arab terrorists. "From their point of view we are aliens from outer space who have landed and trespassed on their land [. . .] We promise [. . .] that we've come to free them from backwardness, ignorance and feudal oppression, [but] what do you think? That they should hand over the keys to the whole land just because our ancestors lived here once? There was a terrible war and they themselves made it a simple question of either us or them, and we won and took it from them. It's nothing to boast about."

Of course, "If they'd beaten us there'd be even less to boast about. They wouldn't have left a single Jew alive. And it's true that there isn't a single Jew living in their sector today." But from all of this, Oz came to paraphrase Marx: "Power," he concluded, "is the opium of the ruling class."

Oz also learned to make do without heroes or villains. Real people were neither, as he knew from his own family. A scholarly uncle, whom he worshipped, grew out of fashion and was forgotten by the public. His mother's depression ended in suicide, and his intellectual father avoided talking about it, as if her life were "a censured page in a Soviet encyclopedia." Oz seems to have concluded that affairs of state—even the Israeli-Palestinian conflict—were more than morality tales of good and evil. In 1978, he helped found the organization Peace Now, a dovish alternative to the policy of the very Menachem Begin whom his father had adored and who had become prime minister the previous year. In 2008, Oz supported a military incursion into Gaza because of repeated missiles being launched from there against Israeli settlements. But he remained an opponent of occupation and a regular critic of military behavior that went beyond the proper bounds of self-defense.

Early on, Oz took to writing letters to the editor of *Davar*, the official newspaper of Mapai, Israel's dominant, socialist party during the founding years. Ben-Gurion himself liked one of these letters enough to invite Oz to discuss it, and when they met, Oz was surprised to discover that even this founder of the State—the man whom his mother called the "Prime Minister and Minister of Defense," pronouncing it "as though she had said 'The Holy One Blessed Be He'"—even he was barely five feet tall!

Ben-Gurion becomes a metaphor for Oz's entire memoir, which reduces all of mythic Israel to real-life size, without, however, doing violence to its greatness. Oz loves, appreciates, and celebrates the Land of Israel throughout his writings.

A Tale of Love and Darkness is a story of growing up—as a Jew, as an Israeli, and as a human being. It is a brilliant writer's account of Israel, Zionism, the Jewish condition post-Holocaust, and the ordinariness of even Amos Oz's extraordinary family—hence the ordinariness of us all. Jewish history becomes a prism through which to view the universal condition of humanity at its ordinary best.

8

The American Experience after World War II

The Conversation Is Renewed

☙❧

World War II marked Jews as it did no other peoples: in large part, the war had been fought over Jewish bodies, victims of Hitler's "Final Solution." But on the very heels of the Nazi defeat, the State of Israel was proclaimed. Jewish fortune in the twentieth century is often seen as revolving around these two singular events: horrific destruction on one hand, and miraculous resurrection on the other.

There is, however, an equally important third strand to the Jewish conversation of our time: the rise of American Judaism to prominence. America came out of World War II as victor, its war machine prepared to spin off any number of peacetime technological advances, and its population anxious to take up ordinary lives again—enriched, however, by automobiles, refrigerators, television sets, and other new technology.

The postwar years saw the formative decision to invest in an interstate highway system, whose concrete cloverleaves and asphalt beltways allowed the expanding urban population to move ever farther into suburbs. Reluctant to have babies during the war, Americans made up for lost time with bumper crops of baby boomers, who, as adults, would leave their mark on America like few generations before. Part of that mark was religious, because President Eisenhower insisted that Americans demonstrate their opposition to godless communism by adhering to their religion of choice. The result of all this, for Jews, was an institutional religious revival with newly designed and child-centered synagogues dotting the suburban landscape, even in areas where Jews had hitherto been unwelcome.

The 1950s were not quite as blissful as we like to remember them, however. The Cold War was real, as was the House of Representatives Un-American Activities Committee and Senator Joseph McCarthy's charges that America was being sold down the river by communist sympathizers, many of whom were said to be Jewish. Rampant fears surfaced most dramatically in 1951, when Ethel and Julius Rosenberg, an American Jewish couple, were found guilty of spying for the Soviet Union and executed two years later.

Especially in suburbs that had been closed to Jews before the war, Jews felt they had to demonstrate their right to belong, so they welcomed Eisenhower's openness to "the religion of one's choice," and joined fellow suburbanites in demonstrating their patriotism by turning to religion. In 1950, *Partisan Review*, a journal for intellectuals, many of them Jewish socialists, reported with some concern, "One of the most significant tendencies of our time has been the turn to religion among intellectuals and the growing disfavor with which secular attitudes and perspectives are now regarded in not a few circles that lay claim to the leadership of culture." It went so far as to predict, "If the present tendency continues, the mid-century years may go down in history as the years of conversion and return." Overnight, it seemed, synagogues (like churches) were dotting the new suburban landscape, as Jews (like Christians) affiliated denominationally.

The critics at *Partisan Review* need not have worried. Even the "newly religionizing" Jews mostly hailed from eastern Europe; they still identified as Jews in ethnic, rather than religious, ways. Synagogue affiliation symbolized loyalty as an American, and it transmitted an ethnic Jewish education to all those baby-boomer children. But by no means were their parents anxious to become seriously religious.

If Judaism was not essentially a religion, however, what exactly was it, now that it had exhausted its immigrant energy of the early 1900s and, for the most part, had escaped poverty and graduated to the suburbs? Was socialism still an option, given the Rosenberg trial, McCarthyism, the communist scare, and the Stalinist betrayal of all that Jewish socialists had embraced? How would the new State of Israel shape Jewish identity in the Diaspora? And what about the Sho'ah—how would the dawning recognition of the Holocaust fit into the new identity mix?

Postwar Jewish identity in America was a mixture of three things: pride in Israel (making sure Israel survived and prospered); the solemn promise "Never Again" (saving Jewish lives wherever they might be threatened, most particularly in Arab countries and behind the iron curtain); and residual socialism (identification with the social welfare system championed by Democrats and built on President Roosevelt's New Deal). Jews in suburbia were Israel enthusiasts, defenders of Jewish rights worldwide, economic liberals, and political Democrats.

But within these broad parameters, much remained open for discussion. To begin with, anti-Semitism was by no means dead; it just went underground, in what Laura Hobson would call "a gentleman's agreement" to blackball Jews from membership in country clubs, have real estate agents exclude Jews from certain neighborhoods, and limit corporate advancement to Jews in business. Religiously speaking, Orthodoxy seemed on the way out as nominal Orthodox Jews began joining the Conservative movement. But simultaneously, Hasidic rebbes who had escaped Hitler began arriving, giving Hasidic Orthodoxy new life in America. Heated conversation arose over the nature of Judaism, generally, in postwar America; the nature of the Conservative movement (to which most Jews belonged at the time); and how European Hasidism would adapt to American life.

By the 1960s, the baby boomers in America were attending universities in record numbers, with many Jewish academicians as their faculty. Especially at Columbia University, a group of intellectuals emerged as a significant voice in framing the nation's cultural agenda. The Eichmann trial (as we saw) had raised the Holocaust to consciousness, and Israel's Six-Day War made Jews take greater pride in Jewish peoplehood. The counterculture, meanwhile, dealt a severe blow to suburban religion, which paled in importance compared to the liberation movements and student unrest that were changing the face of American life—whether on campuses or in street riots that broke out in Detroit, Los Angeles, and elsewhere. So Eisenhower's faith in religion was on its way out just as renewed emphasis on the Holocaust and on Israel was reaffirming Jewish ethnicity.

Conversation on the long-term issue of ethnicity's lasting power had not yet been faced. That would come by century's end—one of the topics of Part Nine. The conversation here belongs to the heady era of postwar suburbia, the golden years of Conservative Judaism in particular, Jewish ethnicity at its triumphant best, and the baby boomers who would remake much of America—and Jewish life along with it.

Peace of Mind
(1946)

Joshua Loth Liebman (1907–1948)

"This is the gift that God reserves for His special proteges. Talent and beauty He gives to many. Wealth is commonplace, fame not rare. But peace of mind—that is the fondest sign of God's love."

Our age of spiritual searching has taught us the supreme value of "peace of mind." From the hundreds of self-help books that come out every year to the boom in therapies of all kinds, our culture is awash in ways to find it. But the phrase did not enter everyday speech until Joshua Loth Liebman's masterpiece put it there. The year it was published, nearly every educated American was devouring it—and this was long before pop-spirituality and self-help became the rage. It was quite a breakthrough for a book such as this one to hit the bestseller charts—especially since the author was a rabbi.

It not only hit the charts; it stayed there. Except for Norman Vincent Peale's 1952 classic, *The Power of Positive Thinking*, it has sold more copies than any other book in its class. In fact, since *The New York Times* began keeping track (1942), only two other books of a similar spiritual nature have even made it to the top (*On Being a Real Person*, by Harry Emerson Fosdick [1943], and *Crossing the Threshold of Hope*, by Pope John Paul II [1994]). *Peace of Mind* may well be the most lyrical and literary guide to spiritual self-help in American publishing history.

In 1946, the wider American public had yet to discover rabbis as sources of wisdom for anyone other than Jews, and even Jews considered them experts on Jewish texts and history, rather than on spiritual guidance. The very word "spiritual" was not yet widely used by Jews, and the notion of Judaism as a legitimate path of religious expression had yet to permeate America's (then still mostly Christian) consciousness. That idea became more commonplace only in 1955, when Will Herberg's *Protestant-Catholic-Jew* (see page 239) posited a Judeo-Christian heritage as the popular backdrop for American religion. And even then, Judaism was never thought of as addressing the life of anyone who hadn't been born Jewish and who wasn't, as it were, already "stuck" with it.

Liebman's idea of "peace of mind" as a basic human need was inspired by Mordecai Kaplan, the founder of Reconstructionist Judaism, whose work all liberally inclined rabbis were anxiously devouring. Kaplan had identified God as a part of nature, what he called "the power that makes for salvation"—an idea that came to him by combining the wisdom of Judaism with the insights of philosophy and sociology. Liebman added psychology, no mean feat at a time when many Protestant religious authorities viewed Sigmund Freud as virtually demonic. Copernicus had decentered earth by showing it to be but one of many planets circling the sun. Darwin had exposed human beings as just another species in the evolution of life. And now Freud had uncovered base animal instincts in human beings. How could humans be just "a little lower than the angels," as Psalm 8 puts it, but also harbor instinctual drives toward patricide and incest, as Freud charged?

Liebman found no conflict here. He saw the presence of God not just in sacred texts and heartfelt worship but in scientific discovery as well. Scientific revelations were, in fact, the best demonstration of the exalted status of the human mind that made them—because only beings who are "little lower than the angels" could be scientists in the first place. Liebman's championing of psychology is, therefore, not just the plea of a scientific universalist. It also derives from his Jewish understanding of human nature as inherently driven to reveal the profundities of creation.

Liebman had particularly high regard for the values that "prophetic religion contributes to the synthesis of human knowledge." But by "prophetic," Liebman meant more than the great biblical voices like Micah, Jeremiah, and Isaiah. He was equally impressed with the grand gamut of human inquiry beyond the classical prophets of the Bible: individuals such as Montaigne, Einstein, Emerson, Marcus Aurelius, William James, T. S. Eliot, Plato, Shakespeare, Tolstoy, and Dante, all of whom he cites with abandon. Liebman, therefore, was not just a Jewish voice, but the kind of Jewish voice that surfaced from the amalgam of traditional Jewish wisdom and Enlightenment faith in human reason—the hallmark of liberal Judaism.

And not just liberal Judaism in general, but the classical era of Reform Judaism in particular, going all the way back to Isaac Mayer Wise, who had founded Hebrew Union College precisely to train rabbis in the universal truths of the human spirit that he saw exemplified in Judaism.

Liebman was a child prodigy who entered a joint program of Hebrew Union College and the University of Cincinnati next door when he was just thirteen years old! By combining Isaac Mayer Wise of his youth with Mordecai Kaplan of his adult years, Liebman came to exemplify the universalist Jewish vision at its best.

These days, Reform Judaism has recovered Jewish particularism—reaccenting the significance of Jewish peoplehood, for example, not just the universality of the human family. But Liebman represents the best of a former age: faith in human reason in general, science in particular, and the prophetic vision of world peace above all else. By the 1930s and '40s, he had become the epitome of Judaism's liberal conscience.

From 1934 to 1939, Liebman served as rabbi on Chicago's South Side, but he is best known for his next nine years as a rabbi of Boston's Temple Israel, before dying tragically of a heart attack when he was only forty-one.

Liebman sometimes speaks as a universalist—he proudly cites Kant's judgment that God is present in the starry skies above and the human conscience within. But he is first and foremost a rabbi, with expertise in the Jewish part of the universal moral equation. When he discusses grief, he cites the biblical Job and the Talmud. On death and immortality, he gives us imagery from the modern Jewish poet Hayyim Nahman Bialik. His personal credo (a section that, by itself, makes this book worth reading) is the testimony of Liebman the Jew coming to terms with modern science.

If literature were a form of music, *Peace of Mind* would be positively symphonic. It begins with Freud's psychological underbelly of human nature, but it ends with a stirring affirmation of the human desire to lead lives that matter. If peace of mind, the quality, is what we seek, *Peace of Mind*, the book, is the best first step to getting there.

Gentleman's Agreement
(1947)

Laura Z. Hobson (1900–1986)

"From the bedroom, his voice came clear and efficient. '—check on reserva-
tions for five days starting Sunday for Mr. and Mrs. Philip Green of New
York.' [. . .] 'One more thing,' Phil said, 'Is your inn restricted?' [. . .]
'Well, I wouldn't say it was "restricted."' The voice sounded plaintive. 'Then
it is not restricted?' 'Ah—may I inquire. Mr. Green, are you—that is, do you
yourself follow the Hebrew religion, or do you just wish to make sure that—
[. . .] You see, we do have a very high-class clientele and naturally—.'"

Laura Hobson was a remarkable woman. Born in New York as Laura Zametkin, she was the daughter of Jewish socialists—her father had actually been tortured by czarist police before escaping to America. Upon arriving, he became the editor of *The Forward* (*Forverts*), the most popular Yiddish daily on the Lower East Side; her mother became an independent reporter for *The Day* (*Der Tag*), its best-known competitor.

From her parents, whom she described as "broad-minded agnostics," she inherited a lifelong concern for social causes and equal rights for women. She was an early female graduate of Cornell University in upstate New York, majoring in religion, of all things. But she remained irreligious. After several love affairs and a writing hiatus in Tahiti, she found her way to Time Inc., publisher of *Time* and *Fortune*, where she worked her way up the ranks, eventually becoming part of the team that launched *Life* magazine. As a committed feminist, well ahead of her time, Hobson volunteered to drive trucks transporting troops during World War II. As a committed liberal, she opposed American isolationism, McCarthyism, and the Vietnam War, while supporting the civil rights movement and the American Civil Liberties Union (ACLU). In 1930, she married Thayer Hobson, who owned the publishing company William Morrow. The marriage ended in divorce five years later. She had two children, both of whom she raised alone and while working.

Much of her writing is semiautobiographical and writing "with a cause." Her life as a single mother, for example, was portrayed in *The Tenth Month* (1970); *Consenting Adult* (1975) presents the situation of a homosexual son. Her claim to fame, however, is *Gentleman's Agreement*, which portrays the subtle yet effective form of anti-Semitism existing in corporations and country clubs in America even after World War II.

Hobson herself identified more as a universalist than as a particularistic Jew. Still, the lingering and insidious anti-Semitism that she encountered forced her to respond. "I am a plain human who happens to be an American," she explained. "But so long as there is anti-Semitism in this country, so long as it remains an advantage not to be Jewish, I can never simply say, 'I am an agnostic,' but must say, 'I am Jewish.'"

Gentleman's Agreement became the immediate subject of fierce reviewer debate. *The New Yorker* castigated Hobson for presenting "a slick treatment of a subject that deserves a great deal more than slickness." The *New York Herald Tribune*, however, called the novel "a first-rate story [about anti-Semitism] in which the author looks behind the demon's ears and down its throat, and tells what she sees." The reading public agreed with the *Herald Tribune*, turning *Gentleman's Agreement* into a major bestseller; looking back in 1983, *Publishers Weekly* called it "a landmark novel." Director Elia Kazan made the novel into a movie starring Gregory Peck as the all-American and perfectly Protestant reporter who poses as a Jew to explore the anti-Semitism that exists just below the gentlemanlike surface of the nation.

Jews were very much on the mind of America back in 1947. With television in its infancy, movies were a major source of information, and movie theaters carried news clips prior to every feature film. It was impossible to attend a movie without seeing gruesome scenes from liberated concentration camps and growing discussion of the proposed State of Israel, which would become a reality the very next year.

Pre–World War II anti-Semitism in the United States had reached a height in the 1930s with the Catholic priest Charles Coughlin, whose weekly radio broadcasts spewed outright hatred of Jews. His Protestant equivalent was Gerald L. K. Smith. They were joined by Senator Theodore G. Bilbo and Congressman John E. Rankin of Mississippi, whose staunch nativism had urged America to stay out of World War II altogether. Jews epitomized the object of xenophobic hatred at the time—many of them were recent immigrants who were steadily moving up the social ladder and threatening the old-time white Protestant elite.

Post-Holocaust anti-Semitism was harder to spot because it went on behind closed doors, largely unacknowledged. American soldiers returned home proud of the values that had underwritten their fight against tyranny—most particularly, the Statue of Liberty's implicit promise that here, the "huddled masses" would be welcome, equal, and free. Coughlin, Smith, Bilbo, and Rankin belied all that America prided itself on. But below the inviting surface, Jews were still not welcome everywhere.

This subtle postwar anti-Semitism is the world that *Gentleman's Agreement* takes on with gentle fury. The enemy is not outright bigots, but quiet ones, aided by all the nice Americans who turn a blind eye to prejudice, not because they dislike Jews all that much, but because they dislike standing up for principle even more. The novel's hero is Philip Schuyler Green, who is hired by John Minify, the publisher of a liberal magazine, to write an exposé on anti-Semitism. Green has made a name for himself as an unorthodox investigator, and decides to approach his assignment by pretending to be Jewish himself, and then to observe what happens. Green soon meets Minify's niece, Kathy Lacey, who seems liberal enough but who eventually displays anti-Semitic tendencies without even realizing it. Typical of the snubs that Philip encounters is a party that Kathy's Connecticut family throws for the couple when they announce their engagement. Thinking Philip is Jewish, guests suddenly discover that they are just not able to attend.

Even Jews are infected with a form of self-hatred. Green's secretary turns out to be Jewish; she got the job by changing her name from Estelle Wilovski to Elaine Wales. When Minify acts on his liberalism by ordering his human resources manager to hire Jews, Elaine herself objects, fearing "the wrong kind" of Jew might apply, thereby putting her own job in jeopardy.

The novel explores the ins and outs of all these twisted relationships that paper over prejudice to such an extent that even those who hold it are unaware of it. There is nothing particularly evil about Kathy's Connecticut relatives, or about Kathy herself—much less Elaine; they are all victims of an insidious system where anti-Jewish bias has become embedded deeply enough that it can be denied.

Gentleman's Agreement is a Jewish book, because it deals with the scourge of anti-Semitism as it was usually practiced in America; it is Jewish also because of its author, who was not religious, but who saw herself acting as a Jew when she wrote it. The book is testimony to the many Jews who filtered prophetic consciousness into active opposition to the evils of their day.

Protestant–Catholic–Jew
(1955)
Will Herberg (1901–1977)

"[American churches and synagogues have become] a kind of emotional service station to relieve us of our worries. On every ground, this type of religion is poles apart from authentic Jewish–Christian spirituality."

No doubt about it, a single book can change the way we think. *Protestant-Catholic-Jew* did that in memorable fashion. When it first appeared, it attracted reviews by extraordinary religious figures of the day. Protestant theologian Reinhold Niebuhr, for example, judged it "the most fascinating essay on the religious sociology of America that has appeared in decades." It was republished in 1983, with an introduction by Martin Marty, the dean of historians of American religion. Looking back, Marty declared Herberg's book "the most honored discussion of religion in mid-twentieth-century times." To be sure, it had its faults, but the faults might not have become public knowledge without the many experts who studied it in minute detail. It remains a benchmark of religious writing, and it addressed one of America's most religious eras since its founding—with special importance for America's Jews. Herberg clearly saw the dilemma of Jewish identity then, and unintentionally, he also prepared us to understand the Jewish challenge today.

Perhaps even more fascinating than the book is its author. Herberg was a genius and a man of extremes—he frequently changed positions, every one of which he believed passionately at the time. After graduating high school at age sixteen, he turned to Marxism; but then shifted radically from the left to the right, becoming increasingly conservative in his views. As a conservative, he returned to religion, even considering conversion to Christianity, until Reinhold Niebuhr convinced him to deepen himself instead in his native Jewish faith. Deepen himself he did, to the point where he distrusted all secular ideologies, including the liberalism that produced Lyndon B. Johnson's Great Society and the Civil Rights Act of 1964. His opposition was not to the principle of equality, but to the notion that social justice rooted in a liberalized social system could take the place of religious faith. He even distrusted the oratory of Martin Luther King, Jr., because it reminded him of "rabble-rousing demagoguery." A *New York Times* review of his life by Richard Wightman Fox proclaimed Herberg to be "always in love with absolutes." Herberg wrote *Protestant-Catholic-Jew* as a joint exercise in theology and sociology, even though he had no professional training in either. He was, however, an astute intellectual who knew how to write, who read every social-scientific survey around, and who saw within them a compelling pattern.

Herberg's general argument is simple but not simplistic. The American religious renaissance after World War II was America's means of hammering together an amalgam of diverse peoples whose grandparents had settled here as immigrants. To do so, it encouraged everyone to identify as a Protestant, Catholic, or Jew. In the interests of forging this national identity, the three faiths (which had been virtually at war with one another for centuries) had to mute their historical differences and grant each other legitimacy as equally authentic expressions of Americanism. Indeed, to say that one did not belong to any of these three faiths was nothing short of being un-American.

This religious rapprochement came at a price, however: the watering down of religious specificity. "Faith in the living God of the Bible" had given way to "faith in nothing in particular"—just "faith in faith," as a healthy and moral virtue in and of itself. By making "religion in America so thoroughly American," the country had reshaped God into the "champion of America, endorsing American purposes and sustaining American might." But shouldn't religion be less self-satisfied and more demanding—a call not just to our higher selves but also to the demands of a Higher Power, to the God with whom Jews made a covenant on Sinai, and who remains the same commanding voice even in liberal, secular America?

Herberg knew full well the extent to which eastern European Jews had arrived in America less as members of a religion than as an ethnicity. His own parents had epitomized the first-generation immigrants who arrived here as "a Jewish proletariat," less faithful to God than they were to socialism, unionism, and even communism, all of which Herberg himself had abandoned. It was not enough, he felt, to be Jewish just by custom, lifestyle, friendship networks, and values. Claiming religious membership was not conviction, and Herberg called for conviction.

Hence his theological qualms about religious vapidity. Jewish affiliation skyrocketed in the 1950s; Jewish faith did not. Just by building synagogues and calling themselves a religion, American Jews could retain group solidarity with the traditional Jewish values of family, charity, education, and Jewish continuity (especially via the State of Israel); but they did not, on that account, have to embrace a genuinely religious life. They were already cultural Jews and could remain that way. They were not religious and didn't have to be.

Herberg was not altogether prescient when he wrote *Protestant-Catholic-Jew*. He did not predict the liberal 1960s and reactive 1970s that polarized hitherto homogeneous religious groupings around social issues; he could not have known, for example, that evangelical churches and Jewish Orthodox groups would work together across faith lines to oppose abortion but support public aid to private religious schools; nor that liberal Jews and liberal Christians would join forces on these same issues from *their* standpoints. He could also not have foreseen that subsequently, with the hermetically sealed borders of the three faiths becoming porous, Jews would marry Christians in droves, or leave Judaism altogether in favor of Eastern faiths, particularly Buddhist spiritual practices. In his analysis of American religion, he neglected to consider Eastern religions altogether, overlooked African American religion as marginal, and did not envision the diverse search for spiritual meaning that set in by the 1960s. But he did correctly assess major trends of religion in America in the 1950s—and he saw through them. For many Jews, religious institutions were really continuations of ethnicity in a socially acceptable guise.

The Jewish American story since then—and ongoing—is the unraveling of an identity and culture based on ethnicity. With interfaith marriage a major factor, and Yiddish virtually dead, most Jews have no reason even to try recovering their ethnic heritage. Increasingly, then, Jewish continuity will depend on the ability to transcend that inherited ethnic glue with compelling spiritual meaning.

Anyone intent on understanding the challenge facing present-day American Jews should turn to Will Herberg's brilliant classic, which laid bare its soul fifty years ago. Put differently, without understanding what constituted Jewish identity back then, it will be difficult to define a successful Jewish identity for tomorrow.

Conservative Judaism
(1955)

Marshall Sklare (1921–1992)

"Conservativism resulted, in part, from the feeling [. . .] that ethnic solidar-
ity would have to be perpetuated chiefly under religious auspices."

Marshall Sklare has the rare distinction of having launched a whole new field of Jewish endeavor: the sociology of Judaism. When he first graduated, he was unable to obtain a university appointment, since no academic positions in the field even existed back then. From 1953 to 1966, therefore, he worked for the American Jewish Committee, an organization established in 1906 (in the wake of the Kishinev pogrom three years earlier) to protect Russian Jews from violence. By the 1950s, that mission had expanded to include the monitoring of civil rights violations against all people. To accomplish that task, the Committee established a division of scientific research that Sklare directed. He was eventually appointed as professor of sociology at New York's Yeshiva University. Since then, sociology has become a favorite Jewish discipline, whose founder remains a standard worth aspiring to.

Sklare's best and most significant book remains his pioneering study of Conservative Judaism, the primary denominational address of American Jews in the 1950s. In addition, Sklare's prescience illuminates the Jewish situation today.

Conservative Judaism in America has been around since the turn of the twentieth century, when eastern European Jews began arriving in large numbers. Finding the Old Country ways of the new arrivals embarrassing, Reform Jews of German origin (who had already made it in America) established the Jewish Theological Seminary of America as a place where the new immigrants would feel comfortable. Only after World War II did Conservative Judaism flex its institutional muscles, send the Reform board packing, and engage in vigorous debate about what Conservative Judaism should represent.

Unlike Reform, Conservative Judaism would retain allegiance to Talmudic law; unlike Orthodoxy, its interpretation of that law would take into consideration the evolution of historical circumstances from the time when the law had first been promulgated. Reform did not support

Zionism; Conservative Judaism was fiercely Zionist. In terms of worship, Reform Judaism used an organ and prayed in English and Hebrew. Conservative Judaism would have no musical instruments and use only Hebrew. Its worship would be fully traditional and fully in keeping with the ambience of eastern Europe, but it would be aesthetically attractive and would feature mixed seating of men and women. Because American Jewish shopkeepers had to work on Saturday, Reform synagogues had moved their main worship service to Friday nights. Conservative congregations would retain Saturdays as the primary time for prayer. Both Reform and Conservative differed from Old World Orthodoxy in accenting decorum, but Reform synagogues were marked by congregational passivity, as worship was led by professionally trained singers, a choir, and a rabbi who read most of the prayers alone while congregants followed along in silence. Conservative worship would engage worshippers who would be trained in Hebrew and attend regularly enough to be able to pray actively in the style of worship known as *davening*—the traditional mode of prayer by which the cantor leads off each paragraph, but the congregation prays along actively in an audible undertone.

But much of this was still theoretical when Sklare's *Conservative Judaism* was first published in 1955—the reality of Conservative synagogues back then was much different. Over 50 percent of Conservative synagogues described by Sklare featured late Friday night services; a choir and (often) an organ led worshippers in prayer, with "inactivity as its dominant characteristic." There were no Conservative camps or day schools yet. Conservative Jewish men, too, had to operate shops on Main Street, and had to miss Shabbat morning services.

Since then, the Conservative movement has specialized in education and boasts a significant cadre of day-school graduates who not only attend but actually lead morning services in vibrant Conservative synagogues across the country. But Conservative Judaism is losing members to Orthodoxy and Reform, raising the question of why Conservative Judaism has not continued the growth that Sklare observed immediately following World War II. To be precise, some 42 percent of all American Jews in 1970 said they were Conservative; by 2000, only 34 percent said so. By contrast, the percentage of American Jews associating with Reform in 1970 stood at 32 percent, but grew to 42 percent by 2000. Orthodoxy, too, has grown from 5.5 percent in 1990 to 9 percent in 2000. Enter Sklare's prescience: he celebrated Conservative Judaism—he was Conservative himself—but he predicted the problem that Conservative Judaism faces today.

To begin with, he saw that any religious turn to the right in America at large could send some Conservative Jews back to Orthodoxy; and indeed, that has happened. But the larger problem emerges from the dominance of ethnic identity over religious sensibility. We have seen how suburban religion grew in the postwar years as an expression of being good Americans, God's loyal force against atheistic communism. So Conservative Judaism grew because institutional religion was growing, not because Conservative Jews necessarily believed in the theology of the movement that they joined.

Enter Sklare's prescience a second time. He was the first to see that if it was not the theology that was attracting Jews to Conservatism, it had to be something else that drew them there. As he put it (in sociological terms), they were "an ethnic church," zealous mostly for its ethnicity, its comfortable retention of eastern European Jewish style, albeit modernized for American taste. Sklare warned that ethnicity might have a limited future, however, and if ethnicity went, so, too, would Conservative Judaism. Ethnicity, he explained, was a bulwark against "anomie, the atomization and disorganization" typical of the rapid social change that Jews experienced as they left the ghetto. But "the direction of movement in our society is toward the discarding of ethnic identification." As the most ethnic of the Jewish denominations, Conservative Judaism would be especially threatened.

Another aspect of Sklare's prescience applies to *all* synagogue bodies today. He ended his book wondering why rabbis provide Conservative Jews with no doctrinal definition; indeed, when he asked them, laypeople in the movement did not know what they believed. But Jews were arrayed hierarchically then, by class: the upper class was Reform; the lower class, Orthodox; the middle class (the majority), Conservative. When class defines who we are, we need no beliefs to do so. But eventually, Sklare warned, we will "feel a need for ideological differentiation which will function in compensation for lack of class and status differentiation." That time has come.

Marshall Sklare is readable for his clarity on the past, but also for his predictive capacity for today—not just for Conservative Jews, but for us all, half a century and more from the time he first showed us what the sociology of Judaism could look like.

The Complete Stories
(1997)

Bernard Malamud (1914–1986)

"It's always like that with the Jews. Tears and people holding each other."

The most obvious choice for one of Bernard Malamud's books here might be his novel *The Fixer* (1966), the story of Mendel Beiliss, an ordinary Jew who was charged and tried in czarist Russia for killing Christian children in order to use their blood for Passover. This medieval "blood libel" had become such a central part of anti-Semitic lore over the centuries that, for example, on August 17, 1840, the *Times* of London carried a front-page translation of the entire Passover seder, to explicitly show its readers that this ritual does not call for Christian blood to be used. *The Fixer* was Malamud's fourth novel, and earned him both the Pulitzer Prize and the National Book Award.

It was perhaps also his most inherently Jewish work, a story unthinkable without the Jewish experience: its Passover ritual, the Christian Easter that Passover spawned, and the medieval "blood accusation" against Jews. But even here, Malamud's vision is universal. He identifies with Jewish suffering, powerlessness, and internal courage in the face of fate— but he universalizes them as a metaphor for human experience writ large.

Hence the choice here of Malamud's short stories, which reveal the author's insight into the human condition as nothing else. They span almost half a century, from 1940 to 1986, and are a spectacular example of the short story literary genre, for which Malamud is especially known. His longtime editor, Robert Giroux, cited Malamud's own pronouncement on himself: "My writing has drawn, out of a reluctant soul, a measure of astonishment at the nature of life [. . .] Working alone to create stories is not a bad way to live our loneliness."

Malamud was born in Brooklyn, the son of a poor grocer and a mother who died when he was fifteen. He worked briefly as a teacher, but left for the solitude of civil service work, which enabled him to reserve part of each day for writing. Eventually, he returned to teaching, completing his life as a prolific writer and professor at Bennington College.

He was enthralled with the themes of existential loneliness, life's innate ugliness, and the human propensity for little acts of defiant heroism. His imagination parallels the surrealism of Marc Chagall (1887–1985), with its imaginative world of suspended souls in flight and fiddlers on the roof. Malamud's heroes are little folk, overwhelmed by the dreariness of ordinary life, but able to show flickers of equally ordinary heroism.

Take Manischewitz, for example, a tailor "on whom suffering was wasted, because it went nowhere but into more suffering." A fire destroys all he owns; his son dies in a war; his daughter absconds with a no-good lout; he himself develops backaches that cripple his capacity to work; his wife (who takes in washing and sewing) develops shortness of breath and is about to die. Along comes Alexander Levine, an African American from Harlem and a victim of poverty himself—the most unlikely self-styled angel. When Levine arrives with the promise of salvation, Manischewitz chases him away; but when he has nothing left but hope for the impossible, he summons up the strength to track him down. Read the story to find out the rest. It's called "Angel Levine."

Malamud's central characters are not all Jewish. He promises a description of the human condition, not just the plight of this or that specific Jew. Tommy Castelli owns a tiny candy store "in a tenement-crowded kid-squawking neighborhood with its lousy poverty" that he never could escape because "everything had fouled up against him." He despises life to the extent that "usually the whole day stank and he along with it." He is humanized by ten-year-old Rosa, who comes regularly to buy tissue paper. But one day, he discovers that her real purpose in visiting his store is to steal candy bars. And then what? Does he turn her in? Or does he let her find a little sweetness in life, even at the cost of thievery?

Malamud has an ear for dialect, a soul with empathy, a conscience for morals, and a brilliance of expression. In "The Jewbird," a crow named Schwartz (naturally) takes refuge in Harry Cohen's Lower East Side flat and requests a bite of herring, speaking "Yinglish" (a combination of Yiddish and English): "If you'll open for me the jar, I'll eat marinated, [and] would be glad to see once in a while the *Jewish Morning Journal* and have now and then a *schnapps*." The ultimate irony is what makes the crow Jewish: not just his dialect but his fate! Harry attacks the bird, first buying a cat to torment the poor creature, and eventually wringing its neck. Harry's son Maurie finds Schwartz "in a small lot by the river, his two wings broken, neck twisted, and both bird-eyes plucked clean." Who did it, Maurie asks. Harry's wife, Edie, who has no idea that her husband is the culprit, responds immediately: "Anti-Semites!" Even victims sit precariously on the cutting edge of becoming persecutors. With its mixture of gallows humor and dead seriousness, "The Jewbird" is Malamud at his incisive best.

By the 1980s, Malamud's style had shifted to surrealistic treatises of real-life characters such as Virginia Wolff and Alma Mahler (the wife of composer Gustav Mahler). But his stature lies in the way he applied the sensitivity of the Jewish experience to everyday life, a world where perennial victims somehow show the undying faith of Manischewitz, the saving grace of Alexander Levine, the unexpected compassion of Tommy Castelli, and (at times) the demonic cruelty of Schwartz the crow's tormenter. One suspects that we are all one or the other of these human possibilities; God help us, it will never be Harry Cohen.

The Tenth Man
(1959)

Paddy Chayefsky (1923–1981)

"He still doesn't believe in God. He simply wants to love, and when you stop and think about it [. . .] is there any difference?"

Even though Senator McCarthy wanted Americans to believe otherwise, relatively few Jewish immigrants actively fought for socialism, much less communism. Many more, however, had embraced the atheism that socialism carried with it. And many who could not go that far were at least less disposed to believe in God.

Not that they actively denied the divine. They just didn't discuss it. The world was filled with too many immediate problems: recovering from Hitler and the Holocaust, saving Jews in the Soviet Union, assuring the survival of the young State of Israel. These were obvious items of concern for Jews who had seen 6 million of their people perish. They had perished, moreover, regardless of religious commitment—making Judaism something other than just a religion (such as their Protestant neighbors displayed). So perhaps they didn't believe in God. But so what? They didn't really *not* believe in God, either. They just gave God little thought. Did they thereby cease being Jews? Of course not! They were certainly proud members of the Jewish People, with some vague sense of the Jewish People's ultimacy, and—perhaps—a divine mandate, too, even though they were not all that sure about the divine.

Matters of God and religion aside, socialism itself was becoming less attractive as America entered its boom years following World War II. A more probable path than socialism was full participation in the economic boom that followed the war. To be sure, the boardrooms of large corporations were still closed to Jews, but Jews could go to college and become independent entrepreneurs or professionals—doctors, lawyers, and accountants—for whom advancement was based on merit alone.

By the 1960s, then, Jewish men, at least, were quite likely to be hardworking professionals with a college degree. They lived in the suburbs, belonged to a synagogue, but had little patience for conversations about God, spirituality, and matters of religion.

One such man is Arthur Landau, the chief male character in Paddy

Chayefsky's remarkable Broadway hit, *The Tenth Man*. Although ostensibly a comedy, it is more accurately described as a dramatized reflection on the great questions of faith (or lack of it) in the postwar generation of successful Jews moving to upscale suburbs from the inner cities. The drama probes issues of God, human value, and the spiritual emptiness that material success cannot dissipate.

It presupposes a widespread kabbalistic folk belief from eastern European mystical lore: the transmigration of souls. When we die, it was taught, our souls move on to inhabit other bodies just being born. Sometimes, however, they act perversely, entering the body of someone who is already alive, and contending with the soul already there. In such a form, they are called a *dybbuk*. The Yiddish playwright S. Ansky had experimented with this theme in 1920, and Paddy Chayefsky returned to it in *The Tenth Man*, which was first performed at Manhattan's Booth Theatre in November 1959.

The scene is a small, failing Orthodox synagogue on Long Island, where some old men, bored with life, come daily for prayer. Some don't even believe in it. "I'm an atheist," says one of them. "If I had something better to do, would I be here?" Present also, however, is a kabbalist, an expert in dybbuks and the eerie folk ritual of exorcising them.

The lines are brilliantly drawn: on one side is the kabbalist, whose overwhelming piety has led him to round-the-clock prayer for days; on the other is Arthur, an attorney who admits to believing "not one damn thing." Even the rabbi has lost his faith, having been ordained into a materialistic world where rabbinic success lies in attracting congregants through "a bazaar and raffles" and even a synagogue Little League team ("a marvelous gimmick"). "It would please me a great deal," he admits, "to believe once again in a God of *dybbuks*." Schlissel, a "leftover" communist and unbeliever, but a daily worshipper anyway, comments wryly, "Religion has become so pallid lately, it is hardly worthwhile being an atheist."

The clash over belief and identity occurs because one of the men gathered for prayer has "kidnapped" his schizophrenic granddaughter, Evelyn, from a mental institution and brought her to the synagogue. He believes that a dybbuk has possessed her and hopes to arrange an exorcism, rather than have her rot for the rest of her life in a psychiatric ward.

Traditional Jewish prayer requires a minyan (a quorum) of at least ten men. So Arthur, too, has been kidnapped, after a fashion—hauled in off the street with the plea that he is needed as the requisite tenth man. He, more than Evelyn, it turns out, is in mental despair. He spends his first few minutes closeted in the rabbi's office phoning his psychiatrist, because he has been "blind drunk for three days" and in a blackout from it all. Like the rabbi, whose desk he sits at, he has sworn off all belief, even belief in a classless society, but not for any ideological reason. He is simply jaded—hence his despair. "I left the Communist Party," he says, "when I discovered there were easier ways to seduce girls."

He became the very capitalist he once despised, a lawyer who "began to work day and night at my law office [. . .] began drinking myself into a stupor [and] pursuing other men's wives [. . .] I managed to avoid my wife entirely. For this deceit I was called ambitious and respected by everyone, including my wife, who was quite as bored with me as I was with her." Evelyn is indeed a schizophrenic, but because she is not altogether "of this world," she is able to see truths that escape everyone else. As Arthur falls in love with her, he explains, "I never met anyone in life who wanted to know the meaning of life as much as you do." Who is really possessed here: Evelyn or Arthur?

Sidney "Paddy" Chayefsky grew up in the Bronx, the son of immigrants from Ukraine. He served on the German front in World War II, was wounded by a land mine, and wrote his first play while recuperating in an army hospital in England. After a brief stint in Hollywood, he returned to New York and established his reputation in the then young medium of television. One of his teleplays, *Marty*, was converted into a movie that earned several Academy Awards in 1955. Well established now in both television and film, Chayefsky moved on to several Broadway hits, including *The Tenth Man*.

Chayefsky was known for his quick wit and sharp intellect—drama critic Martin Gottfried said that he treated "the life of the mind" as "a participant sport." He had a fine ear for the Yiddish witticisms with which he grew up, some of which found their way into his work—as when one of the synagogue goers in *The Tenth Man* reflects, "My daughter in law, may she grow rich and buy a hotel with a thousand rooms and be found dead in every one of them." Dialogue like this captures the subculture of these old Jewish men who care deeply for each other, but who mask that care in the toughness of Yiddish curses and a parody of Talmudic argumentation. Beneath the humor, *The Tenth Man* pierces the essence of Jewish ennui in the middle of the twentieth century; and it presages the ubiquitous conversation about the meaning of life and the search for spirituality that would become commonplace by the beginning years of the twenty-first. In anticipating that search, Chayefsky has given us a play that speaks as much to our time as it did to his.

Goodbye, Columbus
(1959)

Philip Roth (born 1933)

"Once I'd driven out of Newark [. . .] the sun itself became bigger, lower, and rounder, and soon I was driving past long lawns which seemed to be twirling water on themselves, and past houses where no one sat on stoops, where lights were on but no windows open, for those inside, refusing to share the very texture of life with those of us outside, regulated with a dial the amounts of moisture that were allowed access to their skin."

Immigrant groups in America have generally settled in inner-city ghettos, then moved to city neighborhoods just beyond, and later still, "graduated" to the suburbs. But suburbs were of negligible importance until the economic expansion following World War II and the rise of the automobile economy, with its accompanying grid of highways to provide easy access to them. There were exceptions to this late start, such as New York City, where railroads had long carried commuters to prosperous suburban counties, and where a few prewar highways wound picturesquely through largely rural areas. In the 1920s, F. Scott Fitzgerald placed his Brahmin hero in *The Great Gatsby* on Long Island's famed Gold Coast, but postwar prosperity and four-lane highway access to the suburbs sounded the death knell of their utter exclusivity, and no one announced this drastic change more loudly than Jews.

They arrived with the "wrong" religion, the "wrong" ethnicity, and the "wrong" politics, having become FDR Democrats through and through, with a touch of their parents' socialism to boot. The longtime WASP residents whose neighborhoods the Jews "invaded" saw them as unrefined, noisy, and pushy. So Jewish suburbanites labored, as an old saying goes, to be "just like everyone else, but more so."

Philip Roth became the quintessential chronicler of the period. He was born and raised in a mostly Jewish part of Newark, New Jersey, the son of a lower-middle-class Jewish family. He recalls the singular overwhelming sense that the world was made of "us" (the Jews) versus "them" (everybody else). From a high school where 90 percent of the students were "us," he went on to Bucknell University, in the middle of Pennsylvania, where he first encountered a majority of "them," a novelty that informed his undergraduate fiction writing, later described as "refined [. . .] no Jews, no Newark." In *Goodbye, Columbus*, the collection of one longer story (providing the book's title) and five short stories that won him a National Book Award and made him famous, Roth explores the culture gap between the "us" of his childhood and the "them" of America's suburbs—whom his unrefined Jewish suburbanites perceive as *goyim*.

Roth is a serious satirist with a bite. His devastating picture of childhood education comes through in one of the better-known stories of the collection, "The Conversion of the Jews," which pits little Ozzie Freedman against his Old World teacher Rabbi Binder. When Binder threatens Ozzie—"I'd never get bar-mitzvahed if he could help it," as Ozzie puts it—we see the challenge of Jewish education to this day: many Jews join synagogues with one key goal in mind—their children's bar (or bat) mitzvah.

Given their attenuated religious education, Roth's characters would surely never have heard of Judah Leib Gordon, a nineteenth-century Jewish teacher and poet from Lithuania who had experimented with the dual identity of ghetto-Jew on one hand and world citizen on the other. But they practice Gordon's patented advice as if they had invented it: "Be a Jew at home and a man in public." *Goodbye, Columbus* is a not altogether likeable portrait of Jews trying to become "hyphenated" Jewish-Americans—and living mostly in the hyphen.

Of all the short stories here, Jewish ambivalence comes through best in "Eli, the Fanatic," the chronicle of a Jewish neighborhood that is taking shape in Woodenton, a fictitious community near real-life Scarsdale, the very prosperous Westchester County village where Jews know they have arrived. Eli Peck, a Jewish lawyer who commutes to Manhattan, is deputized by his Jewish neighbors to fight a zoning battle against a certain Rabbi Tzuref, who is planning to establish a traditional yeshivah right there in Woodenton. Tsuref's very name is telling—change the final "f" to the look-alike sharp "s" letter in German script, and you get the Yiddish *tsuress*, "trouble." To Eli and his peers, what the yeshivah students learn is not as important as how they dress. What will happen when Jewish teachers and students show up in Old World Hasidic black coat, black hat, and dangling *tsitsit*—the tassels Orthodox Jews attach to undergarments in order to fulfill the biblical commandment of Numbers 15:38–39, "Make tassels [. . .] that you may look at them and recall all the commandments of the Lord"? What actually *does* happen is that Eli himself becomes a "fanatic," adopting Hasidic clothes himself.

"Goodbye, Columbus," the lead story here, features Neil Klugman, a native of Newark who has graduated from Ohio State University and settled in Short Hills, an "*uber*-wealthy" New Jersey suburb where upscale Jews were moving in droves. Neil is out of his league there; neither a businessman nor a professional, he holds down a dead-end job in the library. The plot revolves around his sexual summer fling with Brenda Patimkin, the epitome of a "Jewish American Princess." Utterly vacuous, Brenda spends her days playing tennis and working hard at looking good. Her father, once a scrap metal dealer, has successfully parlayed his traffic in junk into Patimkin Sinks, a business that earns enough money to let Brenda shop on Manhattan's Fifth Avenue (she gets her diaphragm fitted across the street from Bergdorf Goodman). Her sister is an obnoxious brat, her brother a hopeless jock. The entire Patimkin family is pretentious, without a single redeeming virtue.

Talk about hanging dirty laundry out in public! Roth's cruel portrayal of Jewish suburbia had just enough truth in it to be recognized as real. There was another side to it, of course: real-life Patimkins belonged to a synagogue, gave liberally to charity, supported socially advanced causes, were good citizens, and made their children into educated, responsible Americans. But Roth's focus is the emptiness of suburban life, where what matters most is the conspicuous consumption that Jews hoped would demonstrate their right to belong.

Ten years later, his third novel, *Portnoy's Complaint*, only worsened the scandal, since it dealt with the sexual ambivalence of second-generation Jewish men, whose desire to pass as Americans attracted them to non-Jewish women. By then, it was commonplace to hear Roth being chastised as a Jewish anti-Semite, perhaps the worst epithet a Jew can bestow on another. The charge was false, of course—it said more about the insecurities of the Jews who made it than it did about Roth, whose later books, in any event, are more patently universal than they are particularistically Jewish, even when they feature Jewish characters at their center.

All of Roth's work is worth reading, but there has been nothing quite like *Goodbye, Columbus* to reveal the deep flaws of Roth's own upbringing, which depended entirely on "us" versus "them." Like no one else, Roth described the bankruptcy of suburban social climbing rooted in a drive for material success, with nothing deeper than the material.

New York Jew
(1978)

Alfred Kazin (1915–1998)

"I lived my life among brilliant intellectuals."

Every once in a while, a social cauldron of energy brings together a network of minds that leave their mark on the world. One of the most famous intellectual crowds like that was the Bloomsbury group in London in the early twentieth century. It included such luminaries as authors Virginia Woolf and E. M. Forster, art critic Clive Bell, and economist John Maynard Keynes. Intellectuals do leave their mark—on art, on taste, on students, and on historians who find them to be notable chroniclers of their times.

What the Bloomsbury clique was to early twentieth-century England, a loosely linked set of Jews were to mid-twentieth-century New York. For a short period of time, they defined literary tastes and intellectual issues, were coveted by society, and recorded the America that had welcomed them (and their parents). Among them were such luminaries as Daniel Bell, Paul Goodman, Irving Howe, Norman Podhoretz, Philip Rahv, J. D. Salinger, Delmore Schwartz, Lionel Trilling—and Alfred Kazin. Most of them had grown up in New York City, which they proudly called their home. There were also sometime members like Saul Bellow and Isaac Rosenfeld, who came and went from their native Chicago, and other outliers, too—Leslie Fiedler, for instance, who taught at the University of Montana. But the center of intellectual gravity was the English Department of New York's Columbia University. The writings of these intellectuals filled the pages of *Partisan Review*, the foremost literary journal of its day and a centerpiece of moderate left-wing advocacy (socialist but anti-Stalinist). They were also behind *Commentary* magazine, a prominent outlet for largely Jewish intellectual opinion.

These (mostly) men of letters represented a larger post–World War II phenomenon: this was the era during which American Jews—just one or two generations removed from the Lower East Side ghetto—virtually blanketed academia. The immediate cause was the GI Bill of Rights of 1944 that paid tuition for war veterans to go to college, the coveted destination that had been drummed into Jewish children's heads from the moment their parents landed on America's shores.

We have seen how the American government virtually ended eastern European immigration in 1924, and how universities followed suit by limiting the number of Jews accepted as students—and hired as faculty. A major exception was Lionel Trilling, who had become Columbia University's first Jewish tenured professor in 1939. After the war, America became used to Jewish intellectuals who had escaped the Nazis: Hannah Arendt, Bruno Bettelheim, Albert Einstein, Erik Erikson, Erich Fromm, Kurt Gödel, and many more. Universities eliminated their quotas, and by 1969, an astounding 34 percent of university faculty members across America were Jews. Many young Jews headed for Columbia University as students, and some stayed on as faculty, drawn to the incisive brilliance of Trilling.

Alfred Kazin rose to prominence in the midst of this heady academic crowd and wrote a sparkling memoir of it: *New York Jew*. Kazin's personal life is itself fascinating, and he pulls no punches describing it. He grew up in Brooklyn, the son of Russian immigrants, and attended New York's City College and Columbia University (despite the quotas at the time). He was thrice-married and had two children. Not that he was home much. He loved to travel and make any place away from home his home for a while. Rejected by the army for physical reasons, he spent much of World War II in California, North Carolina, and elsewhere. Parts of the book even take place in England and Germany right after the war.

Kazin's other works include *On Native Grounds* (1942), a critical history of modern American literature, and *A Walker in the City* (1951), a memoir of his Brooklyn childhood in which he described what it was like looking across the East River to Manhattan, seeing its skyscrapers and knowing that "beyond, beyond, beyond was the city." He was always aspiring to the "beyond, beyond, beyond," not just geographically but spiritually. He never turned his back on Judaism, but like so many of the Columbia University crowd he wrote about, his true religion was literature. What Talmud had been to European parents, world literature would become for their academically sophisticated children.

The challenge for this scholarly crowd was to remain Jewish but to be broader as well, not just in literary and cultural scope but politically, too, in tune with the suffering of humanity as a whole. They were liberal universalists who thrived on ideas and people of all sorts. Kazin spends great chunks of his memoir describing the economist Kenneth

Galbraith, the writer and film critic James Agee, and publisher Henry Luce at Time Inc. Kazin had been hired there to commission a series of cultural essays to demonstrate that this was "the American century." He chronicles his time with the poet Robert Frost, whom he labels "a fascinating, direct and ruthlessly troubled man [. . .] who was teasingly attracting to himself admirers and possible biographers." He adored Hannah Arendt, who knew everything and lectured everybody on just about anything. He did not take well to the Sixties, with their "inflamed sexual language and bravado" and the "immodesty of scale" that he saw in the painters Jackson Pollock and Mark Rothko. He reflected on the heady excitement of the Kennedy White House, when "everything was suddenly possible because intellect was in charge."

His images of postwar life are not all heroic bravado, however. We also get intimate pictures of pathos, sometimes the underbelly of greatness. After Isaac Rosenfeld moved to New York's Greenwich Village in 1941, he held nightly soirees with guests who had somehow located the obscure Village haunt, and then "climbed up four flights and found their way into the apartment [. . .] as if they never planned to find their way out again." In the end, poor Rosenfeld died miserably alone back in Chicago. Another example is Edmund Wilson, probably America's greatest (certainly most prolific) literary critic, who seemed immensely self-assured but aged badly, and is last seen here "drunk and defiant," so lost that an onlooker says, "Really, shouldn't someone look after the poor man?"

Despite his universalism, Kazin remained a passionate Jew, shattered irrevocably by the Holocaust. He saw himself and all his Jewish friends living "in the abyss of modern culture," the extermination of the Jews. "We believed in nothing," he wrote, more than in "the life of the mind. But the life of the mind," he held, thinking of Hitler's gas chambers, "was of no use unless it addressed itself to gas."

New York Jew recalls the Jewish presence in America's intellectual space not too long ago—yet endlessly distant: New York's cultural life was flourishing, America was on top of the world, and everything seemed possible.

9

Jewish People,
Jewish Thought,
Jewish Destiny Today

The Conversation Continues

☙❧

By the year 2000, the condition of world Jewry had changed beyond what anyone could have imagined just half a century earlier. In 1950, the Holocaust was still fresh, Israel had barely been born, and Stalin was persecuting Jews behind the iron curtain. Just fifty years later, the State of Israel was reasonably secure and on its way to becoming one of the great scientific and entrepreneurial centers in the world. In Europe, Jews were resettling communities where Hitler had virtually eliminated their parents and grandparents. The Soviet Union had fallen, and Jews had abandoned it in droves for opportunities in countries round the world—some 900,000 had come to Israel alone. In most of the nations where Jews lived, anti-Semitism was largely a memory.

Concerns over Jewish safety worldwide had not entirely disappeared, however. Israel remained beleaguered by threats from terrorist groups and from neighboring states like Iran, but its continued existence as a haven for oppressed Jews was no longer in doubt, and fears for Israel's safety were tiny compared to what they had been in the 1960s and '70s. So Jewish conversation now extended beyond the immediacy of Jewish *survival* to encompass long-term concerns about Jewish *meaning*: not just *whether* Judaism would survive but *why* it should; and if it did, what it would look like. These were internal questions of the Jewish soul.

Of all the Diaspora communities, attention has focused primarily on the United States, if only because the Jewish population there is so massive. As of 2010, it had some 5,275,000 Jews (the second- and third-largest Diasporas, in France and Canada, had only 483,500 and 375,000 Jews, respectively). Questions about the Jewish future were highlighted when a 1990 survey revealed that except among the Orthodox, the American Jewish population was declining. Liberal Jews increasingly tend to marry outside of Judaism, have fewer children in any event, and are less likely to raise those children as Jews. Still, Reform, Conservative, and Reconstructionist Judaism continue to represent the vast majority of America's Jewish population. Less than 10 percent claim to be Orthodox.

These American concerns are echoed elsewhere. Part of today's Jewish conversation is about the ability of non-Orthodox Judaism to speak meaningfully to this new century. What, exactly, does non-Orthodox Judaism stand for?

For years, Diaspora Jews have been able to avoid that question because their Judaism was ethnic as much as it was religious. They lived vicariously through identification with Jewish suffering, on one hand, and pride in Israel, on the other. With the dimming of immigrant memories, however, the era of ethnic Judaism (at least in America) is ending. Without obvious ethnic ties, and with no Orthodox faith in halakhah as the God-given law for all time, what binds liberal Jews together?

The most obvious alternative is a revival of Judaism as a religion. It is not *just* a religion, of course—Jews are a people, a culture, and even a civilization (in the judgment of theologian Mordecai Kaplan). In the United States, people of every background are engaged in a spiritual search of epic proportions. Unlike most other industrial and postindustrial countries, where religion has lost a great deal of its popularity, America remains a highly religious country. The growth of Jewish Orthodoxy is attributable not just to demography, but also to its taking religion seriously. Modern Orthodoxy has particularly benefited from the ideas of Joseph B. Soloveitchik (see page 287), for whom religious thought was paramount. Additionally, Hasidism, which was virtually obliterated in Europe, has reestablished itself in America, especially in the form known as Chabad (or Lubavitch); and Hasidism has brought its own brand of spirituality.

Overall, however, with ethnicity commanding Jewish loyalty during much of the past century, Judaism's spiritual message has received insufficient attention. Non-Orthodox Jews, too, therefore, have turned increasingly to conversations on spirituality and theology, as liberal Jewish theologians offer novel visions of what a religious—but modern—Judaism might look like. The feminist revolution, in particular, has challenged theological and ethical assumptions—not just the role of women, but the makeup of synagogues, the hierarchical organization of communities, and the nature of power. The openness to think spiritually, and differently, has increased the visibility of Kabbalah. Today's spiritual conversation has been immeasurably supported by new translations of almost all Jewish classics—Talmud, midrash, responsa, medieval philosophy and mysticism—that are now readily available.

The surest sign of today's renaissance in Jewish creativity is the explosion of Jewish publishing beyond anything ever known: Jewish sociologists explore the nature of Jewish communities; Jewish historians unravel the Jewish past; rabbis unveil Jewish insights into death and mourning; more and more books address Jewish spirituality; more and more novelists apply Jewish imagination to life's contemporary challenges. The Jewish conversation has become less insular as well—Jewish voices appear increasingly in mainstream life.

Despite the 1990 survey, therefore, Jews in America remain optimistic. They recall an earlier time when pundits warned of imminent disappearance through assimilation; a lead article in the May 5, 1964, issue of *Look* magazine was titled "The Disappearing American Jew." Observers have noted wryly that Jews are still around, while *Look* magazine ceased publication a long time ago. More positive voices, therefore, have turned the conversation away from dismal prognoses of Jewish demise to the productive questions of what a post-ethnic Jewish existence will look like.

A new world is being born, and with it, a new chapter in the global Jewish conversation is beginning.

Choices in Modern Jewish Thought
(1983)

Eugene B. Borowitz (born 1924)

"I come to the work of intellect as a Jew first and as a reflective thinker second. What I believe may be obscure, wavering, and difficult to put into words. But to deny it would be false to who I truly am [. . .] I try to base my life on it."

"What exactly is Borowitz doing? Jews do history, not theology. What is Jewish theology, anyway?" These were the questions that some of Eugene Borowitz's older colleagues pondered in the 1960s, when Borowitz, virtually singlehandedly, put together what has since become the thriving discipline of modern Jewish theology.

His colleagues were baffled because they belonged to a generation that understood Judaism as so thoroughly a historical phenomenon that the study of Jewish thought for its own sake, rather than as an index of Jewish historical existence in some place or other, seemed foreign. Even medieval thinkers such as Moses Maimonides and Judah Halevi were studied as products of the historical periods that bore them, not as thinkers able to inform thoughtful Jews today of why and how they are Jewish. For much of the twentieth century, the "why" was ineradicable anti-Semitism on one hand and unabashed Jewish ethnicity on the other. The "how" was the obvious enumeration of the Jewish sacred acts called *mitzvot*, the "commandments" that constitute Jewish law.

But what if neither anti-Semitism nor ethnicity can provide us with the grounds we need to profess life-shaping beliefs? And what if Jewish law is no longer self-evidently an unchanging reality that God provided on Mount Sinai? Jews must still be called to some kind of Jewish duty, Borowitz has insisted, but that duty is not discernible simply by reading traditional Jewish texts such as the Talmud and responsa. Today, it requires a theological rationale if it is to maintain its hold on us, because loyalty to tradition is increasingly matched by our sense of freedom from it.

Now in his eighties, Eugene Borowitz is arguably the most influential liberal Jewish theologian in the world—having taught generations of students at Hebrew Union College–Jewish Institute of Religion in New York, and written one book after another explicating Jewish theology for moderns. He is at home, as well, in modern philosophy and Christian thought; he has applied the philosophy of language to rabbinic literature and composed a guide to Christology for Jews. But his true love is the gamut of Jewish theological options, which he has been exploring for half a century.

His magnum opus, most people would agree, is his own theology of postmodernism, *Renewing the Covenant*, published in 1991. *Choices in Modern Jewish Thought*, however, is a spectacular summary of the entire field; its second edition, from 1995, includes a retrospective on *Renewing the Covenant*—enough for readers to get its general message, and to situate it against the other options that Borowitz describes. It also includes a chapter on Jewish feminism, penned by the prominent scholar and theologian Ellen Umansky.

The question to which Borowitz has dedicated his life is "How to be both truly modern and robustly Jewish?"—and *Choices in Modern Jewish Thought* is quite clearly the best set of essays on that question, as well as on every other central question that has vexed most major Jewish thinkers of modern time. It presents an overview of Jewish theology in a single volume, with quintessential Borowitzian clarity.

It begins with the hardest options for today's readers to understand: the German rationalists Hermann Cohen (1842–1918), a pioneer of Judaism as ethical monotheism, and Leo Baeck (1873–1956), who accompanied his people to a concentration camp rather than accept an invitation to personal safety. Cohen cannot be appreciated without a prior grounding in the philosophy of Immanuel Kant; Baeck sought to provide a sense of God's mysterious presence in history—not an easy concept to get across. But Borowitz is able to translate the depth of even these thinkers in a way that makes them accessible to readers.

Later chapters synopsize better-known figures: the Jewish pragmatist Mordecai Kaplan; the poetic traditionalist—and insistent voice of conscience—Abraham Joshua Heschel; Orthodoxy's best-known philosophical advocate, Joseph B. Soloveitchik; and the forerunners of existentialism, Franz Rosenzweig and Martin Buber. Buber is especially important to Borowitz, who draws his own theological sustenance from Buber's concept of God whom we encounter in relationship.

What makes this book even more outstanding are the chapters on responses to the Holocaust, intellectual bases for Zionism, a modern return to Jewish mysticism, and Umansky's essay on feminism. At last, we get to the personal theology that Borowitz (an avid reader of existentialism and postmodernism) himself espouses.

Typical of Borowitz's appealing style is his foray into existentialism—"Nothing in the world is as real to us as our own being"—and his commitment, therefore, to root his theological investigation in the reality of human beings leading their lives, rather than in ideas laid out logically in some objective but humanly distant system. Critical to him is Buber's "life of dialogue": the "I-Thou" relationship by which we know God the way we know people, and the "love that commands" because it arises from such intimate knowledge. In the end, "we must live up to the self we have come to know ourselves to be, through our relationship[s]," writes Borowitz.

Equally gripping is Borowitz's analysis of post-Holocaust history as a kind of intellectual death. For liberal Christian theologians, the horrors of Auschwitz produced the "death of God." For Jews, however, "What 'died' was not the biblical-rabbinic God moderns did not largely believe in or teach but the one they did: humankind, themselves."

Until Borowitz, twentieth-century Jews studied Jewish law, deduced Jewish commandments, practiced social justice, and assumed that someday, somehow, history would bring about a "messianic era." But with few exceptions (such as the thinkers Borowitz summarizes here), they did not express any of this in a coherent set of theological principles. They took it all on faith, but did not spell out what that faith might be or how it might be held. Borowitz insists on our coming to terms with what we believe, and why we have a right to believe it altogether.

Borowitz is a postmodernist, in the sense that he critiques modernists who assumed the certainty of reason and of historical evolution toward a better tomorrow. Surely, Borowitz counters, the historical traumas of the twentieth century make it difficult to accept the inevitability of human progress anymore. We are therefore thrown back upon the possibility of a God beyond history, and the wisdom of our own people's traditions, not just universal truths of humankind in general. Not that we need to give up on liberalism, however. Ever the liberal, Borowitz insists on personal autonomy: "God and particularity set the context within which people make up their own minds." Yet personal autonomy must inevitably be part of one's communal relationship with the divine.

This is the single best book on modern Jewish thought and theology—a masterful exposition of an entire field by the master who put the field together in the first place. By the end of it, you may be tempted to tack up summaries of each intellectual position on the walls around a room and then find a comfortable place at just the proper distance from each one, thereby staking out your own position and proclaiming, "Here I stand."

Judaism as a Civilization
(1934)
Mordecai M. Kaplan (1881–1983)

"The sooner Jews will come to think of that which unites them as a civiliza-
tion, the sooner will they overcome the process of disorganization which
is reducing them to the status of a human detritus, the rubble of a once
unique society."

Mordecai Kaplan's revolutionary conceptualization of Judaism as a civilization is as relevant today as it was when he wrote it more than three quarters of a century ago. He is still the most influential, and the most controversial, of all North American Jewish thinkers. The Reconstructionist movement, which claims him as its ideological founder, is relatively tiny, but only because Kaplan's far-reaching critique was largely co-opted by Reform and Conservative Jews who integrated it into their thinking without abandoning their own denominations. Indeed, Kaplan never ceased believing that he spoke to all modern Jews who knew in their hearts that Judaism had to be radically "reconstructed" for the modern era. He hoped to unite Jews, not divide them further, by offering a definition of Judaism that everyone could accept.

But his definition carried with it a theology that was anything but unifying, to the point where in 1945, some Orthodox rabbis burned copies of a prayer book he had edited, a sign of their excommunicating him for "atheism, heresy, and disbelief." Others, who stopped short of actually burning his writings, declared his philosophy "the destruction of the Jewish faith and a definite abrogation of Jewish tradition." Even at New York's Jewish Theological Seminary, where he taught, tradition-alist colleagues on the faculty denounced him publicly, all the while watching more and more of their students side with him. No modern Jewish thinker polarized Jewish opinion as Kaplan did.

First and foremost, he had the audacity to deny the existence of a supernatural deity. His rationalist hero, the medieval philosopher Moses Maimonides, had shocked twelfth- and thirteenth-century readers by attacking the doctrine of God's anthropomorphism (God as humanlike); Kaplan saw himself as taking the next logical step. If God is not a "person," God is also not "supernatural." God should be redefined as a part of the natural universe, "the power [inherent in it] that makes for salvation."

By "salvation," he meant something altogether natural, not what happens to the soul in the afterlife, but the satisfaction in the here and now that comes from working alongside others for moral good. God is as much a part of the universe as the law of gravity. Bodies have weight, or mass, and something within the universe attracts such bodies to each other. We call that gravity. So, too, humans have urges to associate with others and labor together for the common good. Something in the universe draws us to each other for that end; we call that God.

Kaplan was taking vocabulary that is usually associated with other-worldly religious concerns and reapplying it to "natural" scientific processes, a method that he learned from philosopher John Dewey (1859–1952), a spokesman for the philosophical school known as American pragmatism (or instrumentalism, as Dewey preferred to call it). Pragmatism insisted on defining concepts by how they function, rather than by what they "essentially" are. However Jews define God's essence, they understand God as *functioning* to underwrite the sense of personal wholeness and social solidarity that they get when they do the right thing.

In whatever way people decide to round out the functional description of God, it would be unethical and even irrational to imagine such a Power singling out any specific People for special attention. So Kaplan denied the age-old doctrine of Jews as a Chosen People and went so far as to edit the liturgy accordingly. An ancient benediction that many Jews learn as children affirms God "who chose us from [*mikol*] all peoples." Kaplan altered the benediction to read, "chose us *with* [*im kol*] all peoples."

The traditionalists who burned his prayer book knew full well that Kaplan denied the absolutism of Judaism as the only (or even the most) true religion. But Kaplan defined Judaism as more than a religion, and it is here that he made his greatest contribution. The very idea of Judaism being solely a religious creed, like Lutheranism or Roman Catholicism, was (as we have seen) a relatively recent phenomenon launched when Napoleon made Jews say so as the price of attaining citizenship in modern nation-states. By the 1930s, however, when Kaplan burst upon the scene with *Judaism as a Civilization*, most Jews no longer believed that anyway. Many of them were Zionists or socialists, and neither of these ideologies demands a prior religious commitment. But Zionism is an undeniably *Jewish* ideology, and even Jewish socialism can be as much "Jewish" as it is "socialist," if it borrows its socialist aspirations from the age-old prophetic and rabbinic commitment to justice and equality.

For Kaplan, the only way to make room for these alternative brands of Jewish commitment was to make clear that Judaism, while religious, is also broader than religion. So he called it "a religious civilization." American Jews, he held, are party to two great civilizations, the Jewish and the American. Kaplan valued them both as parallel paths to goodness. He thereby became the quintessential philosopher of "American Judaism."

On the face of it, Kaplan was the least likely person to have redefined Judaism so radically. He had come to America as the child of immigrant parents from Lithuania, then received a traditional education and gone on to study for the rabbinate at the Jewish Theological Seminary, after which he served as rabbi to an Orthodox congregation for seven years. He then returned to the Seminary as dean of its newly established Teachers Institute. He was eventually promoted to a professorship in homiletics, midrash, and philosophy of religion.

But he had also been a student at Columbia University, where he had encountered the scientific study of religion and the mentorship of John Dewey, and in 1922, Kaplan established the Society for the Advancement of Judaism, a synagogue on New York's Upper West Side that devoted itself to instituting his ideas.

Kaplan lived to be 102 years old, after personally spanning a century of changes unlike anything Jews had ever seen. In 1934, when he wrote his magnum opus, Jews were not yet halfway through that singular century, certain only that they were an ethnic group for whom Jewish peoplehood was an obvious reality, for better or for worse. Many Jews thought it was "for worse," given their experience under the czars, the anti-Semitism that followed World War I, and Hitler's recent accession to power in Germany. Even in America, quotas by corporations and universities limited Jewish advancement. Why, then, be Jewish?

Kaplan answered that question by providing a transcendent justification for Jewish ethnicity, not by celebrating the banal kind that knows only Jewish food, Jewish jokes, and Jewish nostalgia, but by honoring the deepest sense that Jews have of Jewish peoplehood as a significant chapter in the course of human evolution. Uncertain about God and about pretty much everything else, Jews welcomed Kaplan as a prophet of human hope and a guarantor of Jewish significance. To be sure, Kaplan's naturalistic understanding of God and his denial of Jews as the chosen People have always had their detractors, but today, as much as ever, he remains the greatest spokesman for Jewish peoplehood with purpose.

The Sabbath
(1951)

Abraham Joshua Heschel (1907–1972)

"Creation is the language of God, time is His song, and things of space the consonants in the song. To sanctify time is to sing the vowels in unison with Him."

Imagine an idea simple enough to be understood immediately, and overpowering enough to be remembered forever. Imagine, further, an author who etches that idea in prose so powerful that it makes most poetry pale in comparison. More still, the author offers not just an extraordinary idea, but an entire passionate philosophy. Imagine all that, and you have Abraham Joshua Heschel's *The Sabbath*.

The Jewish Sabbath falls on Saturday, the seventh day of the week according to the Bible, a reminder of, and tribute to, the day God rested from the work of creation. "Work," however, was peculiarly defined by the Rabbis of antiquity to include such tasks as writing, sowing seeds, tearing or ripping anything, and lighting a fire. That definition followed from a close reading of the book of Exodus, which lists the ban on Sabbath work immediately after describing the sanctuary that the Israelites built during their desert wandering. The conjunction of the two led the Rabbis to interpret "work" as the tasks that went into the sanctuary's construction.

Other things, too, were forbidden, including activities that are technically not "work" (because they did not go into erecting the sanctuary) but demand undue strain anyway, and normal weekday activities that would detract from the holiness of the day. Ringed round with so many "negatives," the Sabbath can be perceived as a burden—until, that is, you come across Heschel's masterpiece on the subject.

The core idea here is stunning. From its very inception in classic Greece and Rome, Western civilization has been consumed with *things*. The Romans thought immortality came with monuments; we measure our worth through material possessions. "We have fallen victim to the work of our hands, as if the forces we have conquered have conquered us." We multiply things to make us happy, never realizing that "things, when magnified, are forgeries of happiness." Dedicating ourselves to creating ever more and better things is an exercise in "embezzling our own lives." Even God is conceived as a "thing" out there somewhere.

A consequence of our virtual worship of "thingness" is Western civilization's fetish with buildings, and the bigger the better—from Baroque palaces to suburban McMansions. Some of these buildings are indeed fine things—the cathedrals of western Europe, for example. As beautiful testimonials to the spirit, Heschel has no objection to them. But they are foreign to Judaism, he insists. They exist in *space*, whereas Judaism elaborates *time* as the ultimate realm of the spirit. The Sabbath, Heschel concludes, is Judaism's "cathedral in time," created by God on that all-important seventh day when, by resting, God (paradoxically) made something: rest. Ever since, we rest as well, and define rest as the absence of work, of building things. On *Shabbat* (the Hebrew word for "Sabbath"), we achieve freedom from things to which we would otherwise be enslaved.

That does not mean that Judaism denigrates weekdays and the work attached to them. "The faith of the Jew is not a way out of this world, but a way of being within and above this world; not to reject but to surpass civilization. The Sabbath is the day on which we learn the art of surpassing civilization."

What amplifies Heschel's message is the support he draws from the fullness of Jewish tradition. No one knew it better than he, a direct descendant of one of the greatest Hasidic rabbis of all time, the Apter Rav (1748–1825), after whom he was named. Born in Warsaw, Heschel studied in Berlin, and in 1939 was able to flee from the Nazis, first to London, then to New York. From 1945 to 1972 (the year he died), he served as a revered teacher at the Jewish Theological Seminary, but so familiar has he become, and so frequently is he cited, that it is not unusual for people to assume he is still alive.

Heschel wrote one memorable book after another, including two notable theological statements, *Man Is Not Alone* (1951) and *God in Search of Man* (1955), that are bookends of the human condition. Seeing the Bible as God's word to us, he insisted that it be apprehended from God's own authorial point of view. He advocated the perspective of "radical amazement" at the fact that there even is such a thing as "being," rather than nothing at all. Recovering our sense of awe "that anything is" opens us to the reality of the divine, without which "nothing would be."

In addition, Heschel fought the classical notion of cognition being the be-all and the end-all, saying that God must "feel," not just "know."

The prophets of the Bible had sympathized with God's feelings. God's will arrives not with icy indifference, then, but with the kind of passion that we should emulate as we go about bettering the world. We require a leap of passionate action, instead of coldly rational faith.

True to his own demands, Heschel dedicated his life to social activism. In 1963, at a national conference on religion and race, he gave a memorable address recalling the "first conference on religion and race," in which "the main participants were Pharaoh and Moses"—from which he drew the biblical lesson of "the monstrosity of inequality." Two years later, he marched with Martin Luther King, Jr. in Selma, Alabama, and proclaimed, "Our march was worship. I felt my legs were praying." He later co-chaired the organization Clergy and Laity Concerned About Vietnam, leading the religious struggle against what he saw as an unjust war.

The Sabbath is perhaps the most memorable of Heschel's many books. Like the others, it is studded with poetic truths, such as "live and act as if the fate of all of time would depend on a single moment"; "to have more does not mean to be more"; to enter the holiness of the Sabbath, we "must first lay down the profanity of clattering commerce"; time is "eternity in disguise"; "labor without dignity is the cause of misery; rest without spirit is the source of depravity."

Heschel's daughter, Susannah (see page 290), a theologian in her own right, provides a stirring introduction to the 2005 edition of *The Sabbath*, including memories of growing up in her parents' home. Her father fought the trend to demote religion into a mere "means to psychological health." At the time, she says, "even among rabbis and Jewish leaders, a rejection of Jewish mysticism, Hasidism, and even of theology and spirituality was common. It was as if they desired a religionless Judaism—a Judaism without God, faith, or belief. For them, the Sabbath interfered with jobs, socializing, shopping, and simply being American." It is impossible to read *The Sabbath* and still hold such views. The Sabbath, the sacred, God's reality, and human responsibility—these all come together here in a vintage treatise by a Jewish master.

Eclipse of God
(1952)

Martin Buber (1878–1965)

"Eclipse of the light of heaven, eclipse of God—such indeed is the character of the historic hour through which the world is passing."

No single theologian has impacted contemporary Jewish thought more than Martin Buber. He was born in Vienna, but was highly influenced by his grandfather Solomon, with whom he lived in Lemberg (Lvov, Ukraine) from 1881 to 1892. Solomon had edited scientific versions of midrashic texts, and saw to it that Martin received a thorough classical Jewish education. In 1896, Martin attended university in Vienna (and later in Berlin), majoring in philosophy. About the same time, he became fascinated by the stories associated with Hasidic masters.

Solomon had also imbued his grandson with a love of Zionism, especially the cultural variety taught by Ahad Ha-am, which Buber brought with him to Palestine when he moved there in 1938. He had already broken with mainstream political Zionism because he believed a Jewish state should be morally superior to the nationalistic entities he saw around him. He therefore advocated ongoing dialogue between Jews and Arabs, who would (he hoped) one day share a single Jewish-Arab state. Although ultimately marginalized from the political process, he remained a revered teacher and visionary, and from 1960 to 1962, just a few years before he died, he served as the first president of the Israel Academy of Sciences and Humanities.

Buber's everlasting reputation derives primarily from his notion of how we know God—what he called an "I-Thou" relationship. His most famous work is, therefore, *I and Thou* (first published in German as *Ich und Du*, in 1923), the signal announcement of his concept.

Buber is included here, however, with *Eclipse of God*, a book he put together in 1952 as a mini-retrospective on his thinking. The bulk of the work is a set of lectures he had just given at Yale University, but other parts go back as far as 1929, just six years after *I and Thou* had appeared. *Eclipse of God* addresses the central question of why so many people deny the reality of God—why, to put it differently, the presence of God is not obvious. His answer is a stunning metaphor: God is in eclipse.

Buber's thought revolves around what philosophers call intention-ality. Our lives are made of mental acts: wishing, arguing, stating, or questioning, for example. These depend on the *intention* behind them, the way we wish to engage with the world. Buber looks at two such ways of engaging, two ways by which we know anything.

The more obvious is the detached scientific standpoint, where we find ourselves talking *about* something. We also interact with people that way, as a means to an end: discussing price with a salesperson or asking directions of a passerby. Buber calls these "I-It" relationships. By contrast, when we really want to know people, rather than just deal with them, our interest transcends what they can do for us, and we allow ourselves to become totally open to them. If they do the same, meeting us as well with total openness and honesty, there occurs a uniquely pow-erful moment called "I-Thou." Emblematic of this I-Thou moment is the image of a child who "silently speaks to his mother through nothing other than looking into her eyes."

The translation "I and Thou" somewhat misses the force of the German original, "*Ich und Du*," which deliberately utilizes the famil-iar form of the pronoun "You." The moment of an I-Thou meeting is not necessarily intimate, but it is intensely personal, because both par-ties open themselves to each other in complete honesty. What passes between them is a momentary bond of mutuality that cannot be ade-quately captured in after-the-fact interpretations—which are inevitably just I-It descriptions, after all.

Much follows from I-Thou relationships. Because they make mutual demands upon the two individuals, we get ethical responsibility. We also discover God in such moments, for the reality of God underlies, and is reflected in, the miracle of a genuine meeting.

We can also have an I-Thou relationship *directly* with the divine, the way we do with people; but unlike people, whom we often encounter as an It, God is knowable only as a Thou. God's uniqueness lies in this very fact: God "can never become an object" for us. Since I-Thou rela-tionships cannot be reduced to I-It explanations, descriptions of expe-riences with God will always fall short of being convincing. They can only be pointed to.

All of this forms the background for *Eclipse of God*. In a trenchant critique of our time, Buber takes on a panoply of modern voices—Marx, Nietzsche, Heidegger, Sartre, Jung, and others. None of them grasp the significance of a living divine presence open to us as a Thou, says Buber. Without a relationship with the divine as a Thou from which ethical demands must emanate, these thinkers are trapped in pure subjectivism.

Jung, for instance, confuses inner psychological reality with the independently existing God. Another example is Nietzsche. His proclamation "God is dead" led to Jean-Paul Sartre, who, having no God, concluded, "All is permitted." Not so, warns Buber. The fact that we cannot find God does not imply there is no God to find. As to ethical relativity, "One can believe in and accept a meaning or value, one can set it as a guiding light over one's life, if one has discovered it, not if one has invented it." And Marx can be faulted because, accepting no divine source of moral absolutes, he arbitrarily declared as "true" whatever benefits the proletariat—just the reverse of Nietzsche, who denounced those very moral judgments as "slave morality," the kind of right and wrong that underdogs in history always proclaim, without admitting that they have invented it for their own benefit.

Buber therefore demanded a return to ethical objectivity: the insistence that some things are simply right, and others simply wrong. That conviction arises only out of our encountering the I-Thou experience of God (directly and through others), where ethical obligation becomes manifest. Tragically, we find it hard to meet God nowadays—because God is in eclipse. But the eclipse is not God's doing. Buber puts the blame for it thoroughly on us, the human partner in the relationship. We have closed ourselves off from God, and then claimed that God is not there.

The eclipse of God also came to be used (by Buber and by others) as a compelling metaphor for God's absence during the Holocaust. This time, however, no human blame can be attached to what happened. It is not as if the victims, who sought in vain for God at the time, were in any way at fault. God was just mysteriously and inexplicably in eclipse.

Unlike some philosophers who grow old after a while, Buber seems eternally fresh, always commenting on the current condition of the world. He writes in bursts of thought colored by memorable aphorisms, so no summary can do him justice. He is not easy to read, but *Eclipse of God* is a rewarding starting point.

My Name Is Asher Lev
(1972)

Chaim Potok (1929–2002)

"Art is a religion [. . .] Art is not for people who want to make the world holy."

Asher Lev is the only son of Hasidic parents in Brooklyn. They belong to a Hasidic group called the Ladovers, modeled (one suspects) on the Lubavitch (Chabad) Hasidic dynasty. At their rebbe's behest, Asher's father and mother travel regularly to the ends of the earth, it seems, to establish Ladover communities. The time is the 1950s and '60s, and the backdrop is Stalin's persecution of Jews. But the novel is not about Jewish suffering. It is about the suffering of the human condition, and the artist's role in revealing it.

For Asher Lev is an artist, rather than the yeshivah student his father had dreamed of having. Asher is actually a fictitious youthful version of the author himself—Chaim Potok, too, had been raised as a yeshivah student in a Hasidic environment in New York City. As a teenager, he was inspired by James Joyce's *A Portrait of the Artist as a Young Man*, the study of a man who abandons religious tradition for the "higher calling" of art. Potok left his Hasidic upbringing and became a Conservative rabbi in 1954, the recipient of a Ph.D. in philosophy from the University of Pennsylvania in 1965, and, above all, a writer. He became widely known with his first novel, *The Chosen*, in 1967. In later life, Potok even turned to painting, taking his imagery from his own novels.

Lev's story, then, is partly Potok's; but equally, it is the story of anyone faced with a compelling religious heritage on one hand, an artistic search for truth on the other, and no easy way to resolve the tension between them. *My Name Is Asher Lev* stands out because it is not just another trite example of the struggle between traditionalism and secularism. It is the conflict between the particularism of tradition and the universalism of art.

The plot revolves around the artist's demanding search for honesty—a compulsion, really, over which the true artist has no control. It is an internal drive, a matter of the heart. Indeed, in Hebrew, *lev* is the word for "heart"; and *asher* means "happy," but also "walking straight," as in being true to one's path. Here is the story of an artist who follows his passion for truth and discovers at the end who he is. Asher Lev has remained true to himself.

Asher's parents understand none of this. They deprecate art as a sheer waste of time, although his mother is willing to settle for the notion that her son at least makes the world pretty. She eventually learns that art is the very antithesis of prettifying reality. It is laying bare the pain, anguish, and torment of human life. Its epitome is Picasso's *Guernica*, the overpowering artistic masterpiece that reflects the bombing of innocents during the Spanish Civil War. From *Guernica*, Potok said, he learned how art "redeems the horror of reality."

Asher Lev has an artist mentor, Jacob Kahn (modeled after the sculptor Jacques Lipchitz), who warns his student not to become an artistic whore, dulling the world's sensitivities by kitschy images of fiddlers on the roof or "pretty calendar pictures of Abraham and the angels or Rebecca at the well." Artistic whoredom is tempting—just paint what people like; true art, by contrast, risks revelations that bring dire consequences.

These revelations come from the nexus of real life and artistic tradition. The first provides the subject matter of a work; the second determines what counts as a successful artistic rendering of it. As a Jew, Asher Lev has heard about real life, especially from his Holocaust-haunted parents, but also from the Talmud, which speaks plainly about worldly affairs like agricultural species, business contracts, and weights and measures—the realities of everyday existence. But he knows nothing of artistic tradition, the legacy of Western art, which Jacob Kahn must introduce him to. First come nudes, just "naked women" to his disgusted father, but to Asher "the artist's personal vision of a body without clothes." Worse still, for his father, Asher is taken by the most dominant image of suffering in Western art: the crucifixion of Christ. While maturing in Italy as an artist, he stands transfixed before Michelangelo's *Pieta*: "I was an observant Jew; yet that block of stone moved through me like a cry—like the echoing blasts of the shofar." The crucifixion motif goes beyond what even his mother can bear. She has always supported her son, furtively buying him art supplies behind his father's back, but even she gives up: "Where your painting has brought me!" she laments. "To Jesus."

On the surface, Asher Lev never leaves Judaism. But beneath the veneer of outward prayer and practice, he has inexorably transcended it. His religion now is art—and his father knows it. Asher justifies his nudes by explaining, "Papa, I am part of a tradition [. . .] the art form of the nude is very important to that tradition," a tradition begun by "the Greeks." His father sighs. "Ah, the Greeks. Our old friends, the Greeks."

For Asher's father, Judaism's holy war against Greek paganism is more than two millennia old; he is still fighting it, and Asher has gone over to "the other side"—in kabbalistic terminology, the *sitra achra*, which is responsible for the world's pain. Ironically, in Asher's understanding, precisely that is the artist's duty: to make us come to terms with pain.

Leafing through one of Jacob Kahn's art books, Asher reads, "Every great artist is a man who has freed himself from his family, his nation, his race." That, he discovers, is the very path to freedom he is on. It leads him relentlessly, in the end, to create a painting so outrageous that he crosses the line; the rebbe, who had supported him in hope of saving him from total apostasy into the Religion of Art, declares him anathema to the community. Shunned by its members, Asher separates from old friends, neighborhood, and family. At one and the same time, he is an outcast—and he is free. The reader is left wondering if this freedom is worth the pain. But did he have any choice, really? Asher Lev the artist has become part of the pain that his art reveals.

When *My Name Is Asher Lev* came out, it was reviewed by *The New York Times* as "little short of a work of genius." In the last hundred pages or so, as the book's themes come hauntingly together, one suspects that is an understatement. The compelling climax will keep you up all night. And the story itself is as engaging a tale of internal human conflict as one is likely to find.

Haggadah and History
(1975)

Yosef Hayim Yerushalmi (1932–2009)

"Remember this day, on which you went free from Egypt, the house of bond-age, how the Lord freed you from it with a mighty hand" (Exodus 13:3).

There is nothing like a seder, the festive dinner that introduces the annual Jewish springtime holiday of Passover. The seder is more widely observed than any other Jewish ritual. Religious or secular, young or old, Jews everywhere, it seems, feel called to remember how "we were slaves in the Land of Egypt, and God freed us."

Part of the seder's magic is that it takes place around a table in an ordinary home. When Christianity became the official religion of the Roman Empire, it moved its rituals to increasingly lavish churches and cathedrals, while Judaism made do with more modest synagogues alongside the original locus of religious life—people's homes. Even in modern times, when Jews have become free to design great synagogues (see page 326), the parallel centrality of the home remains. Overwhelmingly, the first night of Passover finds Jews—and, these days, non-Jewish friends as well—in someone's home to celebrate the miracle of freedom.

The ritual script for the seder is called a *Haggadah*, from the Hebrew verb "to narrate." It narrates the story of the Exodus. But the tale is told midrashically—that is, it assembles bits and pieces of midrash (and halakhah, too) into a kaleidoscope of imagery from across the centuries. Central to the account is the overarching lesson of Jewish history: the escape from degradation to dignity. Midrash enters in, for example, when degradation is variously described as enforced from without (slavery) or imposed from within (idolatry). The telling is preceded by "The Four Questions," which, nowadays, the youngest child asks, to draw attention to the uniqueness of the Passover evening. The midrash takes over again by describing four different children (one wise, one wicked, one simple, and one not capable of asking), each of whom requires a different answer. The telling ends with psalms of praise.

The entire ritual occurs in the context of a sacred meal, liberally supplied with symbolic foods and ritualized efforts to retain the interest of both children and adults—a series of after-dinner songs, for instance.

But the serious message of deliverance is never far from the surface: a concluding call to open the door for Elijah, for example, who (it is hoped) will inaugurate the arrival of the messiah and the onset of final messianic redemption; and the Haggadah's concluding master metaphoric hope: "Next year in Jerusalem."

From the 1300s on (and, to some extent, even before), the Haggadah has attracted elaborate artistic attention. Other prayer books, too, have invited pictorial art, but not nearly as frequently, since the seder is a home event, allowing for personalization in ways that communal synagogue worship does not. But only the richest of Jewish families could afford an illustrated Haggadah that had to be privately outfitted with paintings and calligraphy by an artist and a scribe.

With the invention of printing in the fifteenth century, however, and with the establishment of Jewish publishing houses in the sixteenth and seventeenth centuries, artistically adorned Haggadahs became affordable in print runs large enough to make it likely that they would survive. Such Haggadahs found their way to library collections, where they have largely languished unseen and unappreciated.

But they need remain unseen and unappreciated no more—thanks to the distinguished historian Yosef Hayim Yerushalmi, who taught for many years at Harvard and Columbia universities. His *Haggadah and History* assembles full-page facsimiles from these Haggadahs, along with explanations of their art and the stories of their creation. This is a coffee-table book worth leafing through and pausing over, again and again, for the tales that lie behind every single page.

Take the sixteenth-century Haggadah from Frankfurt am Main. Johann Pfefferkorn, a Jewish apostate to Christianity, had orchestrated the burning of Jewish books by publishing a pamphlet illustrating "how the blind Jews celebrate their Easter." Pfefferkorn represented the Dominicans of Cologne, who opposed the rise of humanism, a movement that supported Hebrew studies by Christians. The Franciscans were no friends of the Jews, but were not happy to see the rival Dominicans enjoying the spotlight. To counteract them, the Franciscan monk Thomas Murner translated the Haggadah into Latin and published it with illustrations, as a demonstration that Pfefferkorn's charges were scurrilous.

Jewish history comes alive in Yerushalmi's book, through imagery that unfailingly evokes tears of sorrow and of joy, especially in the modern era, with its two pivotal events, the Holocaust and the founding of the State of Israel. A 1934 Polish Haggadah parody pictures Ze'ev Jabotinsky (as "a modern Moses") petitioning England's King

George V (as "Pharaoh") to honor England's 1917 commitment to let Jews reestablish a homeland in Palestine.

We find here also a World War II Haggadah hastily typed and outfitted with hand-drawn illustrations by Palestine's Jewish Brigade, which fought alongside England and celebrated Passover in the battlefield. Another Haggadah, this one copied from memory by a rabbi in a concentration camp, adds the hope, "May this be the last Haggadah in exile." A postwar Haggadah is dedicated to the Jewish refugees interned in displaced persons' camps in Cyprus—its cover portrays a ship illegally transporting Jews to their ancestral home.

Many Haggadah covers impacted by the Holocaust depict the promised land of the Bible as the modern-day state to which Jews from concentration camps can find their way home. But there are also darker images: biblical Egyptian taskmasters dressed as Nazis; a Jew lying half-dead on the ground, accompanied by a Yiddish poem that passes judgment on the era (and on God!): "I had a dream, a terrible dream / that my people are no more [. . .] Alas, alas, my dream has come to pass."

There is wry humor in this book, as well: a Chicago Haggadah from 1883 plays on the midrash of the four children by displaying a grown-up "wicked son" smoking a cigarette instead of attending to the service; another, the Geismar Haggadah from 1927 Berlin, provides a stick-figure drawing of the "wicked son" thumbing his nose at tradition. Sometimes, the humor is unintended. Ezekiel 16:7 likens Israel to a young woman with "fashioned breasts." A Prague Haggadah from 1526 illustrates the verse. The same woodcut is carried in a 1603 Venetian Haggadah, but someone has censored it by rubbing out the breasts and adding the heading, "This is a picture of a man."

By the time of his death in 2009, Yerushalmi had established his reputation as one of the leading historians of the Jewish experience. His 1982 book, *Zakhor*, is widely cited for exploring the rise of historical consciousness in Judaism; and his 1991 study, *Freud's Moses*, is a brilliant exposition of Sigmund Freud's Jewishness. Either one of these masterpieces could have been included here. But *Haggadah and History* is a book to return to year after year at Passover time. There is nothing like approaching the holiday with our own Haggadah in hand, and the Haggadahs of history in our mind's eye.

Community and Polity
(1976)

Daniel J. Elazar (1934–1999)

"The American Jewish community, like the United States generally, is an exceedingly complex organism."

If Judaism is a conversation, Jews must be adept at conversing. Conversations do not just happen, however; they take a shared understanding of what a conversation is about, what is appropriate to say, who gets to say it, and what the goal of the conversation is in the first place. The ways we organize our conversations vary.

While individuals can speak for themselves, however, whole communities cannot: they need organizations to do so. Throughout history, Jews have had to revise old ways of organizing their communities, a decision that evolves by way of an artful interchange between Jewish tradition and the surrounding culture in which Jews find themselves.

Much depends on what authority—if any—the conversationalists have to speak on behalf of others. In Europe, prior to the Enlightenment, Jews belonged to officially recognized communities; specifically designated Jewish officials represented the community to the government. The Enlightenment and emancipation ended these autonomous Jewish communities by recognizing Jews as individual citizens whose corporate loyalty lay with the state alone. Jews now participated in the Jewish community solely by choice, and only for limited purposes.

This is especially true of the United States, which began as a quintessentially modern society by breaking free of traditional European constraints and organizational patterns—and which separated religion from state so that Jews were left free to develop in any way they wished, with absolutely no governmental mandates or restraints upon how they did it. The organizational structure of American Jewry is, therefore, of particular interest, especially when one considers its global importance. It is the largest Jewish community outside of Israel and the wealthiest Jewish community in the world. Whoever speaks on behalf of American Jews speaks to a worldwide audience. The problem is, it is never quite clear who speaks for American Jews in the first place.

For the many centuries prior to the American experience, the leading conversationalists were rabbis, who represented whole communities as the official voice of Jewish tradition. With emancipation, however, rabbis had to make room for secular ideologues—who spoke as socialists, Zionists, or territorialists—and for wealthy individuals (like the Rothschilds of Europe) who represented no particular ideology, but whose very wealth gave them prestige and social standing. In America, therefore (as in democracies generally), rabbis now speak primarily as spiritual leaders of synagogues, where they share power with lay boards that have legal and financial responsibility for their synagogues' welfare. But less than 50 percent of American Jews belong to synagogues, and Jews find themselves represented also by other organizations that have arisen over time to advance one Jewish interest or another. These organizations compete for members and financial support. Some have their own rabbinic leaders, and some do not. Some remain local and tiny, while others enjoy national stature. In a democracy, anyone can set up an organization and hope for the best.

How does one make sense of a dizzying list of Jewish organizations that includes federation, Hadassah, B'nai B'rith, the American Jewish Committee, the Jewish Agency, the Anti-Defamation League, Jewish Community Centers (JCCs), and so on? Without a "map," even the most intrepid organizational pilgrim is likely to be lost. *Community and Polity* is such a map, drawn by a master cartographer, Daniel Elazar, who served as professor of political science at Temple University in Philadelphia and founded and directed the Center for the Study of Federalism. He authored or edited over sixty books, and took a special interest in the organizational complexity of the Jewish world, much of which he influenced as consultant to most of the organizations he describes, not just in America but as far away as South Africa, Canada, Australia, and Israel.

True to the book's title, Elazar begins by characterizing the Jewish *polity*, the individual Jews whose central challenge is "maintaining Jewish life in a truly voluntaristic and open society." We should picture concentric circles of Jewish engagement. Ten percent of America's Jews constitute the *core*: their daily lives revolve around Jewish concerns, events, and causes. Another 12 percent are *engaged participants* who demonstrate some significant "avocational" interest in the things that the core organizes. Beyond that second circle are the 25 to 30 percent of *affiliated Jews* who pay dues to synagogues and other organizations but do not attend regularly. Another 25 to 30 percent care enough about having a Jewish community to be *occasional financial supporters* of the organizations that comprise it, even though they themselves barely frequent the events these organizations sponsor and take little ongoing interest in the work these organizations do. Yet another 20 percent are *peripherals* who are hardly Jewish at all: they say they are Jewish, but support no Jewish organizations, have few Jewish friends, and keep almost no Jewish customs. A final circle—the rest—is more marginal still, having joined churches, perhaps, even though they say on surveys that they are, in some ways, Jewish.

The Jewish core has organized this polity for a multitude of ends: defense against anti-Semitism, internal communal philanthropy, saving Jewish lives abroad, aid to Israel specifically, cultural pursuits, and religion.

Elazar charts the organizational structure of the Jewish community and explores the historical events that brought its individual institutions into being. The American Jewish Committee was a response to anti-Semitic outbreaks in Russia, particularly the Kishinev pogrom of 1903. Hadassah is the 1912 brainchild of Henrietta Szold, a scholar, social worker, writer, and all-around activist who galvanized women in support of a Jewish homeland. The massive influx of eastern European immigrants in the United States after 1881 spawned a variety of local self-help organizations, which coalesced by the 1950s in order to coordinate fundraising and allocation of resources. These became known as federations, and pretty much every local Jewish community now has one (see page 296).

As the twentieth century progressed, these federations collaborated across communal lines to raise the astounding sums of money necessary to support hospitals and schools, coordinate help to Israel, and save persecuted Jews in communist Russia—to name but a few of the causes that have, by now, turned this network of federations into a virtual Jewish government. It cannot officially tax anyone, of course, but its sophisticated fund-raising capacity collects hundreds of millions of dollars annually. This money is then allocated to humanitarian, educational, and cultural concerns worldwide.

Community and Polity was published in 1976 and revised in 1995. It is an encyclopedic "Who's Who" of the complex organizational web that drives Jewish life in America (Canada is quite similar). It provides an excellent answer to the question: What really is the Jewish community—and through which organized venues do Jews converse about the Jewish future?

A Guide to Jewish Religious Practice
(1979)

Isaac Klein (1905–1979)

"The unique character of Jewish life, the factor responsible for the endurance of the Jewish people, the ingredient that gave holiness to its existence, is the mitzwot, the performance of religious commandments."

Judaism defies modern definitions of religion, because it is not primarily a system of belief. But religions in antiquity were never about belief alone. Roman law included Judaism as a licit religion because the Latin *religio* (from which we get "religion") included the sense of obligation, and Judaism patently qualified as that. By the fourth century CE, a newly Christianized empire was heading toward the recognition of only one such *religio licita*, Christianity. But for centuries, the Christian religion, too, might adequately have been subsumed under the concept of obligation, since "religious" was as much a noun as an adjective: it denoted monks, priests, and nuns who gave over their lives to the specific obligations of serving God and the church, and who, on that account, were society's "men and women religious." Our attitudes toward religion today, however, are very much formed by the Protestant Reformation, which made much of doctrinal differences, leaving us with a clear sense that religion is a matter of faith. And Judaism simply does not fit that definition.

To be sure, faith is not irrelevant; Jews cannot believe just anything. Nineteenth-century Jewish reformers, for example, made much of Judaism's core belief in a single Deity—they called it ethical monotheism. But when they met to discuss how best to modernize the medieval Judaism that they had inherited, they turned largely to matters of obligation, because Judaism is essentially a program of action, a recipe for daily living, a system of various do's and don'ts—"Thou shalt" and "Thou shalt not." Committed Jews do *not* so much need a guide to religious belief as they need a guide to religious practice, and since 1979, Isaac Klein's *Guide to Jewish Religious Practice* has been the one that most Jews turn to.

Its roots lie within the Conservative movement in the 1960s, when Louis Finkelstein was chancellor of the Jewish Theological Seminary in New York. Finkelstein led the Conservative movement from 1940 to

1972, a golden age for Conservative Jews. In the early 1960s, Conservative Judaism was celebrating the height of its success, its number of synagogues having doubled since 1949. But the movement was hardly unified on what, exactly, Conservative Judaism demanded. On the right, it included Jews who were practically Orthodox; on the left were many who had sided with Mordecai Kaplan, a professor at the Seminary but a "renegade" thinker who had already founded an alternative ideology of Reconstructionism. Still others were Jews ethnically but kept almost nothing of Jewish law.

So Finkelstein asked Isaac Klein to devise a series of pamphlets addressing specific aspects of Jewish observance. Klein had distinguished himself academically by graduating both from Yeshiva University and the Jewish Theological Seminary; then earning an advanced degree in Jewish Law from the Seminary under the tutelage of the legendary Talmudist Louis Ginzberg; and a Ph.D. in Jewish philosophy from Harvard as well. He was the perfect candidate for the task.

In 1979, Klein's pamphlets were compiled in this singularly magnificent summary of traditional Jewish law, modified by modernity. It followed from the Conservative movement's theological concept of legal evolution, according to which Jewish law remains as binding as ever, but must be interpreted as a set of statutes that is newly understood in every era.

Everything is here: the life of prayer; the Jewish schedule of holy days and festivals; the requirements for a Jewish home; and the Jewish life cycle—all beautifully organized in concise chapters, along with a wonderfully detailed index that makes it possible to look up virtually anything you might like to know. What is the content of the daily synagogue service? How are prayers altered for the second day of Passover? How do you blow the shofar on Rosh Hashanah? What are the rules that define separating milk and meat products at home? How do you make your kitchen kosher, if it isn't kosher already? Why do bride and groom fast on their wedding day? What are Jewish grounds for divorce? What mourning practices govern the first three (or seven) days, the first thirty days, and then the first year, after burial? Why, when, and how do Jews erect a tombstone over a grave?

Klein's compendium goes deeper than the obvious. He explains the entirety of the Jewish calendar, for example: immediately relevant things such as why some months have twenty-nine days and some have thirty, but also the incredible complexities of the entire calendrical system. We get not just the list of foods that may or may not be eaten on Passover but also the rationale behind every ruling. Are you planning a wedding? Klein provides every step of the Jewish route to marriage, how every ceremony is conducted, where it happens, and why it is as it is.

But his book is much more than just a list of dos and don'ts. It is an elegant summary of the thinking that underlies each and every practice, and a handy way to learn about any aspect of Jewish law that piques our interest.

To be sure, this is the Conservative movement's guide to Jewish practice. But the denominations in Judaism are all alike in their high regard for classical Jewish sources. They may arrive at different conclusions after consulting those sources, but they all attend to the same Talmuds, the same medieval codes, the same precedential rulings (the responsa), and so on. Klein's summary of the rationale behind tradition is, therefore, not necessarily denominationally specific. Orthodox, Reform, and Reconstructionist authorities will differ in interpretation here and there and will have their own sense—given this legal history—of what Judaism demands. Also, this is not even the final word for Conservative Jews, whose standing Law Committee regularly reviews old decisions in the light of new understandings. But Klein's *Guide* is not so much a book of prescriptions as it is a collection of explanations. As such, every reader can benefit from its mastery of scholarship, organization, detail, and presentation.

Best of all, *A Guide to Jewish Religious Practice* is for readers at all levels of Jewish knowledge. Specialists can look up what they somehow never learned or have forgotten, while beginners can make a starting foray into whatever subject they find interesting. Many rabbis keep Klein's masterpiece within easy reach on the bookshelves just over their desks. Many more committed Jewish laypeople could and should do likewise.

When Bad Things Happen to Good People
(1981)

Harold S. Kushner (*born 1935*)

"There is only one question which really matters: why do bad things happen to good people?"

Harold Kushner's son, Aaron, was born with progeria, a rare disease that ages a child virtually overnight and kills him of "old age" while he is still young. The doctor warned his parents that Aaron would look like a little old man, but die a teenager. And so it was. Aaron died two weeks before his fourteenth birthday.

What does a rabbi do when personal tragedy shatters faith? Rabbi Kushner wrote a book, "not an abstract book about God and theology [. . . but] a very personal book, written by someone who believes in God and in the goodness of the world, someone who has spent most of his life trying to help other people believe, and was compelled by a personal tragedy to rethink everything he had been taught about God and God's ways."

Kushner's first step was to see what other people had said when confronted with tragedy. What he found was that all such books (and there are many) "were more concerned with defending God's honor [. . .] than they were with curing the bewilderment and the anguish of the parent of a dying child."

There are only a small and finite number of standard responses, and Kushner reviews them all, patiently dismissing them as the sort of thing pastorally minded rabbis might say but shouldn't:

(1) "Maybe you did something wrong to deserve this punishment." This is the classical response given to the biblical Job, but Job rejects the charge—as does the author of Job, who introduces Job as perfectly righteous. What could little Aaron Kushner have done to deserve his terrible disease? "You deserve it" is the worst response of all, since it engenders undeserved guilt, further victimizing the victim.

(2) "It will all turn out to be fair in the end." But, alas, it doesn't.

(3) "God has His own reasons." This response sees suffering as part of God's inscrutable plan, far beyond the capacity of mere human beings to comprehend. We may even be told that it is a privilege to be taken by God as part of God's larger vision. "'Tell me not why I must suffer,' goes a familiar medieval Christian prayer, 'Assure me only that I suffer for Thy sake.'" But is there any such grand design at all? Kushner cannot bring himself to believe it.

(4) "God is above our mortal and limited view of morality." This is like the argument "God has his own reasons," only worse. We are asked not only to question an almighty God, far beyond our ken, but to do so even though God may not actually have a larger plan in mind. If God had a plan, there would at least be a reason for the untimely death. Without one, God becomes a whimsical tyrant, acting immorally. "Is it credible," Kushner asks, "that a good God would give us a system of morals that He Himself does not keep?"

(5) "Suffering is educational. You will be a better person for it." Kushner admits he has become a better person, rabbi, and counselor because of Aaron's death, but no one would ever consider the gains worth the loss. However much he may have benefited in lessons learned, skills acquired, or wisdom attained, he would give all that back in an instant, if he could thereby regain his son.

(6) "God tests us." Then God is a sadist. Kushner recalls the 1960s, when it was fashionable to say that "God is dead." One bumper sticker back then read: "My God is not dead; sorry about yours." Kushner counters, "My bumper sticker would read, 'My God is not cruel; sorry about yours.'"

Another way of looking at this great pain is through the issue of prayer. Given the ubiquity of victims who suffer pain or die young, as Aaron did, Kushner asks what might be the hardest question of all: Why doesn't God answer prayer?

The only rational conclusion, says Kushner, is that God would—if God could. Remember, by his own testimony, Kushner is a believer. It is just that his beliefs about God have changed over time. A truly good God who is all-powerful to effect change would grant prayers for healing; so God must not be all-powerful. God, in Kushner's view, must have created the universe so that it operates according to the laws of nature, which inevitably bring pain as well as happiness. Accidents happen all the time, creating random tragedy—as when a drunken driver hits one car rather than another, or one plane goes down over the sea while other planes nearby do not. These are horrible, but random occurrences, and have nothing to do with God; they are just the natural world at work.

Why does the Bible have God say, "Let us create mankind in our own image" (Genesis 1:26)? Who is God talking to? Kushner thinks God is addressing the lower forms of life already created. God is, in effect, establishing the rule of evolution, saying human beings will be created by God but evolving from animals. We, no less than animals, are both victims and beneficiaries of natural law.

But human beings are unique, Kushner contends. To understand human uniqueness, he addresses yet another rationale that is frequently offered to the suffering: God may burden us with pain, but never more pain than we are able to handle. In other words, God first gives us strength, and then adjusts the pain quotient so that it is not more than the amount of strength we have been allotted. Just the reverse is true, Kushner insists. First we get the pain—not from God but from fate. What God sends us is the strength to handle the pain we already have. And that is our salvation, such as it is. Prayer may not evoke a cure from God, but it strengthens us and brings us together in a common cause. "It taps hidden reserves of faith and courage that were not there before."

So there is no inherent meaning in suffering. Suffering just *is*, for no good reason at all. But after the fact, we, ourselves, can give it meaning by focusing on the question "Now that this has happened to me, what am I going to do about it?"

When Kushner asked himself that question, the answer was clear: write a book. He waited until "I had gone beyond self-pity to the point of facing and accepting my son's death" and concluded, "This had to be a book that affirmed life."

It does just that, as the millions of people who have read it by now can testify. Those for whom traditional responses sound increasingly hollow should find Kushner's naturalistic answer a welcome breath of honesty. The message of *When Bad Things Happen to Good People* should send the suffering back to life, no less than it did the man who wrote it.

Halakhic Man
(1983)
Joseph B. Soloveitchik (1903–1993)

"Halakhic man approaches existential space with an a priori yardstick, with fixed laws and principles, precepts that were revealed to Moses on Mt. Sinai: the imaginary bridging of a spatial gap less than three handbreadths; the imaginary vertical extension, upward or downward, of a partition; the imaginary vertical extension of a roof downward to the ground; the bent wall; the measurement of four square cubits, ten handbreadths, etc., etc. He perceives space by means of these laws just like the mathematician who gazes at existential space by means of the ideal geometric space."

What theology is to Christianity, Jewish law—halakhah—is to Judaism. Imagine the two thousand years of theological tracts, commentaries, disputations, argumentations, and just plain fiats laying down what a pious Christian should believe; apply that image to Jewish law, and you have a rough idea of the sheer magnitude of what goes into seeing the world as a halakhic Jew. Christian belief, of course, implies behavior as well, just as Jewish law presupposes belief. But Christians begin with theology, while Jews begin with law.

But halakhah is not narrow legalism, it is all-embracing: a way of thinking, an entire philosophy, and its own form of spirituality. It covers not just morals and ritual, the categories we normally associate with religion, but also civil law, sacrificial law (for when the Temple once stood), and even criminal law, insofar as Jews ever had the ability to exercise it. Assigning ownership to lost property, punishment for theft, honesty in business, slanderous talk, daily worship, forbidden foods, washing one's hands, appropriate clothing, sexual relations, building a synagogue, propriety in public, saying grace after meals—all of this is halakhah. Jews who follow it are called halakhic.

Since it is the very heart of Torah, Jews do not just *follow* halakhah; they *study* it as well. Even Jews who do not keep halakhah read it to learn its philosophical and moral lessons, and to formulate their conversation in terms of its concepts. Indeed, study of Torah is itself a halakhic demand, perhaps (according to some) the most important one of all, since Judaism would disappear without it—Judaism is unthinkable without the Talmud, the responsa, the legal codes, and the vast mass of legal literature they have spawned.

Contemporary Jews of all denominations take halakhah seriously, but unlike Jews in premodern times, they are not all halakhic. They differ on the details of individual precepts, on how to determine those precepts in the first place, and on how bound we are to follow them after they are determined. Premodern Jews, too, had differences: since Judaism has no hierarchy, for example, they had to balance contradictory legal opinions issued by equally respected masters. Modernity, however, did more than challenge individual Jewish laws; it threw the entire Jewish legal system into question.

When Jews were emancipated from their servile medieval status, the Jewish courts and judges of the ghettos were replaced by the legal system of their respective nation-states. Without such Jewish courts and judges, however, the charge to observe rabbinic law became unenforceable, backed only by moral suasion. But moral suasion depends on community pressure, and as Jews left their ghettos, even moral suasion dissipated.

As we have seen, Jews were also exposed to the intellectual ferment of the Enlightenment—the scientific study of history, for example, which questioned the divine origin of the Bible and which relativized the rabbinic legal giants of the past, by understanding them in their historical contexts: crucial in their times, but potentially irrelevant once those times had passed.

Not just sociologically (the disappearance of an autonomous legal system) and historically (the belief in evolution) but theologically, too, modernity has undermined halakhah, by casting doubt on the existence of a personal God who issued immutable rules on Mount Sinai and who actually cares if Jews keep Jewish law altogether. Without such a God, the commanding nature of halakhah is hard to accept. Hence the importance of *Halakhic Man*. No other scholar comes even close to Joseph Soloveitchik in providing a compelling modern raison d'être for halakhah, by portraying the philosophy and psychology that halakhah presupposes.

Soloveitchik differentiates three paradigmatic personality types: halakhic, cognitive, and religious (he calls them Halakhic Man, Cognitive Man, and Religious Man). Cognitive, for him, means the mentality of the scientist, bent on explaining the world by unveiling the necessary laws by which it operates. The halakhic personality also focuses on the world, but with the altogether different intent of imposing halakhic law upon it. The religious personality is the mystic, who yearns for spiritual experiences beyond the laws of physics and seeks holiness beyond the earthly realm. Not content with *seeking* holiness, the halakhic point of view actually *confers* holiness upon the earthly realm, by executing halakhic decisions upon it. In so doing, the halakhic personality completes the creativity begun by God when the cosmos came into being. Access to halakhah, moreover, is open to anyone who wants to study it; the halakhic type sees it, therefore, as the quintessential democratic portal to God.

As law, halakhah is a life of action, not just thought, but the most important action the halakhic type can take is thoughtful study, even when such study is not immediately relevant. Nothing is moot in a legal system that exists not only for practice but for its own sake, as a mirror of God's own mind. So a halakhic person seeks halakhic understanding of everything, even of matters that are no longer applicable—such as sacrifice and the laws of ancient agriculture. The entirety of halakhah can be seen as the Jewish equivalent of a Platonic ideal universe, beyond the limitations of the world of our senses that we actually experience: the sensory world is imperfect; it requires human agency to be perfected. And the system of human agency that God entrusts to us—God's creatures—is halakhah.

Reading Joseph Soloveitchik is a treat, not just because of what he wrote but also because of who he was. Born into an illustrious rabbinic family in Poland, the young Soloveitchik was taught by his father, himself a famous halakhist. Joseph shocked his family by going off to pursue secular studies in Berlin, where he received his doctorate in philosophy. On the eve of Hitler's accession to power, in 1932, he left Europe for Boston, then taught in the rabbinic school of Yeshiva University in New York, and became its director in 1941. Sometimes called "the Rav," meaning, the teacher and rabbi par excellence, Soloveitchik combined mastery of halakhah with profundity of thought in general—Western philosophy no less than Talmudic literature. To call him revered is an understatement.

As it is not just law but also the philosophy behind the law, halakhah is a kind of Jewish metaphysics, a way of measuring the world by what God wants us to do in it. Judaism is a distinctive approach to reality, and the concepts of halakhah are central to that approach—the quintessentially Jewish way of talking about life. No one understood that better than "the Rav," whose *Halakhic Man* is the very best way to appreciate what halakhah is all about.

On Being a Jewish Feminist
(1983)

Susannah Heschel (born 1952) (editor)

"The Jewish woman has been a golem [a mythical Frankenstein, who was disabled by removing the divine name from its person]. She cooked and bore and did her master's bidding and when her tasks were done, the divine name was removed from her mouth. It is time for the golem to demand a soul" (from the essay by Rachel Adler).

Most people who have grown up since the 1970s will find it hard to imagine contemporary Judaism without feminism. The battle of Jewish women for equality isn't over yet—there are still very few women heading up major Jewish organizations, and the strength of Jewish women's voices varies from country to country—but, except among the Orthodox, Jews have become used to women as clergy, synagogue presidents, and communal leaders of every sort. Susannah Heschel's exceptional collection of essays marks the state of Jewish feminism in the early 1980s, after a decade or so of social ferment. Things have changed since Heschel put this book together, but the early and basic terms of the debate were in place by then, making *On Being a Jewish Feminist* a superb starting point for tracking the feminist revolution in Jewish polity and policy that is still under way.

Heschel, a professor of Jewish Studies at Dartmouth College, provides an introduction that sets the historical stage. Feminism began with baby boomers coming of age in the tumultuous 1960s and '70s. Earlier Jewish women seeking liberation had to "break off and struggle alone." Contemporary Jewish feminists converted individualized unrest into a social movement that fought to have women counted in a minyan (the quorum of ten adult Jewish worshippers necessary for communal prayer), be admitted to places where sacred text is studied, and be ordained as rabbis—to name just the most obvious issues.

Not surprisingly, the issue of female rabbis has been especially hotly contested. When Heschel compiled her anthology, her own Conservative movement had not yet ordained women—that would happen two years later—but the Reform and Reconstructionist movements had done so in 1972 and 1974, respectively. The first Jewish woman in Great Britain was ordained in 1975; that same year, the Reform movement in Israel established a rabbinic program for both men and women. In no case was the decision to ordain women made without struggle, acrimony, and rancor.

Heschel records some of the arguments that were used to oppose this move—not just issues of Jewish law that would have to be changed to admit female rabbis, but also pseudo-theological claims, such as the charge that the traditional role of women as mothers and homemakers was "designed by Almighty God Himself." Most difficult of all to contend with were psychological fears that sound laughable now. Female rabbis, it was said, would "sacrifice masculine self-confidence and biological zest"; and a woman officiating at services would pervert prayer, because she would be "likely to encourage erotic fantasies" among the men present.

Perhaps the core of the struggle is the extent, or even the possibility, of achieving women's equality in a system where Jewish law (halakhah) is fundamentally opposed to them. In her essay here, Judith Plaskow (who would go on to write the first great feminist theological critique, *Standing Again at Sinai*, in 1990) takes Cynthia Ozick (see page 311) to task for not realizing that "the subordination of women within Judaism is rooted in theology, in the very foundation of Jewish tradition [. . .] The Jewish women's movement [. . .] has focused on getting women a piece of the Jewish pie; it has not wanted to bake a new one." Ozick would indeed prefer that Jewish women have a piece of the already existent pie, the fundamental ingredient of which certainly is halakhah. Rachel Adler (who would compose another signal theological treatise, *Engendering Judaism*, in 1998) also argues for change from *within* halakhah, rather than abandon the halakhic enterprise altogether. But change from within will not come easily, because halakhah has marginalized, ignored, and erased women from consideration, to the point where they have become "the Jew who wasn't there."

Historians and social scientists weigh in as well. Paula Hyman (whose work includes editorship of Puah Rakovsky's *My Life as a Radical Jewish Woman*; see page 143) takes issue with critics who fear the demise of Judaism because of low childbearing rates and therefore urge women to leave the workplace and have larger families. "The Jewish working mother," she counters, "has a long and noble history [. . .] The image of the *Yiddishe mamma* spending all her time and energy" with children and homemaking is a "myth." Lesley Hazleton (author of *Israeli Women* [1977]) warns against surrendering to "the new direction in Israeli women's fantasies [. . .] a deep yearning for the protected yet vulnerable times of yore, when men indeed 'did' and women indeed 'were.'" Mimi Scarf (who published *Battered Jewish Wives* in 1988) blows the whistle on a culture that naively imagines "marriages made in heaven," when what we get is "battered Jewish wives." And Deborah Lipstadt (well-known for her denunciation of Holocaust-deniers) exposes the absence of "Women and Power in the Federation."

As one would expect from a feminist collection of essays, we get ample testimonial to Jewish women in search of authentic Jewish experience. Sara Reguer describes what it was like going to synagogue daily to say *Kaddish* (the memorial prayer) for her recently deceased mother, but having to do so while sitting in the women's section of the synagogue: one man even told her to recite it quietly so that he would not have to hear her. On the positive side, Arleen Stern remembers the thrill of learning how to chant the Torah as an adult: "The feeling of relief and exhilaration," she says, "brought me close to tears." Lynn Gottlieb's poetry celebrates Passover housecleaning. Laura Geller, another of the few Jewish women to be ordained in the 1970s, and the first to bear a child while serving as a rabbi, argues that the very existence of female rabbis allows congregants—all congregants, not just women—to transcend the childish notion that God must be a man. The result is an entirely new way to relate to God, requiring such adult questions as "What do I believe about God?" and "How do I speak to God?"

Jewish feminism is still in process. Every movement is, but especially feminism, which is a liberation movement for all women and fights the notion that the social roles by which we define anyone are somehow inherent in the way the world is, rather than a decision that we make as a culture—and can unmake or remake, if we wish. By definition, then, Jewish feminism can hardly be a single issue. New waves of feminist consciousness arise with every new generation, each one nourishing the ongoing Jewish conversation.

But this book sets the stage for them all—it is the group testimonial of the earliest wave of Jewish feminists. Its many voices help readers see that Jewish feminism is a rich tapestry of debate, not a single thread of thought. Serious people differ seriously, and feminism is serious.

The essays here make it abundantly clear that admitting women to Jewish learning, authority, and power has constituted a radical shift of perspective—probably *the* most radical shift since the Enlightenment, and rivaling the Enlightenment itself as a revolutionary change in consciousness. As an index of how the whole revolution began, there is nothing better than *On Being a Jewish Feminist*.

The Gate Behind the Wall
(1984)

Samuel C. Heilman (born 1946)

"For the last sixty years, without exception, had a group been gathering around these tables to review the Talmud. Here was the great Jewish chain of being that begins with Moses at Sinai."

Bus number 9 snakes through every conceivable neighborhood of the magical city of Jerusalem. It skirts the ultra-Orthodox Jewish quarter of Meah Shearim, where life proceeds as much as possible as if the world had never heard of Napoleon, Darwin, and Mickey Mouse; then, later, it drops off graduate students at the world-renowned Hebrew University, Meah Shearim's very antithesis. Bus number 9 is a metaphor for multiple identities, and, by extension, internal psychological conflict that can become self-discovery—the subject of this book.

Its author, Samuel Heilman, is a prominent professor of sociology in New York and a modern Orthodox Jew who defies what social scientists laughingly call "Bongo-Bongoism." The term refers to the tendency of aspiring anthropologists to study far-off tribes no Westerner has ever seen, and ever after—whatever the question, on whatever topic—to respond, "I don't know about that, but the 'Bongo Bongo,' where I did my work, do it this way."

Being a Jew himself, Heilman reasoned, he would more easily understand his subjects if they were Jewish, too. Why study cultures he knew nothing about? He had already applied that logic to an earlier study, *Synagogue Life* (1976), a fascinating look at what went on at the Orthodox synagogue he attended. In *The Gate Behind the Wall*, Heilman once more set out to investigate what he already knew a lot about: traditional Jewish study called *lernen* (Yiddish for "learning"). There are different styles of lernen, but they all share a passion for the Talmud and its offshoots: midrash, responsa, biblical exegesis, and commentaries upon commentaries upon commentaries. In some cultures, people aspire to be artists, monks, or millionaires. Jews learn how to navigate the densely packed arguments of holy books.

True to its subtitle, *A Pilgrimage to Jerusalem*, Heilman's book is also the odyssey of a scientific researcher who discovers that the object being researched is himself. Every day, he leaves his Jerusalem apartment in search of a *lerning* group to match his soul. Accustomed to being the professor, and by no means new to Talmud study, he nonetheless finds himself a relative beginner, scurrying to keep up with classmates who are ordinary bank tellers, managers, shopkeepers, and metal workers by day, but adept Talmudic literati by night.

He first encounters a gaggle of men studying laws of temple sacrifices as if the ancient sacrificial cult were still around, and they must figure out what offering to bring (and how to bring it) that very day. They are so thoroughly caught up in their subject that, for them, "there was now and no then"—whereas in Heilman's world, "past is past and present present, and one simply learns to dim the lights in one room while passing into the other."

His "pilgrimage" leads him to a pious bookseller who has never heard of Adam Smith or Karl Marx, and in defiance of predictions that either one would have made, asks Heilman *not* to buy a lot of his books. Sacred texts, he says, are "what you live for, not what you live off." You do not possess them; they possess you. He has only contempt for people who purchase a library's worth of books and master not a single page or volume in it.

As he travels from one pious group to another, Heilman eventually comes across a set of ultra-Orthodox (Hareidi) Jews led by a descendant of perhaps the most enigmatic Hasidic leader of all time, Nahman of Bratslav. Every bit as inscrutable as his movement's founder, this man is a walking Jewish library, his every utterance a double entendre from the Bible or Talmud. Heilman is directed through Jerusalem alleyways and courtyards that seem to go back centuries in time, each one housing *lerners* and their families who, one suspects, are holding on to lives that they perceive as inherited directly from the Middle Ages. Heilman's Jerusalem classmates had pursued their Talmudic lernen as an avocation—a serious one, to be sure, but still, just an after-hours avocation. These Hareidi men, by contrast, do virtually nothing else. They are fundamentalists who never read a newspaper, never vote, have no hobbies, barely have jobs, and make do with poverty because they spend every waking hour lerning and praying; their wives (who practice no birth control as a matter of religious principle) are constantly pregnant, keeping house, watching over children, and supporting their husbands in their sacred duties.

These lerners are not, however, ignorant—far from it. In their own way, they know infinitely more than Heilman, who is in awe of the way they tease out meaning from arcane and ancient texts. With time and study, he reaches the point where he has "ceased dismissing opaque Talmudic dicta as beyond my comprehension," or, worse, as being so absurd as to make attempts to understand them ridiculously unworth the effort. "Words, phrases, and ideas that seemed unintelligible could be penetrated, and when we managed to interpret our way through such a text, those were the moments of highest intellectual and emotional drama."

The Gate Behind the Wall is a cascade of such moments, for Heilman is the participant-observer at his lyrical best: with keen detail, he observes the intricacies of a bygone era that has never quite gone by; then participates in the very rites he is describing; all the while reflecting inwardly upon his own personal journey, as bus number 9 takes him ever deeper into his Jewish soul.

This world of men will remain foreign to women readers. Nowadays, in modern Jewish circles (including modern Orthodoxy), lerning is open to women, too. But here, in ultra-Orthodox Jerusalem, women are appendages to their husbands' quest for the sacred. Their barriers of gender, however, are not altogether different from what Heilman calls his own "barriers of biography" that keep him at a distance from the inner core of the lerners he encounters. He is kept standing just outside the gate, never without a wall that bars his complete entry.

There is nothing like this book to take the modern reader into the esoteric depths of Jewish lerning—and there is nothing like lerning to draw modern readers into the profundity of Jewish tradition. *The Gate Behind the Wall* is a must-read for appreciating the study of Torah as a quintessentially Jewish mode of spirituality.

Sacred Survival
(1986)

Jonathan S. Woocher (*born 1946*)

"When our children and grandchildren gather in years to come, let them say that each of us responded Hineni *['Here!']—that we made a difference. If we act now, we—you and I—can take part in a future for the Jewish People even brighter than our glorious past. And the Jewish People can live forever.* Am Yisra'el Chai *['The Jewish people lives']."*

Thanksgiving and Memorial Day are important holidays in the United States. The first dates back to 1863, when President Lincoln announced a day of gratitude for "these bounties, which are so constantly enjoyed [. . .] the ever watchful providence of Almighty God." Memorial Day, too, goes back to the Civil War, a day to remember the soldiers fallen in the Union cause.

Despite America's official separation of church from state, it is hard not to see these two holidays as religious, and in 1967, the sociologist Robert Bellah identified them as signs of an American "civil religion," the "social glue" that binds people together, using the full array of symbols, holy days, and rituals that we normally associate with religion.

What about American *Jews*? As Americans, they observe American civil religion like everybody else. But do they also celebrate a *Jewish* civil religion that galvanizes their behavior?

Apparently they do. This revelation came in 1986, with Jonathan Woocher's breakthrough study of the Jewish federation movement—in the United States, chiefly, but in Canada as well. Woocher had received a doctorate in religious studies from Temple University, and then taught at Brandeis University. In 1986, he left academia for the Jewish Education Service of North America (JESNA) in New York City and has worked there ever since. JESNA was formed in 1981 as a national resource for Jewish education of every facet, and has remained closely allied to the very federation system that Woocher describes.

It is difficult to overemphasize the importance of "federation," as Jews generally call it. No other organization even remotely comes close to federation's collective strength, its ability to raise and distribute vast sums of money for Jewish causes, and its ability to influence Jewish life both locally and abroad. It operates independently of synagogues, is entirely secular, and receives relatively little national publicity. It is indeed best likened to a voluntary government for Jewish affairs.

In free societies like Canada and the United States, the government cannot compel Jews to constitute their own community. Still, most North American Jews want to contribute to specifically Jewish causes such as Jewish camps and educational institutions; they also want to protect Jews from anti-Semitism, nurture the Jewish homeland of Israel, and support Jewish well-being around the world. Such extensive philanthropic causes require some form of self-government to organize them.

Attempts at self-government in America go back to 1877, when immigrant Orthodox Jews tried to establish a *kehillah* (community) in New York City. It was to be directed by a chief rabbi, invited from Europe to fill the post. But the European conditions of the time could not be imported with him, and the experiment quickly died. In 1909, Reform rabbi Judah Magnes launched a second effort, also in New York City, but for all Jews, not just for the Orthodox. In place of being organized around the leadership of a chief rabbi (the European model), Magnes foresaw a democratic federation of local organizations that ceded some of their power to professionalized bureaus—a Bureau of Jewish Education, for example. By 1916, this kehillah had failed as well, but its bureaus were set free to seek independent funding.

Meanwhile, a variety of Jewish welfare and education agencies were taking root, and by the 1950s, these were being merged with communal efforts established in the 1930s for Jewish relief overseas. The stage was being set for a national federation of local federations.

By the time of Woocher's book, these federations had become the most powerful Jewish organization in North America, and indeed—save for the government of Israel—for Jewish life worldwide. On any given day, and in every city with a Jewish population of consequence, a host of professional federation workers direct grants to a number of causes: Jewish educational initiatives; outreach efforts to the unaffiliated; fact-finding missions to investigate the state of affairs for Jews in countries like Cuba, Romania, or Russia; programs to stem anti-Israel propaganda on campuses; food deliveries for Jewish shut-ins; the ongoing work of maintaining such institutions as a Jewish cemetery, a Jewish nursing home, Jewish camps, Jewish community centers; and much more. This is big business, requiring vast sums of money, which other professionals raise in an annual campaign for contributions. Each local federation is run by an executive director, who is answerable to a lay board.

But the federation represents the local Jews it serves, so the professionals work alongside volunteers who take time off work or attend after-hours meetings to determine policy for the various efforts and agencies in question. These same volunteers also head up the fund-raising efforts and are expected to give liberally themselves.

Some members of this virtual army of volunteers and professionals would call themselves religious. But many would not. They are secular, they would say, committed to the survival of the Jewish People, not Jewish religion. Woocher demonstrates, however, that even they are motivated religiously: not by the official religion called Judaism, perhaps, but by an alternative set of values, beliefs, and obligations—a Jewish civil religion that is sacred in its own way. It is not just survival, but *sacred* survival that matters to them.

Religions have rituals, a sacred calendar, liturgies, pilgrimages, a sacred tale, and a transcendent purpose allied to an ultimate authority or source of value. Federation has all of this.

Take liturgy: the central liturgical expression of Jewish faith is the *Sh'ma* (meaning, "Hear . . ."): "Hear O Israel, The Eternal is our God, the Eternal is One." Federation secularizes that into "*We* are One," a reflection of the hope that Jews will support each other worldwide. For its pilgrimages, it sends supporters on "missions" to Israel, sometimes by way of the ruins of Hitler's death camps: the State of Israel is a central shrine, and Jewish survival in the face of danger is the highest religious imperative. Appropriately, federation's sacred tale is not the Exodus from Egypt but the Holocaust in Europe; not the desert wandering of millennia ago but the post–World War II trek back home to the new Jewish state. As for a sacred calendar, federation sponsors its own "Super Sunday," an annual fundraising day for volunteers nationwide to staff phone banks, raising donations to the sacred cause.

But can civil Judaism alone sustain Jewish continuity? Will the next generation also be moved to sacrifice time, money, and energy to federation's cause? *Sacred Survival* suggests it will not, making it necessary reading not just for the information it contains, but for the challenge it poses—the ultimate failure of civil religion to motivate the post-ethnic Jewish community that is coming into being. To continue successfully, federation will require a more transcendent sense of purpose than what civil religion provides. It is too soon to count federation out, but anyone serious about its mission ought to confront Woocher's sterling critique of what makes federation tick.

Jewish Literacy
(1991)

Joseph Telushkin (born 1948)

*"At a time when Jewish life in the United States is flourishing, Jewish igno-
rance is, too. Tens, if not hundreds, of thousands of teenage and adult Jews
are seeking Jewish involvements—even Jewish leadership positions—all the
while hoping no one will find out their unhappy little secret:* They are
Jewishly illiterate.*"*

So begins this marvelous compendium of everything you need to
know about Judaism to claim basic literacy. As such, this is a single-
volume, encyclopedic dictionary of Jewish life, broad enough to say
something about pretty much everything Jewish, yet deep enough on
every page to make it all worth reading. The choices are spectacular, and
the style is compelling.

There was once a time when, as a matter of course, most Jews knew a
good deal of the information that this book contains. Raised in ghettos
where general education was unknown, Judaism was the totality of the
official—and unofficial—curriculum of concerns. Even making a living
and running a home were governed by the Talmudic tradition that makes
Judaism what it is. Jews automatically marked the Jewish calendar, lived
by Jewish law, and studied Jewish classics. They heard Bible stories within
every synagogue service, knew biblical names as well as they knew their
own, recited prayers from memory, and considered Hebrew their holy
tongue. But those days are long gone. Even well-educated Jews today are
likely to have missed a lot of what once passed for obvious and elementary
Jewish knowledge. This is just the right volume to fill in the gaps.

It is divided both historically and topically—that is, the first ten parts
go from biblical to modern times, with excurses on topics that people
today ought to know about. The last five parts diverge from chronology
to cover subjects that transcend time: the nature of Jewish texts, the
Jewish calendar, Jewish ethics and beliefs, the Jewish life cycle, the synagogue, and prayer. Here and there, Telushkin's discussion is illustrated
by pithy quotations and suggestions for further reading.

The impetus for this work was *Cultural Literacy*, a controversial bestseller from 1987 featuring 5,000 things every American (presumably)

ought to know. "Eighty percent of the listed items have been in use for more than a hundred years!" its author, E. D. Hirsch, declaimed from his vantage point as professor at the University of Chicago. Predictably, his effort to prescribe a classical canon of information was attacked by many as sexist and racist, not to mention outdated, in that it privileged classical information over such recent concepts as software or (one might add today) iPods, blogs, and webcasts. Hirsch remained undeterred.

There is something to this critique, since any cultural canon is formulated by privileged classes—for Judaism, that traditionally meant men (not women), and Ashkenazi (not Sephardi) Jews. But Telushkin finds a good middle ground. His discussion of "the most important things to know about the Jewish religion, its people, and its history" (so the book's subtitle) is indeed classically biased—how could it not be?—but he does not, on that account, disparage modern innovations, and he provides a balanced set of terms, each of them described in an equally balanced way. He has, for example, entries on women rabbis and on patrilineal descent, the North American Reform movement's decision in 1983 to count as Jewish not just children of a Jewish mother (the so-called matrilineal descent, which has been the traditional Jewish yardstick)—but also children of a Jewish father. If Telushkin's list of entries prejudices the past, it is because there is so much "past" to cover, especially for Jews, who value memory and tradition so highly.

So here is the education you probably wish you had had, the big things and the little ones. Do you want to know when and why Jews were expelled from medieval England? Why Moshe Feinstein (Reb Moshe) was crucially important to modern Jewish law? The difference between a *kibbutz* and a *moshav* (two alternative forms of socialist cooperative practiced in early Zionist days)? *Jewish Literacy* is a mine of information; the questions are as fascinating as the answers, which invariably arrive in readily readable summaries.

Some of it is technical (example: the Talmudic regulations of *m'lakhah*, *eruv*, and *muktse*, categories that define what counts as work on Shabbat); some is historical (one entry addresses why many southern Jews came to America through Galveston in Texas, not via New York's Ellis Island); some is quite basic (such as recapping the story of David and Goliath); and some is more advanced (the evolution of Reform Judaism from the Pittsburgh Platform of 1885 to the Columbus Platform of 1937, for instance).

Some of this knowledge is available elsewhere. Any good encyclopedia or dictionary provides information on terms, events, people, and literature. But *Jewish Literacy* offers something unique: more than the snappy one-line dictionary definition of Shabbat, but less than the encyclopedic treatise that goes deeper than what most people probably want to know. And where do you go to get something as broad as basic Jewish beliefs and basic Jewish ethics?

The task of selection is especially crucial in these two areas of beliefs and ethics, where readers require evenhanded discussions that favor neither a conservative nor a liberal understanding of Jewish tradition. But Telushkin pulls it off! As to beliefs, *Jewish Literacy* includes entries on what Jews have said about such weighty matters as an afterlife, forgiveness, the chosen people, and theodicy (why bad things happen to good people). As to ethics, we find such entries as "In God's Image" (the belief that being godly ourselves, we must act as God would in the world); "Do not put a stumbling block in front of the blind" (the prohibition against tempting people into sin by, for example, leaving valuable items unattended); "Do not stand idly by while your brother's blood is shed" (the obligation not to turn a blind eye if we see a crime being committed); "For you were strangers in the land of Egypt" (the Jewish responsibility to the homeless, oppressed, or persecuted minorities in the world); and "Who says your blood is redder?" (a discussion of capital punishment). Any one of these is enough to justify Judaism as a religion of depth, justice, and compassion. Together, they provide an astounding testimonial to three thousand years of Jewish experience with the human condition.

Joseph Telushkin is a modern Orthodox rabbi at the Synagogue for the Performing Arts in Los Angeles. He is best known, however, as a compelling author and speaker whose breadth of knowledge led to his description in New York City's *Jewish Week* as a "renaissance rabbi." In *Jewish Literacy*, he takes what could have been an overwhelming set of information and transforms it into a concise and enjoyable exercise in mastering Judaism. Helping that task along is a useful index and asterisks within each entry to designate words and concepts that have their own entries elsewhere in the book. So beware! Opening it on any given page is likely to prove an endless case of looking up everything else, just by following down all the cross references. The good news is that there aren't a whole lot of better ways to pass up a night's sleep.

Hasidic People
(1992)

Jerome R. Mintz (1930–1997)

"They were going to the wild reaches of America, where Yiddischkayt *[the traditional Jewish way of life] was very poor. In general, it was felt, how could they leave Europe?"*

Most Jews in America are unidentifiable by their outward appearance. Not so Hasidic Jews, a fundamentalist branch of Judaism whose leaders still dress to look like their eighteenth-century founders in eastern Europe. Even ordinary Hasidic men are readily recognizable in their black hats, white shirts (usually with no necktie), and long black coats. Among the roughly 8 to 9 percent of American Jews who are Orthodox, 5 percent are Hasidim. In an effort to retain strict adherence to Jewish law and culture as their leaders recall it from their European past, these Hasidic Jews avoid such modern innovations as TV, movies, fashion, radio, and newspapers.

Most North American Hasidim arrived as refugee survivors of the Holocaust, settling in such Brooklyn neighborhoods as Williamsburg and Crown Heights (and, later, Borough Park). By now, most of these Hasidic communities have followers in cities all over the world.

A closer look at Hasidic clothes (among the men) reveals a host of features that designate hierarchical status ranging from regular followers to the rebbes, the charismatic rabbinic leaders who usually trace their lineage back to dynastic beginnings in the eighteenth or nineteenth centuries. Believed to enjoy privileged communion with God, the rebbe directs even the most intimate affairs of his followers. They visit him regularly, venerating him as an all-knowing seer and wonder-worker whose word is law.

There are many such rebbes, each with his own fervent (and sometimes militant) followers. Their titles, like Satmar and Lubavitch (the two groups most discussed here), tend to denote a place of European origin, usually a small town or village in eastern Europe, a name their descendants carry proudly in their new homes. They reproduce other vestiges of the Old Country, too—their characteristic garb, as we have seen, but also their preference for Yiddish as their mode of communication. Most outside observers lump them all together, a major mistake, since they oppose each other, sometimes with the same intensity as they oppose their common enemy, Jewish acculturation to modernity. *Hasidic People* is the descriptive map of some of the best-known Hasidic groups in North America, written with sociological dispassion and historical precision. The book received a National Jewish Book Award in 1993.

Jerome Mintz was a prominent anthropologist at Indiana University who had made his name studying Casas Viejas, a Spanish village where inhabitants had been put to death by the leftist government in 1933. His book *The Anarchists of Casas Viejas* (1983) was widely praised and was followed up by two other books and several films on the subject. In *Hasidic People*, Mintz returned to the Jewish world in which he had been raised, writing what he calls "a social history" of a community that is so zealous of its privacy that it rarely allows outsiders in at all. Mintz praises his subjects for their piety, especially the "enthusiasm and joy they bring to the punctiliousness of Orthodox Judaism." They believe that "the fate of the Jewish community is tied to fulfillment of the mitzvot [God's commandments]." Failure to fulfill these commandments has resulted in "exile, delay in the coming of the Messiah, and, according to some, the terrible tragedies" of the twentieth century. With so much at stake, each Hasidic community argues its positions vehemently, certain that the fate of all Jews, and even the world, depends on its own understanding of God's will. Mintz gives us both sides of the equation: the ultrapiety and spirituality, on one hand, and the bitter argumentation among rival factions, on the other.

These Hasidim did not usually arrive in New York until after World War II because their rebbes, fearing American openness and freedom, had kept their followers in Europe until last-minute flight was the only way to avoid total obliteration by the Nazis. There were exceptions— the Boyaner rebbe, for example, arrived in the New World in 1927, claiming descent from the great-grandson of Dov Baer of Mezeritsch, one of the earliest Hasidic masters and a direct disciple of Hasidism's founder, the Baal Shem Tov himself. Another early arrival (in 1921) was the Malach, who introduced the characteristic Hasidic black coat to differentiate his followers from secular Americans. When other rebbes arrived later, that dress became commonplace.

Much of *Hasidic People* is the ongoing saga of the especially well-known and influential Satmar and Lubavitch dynasties. The Satmar rebbe, Joel Teitelbaum, reached New York in 1947, with an ascetic brand of Hasidism so stringent that (it was said) except for the Sabbath, the rebbe slept on the floor. More significantly, he set the standard for the religious rejection of the State of Israel, since its very establishment represented a break with Orthodox tradition, according to which only God was supposed to end Jewish exile—and not the Zionists, not even the religious ones, never mind the usual secular variety that established a modern constitution for the State without regard for traditional Jewish law. The Lubavitch rebbes, by contrast, have accommodated to secular learning and support the Jewish state, believing, in fact, that it is a genuine God-sent miracle. Lubavitch philosophy holds that the messiah will come when enough Jews practice enough piety, so its adherents are known for their outreach to Jews around the world.

What makes *Hasidic People* so arresting is not only its author's appreciation of the Hasidic way of life, but also his description of the sectarian rivalries that sometimes reach militant proportions—as when the Malach and the Satmar Hasidim hang an effigy of the Lubavitch rebbe from a telephone pole and set a newspaper office on fire because it takes the Lubavitch side. Given the fact that a rebbe's headquarters is also called a court, we should not be surprised to find considerable palace intrigue. It is not unusual to find various factions plotting against one another in pursuit of dynastic succession.

But *Hasidic People* is primarily an account of Hasidic doctrine and practice. Women are rarely seen in public here; they have large families and stay at home with their children, while their husbands make what living they must, preferring to spend time with each other in sacred Jewish study. They visit the rebbe for advice and attend Sabbath lessons around the rebbe's table, standing in rapt attention while the rebbe speaks, his eyes closed to indicate mystical union of his soul with the divine. At the same table, they dance, sing, and await the coming of the messiah, convinced that they are on this earth to hasten the day of redemption by their scrupulous attention to God's will. If they fight among themselves, it is because they believe so firmly in matters on which the fate of the world depends. They venerate Jewish learning, heartfelt prayer, and charity beyond the norm. For they know they are in exile, with the arrival of the messiah depending on their own ability to merit it.

The Book of Blessings
(1996)

Marcia Falk (born 1946)

"Let us bless the source of life / that ripens fruit on the vine, / weaving new threads / into the tapestry of tradition."

In 1975, and to considerable fanfare, the Reform movement published *Gates of Prayer*, the first official Jewish prayer book to integrate feminist consciousness. The changes were modest: human beings were no longer only "men," for example, but God was still masculine. That same year, but almost unnoticed, Margaret Moers Wenig and Naomi Janowitz, two undergraduates at Brown University, composed *Siddur Nashim* ("Prayer Book for Women"). It replaced masculine references with feminine equivalents, even for God (God was "Queen," not just "King"); added women's voices from ancient and modern sources; and composed new material reflective of women's experience ("Blessed is she whose womb covers the earth").

Other Jewish women went on to develop their own alternatives, all the while expanding the feminist liturgical agenda. One of the best of these pioneers is Marcia Falk, already a noted Hebraist at the time, whose *Book of Blessings* made her, in addition, the foremost feminist liturgical composer of her generation. Falk grew up in New York, received her undergraduate education at Brandeis University, and was awarded a doctorate in English and comparative literature from Stanford University. A Fulbright scholarship took her to Jerusalem, where she studied Bible and Hebrew literature, leading her to become a spectacular translator of Jewish poetry and a poet in her own right. At a scholarly conference held in 1996, her groundbreaking work in *The Book of Blessings* was recognized at a special session of her academic and artistic peers.

And for good reason! Poetry written originally in Hebrew or Yiddish comes beautifully translated by Falk, who also adds her own poetic versions of traditional liturgy, suitably altered for feminist consciousness. Her own Hebrew is as creative as her English: *nashir l'nishmat kol shem ul'shem kol n'shamah*, for instance, gets translated as "Let us sing the soul in every name / and the name of every soul"; the recurrent "sh" sound in Hebrew is replicated by a redundant "s" in English.

Classic contributors of poems in *The Book of Blessings* include Leah Goldberg, who made aliyah to Palestine in 1935; her contemporary Zelda Schneersohn Mishkovsky (known simply as "Zelda"), who arrived there in 1926; and Malka Heifetz Tussman, who came to America from Ukraine in 1912. The whole volume comes with copious notes and explanations of what motivated each aspect of it.

The Book of Blessings is, therefore, utterly unique, the culmination of a decades-long project by Falk, and a synoptic statement for her entire generation of Jewish women who have urged us to think differently about God, revelation, ritual, relationship, and religion itself. Read *The Book of Blessings* as a manifesto of a generation, a liturgical benchmark against which everything else is now measured.

Unlike some feminists, Falk thinks women can own tradition, rather than having to trash it as hopeless and start all over again. Although innovative to the point of being radical, therefore, *The Book of Blessings* presents itself as a traditional order of prayer, served up with an intellectual banquet of ideas surrounding each entry. Central to Falk's project is scrupulous attentiveness to the power of language as the way we name our world. As she sees it, "We should set in motion a process of ongoing naming that would point toward the diversity of our experiences and reach toward a greater inclusivity within the encompassing monotheistic whole." Indeed, Falk dedicates an entire category of prayer to this process of naming, recategorizing traditional liturgical rubrics as she goes along: instead of the usual "Hallowing God's name" (*K'dushat Hashem*), for example, we get "Hallowing our naming," by which Falk means to empower human beings to be the ultimate namers of reality. At stake is Falk's feminist revision of the power relationship between God and humanity—an understanding that comes through in her treatment of rabbinic blessings especially.

A particularly troublesome "name" that requires revision is the way God is addressed in the traditional formula for these blessings, the most familiar genre of Jewish prayer (dating to the very beginning of the rabbinic period, and commonplace by the time of the Mishnah, around 200 CE). The stylistic hallmark of blessings is the formula "Blessed are You, Lord, our God, King of the universe." Falk faults that kind of naming as "an example of a dead metaphor [. . .] a greatly overused image that no longer functions to awaken awareness of the greater whole." She does not just mean the obvious—referring to God as (masculine) "Lord" and "King." Urging deeper scrutiny, Falk rejects the inherently masculine picture of a transcendent God on whom we lower human beings depend. If God is not a hierarchical "Other," then God must be immanently present throughout creation. Falk's alternative is "Let us bless the source of life," a double entendre, because the Hebrew word for "source" also means "nurturing well," even "womb," and makes the subject of the blessing the same as its object: the God who is immanent within us all.

The Book of Blessings, then, is not just a highly original set of prayers. It is a daring theological challenge. Thinking through her liturgy, Falk asks, "Where is the divine in all of this?" Her answer: "Nowhere, in particular—yet potentially everywhere that attention is brought to bear." Prayer focuses such attention, locating divinity "wherever our hearts and minds, our blood and souls are stirred."

Falk created *The Book of Blessings* "for those immersed in Judaism, and for those standing at its gate looking for a way in." As a woman, she knows what it is like to have "stood like Hannah outside the sanctuary's walls, suffused with longing, or anger, or pain." She intends her liturgy, therefore, as "a new beginning, a new healing." Given her theology of a universal God immanent in all that is, she invites worshippers "to add your own voices to the whole of the community of Israel, and the greater wholes of all humanity, all creation." In so doing, she does away with all binary oppositions, precisely what her thoroughgoing feminism demands. Here is a liturgy that is both remarkably traditional—and, therefore, particularistically Jewish—and at the same time universalistic, since God, not being outside the universe, must be inherent in it.

Witness, for example, Falk's treatment of *Aleinu*—"We are responsible"—the daily concluding prayer that celebrates the responsibility of Jews as God's chosen people. Not surprisingly, Falk will have none of it, neither in Hebrew nor in English. Instead, she offers a moving celebration of our responsibility as humans, occupying our place as part of the whole: "It is ours to praise / the beauty of the world," she proclaims. "May we live with promise / in creation's lap, / redemption building / in our hands."

Marcia Falk's *Book of Blessings* stands out as a liturgical and literary masterpiece that should be studied, prayed from, and assimilated into our communal consciousness. It is a culminating work of a noted scholar and poet who celebrates her generation of Jewish feminism, and does so splendidly.

The Book of Jewish Food
(1996)

Claudia Roden (born 1936)

"Every cuisine tells a story. Jewish food tells the story of an uprooted, migrating people and their vanished worlds."

Is there even such a thing as Jewish food? Claudia Roden repeatedly gets that question, all over the world. She is, herself, a genuine cosmopolitan. Born in Cairo, she moved to Paris and then to London, to study art. Originally a painter, she eventually turned to cooking, influenced, she says, by her grandmothers who had served her eggplant and spinach pies from Istanbul and mint and lamb from Aleppo. She dedicated herself to ensuring that Jewish food traditions like these were not forgotten. *The Book of Jewish Food* is her masterful compendium that has indeed made them unforgettable.

The recipes come with Roden's own narrative—a 1992 gastronomic conference she attended in Jerusalem, for example, entitled "Gefilte Fish or Couscous?" The former—stuffed fish—is a quintessential Jewish dish from eastern Europe; the latter, the national staple of Morocco, is also served in certain Mediterranean Jewish communities. With Roden, at the time, were "cooks from Poland, Georgia, Morocco, Iraq, Kurdistan, and many other countries," some of whom may never have heard of either gefilte fish or couscous. Jewish chefs from India might have served fish, all right, but instead of the gefilte variety, it would have been Samaka Tarator (cold fish with pine nut sauce) or Sardiba (fish and mango salad).

But what makes it all Jewish? Truth be told, Jews in any given community have usually adopted the local favorites that non-Jewish natives ate as well, frequently the least expensive option available, since Jews were usually among the poor. Take, for instance, *holishkes* (sometimes called *kholipches*), Polish stuffed cabbage. "Before the potato, it was the only vegetable apart from the carrot" hardy enough for northern climates and so ubiquitous that "every shtetl smelled intensely" of it. The cabbage leaves could be stuffed with pretty much anything available: inexpensive ground-up meat was common. When potatoes arrived in eastern Europe, they "were eaten every day, sometimes three times a day, at every meal," and not just in season, but all year round, because people "kept tons of potatoes in the cellar for the winter." They "went into everything, even bread and pies." We have inherited potato *kugel* for Shabbat and potato *latkes* for Hanukkah.

But Jewish food wasn't necessarily poor. Although "there is a great deal of 'poor food,' a part of Sephardi cooking was shaped by an aristocratic elite and is a legacy of court traditions."

When Jews left the Old Country (whatever old country it was), along with whatever else they packed for the journey came a healthy dose of nostalgia for old-time recipes handed down from mother to daughter, sometimes for several generations. Those recipes are the bulk of Roden's book; they are still available in ways that other cultural constructs (like scholarly traditions in elite yeshivot) are not. Because food habits die hard, recipes may be the last thing lost to acculturation. Indeed, when assimilation eats away at every other tradition, old-time food may be rediscovered as an easy and pleasant reminder of the warmth associated with ancestral ways. Wealthy suburbanites who eat upscale cuisine and wouldn't be caught dead ordering stuffed cabbage in a restaurant may deliberately cook it at home as a patent, and delicious, way of remembering the Jewish past.

That is especially the case for holidays. Not many Jews can tell you the names of all the special insertions for Rosh Hashanah liturgy, but they know what they will eat for dinner that night. The Rosh Hashanah meal in North Africa is likely to be lamb brains in a sauce of fried garlic, chili pepper, sugar, and tomatoes, and then simmered in tomato sauce for ten minutes. Moroccans, specifically, may precede it with yellow split pea and pumpkin soup. Jews in Asia serve fish balls in tomato sauce, specially rounded to symbolize the cyclicity of time. Alsatian Jews drink the equivalent of eggnog—rum and honey beaten into egg and milk.

Purim evokes something else: triangular pastries called *hamentaschen* (meaning, "Haman's pockets," named after Haman, the archenemy in the book of Esther who tries to kill the Jews but fails). But these are Ashkenazi specialties. Sephardi Jews make "Haman's ears," pasta dough deep-fried in oil (the ones from Turkey come with brandy added to the dough).

Regardless of local variety, Jewish foods everywhere were shaped by halakhah—that much was Jewish to the core. Milk cannot be mixed with meat, for instance. Starting a fire is forbidden on Shabbat, so anything eaten warm on Saturday has to be heated overnight on a low flame lit before dark on Friday. German Jews made a Shabbat stew called *cholent*, a name deriving, perhaps, from the medieval French *chauld* (hot) and *lent* (slow). It could be made of almost anything: goose, sausage (made from kosher meat, of course), barley, and beans were common. Nowadays, people pride themselves on their *cholent* recipes: what was once a simple stew determined by conditions of miserable poverty has become a gourmet special, shared with friends.

The Passover seder is a special case where specific foods are part of the prescribed liturgical ritual. *Charoset*, for example, is described by the Talmud as a paste that is thickened to resemble the mortar from which the Israelite slaves manufactured bricks. American Jews of eastern European heritage make it with nuts, red wine, and apples. But Jews elsewhere have different ideas. As early as the tenth century CE, Mediterranean Jews used combinations of fruit mentioned in the biblical Song of Songs. More recent Egyptian charoset is made with dates, raisins, and walnuts. Turkish Jews add orange zest. In medieval Piedmont, charoset was made by combining chestnuts, almonds, and oranges with lots of sugar. And here's a recipe you will not find in Roden's book— and for good reason: a twelfth-century rabbi reported having attended a seder where he almost broke his teeth on the charoset made with slabs of real mortar, not just the symbolic stuff!

Traditional accounts of history have ignored what Jews ate, largely because they were written by men whose only interest was in doing the eating. But women kept their own records, usually oral, which are very much a part of the Jewish conversation over time. We hear of women in concentration camps who stayed alive by sharing recipes they probably would never live to prepare. Other women, condemned to debilitating disease that robs them of mobility, sight, and sounds have kept their sanity by following the annual holiday cycle and reminding their daughters of the foods they should be preparing come winter, spring, or fall.

"Without food, there is no Torah," say the Rabbis in *Pirkei Avot*. Modern rabbis with historical sensitivity might go so far as to say that Jewish food is its own form of Torah. If you doubt that, try *The Book of Jewish Food*. You will find it very convincing.

The Puttermesser Papers
(1997)

Cynthia Ozick (born 1928)

"Her second thought is about the golem [. . .] Who, Puttermesser sometimes wonders, is the true golem? Is it Xanthippe or is it Puttermesser? Puttermesser made Xanthippe. Xanthippe did not exist before Puttermesser made her; that is clear enough. But Xanthippe made Puttermesser mayor, and Mayor Puttermesser did not exist before. And that is just as clear. Puttermesser sees that she is the golem's golem."

Cyntha Ozick is a prodigious worker, prolific writer, and profound commentator on this mysterious thing called life. More than a "commentator," she is a "creator," for she has said that the existential human task is "to clothe nature [. . .] to impose meaning on being [. . .] to invent civilization." For almost half a century, she has been making over the world for readers of her many short stories, essays, novellas, and novels.

Take *The Shawl* (1989), a harrowing account of a concentration-camp mother who shields her infant daughter from the Nazis by wrapping her in a shawl which she holds tightly to her breast. A few short pages into the story, the child is discovered and tossed to its death onto the electrified wires surrounding the camp. We then follow the mother into her old age, her memories, and her search for the shawl as if it were her personal Holy Grail, a metonymic relic of her martyred child.

The heroine of Ozick's novel *The Puttermesser Papers* is Ruth Puttermesser, a Jewish woman in Manhattan. Single and an intellectual, she is most at home in the Victorian world of George Eliot, but also other great writers such as Thomas Mann, Wallace Stevens, and Anton Chekhov, all of whom get cited here as the broadly humanistic yardstick against which Ruth measures life. When she is not working or reading, she wanders through New York's museums—not just the Metropolitan Museum, but also the lesser-known Frick Collection, Cooper-Hewitt, and the Morgan Library. She makes sure also to take in "the special exhibits at the Jewish Museum," because she is Jewish to her core, not religiously, but culturally: she has studied Hebrew grammar, can quote some Bible and even Talmud, and is familiar enough with Jewish mysticism to know the legend of the sixteenth-century rabbi Judah Loew in Prague, who used the ineffable name of God to create a monstrous golem—the Jewish equivalent of Frankenstein.

Like so many second-generation New York Jews in real life, the fictitious Ruth Puttermesser has gone to Hunter High School in Manhattan; by becoming a lawyer and something of a feminist (in what we assume are the 1960s), she has been somewhat ahead of her time. She has persisted since then in the bureaucracy of the New York civil service and, by age thirty-five, has become assistant corporation counsel in the Department of Receipts and Disbursements (a title both "moveable and fictitious [. . .] the poetry of bureaucracy"). She has "retained the immigrant's dream: merit," but everyone else in the office is a freeloading beneficiary of bureaucratic nepotism. Predictably, Ruth gets canned—so much for merit—and becomes what Ozick has elsewhere described as "something of a New York Don Quixote."

Always wanting a daughter anyway, but unable (or unwilling) to take time out to have one the natural way, Ruth creates one—her own female golem, a supergirl whom she names Xanthippe. The golem shows her gratitude by making her creator-mother the city's mayor; Xanthippe then cleans up city hall, ends crime, and transforms Gotham into a modern urban Eden. But as all golems do eventually, Xanthippe, too, careens out of control. Fortunately, the same medieval mystical source that describes the recipe for making a golem provides the means to bring the creature to an end. So Ruth destroys Xanthippe, and, along with her, the ideal metropolis that she created. (For these two things, there is no shortcut: guaranteeing our children's character and creating the messianic state.)

Twenty years later, Ruth develops a platonic relationship with her literary soul mate, Rupert Rabeeno, a fellow devotee of George Eliot, but an expert also in the tangled relationship between Eliot and her two lovers: George Lewes and (later) Johnny Cross. A literary debate regarding Eliot's relationship to them soon turns into a story within a story, with Ruth and Rupert as the latter-day Eliot and Cross. Again, success proves chimerical. Ruth has no more control over Rupert than she had over her golem. Both worlds—public and private—resist happy endings.

The final two acts of Ruth's life paint her retirement, juxtaposing hilarious comedy with graphic trauma. The first is pure enjoyment: Ruth's discovery of a long-lost cousin seeking asylum (it seems) from Gorbachev's tottering Soviet Union. The second is pure horror, the stuff of Edgar Allen Poe but from a woman's perspective, and not recommended for the fainthearted. Describing it would hardly do it justice; readers will have to learn it for themselves.

Like Ozick herself, Ruth Puttermesser is a well-read Jewish universalist who sees humanity through a literary lens that collapses time and perspective into the closest we will ever come to God—what Spinoza famously called "from the perspective of eternity" ("*sub specie aeternitatis*"). Puttermesser is the idealized persona of an intellectual Jewish New Yorker, for whom Judaism is a pastiche of history and ideals loosely glued together into an identity that is far from religious but no less Jewish on that account.

Cynthia Ozick's heroine typifies the liberal ideal that most American Jews now embrace as their intellectual heritage: an intense search for justice; a virtual worship of culture; a passionate love of the arts; a fierce (some say neurotic) faith in education; and an equally insistent hope for a better day—even if, as Puttermesser herself discovers, again and again, life just doesn't usually work out that way.

Bee Season
(2000)

Myla Goldberg (born 1972)

"Ever since Saul dissected a Snoopy Snow Cone Machine commercial for Aaron at age seven, Aaron has been aware of the manipulative powers of advertising [. . .] As a result, Aaron has grown to mid-adolescence with an eye for label reading. It is at the service's completion, while munching an oneg *cookie, that Aaron realizes he's bought Judaism without consulting the side of the box."*

Until very recently, Jews did not have to "buy" Judaism. But until relatively recently also, people did not buy very much else. "Buying" applied only to a small number of things: even necessities such as food, shelter, and clothing were as often made as bought. By the 1960s, however, the economic boom following World War II had convinced an entire generation of baby-boomer college students that even "experience" was for sale.

Young Saul Naumann, the father figure in Myla Goldberg's novel *Bee Season*, was such a college student, buying experience with psychedelic drugs and sexual adventures. When his drug days ended, he "bought back into" his Judaism, which he had temporarily put on hold, even becoming a cantor and discovering Jewish mysticism—a better route than drugs (he hoped) to spiritual wholeness.

Saul's wife, Miriam, took a different route. She somehow escaped the 1960s without trying either drugs or sex. The raw experience that Saul adored, Miriam avoided, deflecting her energy instead into becoming a workaholic lawyer, "a hummingbird in human form, her wings too fast to be seen without a stop-motion camera."

Saul's parents virtually disinherited him in his hippie years; Miriam's parents died young; and the two of them bonded "over their mutual lack of family ties." They had two children, Aaron and Eliza, raised mostly by Saul, while Miriam pursued her career.

The mystical texts that Saul studies preach the Jewish doctrine of *tikkun olam* (repairing the world). God is said to have created the universe with emanations of divine light captured in glasslike vessels that shattered along the way. The human task ever after has been to act on God's behalf by righting the world's wrongs, and thereby restoring the vessels to wholeness.

Poor passionless Miriam has dedicated her own sad life as well to the wholeness of perfection, but in her own way. Unbeknownst to her husband and children, she has adopted a double life that will unravel her sanity, astonish her family, and horrify the reader. It turns out that she, too, in a twisted way of speaking, has been "gathering up the broken vessels to make things whole again."

Bee Season is about shattered lives hiding under the pretense of fulfillment and the human need to be whole. What attracted baby boomers to Judaism was its promise of quintessential wholeness: what Saul at first wanted from LSD, what he now hopes to find in mysticism, and what Miriam seeks in her double life. But what if Judaism can't deliver it?

By the time Goldberg wrote *Bee Season*, the hunt for wholeness had been reframed as the search for spirituality. The search was well under way when she graduated from Oberlin College in 1993 (thereafter, she lived for a year in Prague and then settled in Brooklyn, where she still makes her home). Critical to *Bee Season,* she writes, was a college course she took on Jewish mysticism. "Everyone's searching for meaning in life," she says.

"Meaning in life" is one of the major ways Jews talk about "spirituality." But they tend not to use the word "spirituality" itself—it runs counter to the cultural and even secular Judaism with which they have been raised. So, too, with Miriam and Saul in *Bee Season*. Miriam never mentions spirituality; but neither does Saul, who must have sought it out in his hippie past. For present-day Saul, institutional Judaism (the worship he leads as an accomplished cantor) and textual Judaism (the study he pursues as a would-be mystic) suffice.

Not so for Aaron, their older child, who finds his father's worship trivial and his study arid. On the day of his bar mitzvah, Aaron has a life-changing epiphany. As he dutifully leads the Hebrew prayers in front of the congregation, "Aaron can sense the approach of something larger, a sea swell building up to a huge wave [. . .] Every person in the room becomes part of him [. . .] He is linked. He feels the theme and variation of forty-six heartbeats [. . .] forty-six pairs of lungs [. . .] For one breathtaking moment, Aaron is completely unself-conscious. He feels total acceptance and total love."

Aaron has suddenly had the kind of mystic awakening that his father, the self-styled master of mystical texts, cannot begin to imagine—Saul does not even notice Aaron's newfound self. Aaron despairs of finding wholeness in his father's mystical forays into pure cognition, which are a far cry from the real thing he glimpsed on bar mitzvah day. So Aaron goes elsewhere: to Hare Krishna.

And then there is Eliza, Aaron's younger sister, daughter of a distant and disturbed mother and a grown-up but somehow-still-hippie father. Eliza goes unnoticed in the Naumann family, until her unexpected spelling competence boosts her into the limelight. She might not understand the words she spells, but she spells them right. Saul makes her his prize pupil, coaching her for higher and higher levels of spelling bees—but with his own motive. The thirteenth-century rabbi Abraham Abulafia believed that mystical union with the divine came through concentration on individual letters—a technique that freed the mind from consciousness of everyday things. Eliza, Saul imagines, may have what Abulafia was talking about. "'Do you mean,' Eliza whispers, 'that I'll be able to talk to God?' [. . .] 'In all my life,' Saul says, [. . .] 'you're the only person I've encountered who might have a chance.'"

As *Bee Season* unfolds, we wonder if *anyone* has a chance. Can Judaism, even the mystical kind, make good on the promise of wholeness?

Every religion faces the question of making good on its promises. In today's "experience economy," the immediacy of authentic personal experience is everything. Can institutional Judaism survive if its very essence as an institution is extrinsic to the direct experience of the spiritual? It is this larger question that *Bee Season* addresses—and it does so brilliantly.

Like Everyone Else . . . But Different
(2001)

Morton Weinfeld (born 1949)

"The Jewish community in Canada is on its way to becoming the second most-important Diaspora community, after the United States. But the quality of Jewish life is higher."

Morton Weinfeld has been monitoring the condition of Canadian Jews since 1977, when he introduced a course on the sociology of Canadian Jewry at Montreal's McGill University—the first course of its kind. He holds a university chair in Canadian Ethnic Studies there and is an outspoken advocate of Judaism as an ethnic way of life. He begins his book with the exuberant pronouncement that "Jewish life in Canada today is as good as it has been anywhere since the Golden Age of Spain." Quite a claim!

Is Weinfeld correct? While no Jewish Diaspora community comes even close to the United States in terms of numbers, worldwide influence, and cultural output, Canada has a lot going for it: it has the second-largest Jewish population in the Americas, and boasts everything from Jewish book fairs and film festivals to an abundance of synagogues. Its two largest Jewish communities, in Toronto and Montreal (with Jewish populations of roughly 200,000 and 93,000, respectively), are widely regarded as spectacularly rich in Jewish opportunity. Other Canadian cities with smaller Jewish populations—Vancouver (roughly 23,000) and Winnipeg (roughly 15,000), for example, are similarly striking, considering their size.

Unlike its neighbor to the south, Canada benefits from a concerted national policy of encouraging cultural, not just religious, diversity—sometimes with outright economic support from a public sector that demands no separation of church and state. This is the so-called salad bowl (not the melting pot) approach to the way modernity molds traditions.

More than a book on Canadian Jews, *Like Everyone Else . . . But Different* is also, therefore, a bold claim for a vibrant Jewish alternative to the religio-centered enterprise in Jewish identity that marks the American experiment next door.

Of all the issues facing Jews in the twenty-first century, the most substantial may well be this one: Can Judaism survive as an ethnicity—largely cultural, that is, and even secular? Or will ethnicity disappear as immigrant memories fade and greater proportions of young Jews intermarry with partners who are not Jewish? Will Judaism then have to emphasize its powerful religious heritage, for seekers who are drawn to Judaism because it offers a spiritual and moral compass to a meaningful life?

Evidence in the United States suggests that ethnicity fades away after three generations, while religion remains enormously popular. Not so in Canada, where Christian Sunday school attendance, for example, has declined from an already low "35 percent in 1975 to 28 percent in 1990." What is slipping, says Weinfeld, is "elite religion," the official beliefs and practices on which religious faith is founded. Judaism, he maintains, never gave much weight to those anyway. Far more important are ethnic traits like Jewish culture, Jewish learning, Jewish community, Jewish food, and even Jewish jokes, which Weinfeld enjoys enough to insert regularly in his book to illustrate his arguments. Canadian Jews actually give their children *more* Jewish education than ever before: Montreal alone allocates over forty million dollars annually to assorted Jewish day schools, some of them patently secular. The curriculum is rarely religious, so much as it is cultural: pride in Jewish history, celebration of Israel, and instruction in Hebrew, which is also taught in many Ontario and Quebec public schools as part of the government's encouragement of "heritage languages."

Canadian Jews are insular. They live in close proximity to one another, making it possible to sustain a rich network of Jewish bakeries, delis, bookstores, and synagogues. They are more attuned to Israel, more conscious of the Holocaust, and more tied to "informal religion" (traditional holiday foods, for instance). Some 19 percent of Canadian Jews still say they are Orthodox (compared to some 8 to 9 percent in the United States), but between 33 and 44 percent of these nominally Orthodox Jews do not actually attend synagogue or lead otherwise Orthodox lives—they do not observe Shabbat, for example. They are Orthodox by ethnicity—that is, they identify with the Old World religious style, which they consider authentic, even if they do not frequent the synagogues that preach it. They may not keep kosher, but they eat at kosher-style delis, and even meet at Chinese restaurants, which have, somehow, become the Jewish thing to do.

Some of this may seem flippant: Why Chinese restaurants? But continuity demands community; community means mixing and mingling together; and while they mix and mingle (even over Chinese food), Jews discuss Israel, deplore anti-Semitism, argue the headlines of the national Jewish press (*The Canadian Jewish News*), and ponder ways to support Jewish causes.

Two-thirds of Canadian Jews have visited Israel; one-sixth can converse in Hebrew. If they do not all practice all the laws of the Talmud, they at least know there is a Talmud, and have spent some years studying it. They have learned to pray in Hebrew, and to read the Hebrew Bible, and to keep the Jewish calendar as a cultural heritage.

Canadian Jews are, for the most part, still fairly recent immigrants. Their story begins in the 1670s, when a storm forced some Jewish traders and merchants from Rotterdam to land their vessel in Labrador (they were subsequently offered title to it by England's King William III of Orange, but never acted on it). A Sephardi congregation in Montreal dates to 1768. But the migration of central European Jews in the 1800s mostly peopled the United States; before the eastern European influx beginning in 1881, the total Jewish population in Canada was under 2,500.

So Canadian Jews are mostly of eastern European heritage, and many of those immigrants arrived only after 1924, when the United States closed off immigration by congressional fiat. Canada remained open until the Great Depression had fully set in (1931). A much larger percentage of Canadian Jews, therefore, still have warm memories of European grandparents. And then there are the more recent Holocaust survivors, who make up only 3 percent of America's Jews, but 16 percent of Canada's.

Perhaps Canada's vaunted Judaism of ethnicity will indeed last— Canada is multicultural in ways America is not, and Jews "are like everyone else, but different." They intentionally invest in ethnicity; they cluster together to practice it; they "have an unusually large repertoire of cultural traits: language, literature, a homeland, festivals, beliefs, art, music, rituals, customs, and foods that comprise Jewish identity."

In every developed country where Jews live, the Jewish conversation today focuses on continuity. Jews survived anti-Semitism; will they survive freedom? What strategies might guarantee survival? And why bother to survive anyway? These are the large and anxious questions that Weinfeld raises, making his study of Canadian Jews a study of and for us all.

Entertaining America
(2003)

J. Hoberman (born 1949) and Jeffrey Shandler (born 1956)

"Popular culture plays a leading role in defining what being Jewish is for many American Jews [. . . It is] an alternative to the organization of Jewish life around religion or political ideology."

On Christmas eve, 1908, police raided several hundred nickelodeons (five-cent movie theaters) throughout New York City because they were open on Sundays and offered images unsuitable to unchaperoned women and minors. Among those who fought back were two Jewish owners, Carl Laemmle and William Fox, who would go on to found what became Universal Pictures and Twentieth Century Fox, respectively. Another Jewish pioneer in the movie industry established Paramount. Metro-Goldwyn-Mayer and Warner Bros. were begun by Jews as well. Entertaining America was becoming a Jewish phenomenon.

Though launched in New York, the Jewish movie business really took off in Hollywood, where it relocated after World War I. Ever since, Jews have figured prominently in an ongoing American love-hate relationship with Hollywood—what J. Hoberman and Jeffrey Shandler call "Hollywood's Jewish Question." The first broadside came in the 1920s, when Henry Ford's rankly anti-Semitic *Dearborn Independent* leveled the accusation that "these Jews think of nothing but money making and sexual indulgence." By the 1930s and '40s, isolationists charged Hollywood with selfishly stirring up anti-German fervor to get America into World War II and save Europe's Jews. In the 1920s, Jewish movie producers had been called "rampant capitalists." By 1947, they were relabeled "communists." And attacks have continued into the twenty-first century, this time from conservative voices that see Hollywood as a "purveyor of 'secular humanist' values or as the provenance of a 'cultural elite.'"

By and large, the Jews behind the scenes have not advertised their Jewish heritage, but *The Jazz Singer* (1927)—widely billed as the earliest "talkie"—starred Al Jolson (himself Jewish) as a cantor's son who abandons his father's sacred calling for show business; in the end, he leaves his Broadway debut on Yom Kippur eve to take his dying father's place chanting *Kol Nidre*, the signature prayer on the theme of "repentance and return." In 1947, Twentieth Century Fox filmed *Gentleman's Agreement*, based on Laura Hobson's successful novel; and the same year, RKO produced *Crossfire*, the story of a hate crime in which the victim was portrayed as a Jew. Charlie Chaplin was not Jewish, but so Jewish was Hollywood that the media kept insisting that he was.

Side by side with the rise of movies came the spread of radio, in some ways the opposite medium, for rather than bringing people out of their homes into a public place, it brought public affairs into private homes. New York's WEVD (founded in 1926, with the initials of socialist party leader Eugene V. Debs) broadcast in Yiddish (but also in Spanish, German, Turkish, Italian, and Japanese) as "the station that speaks your language." On a larger scale, William Paley and David Sarnoff—both of them Jews—were the network chiefs at CBS and NBC, respectively. Remembered best from those early days, perhaps, is Molly Goldberg (real-life Gertrude Berg), whose radio show *The Goldbergs* debuted in 1929, just as the Great Depression was unfolding. As an immigrant Jewish mother herself, Molly provided weekly inspiration for second-generation immigrant families of all sorts.

By the 1940s, television was on its way, and there, too, Jews played a starring role—not just Molly Goldberg, transported to the TV screen, but also a host of comedians who virtually made the new medium their own: Jack Benny, Eddie Cantor, Sid Caesar, George Burns, Gracie Allen, Groucho Marx, Phil Silvers, and Milton Berle (Mr. Television himself). Jewish writers who made television (and movie) history include Carl Reiner, Mel Brooks, and Woody Allen.

Entertaining America offers a panoramic sweep of it all. The book originated as the catalogue for a 2003 exhibition at New York's Jewish Museum. It juxtaposes a running narrative by the catalogue's primary authors (and the exhibition's guest curators), J. Hoberman and Jeffrey Shandler, with short essays and vignettes by other contributors, all of it beautifully illustrated with photos from the original exhibition. Hoberman is known best as a film critic for the *Village Voice*, but he teaches also at New York University; Shandler is a professor at Rutgers University. Both are experts in their field with a rare gift of being able to write for the non-specialist.

Their conclusion, aptly titled "Not the Last Word: A Conversation," raises the serious issues that underlie what would otherwise be just a self-congratulatory celebration of "what Jews have wrought." To be sure, Jews have had an impact on American consciousness, which is to say, "As Jews become more American, America becomes more Jewish."

But if Americans, generally, relate positively to Molly Goldberg or Milton Berle, and if even a film such as *Exodus* (1960; based on Leon Uris's 1958 bestselling novel that celebrates the birth of the State of Israel) is best described as "an American" phenomenon—starring a "pretty blond American Christian nurse" (played by Eva Marie Saint) as heroine—then how is any of this Jewish?

We also need to consider that many of the personalities named in the book did not actually identify as Jews; some (like the early silent film stars Bronco Billy Anderson and Theda Bara) even concealed their Jewishness as best they could. Did they make the entertainment industry "more Jewish" just because they were born to Jewish parents?

In part, suggests Hoberman, *Entertaining America* points to the Jewish insistence on connecting with "a collective Jewish experience." Shandler calls it "the practice [that Jews have] of inventorying Jews [. . .] a common desire to map Jewish presence and Jewish continuity, two constantly contested issues in the modern age"—a response to Jewish insecurity in the face of looming assimilation. If Jews are so present for so long and to so many, Jews surely matter even when they are hardly Jewish—don't they?

But knowing Jews matter is not the same thing as mattering oneself, so "it's the discussion," says Shandler, "the act of getting together and discussing these films and broadcasts—that defines this as a Jewish phenomenon." If beauty is in the eye of the beholder, so, too, is identity, and cultural Judaism, as it has been called, becomes a way for Jews to keep the Jewish conversation going. It may not be the Bible and Talmud, but Jewish films or broadcasts raise the same universal questions of human joy and suffering, alongside the perennial issue of how Jewish experience specifically still matters as well nowadays.

The Jewish Life Cycle
(2004)

Ivan G. Marcus (born 1942)

"If ritual innovation is a measure of a culture's vitality, then the study of Jewish rites of passage should make one hesitate before throwing up one's hands in despair over the future of the present Jewish community."

Once upon a time, everybody was in touch with their respective religious traditions. Religion was a person's "sacred canopy," covering every aspect of life.

With modernity, however, life was carved up into rival and independent spheres of activity: work, school, family, leisure, and so on. Instead of an all-embracing canopy, religion became just one more sphere like all the rest. Certain times and activities were "religious"; most were not. The religious sphere became altogether voluntary. It is hard to go through life without spending considerable time with "work," "school," or "family." But lots of people limit "religion" to events of choice, like favorite religious holidays or life-cycle rituals.

Most people who get married still choose a religious ceremony, and most are buried religiously, as well. In between, depending on their religion, they may celebrate births and first communion or bar/bat mitzvah, mark divorces, and remember their dead. As religious activities like attending regular worship have faltered, life-cycle celebrations have grown in importance, expanding, as it were, to fill the vacuum. Jews have participated in this phenomenon as much as anyone. Even Jews relatively removed from religion become impassioned with wedding plans, obsessed with bar/bat mitzvah preparations, and insistent that their beloved be buried in proper religious ways.

Why do all religions even have life-cycle rituals to which families and friends are invited? Isn't our own personal life cycle just that—personal? Actually, even our "personal" lives are deeply embedded in relationships with others. Despite our high regard for personal autonomy, we want the most important moments of our lives to be recognized by them. We therefore celebrate life's major changes by having family and friends gather round and affirm our role in the larger whole. Religions provide life-cycle templates that give cosmic significance to such mysteries as why we are born, how to understand illness, and what happens when we die.

But religions also specify arbitrary life-cycle moments: times like first communion, confirmation, and bar/bat mitzvah. These are "arbitrary" because they correspond to no precise moment of biological change or development. Religions thereby provide a model of the kind of human life we should lead. These arbitrary stopping-off points in the journey of life reinforce the religious vision of the sort of person God would want us to be.

Sometimes, however, the inherited life-cycle moments are insufficient. That has been the case for women, because traditional religions have usually focused on the lives of men. Traditional Judaism, for example, has bar mitzvah for boys but no parallel event for girls. Nowadays, we have righted that wrong, offering a bat mitzvah as well. But even new ceremonies are not usually made up out of whole cloth—we prefer rooting them in precedents, because we want our lives to be authentic. Millennia-old religious traditions authenticate us as more than the sum of our momentary whims that are here today and gone tomorrow.

Given today's emphasis on life-cycle events, few Jewish books are as interesting and necessary as Ivan Marcus's well-written and properly grounded summary of it all, *The Jewish Life Cycle*. Marcus was a professor at the Jewish Theological Seminary of America before joining Yale University in 1994 as a professor of Jewish history. He is especially well known as an eminent medievalist, an expert at ferreting out both ancient and medieval origins of today's life-cycle rituals. More than a simple how-to book (how to prepare a bat mitzvah or a fun wedding, for example), Marcus provides an engrossing narrative of the Jewish life cycle through history. Reading it is like a treasure hunt for customs that once prevailed but have been lost. One regularly finds oneself muttering out loud, "I didn't know Jews did that!"

Take the wedding ceremony. In biblical days, there was no ceremony at all. A man chose a woman, and, after some negotiation with her family, she moved in with him. Jewish weddings, as we know them, are a post-biblical invention of the Rabbis who defined marriage as a two-part process.

First came formal engagement, a ceremony in which bride and groom affirmed their commitment to each other. In part, the groom gave the bride something of nominal value. By accepting it, she indicated that she was agreeing to the marriage of her own free will. Over time, that became a ring.

The second stage occurred when the bride moved into her husband's home. The word *chuppah* denoted the process of changing living quarters—there was no canopy yet. Only in sixteenth-century Poland did a canopy become the norm, at which time the old word "chuppah" was applied to it. At first, the chuppah was a simple sheet placed over poles. A report from 1617, however, remembers "an elaborate tent with decorated curtains into which the bride and groom were ceremoniously led." By then, Jews were using a prayer shawl (a tallit) as the canopy—an improvement, so to speak, on the ordinary sheet.

Another fascinating example is bar mitzvah, something unheard of until the High Middle Ages. The Rabbis of late antiquity declared age thirteen as the time boys were to be held responsible for adult duties before God, but there was no ceremony connected to it. Frequently, boys fulfilled such duties (like reading the Torah within the worship service) even before their thirteenth birthday, because without clocks and calendars, people did not automatically know how old they even were.

In the medieval church, meanwhile, one of the highest ways to serve God was to become a monastic. In the early Middle Ages, parents would therefore dedicate their children, even as infants, to monastic service. By the twelfth century, however, an increase in piety and large families produced an overabundance of monastic initiates, leading the church to prefer candidates old enough to understand the rigors of a monastic calling. As it happened, Christians had inherited the Roman idea that girls and boys matured at the ages of twelve and fourteen, respectively. So monastic communities insisted that boys reach age fourteen before applying, and people began paying attention to the passing of years and the moment children became adults.

Jews had no monasteries, but they did have adult responsibilities. With age thirteen already on the books in theory, they now began enforcing it in practice, too, as the age when a boy becomes a man. They kept the age of twelve for girls, and when bat mitzvah was finally introduced in the early twentieth century (by none other than Mordecai Kaplan), it became the earliest age for bat mitzvah.

Many of us have been at the events Marcus describes, and wondered how they got to be the way they were. Wonder no more! *The Jewish Life Cycle* demystifies life-cycle ritual by explaining its history, symbols, and practices in a beautifully captivating way. It will make us all the more want to model our lives after Jewish rites of passage that commit us to Jewish history and culture, and make us partners in the Jewish conversation of the centuries.

Synagogue Architecture in America
(2004)

Henry Stolzman (born 1945) and Daniel Stolzman (born 1980)

> *"The search for Jewish identity is especially pressing in contemporary American society [. . .] How do we build buildings that celebrate our Jewish past, serve our contemporary communal psyche, and announce our future?"*

More than any other institution, it is the synagogue that has guaranteed Jewish survival over the centuries. It was commonplace once to date the institution of the synagogue all the way back to the Babylonian exile of 586 BCE, but synagogues actually came into being much later. It is notoriously difficult to date archeological finds with any degree of specificity (and harder still, sometimes, to know what counts as a synagogue in the first place), but in general, synagogues go back only to the time of Jesus (we hear of him attending synagogues on occasion).

Nowadays, synagogues are said to have three traditional functions— prayer, study, and gathering—but originally, they were just places to gather. The very word "synagogue" attests to this origin, because it comes from *sunagein*, the Greek verb meaning "to gather"—a perfect parallel to the standard Hebrew term for synagogue, *bet knesset*, "place of gathering." But by the first century CE, one purpose of such gathering was to study or argue the meaning of sacred texts. The Gospel of Luke, for example, pictures Jesus in a synagogue, pointing to a passage in Isaiah that he took as a prophecy of his mission. A Greek inscription from Jerusalem in the same era (first century CE) records a synagogue administered by a synagogue president (*archisynagogus*) named Theodotus, who gives synagogue functions as "the reading of Torah [. . .] teaching the commandments," and "serving as a hostel for wayfarers." We do not know when the Rabbis managed to import their daily regimen of prayer to synagogues—it may have been as late as the third or even the fourth century CE.

Synagogue architecture through time has combined attention to the synagogue's three central functions with the aesthetic standards of the era in question. The famous ruins of the third-century CE synagogue of Dura Europos in Syria, for example, contain richly painted frescoes with illustrations from the Bible and midrashic literature. The sixth-century

CE synagogue of Beth Alpha in Galilee utilizes Byzantine artistic norms of the time to display mosaics of the Zodiac. Most Enlightenment-era synagogues of Germany looked like churches, but were outfitted with Stars of David rather than crosses to mark their Jewish provenance. Other synagogues of the time celebrated the Jewish fascination with the Jewish golden age in Spain by adopting classical Moorish architecture as their model.

Although *Synagogue Architecture in America* is a survey of American synagogues, specifically, its American samples amply illustrate the search for synagogue spirituality in other parts of the world as well. The book comes with comprehensive histories of synagogue space against the backdrop of American Jewish history on one hand, and the American fascination with spirituality on the other. The authors, Henry and Daniel Stolzman, are father and son; Stolzman senior, a principal of a major New York–based architecture firm, has had a long-time fascination for sacred architecture. Daniel is a writer and filmmaker who has produced and directed commercial, music video, and television projects, including programs for Discovery Channel, History Channel, CNN, and ABC.

Page by page, we discover how well great synagogues reflect the spiritual search of the larger society in which Jews find themselves. The Touro Synagogue (completed in 1763) in Newport, Rhode Island, for example, is the Jewish equivalent of New England colonial churches, with a modest façade that recalls Congregational meetinghouses. But unlike churches of the time that boasted a traditional steeple, synagogues had no obvious external symbolism. Aside from the fact that it was built on an acute angle in order to face Jerusalem, Touro Synagogue's exterior does not look distinctively Jewish or even particularly religious. The inside, however, distinguishes it as the kind of Sephardi synagogue that arrivals from Dutch Brazil would have remembered from their families' histories.

The opposite of Touro's simplicity is Manhattan's Central Synagogue (1872), an imposing Moorish-style structure flanked by towers with large bulbous domes that dominate its exterior, and a brightly colored patterned design covering the sanctuary walls inside. Equally impressive is Temple Emanu-El (1929), just a few blocks uptown, with its enormous stone exterior, massive Romanesque arches, and an inner sanctuary that takes your breath away.

The very opposite of modest, these two synagogues celebrated their congregants' commercial and social success in New York City. Like Touro, however, Central Synagogue and Temple Emanu-El reflect an

328 ຄ One Hundred Great Jewish Books

era when Americans took worship seriously enough to want buildings that focused on worship and solemnity, not socializing. Worshippers were expected to quiet down for the service inside, not engage in animated conversation outside. The external doors lead almost directly into the sanctuary, with barely any space at all to greet or talk with others. The architectural scheme goes back to nineteenth-century churches and synagogues that saw the religious enterprise as the opportunity to engage in uplifting one's moral vision and obtaining the sense of being in the House of God (*Gotteshaus*).

By contrast, in America's suburban synagogues after World War II, worship took second place to education and socializing: education for the many little baby boomers, and socialization for their parents, who spent most of their work week sequestered away alone in offices, homes, and cars. Socializing required room, however. So architects designed smaller sanctuaries next to enormous social halls; a collapsible wall permitted the extension of sanctuary seating into the socializing area for the High Holidays, when crowds would come.

People attending these synagogues in the 1950s expected their worship to display a message of Jewish sophistication, a sign that, culturally speaking, they belonged in their new-found suburban neighborhoods. Especially in Reform synagogues, therefore, but in some Conservative synagogues as well, worship was a somewhat passive congregational affair. The "liturgical action" was directed at worshippers from the *bimah*, the frontal area where rabbi and cantor variously read and sang the service. Being strongly ethnic but also highly educated, the congregants valued high culture more than deep spirituality. The architectural excellence and high aesthetic of the worship mirrored their search.

Their children, however, reached maturity in the 1960s and '70s, when spirituality became a ubiquitous cultural quest. They turned their backs on worship that was, as they saw it, unengaging, and began designing synagogues with intimate worship spaces that accord with Martin Buber's theological emphasis on encountering God's presence within the genuine human relationships that we establish with each other.

The spaces we design for religious purposes are not simply envelopes in which we locate ourselves. They are our stories in process. *Synagogue Architecture in America* explores the American Jewish story as it has unfolded since the arrival of its first Jews in 1654. The illustrations of synagogue architecture that fill this book's lavish pages are spectacular reflections in space of the Jewish conversation in time.

The Rabbi's Cat
(2005)

Joann Sfar (born 1971)

"Jewish people aren't crazy about dogs. A dog will bite you, chase you, bark. And Jews have been bitten, chased, and barked at for so long that, in the end, they prefer cats [. . .] I am the rabbi's cat."

Traditionally speaking, are Jews really not so fond of dogs? Possibly. Talmudic literature is notoriously scant on stories about pet dogs! Not that cats fare any better, but as it happens, the rabbi in this story has a daughter and the daughter has a cat, making the cat, by one step removed, the rabbi's pet, as well.

The Rabbi's Cat is a graphic novel combining three separate stories that first appeared in France between 2001 and 2003. They reflect the changing fortunes of twentieth-century Algerian Jews who confront modernity—a familiar story, of course, but these Jews are Sephardi, not Ashkenazi, and the modernity they encounter is French culture, specifically. (A second volume, with two more stories, was published in English in 2008.)

Sephardi, in this case, designates Jewish exiles from the Iberian peninsula in 1492 who did not move north to the Netherlands and from there to England or the Americas; these Sephardi Jews sailed east through the Mediterranean, settling in the Land of Israel and North African centers along the way. These North African Jewish communities were not altogether new, however. They date back all the way to Roman times, but grew to prominence only under Islam. The region became known as the Maghreb, from the Arabic word for West.

For Jews in the Maghreb, the Tunisian town of Kairouan enjoyed pride of place. Already in 987, Kairouan Jews had written to the leading rabbi of Baghdad, asking him for a history of Jewish tradition, and the resulting responsum, *Iggeret Sherira Gaon* ("The Letter of Sherira Gaon") is, to this day, the account on which historians most base their reconstruction of the rabbinic past. By the eleventh century, an independent school of Talmudic study in Kairouan was being led by such rabbis as Rabbenu Nissim (d. ca. 1050) and Rabbenu Hananel (d. ca. 1055), whose commentaries on Jewish law are studied to this day. One of their students,

Isaac Alfasi (1013–1103), originally from Fez (Morocco), penned a code of Jewish law that later authorities called "The Little Talmud." Over the centuries, however, Kairouan, like the rest of Jewish North Africa, devolved into a backwater bastion of traditionalism.

The Rabbi's Cat is a set of stories by Joann Sfar, one of the most influential young artists in a new wave of Franco-Belgian comic books and graphic novels. He traces his Jewish roots through an Ashkenazi mother and a Sephardi father. The series captures the stresses and strains of traditional Jewish life as Maghreb Jews, particularly in Algeria, bump up against twentieth-century French colonial rule. The cultural gap between old and new is told through the perceptive eyes of the rabbi's cat.

The first story, "The Bar Mitzvah," is pure fable, a reflection of the traditionalist kabbalistic milieu that dominated Jewish life in Arab lands from the expulsion of 1492 onward. In short, the rabbi's cat develops the ability to talk (by eating a parrot), but later loses it because he misuses the ineffable divine name of God. The tale diverges from traditional stories in that the talkative cat struggles philosophically with the ethical issues that come with the gift of language. Can he tell lies about what he observes? Are truths always desirable?

The rabbi's cat also understands the appeal of modern science. His master detests it as "prehensile, predatory, and in the final analysis [a] destructive machine." The cat will have none of this. When overhearing a yeshivah student voicing traditional views like "If you fear God [and do His commandments] nothing bad can happen to you," the cat mutters, "Jerk!"

In the second story, "Malka of the Lions," the cat loses his ability to speak and we are back in the realm of real life. Its master is about to meet modernity. His first challenge arrives in the form of what sociologist Max Weber called the typically modernizing trends of rationalization and bureaucratization—in this case, rules governing the education of clerics in the colonies. The rabbi already speaks Arabic, Ladino, and the local Algerian patois but not French, in which he is newly obliged to show competence. "You've been the rabbi here for thirty years," the cat observes sarcastically, "[. . .] and to lead prayer in Hebrew for Jews who speak Arabic, they want you to write in French."

Of special interest nowadays, when politics so tragically divide Muslims from Jews, is the realization of just how close these two groups once were. Afraid that he has failed the exam, the rabbi pursues the age-old Sephardi custom of seeking advice at the grave of a saintly ancestor. Along the way he meets a Muslim pilgrim seeking counsel at the grave of a Sufi sage. It turns out they are traveling to the same site—we never do find out if the man buried there is a Jew or a Muslim, and it doesn't seem to matter!

The final story, "Exodus," shifts to Paris. A modern Parisian rabbi has spent some time in Algeria and fallen in love with the Algerian rabbi's daughter. To the young man's dismay, his new father-in-law accompanies them back to Paris to observe the life his daughter will have. It will prove a mixed blessing. A nephew who had been reputed to have found fame and fortune there as an opera star is revealed as a mere sidewalk entertainer collecting loose change for impersonating an Arab troubadour. For all intents and purposes, he has abandoned Judaism and is living with a Catholic girlfriend.

Is this the freedom that this modern Exodus makes possible? The Algerian rabbi finds nothing good in Paris: the streets are gorgeous but lack palm trees; the weather is cold and rainy; the people are as cold as the weather. The synagogue is Orthodox, but a veritable study in coldness. "Listen to this silence," the rabbi complains. "There's an echo, you'd think we were in a church. Back home, for Shabbat, we sing."

But the rabbi is not untouched. As the book ends, he is back home in Algeria, preaching on his Parisian experience. "Dear friends," he says, "I met a Jew who ate pork all the time. And on Shabbat, he smoked. And he never prayed [. . .] and quite honestly, I don't think he lived less well than I do. So, my friends, if we can be happy without respecting the Torah, why should we exhaust ourselves to apply all these precepts that make life so complicated?" The congregation shouts expectantly, "Come on [. . .] tell us why, we're waiting!" But the rabbi has no answer. "The truth is, I don't know."

The Rabbi's Cat touches the essence of Jewish life in modernity. Why should we keep the Torah and its many commandments? Algerian Jews who discovered Paris in the 1900s were remarkably like Polish Jews who encountered Berlin or Vienna a century earlier—and not altogether unlike their grandchildren and great-grandchildren in Dallas, Toronto, London, or Buenos Aires. Jewish life and practice can still be compelling. But the conversation about them is increasingly accompanied by the question "Why bother?"

To the End of the Land
(2008)

David Grossman (born 1954)

"The hotel management expects guests to leave when they reach the age of 18!"

Neither the generals who command it, nor the historians who study it, comprehend the terrible reality of war. War's real experts are mothers whose eighteen-year-old children leave home to fight and maybe to die in it. Unlike hotel guests, however, they never really leave; as long as they go off to fight, they remain in the minds and hearts of their parents who worry that they may not return alive. A mother whose child is at war lives in daily fear of the ringing doorbell signaling the news that her eighteen-year-old will never turn nineteen.

Ora is such a woman in Israel. Her son Ofer has volunteered for a top-secret military mission during the Intifada of 2000. To escape the dreaded doorbell ring, she embarks on a hike far from home—as if Ofer cannot die if there is no one home to receive the news. (The original Hebrew title of the novel translates as "A Woman Escaping News.") As her hiking companion, she takes Avram, a man she first met in a hospital when the two of them were young, battle casualties of the 1967 Six-Day War. Avram, back then, had introduced her to a third patient, Ilan.

Except for a first scene that introduces the three protagonists in the hospital, the entire novel narrates Ora and Avram's hike, punctuated by flashbacks that explore the complicated set of relationships that has governed their adult lives since 1967. Ilan, it turns out, eventually married Ora, and the two of them had a child, Adam. Ilan and Avram served together in the 1973 Yom Kippur War, where one of them had to volunteer to serve on the Egyptian front. But which one? To decide that question, they phoned Ora and asked her to draw lots without telling her what the lots were for. Avram lost and was subsequently captured by the Egyptians, who tortured him brutally. He returned to Israel physically and psychologically demolished.

Haunted by guilt for allowing Avram to go to the front, Ilan abandons his family, then later returns but lives alone, ascetic-like, in a shed behind Ora's home. Recently, he has left again, this time taking grown-up Adam with him but not telling Ora exactly where: maybe he is in Ecuador or Peru, she muses, or "hiking [. . .] among the turtles in the Galapagos." While she is hiking "to the end of the land" to escape the dreaded news of Ofer's potential death, Ilan is traveling "to the end of the earth to get away from her."

Adam is Ora's son whom she had with Ilan; but who is Ofer? It turns out that Ora had assuaged her own guilt by nursing Avram back to health; and then slept with him one night to show him that he was still fully a man. Ofer is the child of that union. "It's not the end of the world," she consoles Avram when she breaks the news of Ofer's foolhardy decision to volunteer for special service. But secretly, she fears that it might be. Her journey to the end of the land will cheat fate of its plot to bring about the end of the world.

Their backpacking expedition affords Ora the opportunity to acquaint Avram with the everyday details of Ofer's childhood that Avram has missed. Ofer can hardly die as long as she talks about him, she reasons, so she keeps up a steady stream of recollections, interspersed with memories of Avram, Ilan, and herself along the way.

War is anything but glorious here; it is too much for anyone to bear. So except for Ofer—poor naive Ofer, running off to a battle he could have avoided—all the characters are in retreat, escaping what life has foisted upon them. The writing is sheer genius, page after page of intricately articulated detail about the two landscapes of the journey: the exterior one of Israel's countryside that Ora and Avram traverse, and the interior one that reveals the moral and human contour of the characters' souls.

David Grossman is an Israeli writer of international renown, the recipient of a number of prestigious awards. His work has been translated into thirty languages. In an earlier novel, *The Smile of the Lamb* (1983), Grossman became the first Israeli to address the Israeli occupation of Arab land, and since then, he has emerged as an outright opponent of any governmental policy that establishes settlements there, in effect annexing the territory into "Greater Israel." Very tragically, while working on *To the End of the Land*, Grossman's own son Uri was killed in war—it was the very last day of the Israeli incursion into Lebanon in 2006.

But *To the End of the Land* is no mere political statement; Grossman remains realistic about the horrendous situation that pits two peoples against each other with no apparent solution. His attitude toward Israeli Arabs comes through in the person of Sami, a Palestinian driver whom Ora hires on occasion, most recently to drive Ofer and her to the rallying point for the military call-up. She realizes too late the insensitivity of using a Palestinian to transport her Israeli soldier-son to a rendezvous for battle against the Palestinians, but makes up for it by helping Sami take a gravely ill Palestinian boy to an Israeli hospital, the only place where he can get proper care. To hurry the boy past the military inspection points, she pretends to be his mother. But Sami is unappeased: "You people," he spits out angrily at her, classifying her as the occupying enemy. For her part, Ora cannot get over "their [the Palestinian] culture [. . .] them and their lousy honor, and their never-ending insults, and their revenge, and their settling of scores over every little word anyone ever said to them since Creation."

Neither Ora nor Sami is evil. They are victims "of the fears and the hatred we both drank with our mothers' milk," Ora muses. But the fears and hatred are real because Sami is a Palestinian and Ofer may die in fruitless battle against Sami's people—to no avail on either side. This must be some sacrificial ritual, Ora thinks wryly, as she deposits Ofer at his call-up station: "In every car sits a young boy, the first fruits, a spring festival that ends in human sacrifice."

Grossman's fiction excels in its revelation of the painful contingency of human life, making his story altogether Jewish in its plot and major characters, but equally a vivid insight into the life of everyone, everywhere. Avram is captured and tortured solely because he is Israeli and Jewish. But he is also just Avram, a man, thrown into battle by a quirk of fate, born into a certain time and place and subject to the ridiculous whim of a game—the mere drawing of lots. Ora is a Jewish woman with a Jewish son, but she is also every mother whose son signs on for a war she never planned or asked for.

To what extent, Jews wonder, is the Jewish experience just a particular manifestation of being human? Are Jewish conversations simultaneously ruminations on the universal human condition? Perhaps the three millennia since King David first raised a Jewish emblem over Jerusalem have cast Jews as characters in more than their own private drama. And perhaps it is this universality of Jewish specificity that gives the Jewish conversation depth.

To the End of the Land is so completely and absolutely a reflection on being an Israeli Jew, perpetually at war—but it is also the haunting suggestion that we are all inexplicably thrown into a world where the only alternatives are to run madly away from each other or to clutch each other in mutual recognition that love is as real as loneliness, and that we are born into the world to love.

Start-Up Nation
(2009)

Dan Senor (born 1971) and Saul Singer (born 1961)

"Google, Cisco, Microsoft, Intel, eBay . . . the list goes on. The best-kept secret is that we all live and die by the work of our Israeli teams [. . .] What we do in Israel is unlike what we do anywhere else in the world."

With relentless regularity, newspapers around the world publish reports on Israel's military situation: its ongoing fight for survival; its skirmishes with terrorists; and its wars, its endless wars. But the real news story may turn out to be economic: Israel's emergence as a world leader in science, technology, and innovation. The actual army of Israelis that devotes one month a year to reservist duty is also a virtual army that spends the other eleven months on the global entrepreneurial frontier. *Start-Up Nation* chronicles this economic accomplishment, which goes to the very heart of Israeli culture and of Judaism's age-old emphasis on learning, love of debate, and long-term purpose.

The authors of this book that became something of an immediate bestseller are well positioned to present their facts. Dan Senor is adjunct senior fellow for Middle East studies at the Council on Foreign Relations and a foreign policy advisor to the United States government; Saul Singer is a columnist and former editor at the *Jerusalem Post*. Together, they have amassed the data necessary to make the miracle of Israel's economic turnaround incontrovertible. Israel contains "the highest density of start-ups in the world," for example, "a total of 3,850 start-ups, one for every 1,844 Israelis [. . .] more Israeli companies are listed on the NASDAQ exchange than all companies from the entire European continent." Also, "In 2008, per capita venture capital investments in Israel were 2.5 times greater than in the United States, more than 30 times greater than in Europe, 80 times greater than in China and 350 times greater than in India." Israel is, in sum, "the world leader in the percentage of the economy that is spent on research and development."

All of this was accomplished despite Israel's many wars. From 2000 to 2004, Israel was beset by the second Intifada; but during the same time frame, from 2000 to 2005, foreign investment in Israel's economy (almost none of it by Jews) tripled. That was because in the midst of the fighting, Israel was able to convince the world economic community that it was here to stay. Emblematic of that lesson is Intel Israel, which had designed the elementary chip first used in IBM computers and, after that, the first Pentium chip as well. In the midst of the first Gulf War, with Iraqi scud missiles falling all around them, 80 percent of Intel workers showed up voluntarily to make sure factory orders were met on time.

Visitors to Israel as recently as the 1970s and '80s would never have predicted such an economic turnaround. Israel was virtually a developing country back then, to the point where visitors sometimes brought ordinary bathroom towels and even soft toilet paper as gifts. From 1971 to 1979, inflation rose from 13 percent to 111 percent, on the way to a record 445 percent in 1984. Israelis hoarded telephone tokens, the single form of "currency" that held its value because it was too hard to retool the phone booths every day. A standard joke at the time recommended traveling between cities by taxi rather than by bus, because you could pay the taxi fare at the end of the ride when money was worth less.

Israel's initial aversion to creative business ventures went back to its origins, in fact long before statehood in 1948. Entranced by their socialist ideals, its founders had produced, among other things, one of the most unionized economies in the world, and a fetish for farming and physical labor. Ideological elitists established kibbutzim, the agricultural collectives that abolished private ownership to the point where members needed permission to engage in higher education.

How did Israel overcome all this to turn into a model of business entrepreneurialism? *Start-Up Nation* lists several factors, first among them the army, where virtually everyone's character is formed. Unlike military cultures elsewhere, Israel's army encourages subordinates to question orders received from above. It expects battlefield commanders to make important on-the-spot decisions that other armies kick back up to superiors. Battles that have been fought are revisited again and again, to understand where mistakes were made—not to punish the soldiers who made them but to reward honesty, and to increase the probability of performing better next time around. Young Israelis graduate into the workforce with longstanding friendships made on the field of battle, trust in comrades who have saved each other's lives, and a commitment to start-up values like taking risks and arguing strategy in the hope of improving performance. Veterans are used to a situation where job titles mean less than getting the job done, and where interdisciplinary cooperation trumps established fiefdoms of self-interest. And Israel is a democracy: no ruling power limits creative thought and free speech.

Credit also goes to Israel's insistence on admitting refugees, especially the Russian immigrants who arrived after the fall of the iron curtain: 800,000 new settlers between 1990 and 2000 alone. With 7.1 million inhabitants in 2008, Israel has grown almost ninefold in the sixty years since it was founded. Nine out of ten Israelis are still either immigrants or their children and grandchildren. But here another traditional Jewish value has made a difference: the strong emphasis on education. Russian Jews were already among the educational elite in the Soviet Union (30 percent of the doctors, 20 percent of the engineers), and they arrived in a country where universities had been established as early as 1925 and were considered just as vital to Israeli society as the socialist kibbutzim that were established at the same time.

A handful of other countries can tell somewhat similar stories of success. But Israel's true uniqueness lies in the further fact that Israel is "a country with a motive." What has not changed from the days of its earliest Zionist pioneers is Israel's commitment to a state that can support every Jew who settles there; a haven to which every Jew can turn should anti-Semitism threaten Jewish life again. Like the Jewish People throughout time, Israel has a "core purpose."

Start-Up Nation is a completely secular narrative, scientifically researched and reported. The authors offer no spiritual perspective, therefore. But readers familiar with the Jewish conversation over time may be forgiven if they intuit the age-old Jewish dream of a messianic age—not in traditional religious garb but in the shape of international business ventures that may contribute to world peace better than politics can. It will take a miracle to establish world peace, but Israel is, apparently, a land of miracles, isn't it?

American Jewish Year Book
(since 1899)

American Jewish Committee

"Committed to providing a continuous record of developments in the U.S. and world Jewish communities."

In 1751, there appeared in Paris the first volume of *Encyclopédie*, a collaborative Enlightenment effort to record "each and every branch of human knowledge" in order "to change the way men think." This audacious idea of changing the way we think emerged from the Enlightenment's insistence on replacing medieval thought with the modern scientific perspective, which viewed the entirety of knowledge as a single comprehensive entity that can be studied dispassionately and captured encyclopedically. To be sure, from Aristotle on, Western thought had moved in that direction, but *Encyclopédie* was a quantum leap forward, since it subjected reality to the principal doctrine of the Age of Reason: human beings are essentially alike, part of a single collective—humanity.

By the nineteenth century, the Age of Reason had been replaced by the romantic era, which denied the solidarity of humanity. In its place came nationalism, the belief that national peoples are essentially different from one another. Rather than universal human reason, it was the particularistic German, French, Russian, English (etc.) ways of thinking that were now explored. The Enlightenment concept of a single and universal body of knowledge was dismembered into the romantic idiosyncrasies of individual "cultures," each with its own compendium of history, myth, thought, literature, art, and practice.

Jewish emancipation emerged in the Age of Reason but matured in the romantic era, when Jews decided also to portray a culture of their own. They discovered Jewish history and arrayed Jewish texts as an evolving collectivity called Jewish literature. Jewish romanticism reached its pinnacle in Germany, where scholars applied the latest scientific methods to produce a cultural whole called "Judaism"—the equivalent of what other Europeans already enjoyed. It was only a matter of time until Jews, too, had launched an encyclopedia collecting this data.

The first truly comprehensive such work, therefore, was overwhelmingly the product of scholars trained in Germany (even though it was written in English): the *Jewish Encyclopedia*, published in New York from 1901 to 1906. Its official goal was described in the preface: "Owing to their long history and their wide dispersion, the Jews have been connected with most of the important movements in the history of the human race [. . .] there has been hardly a phase of human thought and activity in which the participation of Jews may not be discerned. While they have thus played a prominent part in the development of human thought and social progress throughout the centuries, there has been no faithful record of their multifarious activity. The *Jewish Encyclopedia* is intended to supply such a record, utilizing for this purpose all the resources of modern science and scholarship."

At stake, also, was a not-so-subtle defensive maneuver. Since the century just ending had been marked by rising anti-Semitism, the editors duly noted that "Jewish history is unique and therefore particularly liable to be misunderstood. The Jews are closely attached to their national traditions, and yet, in their dispersion, are cosmopolitan." The *Jewish Encyclopedia* was an apologia for Jewish cosmopolitanism, precisely the universalist facet of Jewish culture that narrow and nationalistically minded anti-Semites attacked.

The *Jewish Encyclopedia* remains a landmark Jewish accomplishment, the culmination of nineteenth-century German-Jewish scholarship that launched the modern Jewish project of self-discovery with such rigor and care. We are not better scholars today: we just have more sources at our disposal, and benefit from over a century of debate on academic method. Nonetheless, we do live over a hundred years later, and many newer encyclopedias of Judaism have emerged in the meantime. The most pathos-ridden must be the substantial work planned by Polish Jews who hoped it would dissuade Hitler from his commitment to eradicate Jews from the face of the earth. The encyclopedia was never executed; most of its would-be editors were.

The work that eventually did replace the *Jewish Encyclopedia* is the sixteen-volume *Encyclopaedia Judaica* of 1972 (revised in 2006). The project arose in Germany after World War I and was to be published in German, but was halted with the Nazi rise to power. Following World War II, its surviving editors resumed the venture, but German was hardly a language of Jewish publication anymore, and much had changed in any event: Jewish studies in Germany had been eradicated; many potential contributors had been murdered in concentration camps; others had dispersed around the world. So the *Encyclopaedia*

Judaica was restarted in the Jewish cultural capital of Jerusalem, and is now the established Jewish encyclopedia of record.

But standard encyclopedias describe the past, and ever since 1899, there has existed also an ongoing record of the Jewish world in process, an annual updating of the actual state of Jews and Jewish affairs around the world: the *American Jewish Year Book*. It was begun by the Jewish Publication Society (JPS) in Philadelphia, the pioneer Jewish publisher in America. In 1908, its preparation became the responsibility of the American Jewish Committee (AJC), the New York–based organization formed in the wake of the Kishinev pogrom. The AJC describes itself as working "since 1906 to safeguard and strengthen Jews and Jewish life worldwide by promoting democratic and pluralistic societies that respect the dignity of all peoples." Over time, the AJC became the *Year Book*'s publisher as well.

Each and every volume provides vital statistics such as international Jewish demographics, a synopsis of the year's events in Jewish communities worldwide, obituaries of significant Jews who have died, and a list of major Jewish organizations (including their headquarters and contact information). Although the title contains the word "American," the book's purview is global.

Each volume comes with comprehensive introductory essays on matters of moment, written by authoritative experts in the field. In 1998, for example, when Israel celebrated its fiftieth anniversary, the *Year Book* featured "Israel at 50"—one perspective from America and another from Israel, along with retrospectives on "Herzl's Road to Zionism" and "Zionism and the Upheavals of the 20th Century." In 1996, it gave us "Jewish Experience on Film," the way Jews have been treated in the cinema and what movies can teach us about Jewish identity, from *The Jazz Singer* (1927) until today. The 1992 edition focused on "Jewish Identity in Conversionary and Mixed Marriages"; the 1966 volume looked back at the history of "The Church and the Jews" in light of the recently concluded Second Vatican Council (Vatican II); and a year later, readers received a survey of "The Jews in Western Europe Today."

The cumulative result is a serialized version of everything you want to know about the contemporary state of Jews, annually and around the world, as well as feature articles on every conceivable aspect of Jewish culture, religion, history, and identity. Year after year, it remains a singularly significant book to consult. Indeed, there is nothing quite like the *American Jewish Year Book* to remain up to date on the topics that regularly reinvigorate the Jewish conversation.

Book Notes

American Jewish Year Book. New York: American Jewish Committee; Jewish Publication Society of America, since 1899 (appears annually).

American Judaism. Sarna, Jonathan D. New Haven, CT: Yale University Press, 2004.

As a Driven Leaf. Steinberg, Milton. 1939. New York: Behrman House, 1996.

Aspects of Rabbinic Theology. Schechter, Solomon. 1909. Reprint Ed., New York: Schocken Books, 1965, 1972, 1975, 1984.

An Autobiography. Maimon, Solomon. 1793. English Ed., J. Clark Murray, trans., 1888. Reprint Ed., Whitefish, MT: Kessinger Publishing, 2008.

Awake and Sing! Odets, Clifford. In Clifford Odets, *Three Plays by Clifford Odets.* New York: Random House, 1935.

The Babylonian Talmud. Available in many English editions. The most widely used over time has been the edition by Isidore Epstein, trans. and ed., London: Soncino Press, 1935–1952. Newer (and now more commonly used) editions include the edition by Adin Steinsaltz, ed. with commentary, New York: Random House, 1989–1999; the edition by Jacob Neusner, trans. and ed. with commentary, Peabody, MA: Hendrickson Publishers, 2005; the edition by Hersch Goldwurm and Nosson Scherman, eds., Brooklyn: Artscroll Mesorah Publications, 1990–2007.

Badenheim 1939. Appelfeld, Aharon. 1979. English Ed., Dalya Bilu, trans., Boston: D. R. Godine, 1980, 1998, 2009.

Bee Season. Goldberg, Myla. New York: Anchor Books, 2000, 2001, 2005.

The Bible. The Bible exists in countless versions, but this book draws almost exclusively on the one used by most Jews: the Jewish Publication Society of America (JPS) version of 1985. At times, however, quotations come also from the NRSV (New Revised Standard Version), 1989; the King James Version (KJV), 1611; or the New King James Version (NKJV), 1982; on occasion, I supplied translations of my own.

The Book of Blessings. Falk, Marcia. 1996. Boston: Beacon Press, 1999.

The Book of Jewish Food. Roden, Claudia. 1996. New York: Alfred A. Knopf, 2007.

Bread Givers. Yezierska, Anzia. 1925. Reprint Ed., New York: Persea Books, 1969, 1975, 1999, 2003.

The Brothers Ashkenazi. Singer, Israel Joshua. 1936. English Ed., Maurice Samuel, trans., New York: Alfred A. Knopf, 1936, 1945, 1959, 1965; also Joseph Singer, trans., New York: Atheneum, 1980.

Choices in Modern Jewish Thought. Borowitz, Eugene B. 1983. Second Ed., West Orange, NJ: Behrman House, 1995.

Community and Polity. Elazar, Daniel J. 1976. Revised Ed., Philadelphia: Jewish Publication Society of America, 1995.

The Complete Stories. Malamud, Bernard. New York: Farrar, Straus and Giroux, 1997.

The Complete Works of Isaac Babel. Babel, Isaac. 2002. Nathalie Babel, ed., Peter Constantine, trans. Second Ed., New York: W. W. Norton, 2005.

Conservative Judaism. Sklare, Marshall. 1955. Reprint Ed., Lanham, MD: University Press of America, 1985.

The Diaries. Herzl, Theodor. 1922–1923. This exists in several versions, but the one used here is by Marvin Lowenthal, ed. and trans., New York: Dial Press, 1956.

Duties of the Heart. Bachya ibn Pakuda. Ca. 1080. Several translations exist, but the most commonly cited one, which is the one used here, is the translation by Moses Hyamson, New York: Bloch Publishing Co., 1925, 1943, 1945, 1947.

Eclipse of God. Buber, Martin. 1952. English Ed., Amherst, NY: Humanity Books, 1988, 1999.

Eichmann in Jerusalem. Arendt, Hannah. 1963. Revised Ed., New York: Penguin Books, 1976, 1978, 1984, 1987, 1992, 1994, 2006.

Entertaining America. Hoberman, J., and Jeffrey Shandler. Princeton, NJ: Princeton University Press, 2003.

From Beirut to Jerusalem. Friedman, Thomas L. 1989. New York: Anchor Books, 1995.

From Berlin to Jerusalem. Scholem, Gershom. 1977. English Ed., Harry Zohn, trans., New York: Schocken Books, 1980, 1988.

From Politics to Piety. Neusner, Jacob. 1972. Second Ed., Eugene, OR: Wipf and Stock Publishers, 2003.

The Gate Behind the Wall. Heilman, Samuel C. 1984. Reprint Ed., Philadelphia: Jewish Publication Society of America, 1995.

Gentleman's Agreement. Hobson, Laura Z. 1947. Reprint Ed., Cary, NC: Cherokee Publishing Co., 2007.

Goodbye, Columbus. Roth, Philip. 1959. Reprint Ed., Shelton, CT: First Edition Library, 1996.

Guide for the Perplexed. Maimonides, Moses. Ca. 1200. The standard English version for many years was by M. Friedlander, trans., 1885. The most cited version today is by Shlomo Pines, trans., Chicago: University of Chicago Press, 1961, 1963, 1969, 1974, 1979, 1986, 1990, 1999, 2003.

A Guide to Jewish Religious Practice. Klein, Isaac. New York: The Jewish Theological Seminary of America, 1979, 1992.

Haggadah and History. Yerushalmi, Yosef Hayim. Philadelphia: Jewish Publication Society of America, 1975, 2005.

Halakhic Man. Soloveitchik, Joseph B. Lawrence Kaplan, trans., Philadelphia: Jewish Publication Society of America, 1983.

Hasidic People. Mintz, Jerome R. Cambridge, MA: Harvard University Press, 1992, 1994, 1998.

Hebrew Ethical Wills. Abrahams, Israel, ed. 1926. Expanded Facsimile Ed., Lawrence Fine, ed., Philadelphia: Jewish Publication Society of America, 2006.

In My Father's Court. Singer, Isaac Bashevis. 1966. Reprint Ed., New York: Farrar, Straus and Giroux, 1991.

Israel. Gilbert, Martin. 1998. Revised and Updated Ed., New York: Harper Perennial, 2008.

The Itinerary of Benjamin of Tudela. Benjamin of Tudela. Ca. 1173. Different editions are discussed in the entry. The edition used here is by Michael A. Signer, ed., Malibu, CA: J. Simon, 1983, 1987, 1995.

Jerusalem. Mendelssohn, Moses. 1783. Many translations have appeared over time. The one used here is by Allan Arkush, trans., Hanover, NH: Published for Brandeis University Press by University Press of New England, 1983.

The Jewish Gauchos of the Pampas. Gerchunoff, Alberto. 1910. English Ed., Prudencio de Pereda, trans., 1955. Reprint Ed., Albuquerque: University of New Mexico Press, 1998.

The Jewish Life Cycle. Marcus, Ivan G. Seattle: University of Washington Press, 2004.

Jewish Literacy. Telushkin, Joseph. 1991. Revised Ed., New York: William Morrow, 2001, 2008.

The Jewish Prayer Book (Siddur). The most commonly used version is *The Complete Artscroll Siddur*, Nosson Scherman and Meir Zlotowitz, eds., Nosson Scherman, trans. and commentary, Brooklyn: Mesorah Publications Ltd., 1984 (First Ed.), 1986 (Second Ed.), 1990 (Third Ed.), reprinted several times since. Of late, another popular version has appeared: *The Koren Siddur*, Jonathan Sacks, trans. and ed. with commentary, New Milford, CT: Koren Publishers Jerusalem Ltd., 2006, 2009. The edition included here is not a Siddur per se, so much as it is a running commentary on (and a set of essays about) the Siddur: *My People's Prayerbook*, 10 vols., Lawrence A. Hoffman, ed., Woodstock, VT: Jewish Lights Publishing, 1997–2007.

The Jewish Study Bible. Berlin, Adele, and Marc Zvi Brettler, eds. New York: Oxford University Press, 2004.

Jews Without Money. Gold, Michael. 1930. Third Ed., New York: Carroll & Graf Publishers, 1984, 1996, 2004.

Judaism as a Civilization. Kaplan, Mordecai M. 1934. Philadelphia: Jewish Publication Society of America, 1981, 1994, 2010.

The Kuzari. Judah Halevi. Ca. 1140. Several translations and editions are available. The ones used here include the Henry Biberfeld edition, New York: Spero Foundation, 1946, 1957; and the Isaak Heinemann edition, Oxford, U.K.: East and West Library, 1947; republished in New York: Schocken Books, 1964.

Letters to an American Jewish Friend. Halkin, Hillel. Philadelphia: Jewish Publication Society of America, 1977.

The Life of Glückel of Hameln. Glückel of Hameln. 1690s. Beth-Zion Abrahams, ed. and trans., London: Horovitz Publishing Company, 1962. Reprint Eds., New York: Thomas Yoseloff, 1963; and Philadelphia: Jewish Publication Society of America, 2010.

Like Everyone Else . . . But Different. Weinfeld, Morton. Toronto: McClelland & Stewart, 2001.

Maus. Spiegelman, Art. 2 vols. New York: Pantheon Books, 1986 and 1991.

Midrash Rabbah. The most commonly used English translation is by Harry Freedman and Maurice Simon, London: Soncino Press, 1939 (First Ed.), 1951 (Second Ed.), 1977 (Compact Ed.), 1983 (Third Ed.).

The Mishnah: *Pirkei Avot. Pirkei Avot* is available in most versions of the traditional prayer book (Siddur). Classic editions of the Mishnah, as a whole and published separately, are by Herbert Danby, ed., Oxford: Clarendon Press, 1933, Reprint Ed., Oxford: Oxford University Press, 2008; and by Philip Blackman, ed., Gateshead, U.K.: Lehmann, 1965. The newest and most scientific edition is by Jacob Neusner, ed. and trans., New Haven, CT: Yale University Press, 1988.

Modern Jews Engage the New Testament. Cook, Michael J. Woodstock, VT: Jewish Lights Publishing, 2008.

Moses and Monotheism. Freud, Sigmund. Katherine Jones, trans., New York: Alfred A. Knopf, 1939. The edition used here is by James Strachey, ed. and trans., London: Hogarth Press, 1991.

My Life as a Radical Jewish Woman. Rakovsky, Puah. 1954. Paula Hyman, ed., Barbara Harshav, trans., Indianapolis: Indiana University Press, 2002.

My Name Is Asher Lev. Potok, Chaim. 1972. New York: Anchor Books, 2003.

New York Jew. Kazin, Alfred. 1978. New York: Syracuse University Press, 1996.

The Night Trilogy: Night; Dawn; Day. Wiesel, Elie. 1958; 1960; 1961. Reprint Ed., New York: Hill and Wang, 2008.

The Nineteen Letters. Hirsch, Samson Raphael. 1836. English Ed., Bernard Drachman, trans., 1899. Second, Corrected Ed. with commentary by Joseph Elias, New York: Feldheim Publishers, 1996.

On Being a Jewish Feminist. Heschel, Susannah, ed. 1983; Reprint Ed., New York, Schocken Books, 1988, 1995.

Only Yesterday. Agnon, Shmuel Yosef. 1945. English Ed., Barbara Harshav, trans., Princeton, NJ: Princeton University Press, 2000, 2002.

Passage From Home. Rosenfeld, Isaac. 1946. Reprint Ed., New York: Markus Wiener Publishing, 1988.

Peace of Mind. Liebman, Joshua Loth. 1946. Reprint Ed., New York: Simon and Schuster, 1973.

The Penguin Book of Modern Yiddish Verse. Howe, Irving, Ruth R. Wisse, and Khone Shmeruk, eds. New York: Viking, 1987.

The Pity of It All. Elon, Amos. New York: Metropolitan Books, 2002.

Poems. Bialik, Hayyim Nahman. 1891–1934. Several editions of Bialik's poetry exist. The edition relied on primarily here is by Israel Efros., trans., Revised Ed., New York: Bloch Pub. Co., 1965, 1999. The translations used here, however, are original, by Joel M. Hoffman.

Poetry and Stories. Amichai, Yehuda. 1955–2000. Several books of Amichai's poetry are available in English, for example *The Selected Poetry of Yehudah Amichai*, Chana Bloch and Stephen Mitchell, eds. and trans., New York: Harper & Row, 1986; and *Yehudah Amichai: Selected Poems*, Ted Hughes and Daniel Weissbort, eds. and trans., London: Faber & Faber, 2000. The short stories cited come from Yehudah Amichai, *The World Is a Room and other stories*, Elinor Grumet, Hillel Halkin, Ada Hameirit-Sarell, Jules Harlow, Yosef Schachter, trans., Philadelphia: Jewish Publication Society of America, 1984.

Principles of the Jewish Faith. Jacobs, Louis. New York: Basic Books, 1964.

The Promised City. Rischin, Moses. 1962. Reprint Ed., Cambridge, MA: Harvard University Press, 1977.

Protestant-Catholic-Jew. Herberg, Will. 1955. Reprint Ed., Chicago: University of Chicago Press, 1960, 1983, 1994.

The Puttermesser Papers. Ozick, Cynthia. New York: Alfred A. Knopf, 1997.

The Rabbi's Cat. Sfar, Joann. 5 vols. in French, 2001–2006. Discussed here is a compilation of vols. 1–3, English Ed., Alexis Siegel and Anjali Singh, trans., New York: Pantheon Books, 2005. An English edition of vols. 4 and 5 is available also: *The Rabbi's Cat 2.* Alexis Siegel, trans., New York: Pantheon Books, 2008.

The Rabbinic Bible (*Mikra'ot G'dolot*). The English version is *The Commentators' Bible*, Michael Carasik, ed. and trans., Philadelphia: Jewish Publication Society of America, 2005 (Exodus), 2009 (Leviticus), 2011 (Numbers).

Reminiscences. Wise, Isaac Mayer. 1901. David Phillipson, ed. Reprint Ed., New York: Arno Press, 1973.

The Responsa Literature. Freehof, Solomon B. 1955. Philadelphia: Jewish Publication Society of America, 1959, 1963.

The Sabbath. Heschel, Abraham Joshua. 1951. New York: Farrar, Straus and Giroux, 1979, 1981, 2005.

Sacred Survival. Woocher, Jonathan S. Bloomington: Indiana University Press, 1986.

Selected Essays. Ahad Ha-am. Leon Simon, trans., Philadelphia: Jewish Publication Society of America, 1912. Later editions include an edition by Joshua H. Neumann, trans., New York: Tarbuth Foundation, 1967; and an edition by Leon Simon, trans., New York: Atheneum, 1970.

Start-Up Nation. Senor, Dan, and Saul Singer. New York: Twelve, Hachette Book Group, 2009.

Stories. Peretz, Isaac Loeb. Ca. 1889–1915. There are a number of anthologies, including: *Stories of Isaac Loeb Peretz*, Helena Frank, trans. and ed., Philadelphia: Jewish Publication Society of America, 1906; Reprint Ed., Whitefish, MN: Kessinger Publishing, 2010. *Prince of the Ghetto*, Maurice Samuel, trans. and rearranged as a running commentary on Peretz's life, 1948; Reprint Ed., Lanham, MD: University Press of America, 1987. *The I. L. Peretz Reader*, Ruth R. Wisse, trans. and ed., New York: Schocken Books, 1990.

Survival in Auschwitz; The Reawakening. Levi, Primo. 1958; 1965. Stuart Woolf, trans., New York: Summit Books, 1986.

Synagogue Architecture in America. Stolzman, Henry, and Daniel Stolzman. Mulgrave, Australia: The Images Publishing Group, 2004.

A Tale of Love and Darkness. Oz, Amos. 2003. English Ed., Nicholas de Lange, trans., Orlando, FL: Harcourt, 2004.

The Tenth Man. Chayefsky, Paddy. 1959. New York: Random House, 1960.

Tevye the Dairyman. Aleichem, Sholem. 1894–1916. The Tevye stories are found in many places, including *Tevye the Dairyman and The Railroad Stories*, Hillel Halkin, trans., New York: Schocken Books, 1996; and *Tevye the Dairyman and Motl the Cantor's Son*, Aliza Shevrin, trans., New York: Penguin Books, 2009.

To the End of the Land. Grossman, David. 2008. English Ed., Jessica Cohen, trans., New York: Alfred A. Knopf, 2010.

Tormented Master. Green, Arthur. 1979. Reprint Ed., Woodstock, VT: Jewish Lights Publishing, 1992.

The War Against the Jews 1933–1945. Dawidowicz, Lucy S. New York: Holt, Rinehart and Winston, 1975.

When Bad Things Happen to Good People. Kushner, Harold S. 1981. Reprint Ed., New York: Anchor Books, 2004.

Why I Am a Jew. Fleg, Edmond. 1927. English Ed., Louise Waterman Wise, trans., Second Ed., New York: Bloch Publishing Co., 1929, 1933, 1945, 1975.

The Wise Men of Helm and Their Merry Tales. Many collections of Helmite tales exist. The edition used here is the classic by Solomon Simon, 1942. Reprint Ed., Ben Bengal and David Simon, trans., Lillian Fischel, illust., West Orange, NJ: Behrman House Publishing, 1996.

The Yeshiva. Grade, Chaim. 1967/68. English Ed., Curt Levian, trans., Indianapolis: Bobbs-Merrill, 1976.

The Zionist Idea. Hertzberg, Arthur. 1959. Reprint Ed., Philadelphia: Jewish Publication Society of America, 1997.

Zohar. Moses de Leon. Ca. 1287. An older, and only partial, translation is by Harry Sperling and Maurice Simon, London: Soncino Press, 1934, 1956, 1970, 1984. The new and authoritative translation used here is by Daniel C. Matt (it is in process, with 4 vols. published thus far), Stanford, CA: Stanford University Press, 2004–2007.

Index

Acknowledgments

This book presents an idea I have long had: to see Judaism not just as a religion, a culture, or even its own civilization, but as an evolving conversation over time. Appropriately, it began with a conversation—when Jan-Erik Guerth invited me to author it. Given prior writing commitments that I had already made, he offered me the unheard-of opportunity to write the book in my own good time: whenever I could manage it. His magnanimous proposal was too good to turn down. I would at last be given the opportunity to read (or reread) the Jewish conversational record of the centuries. My first and foremost expression of gratitude goes, therefore, to Jan-Erik himself, not only for his vote of confidence in me but for his remarkable expertise as my partner in this venture all along the way. He is a most demanding editor, insistent on the excellence that I, too, value. I could not have wished for a better publisher and editor in what each of us, in our own way, treated as a sacred venture.

More conversations followed, not just with Jan-Erik, but with a host of other conversationalists, whose numbers included pretty much anyone I came across—rabbis and cantors; educators and librarians; academicians everywhere (including, especially, colleagues at Synagogue 3000 and Hebrew Union College); and lay readers of all sorts, in particular, people who had recently discovered Judaism in all its fullness and whose encounter with the Jewish conversation proved especially instructive. Everywhere I went, people greeted my proposal with enthusiasm. I wish I had room to list the names of everyone who offered suggestions, but, failing that, I should mention at least two of them with whom I engaged in sustained conversations over the several years in which this book was taking shape: Dr. Joel Hoffman and Dr. Wendy Zierler. To them, I owe particular gratitude.

The process of working with Jan-Erik Guerth has been extraordinary, not only for the loving attention to editorial and production detail that he offered, but for his full engagement in the Jewish conversational record itself. With regularity, Jan-Erik critiqued my own selection of books, recommended others, and became my conversational partner in everything I had to say. He also surrounded himself with a superb supportive team including proofreaders Anne Louise Mahoney and Robert D. Land, text designer Cynthia Dunne, and cover designer Stefan Killen. This book owes a great deal to them all.